City *of* Tree

City *of* Trees

The Complete Field Guide to the Trees of Washington, D.C.

THIRD EDITION

Melanie Choukas-Bradley

Illustrations by Polly Alexander

University of Virginia Press
Charlottesville and London

UNIVERSITY OF VIRGINIA PRESS
Originally published in 1981 by Acropolis Books Ltd. as *City of Trees: The Complete Botanical and Historical Guide to the Trees of Washington, D.C.* Revised edition published in 1987 by Johns Hopkins University Press.
Copyright 1981, 1987, 2008 by Melanie Choukas-Bradley and Polly Alexander
All rights reserved
Printed in China on acid-free paper

First University of Virginia Press edition published 2008

9 8 7 6 5 4 3 2 1

LIBRARY OF CONGRESS CATALOGING-IN-PUBLICATION DATA
Choukas-Bradley, Melanie.
  City of trees : the complete field guide to the trees of Washington, D.C. / Melanie Choukas-Bradley ; illustrations by Polly Alexander. — 3rd ed.
     p.   cm.
  Includes bibliographical references and index.
  ISBN 978-0-8139-2688-9 (alk. paper)
  1. Trees in cities—Washington (D.C.)—Identification. 2. Trees—Washington (D.C.)—Identification. 3. Washington (D.C.)—Guidebooks. I. Alexander, Polly. II. Title.
  SB435.52.W18C48 2008
  635.9'7709753—dc22

                                                                2008008573

PHOTO BY POLLY ALEXANDER: Azaleas and Dogwoods at the National Arboretum

PHOTOS BY MELANIE CHOUKAS-BRADLEY: Star Magnolia; Kobus Magnolia; Yulan Magnolia; Umbrella Magnolia; Southern Magnolia; Sweetbay Magnolia; Witch-Hazel; Red Maple; Fringe-Tree; Pawpaw; Yoshino Cherry; Weeping Cherry; Kwanzan Cherry; Serviceberry (Shadbush); Cornelian Cherry; Flowering Dogwood; Redbud; Black Locust; Yellowwood; Japanese Pagoda Tree; Blackhaw; European Smoke-Tree; Red Horse-Chestnut; Yoshino Cherry at the Library of Congress

PHOTOS BY RYAN DANIELS: Saucer Magnolia; Flowering Pear; Flowering Crabapple; Kousa Dogwood; Catalpa

PHOTOS BY LORNE PETERSON: White Oak, autumn branching

PHOTOS BY SUSAN A. ROTH: Bigleaf Magnolia; Tulip-Tree; Carolina Silverbell; Japanese Snowbell; Franklin Tree; Dove Tree (Handkerchief Tree); Tamarisk; Stellar Dogwood; Mimosa (Silk Tree); Golden-Rain-Tree; Paulownia; Crape-Myrtle; Chaste-Tree; Street Trees (Ginkgo and American Elm)

In memory of our grandparents:

Gertrude Choukas and Dr. Michael Choukas

Amelia Crane Crosby and Merton Crosby

Madeline Dyer Alexander and Rowland Carpenter Alexander

Eleanor Town Andrews and Thomas Wood Andrews

Contents

Color plates follow page 184

Foreword to the Third Edition

Adrian Higgins, Garden Editor of the *Washington Post*

Trees form the fabric of life in Washington, D.C.—of plant life, certainly, but also of the life of the city and of its inhabitants. If you are a visitor, you will be struck by the astonishing tree canopy of the metropolis, and perhaps too by the farsighted urban planning that limited building heights to approximately 110 feet, or about the height of our oldest and most precious trees. Those of us who call Washington home never take this urban forest for granted. The absence of skyscrapers and the great civic greensward of the Capitol grounds and the National Mall give trees their due.

This book gives trees their due, too. It is a unique acknowledgment of this gift, and of our duty to protect it. *City of Trees* is also a celebration of arboreal Washington, of the magnificence of forested Rock Creek running through the heart of the city, or of the picturesque beauty of the Tidal Basin in April. And the book reminds us that our trees are not just about the past; they are about our role in assuring their future.

There are more than three hundred species of native and exotic trees in the metropolis. Some are well known, others off the beaten track. Still others are famous but located in places, such as the White House grounds, that are off-limits for the most part. Unless you have this book—which brings them all within reach.

City of Trees is a field guide, in the sense that it will direct you to, say, Dumbarton Oaks, where you can identify some of the estate's astonishing specimens. However, if you detect in this book a certain passion blended with the dendrology, it is because the author and illustrator understand that trees are not meant to be studied alone, but to be admired as wondrous living organisms, vast and sheltering. Who could go to Dumbarton Oaks, especially in the fall, and not be awestruck by the low-boughed katsura tree on the south lawn or the silver-skinned American beech on the Beech Terrace? Or, in the early spring, when scilla and glory of the snow appear at the foot of the beech like little blue pixies dancing among the surface roots?

Washingtonians know the bounty of the urban forest, but it is not until it is gathered in its totality, as it is here, that one gets the fullest sense of just how rich it is. Like the katsura and beech, many beloved trees have an aura that fixes in the mind the memory of their setting. I cannot think of the Bishop's Garden at the Washington National Cathedral without summoning up its sentinel Atlas cedars, or of the walled azalea garden at the National Arboretum without recalling the old lace-bark pine and the astonishing mosaic of its trunk.

You hold in your hands the third edition of *City of Trees*. The original edition dates to 1981, and the more familiar revised paperback edition was published in 1987. This third edition has been expanded in a number of directions, not least in acknowledging new Washington landmarks where trees play a vital role. These include the Franklin Delano Roosevelt Memorial, the World War II Memorial, and the National Garden of the U.S. Botanic Garden. Melanie Choukas-Bradley has also expanded the number of tree species listed, and has added descriptions of a number of lesser-known natural areas in and around the city, where trees, especially native species, can be enjoyed in their own habitat. Polly Alexander has executed several new drawings for the third edition, including the round-lobed cultivar of the sweetgum, and the blight-plagued American chestnut, which many fans are trying to resurrect for future generations.

Of course, one of the biggest developments since the publication of the earlier editions of *City of Trees* has been the creation of Casey Trees, established by the philanthropist Betty Brown Casey. The organization has fostered a grassroots advocacy for the continued sustainability of the urban forest, a task that cannot fall alone to the public entities that manage the urban forest on city and federal land. In Mrs. Casey's gift we see echoes of the farsightedness of another Washington tree lover, the District's second, and last, governor, Alexander Shepherd. In the 1870s, "Boss" Shepherd brought sanitation to the fetid area we now call the National Mall, and planted sixty thousand trees. He spent far more money than Congress gave him, God love him.

Today, new, disease-resistant American elms line Pennsylvania Avenue in front of the White House, serving as a metaphor for another era of tree revitalization. More needs to be done. Many of the trees on the Mall and its environs are clearly suffering from the simple effects of human foot traffic. These ills can be reversed, but only if the decline is recognized and the funds to fix it are forthcoming.

Since the first edition of this book, many old and beloved trees in our city have been lost, even in places that gave them the finest care. Trees are long-lived, but they are not immortal. The conservation group American Forests found in 1999 that the city had lost about 30 percent of its heavy tree cover in the preceding three decades. Since that report, of course, the issues of global warming have come to the fore.

Trees need us, and we need trees. They can stand silent for decades, even centuries—sometimes too silent. This book gives them a voice. All we have to do is listen. And buy a good pair of walking shoes.

Foreword to the Original Edition

Dr. John L. Creech, Director of the
National Arboretum, 1973–1980

One day in the spring of 1978 two young women sat across
from me in my office at the National Arboretum. Melanie
Choukas-Bradley introduced her cohort, Polly Alexander, and
then announced, "We intend to publish a book on the trees of
Washington." I wondered if these two young women realized the
monumental nature of what they were undertaking, and whether
or not they had the background to carry out so formidable a task.
But after listening to their plans and seeing their enthusiasm, I
was won over.

There is a wealth of information on trees at the National
Arboretum, plus a vast range of scientific expertise, so I took
the aspiring authors to visit several members of the Arboretum
staff, who agreed to provide technical assistance. As a result, I
was to see this delightful twosome on numerous occasions during the development of their book, as they hurried through the
Administration Building with materials for review with one or
more of the Arboretum staff. Their steady progress has evolved
into a book that portrays the remarkable history and locations
of the important tree collections in the nation's capital, and also
provides technical descriptions of each species along with the
line drawings so essential to a thorough review.

Washington is indeed a "City of Trees," more so than any
other world capital, because of the diversity of the species involved. In a city with so many transient residents and a complex-
ity of federal agencies, the common interest in trees is surprising.
Trees have been planted to commemorate historic, scientific,
and diplomatic events. Other plantings were integral elements
of various architectural plans for the capital, and still other trees
were planted by presidents, congressmen, and visiting dignitar-

ies, in keeping with a tradition begun in the early days of the city. This enthusiasm for trees is of an enduring nature, making Washington, D.C., a special kind of "window on the world." In the spring of 1981, for example, a tree-planting ceremony was held at the Freer Gallery on the occasion of the visit of the Prime Minister of Japan. For the planting, Secretary of the Smithsonian Institution S. Dillon Ripley selected the small flowering cherry, *Prunus incisa*. It is a pendulous form, probably not planted elsewhere in Washington as a commemorative tree. It grows wild in the vicinity of Mount Fuji and was therefore a most appropriate choice.

The trees of Washington hold their own histories, some related to our heritage, others reflecting the views of architects, and still others involving diplomatic exchanges, moments of anxiety, and even amusing side-issues. Some trees have been mislabeled, others displaced by construction (although there are numerous instances where the tree took priority over the building). Because these histories are often relegated to archives or reposited only in the recollections of contemporary scientists and historians scattered about the city, we have lacked a compiled record. Thus, many tourists, and even longtime residents, depart the city knowing only the most conspicuous specimens. With this book, visitors and others can now acquire a new and exciting understanding of the living monuments of the nation's capital.

Walk under the gracious flowering cherries around the Tidal Basin or stand in the majestic grove of Chinese metasequoias (or dawn redwoods) at the National Arboretum. Pause to reflect on the probability that in their distant homelands, people seemingly of a foreign nature are sharing the same sort of experience under the same trees. Or read the complex story of how these trees were introduced into this country. Then you will understand why Washington can truly be called a "window on the world."

Let us hope that those who are the temporary stewards of this gracious heritage of our nation's capital will gain a new insight into the importance of the trees of Washington. For myself, I am simply grateful for the day Melanie and Polly walked into my office at the National Arboretum.

Preface

Melanie Choukas-Bradley

It is a midsummer evening in Washington, D.C. The Japanese pagoda trees are in bloom on Massachusetts Avenue. The dark pink crape-myrtles are out on every block. And the mimosa tree in the courtyard drops blossoms in my hair. It is cool, clear, and breezy. The air feels as if it has never held a drop of uncomfortable humidity. Soon it will be autumn and the air will feel this way every night. The marble monuments will glitter and the Tidal Basin will fill with fallen cherry leaves.

Autumn is my favorite season in the "City of Trees." It is the time of year I imagine Thomas Jefferson returning. In my fantasy, he strolls around the Tidal Basin, amazed at what's been done to the Potomac flats. He smiles when he sees the marble replica of Monticello and its rippled reflection in the water. Walking under the Japanese cherry trees, with their strange, foreign aura, he is overcome with a sudden, inexplicable feeling of peace.

The sun goes down over the Potomac. The pines and hollies encircling Jefferson's memorial darken. Jefferson feels the magnetism of the memorial—*his*, after all—as he slowly circles the basin. A full moon is rising, and the sky is an unnatural blue. As the sky grows darker, the memorial structure seems to glow from within. Mesmerized, Jefferson scales the seemingly endless marble steps and, with a shiver, beholds the mammoth statue of himself inside.

Just then, a most pleasing fragrance seems to materialize out of the night air. Flowers? In November? As he walks over to the holly trees that brush against the pillars, the sweet smell intensifies. But the hollies aren't in flower. At that moment, he sees them: tiny white flowers covering a large, holly-like shrub. Never has he seen this plant in Washington, nor in Charlottesville, nor even in France.

Jefferson turns and surveys the scene. But for the rising moon, nothing is the same as it was in his time. The marsh has become a lake. Horses have metamorphosed into self-propelled machines that are lit up like fireflies. And the capital is filled with trees and shrubs that he—an accomplished horticulturist—has never so much as read about. Overwhelmed, he decides to enter the memorial. And irony upon irony, while every part of the landscape has evolved to an inscrutable degree, there are Jefferson's words, carved into the stone. His thoughts have survived, while all else has vanished.

I am imagining another evening. It is spring. George Washington rides up on horseback from Mount Vernon, where he discovers, lo and behold, that the bowling green, where he planted seedlings more than two hundred years ago, is lined with huge trees!

It is a special kind of Potomac evening. A fine mist, teasing rain, brings out the colors in his favorite combination of trees—the purplish pink redbud and the snow-white dogwood. Never in all his travels, Washington thinks, has any sight rivaled the beauty of a spring evening on the Potomac. And never has he felt more at peace than when riding through this familiar wood, now bursting with soft greens.

Washington remembers the reason for his journey and nudges his horse onward. He finds it peculiar that so much has changed: the traffic on the river has taken to the air on noisy wings, and the old port of Alexandria seems almost landlocked. But what strikes him even more profoundly than the changes he sees are the things that have remained the same. He remembers riding on horseback through these same woods, under the flowering dogwood trees, on just such an evening centuries ago.

As he nears the capital, suddenly one of Washington's worst fears is confirmed. "They've destroyed the view to the river. And with all those monstrosities sticking up everywhere, including that giant obelisk, the President's House probably won't look a thing like the plan." Noticing names and signs for the first time, he sees one that almost makes him fall off his horse. "L'Enfant Plaza? Named for the French engineer I fired?" Surely, it must be another L'Enfant.

Soon, Washington muses, he'll know whether or not the President's House, begun on his hand-chosen site, was ever completed. And if he has time before nightfall, he might even trot up to Jenkins Hill to see if they ever completed construction of the Capitol. His musings are interrupted, however, by the most incredible sight! He won't have to ride up to Jenkins Hill after all, because there it is, rising out of the spring mist, the United States Capitol, looking larger and more glorious than he ever imagined. "And I laid the cornerstone myself!"

Washington's spirits are soaring. Spread out at his feet lies the Federal City of his dreams—and so much of it, from the President's House at one end of the long green Mall, to the Capitol at the other, laid out according to the plan drawn up during his lifetime. And as far as the eye can see, the beautiful groves of trees. "Every man should be able to live for centuries," he thinks, "if this could be his reward."

When I first moved to Washington, D.C., I told my husband, Jim—who had majored in U.S. history—that George Washington and Thomas Jefferson seemed no more real to me than the man in the moon. For me, the history books had failed to breathe life into the Founding Fathers. How strange it is that I have since come to appreciate Washington, Jefferson, and so many other American leaders—not by studying Revolutionary history or reading the Constitution, but through my research for a book on trees!

When Polly Alexander and I began work on the first edition of *City of Trees*, in 1978, we planned simply to fill a need. As I had discovered after moving here from northern New England, local bookstores carried no guide to the magnificent trees of the nation's capital. For weeks, I had tried to identify a massive tree with elm-like leaves that grew across from my Capitol Hill apartment. At the end of two months' time, I had finally made a "negative" identification: it was not an elm tree.

It would be many more weeks before I would find a source to tell me that my mystery tree was a Japanese zelkova. But with one botanical mystery solved, another would inevitably crop up. Polly and I learned to identify southern bald-cypress trees, only to discover that many of them were not bald-cypresses at all, but dawn redwoods from a remote part of China. We didn't believe it possible that we could confuse the Eastern white pine—that beautiful conifer of our New England woods—with any other species. But we did. The rare exotic Himalayan pine, sparsely scattered throughout the city, is nearly a dead ringer. Washington, we found, those many years ago, is a city filled with trees from other continents. And the native American species we came across were just as likely to be indigenous to the Rockies or the Ozarks as they were to the Blue Ridge. Among the American trees we encountered were giant sequoias, Douglas-firs, and several species of magnolias.

As we planned our guidebook, we received assistance from the late congressman Fred Schwengel, in his role as president of the U.S. Capitol Historical Society, who helped us to enlist the financial support of the American Forest Institute and the forest products industry. Jane Spivy Keough, then on the staff of the Smithsonian, put her tireless self to the task of historical and botanical research. Botanists at the National Arboretum and the National Park Service also generously shared their time and expertise. For months, Polly and I criss-crossed the city, gathering specimens of leaves, flowers, and fruit for our own little herbarium. We photographed the trees in all seasons and recorded field notes in our journals. Now, more than twenty-five years later, we have repeated those journeys, with the goal of bringing the reader a completely updated and revised third edition.

Botanical diversity is only one part of the story of the City of Trees. In our original research we learned that George Washington, Thomas Jefferson, John Quincy Adams, and many other presidents were accomplished horticulturists. And that the city of Washington evolved in close accordance with a plan laid out at its founding more than two centuries ago. That plan—largely the work of Pierre L'Enfant, the French engineer hired by President Washington—had called for tree plantings and parks throughout the capital.

While my imagination had never been fully engaged by thoughts of George Washington the Revolutionary War General, I found that I was captivated by accounts of Washington's botanical experiments at Mount Vernon. Standing under living trees he had planted more than two hundred years ago, I felt awed. And I grew to respect the man who was as interested in the construction details of the Capitol building and the White House as he was in the fine points of military strategy and the business of governing a new nation.

Thomas Jefferson, whose legacy I'd always admired, also grew in stature for me as I read about his struggles to save the young city of Washington from the haphazard development that threatened to destroy its natural charm. Like George Washington, Jefferson understood that no blueprint for government could be put to work in a void. Concerned about the sorry state of Pennsylvania Avenue during his presidency, Jefferson drew up plans to line the route from the Capitol to the President's House with Lombardy poplar trees. Eventually, through the efforts of Washington and Jefferson, and like-minded successors, Washington, D.C., came to be known as the City of Trees.

The story contained in these pages is much more than an accounting of various tree-plantings. When George Washington chose the site for the nation's capital, the Tidal Basin—where the world-famous cherry trees have bloomed each spring since the early 1900s—was a Potomac River tidal marsh. This book charts the city's evolution from tidal marsh and woodland to its status as world capital today. The book can be enjoyed for its own sake or used as a guide to the city's trees. Earlier editions have proved useful in other cities and towns—particularly in the eastern and midwestern United States, but also in Europe and elsewhere—as a guide to trees planted along streets and in parks and gardens. Because many urban and suburban trees are non-native, regional field guides are of limited utility in settled areas.

Since publication of the earlier editions of *City of Trees*, much has happened in the nation's capital to change the fortunes of the city's residents and its trees. On September 11, 2001, tragedy struck the city and the nation when a hijacked plane was crashed into the Pentagon, killing dozens of people, on the same day that two other hijacked planes destroyed the twin towers of the World Trade Center in New York City. Weeks, months, and years of anxiety followed, as threats of further terrorism and fear of the unknown haunted those of us living and raising our children in and around the city.

Following the frightening events of that day, I visited the Bishop's Garden of the Washington National Cathedral with my two young children, from whom my husband and I had been separated for many hours during the crisis. There we found comfort in the sweeping branches of the large silver Atlas cedar, the southern magnolias, and the stone sculpture of the Prodigal Son, for which my husband's father and great-grandfather had served as sculptor's models during the 1930s. The trees throughout the city continued to provide a sense of continuity for my family, and all Washington families, during those troubled days.

But the trees themselves had undergone their own traumas. Severe budget cuts for tree maintenance in the latter part of the twentieth century, combined with increased development and other stresses, led to a decline in the city's street trees, and dead and dying trees were apparent almost everywhere. Several of the most historic trees in Washington, including the John Quincy Adams Elm on the White House grounds and the Cameron Elm at the Capitol, had to be cut down because of ill health and old age, and many other arboreal giants have died within the past quarter of a century. These changes are sadly noted in the pages of this edition of *City of Trees*. But if trees teach us nothing else, they teach us to hope. And as had happened previously during the history of the city, just as the future of Washington's trees looked bleakest, help arrived—in the form of increased investment by the city and in the founding of Casey Trees, an organization whose stated mission is to restore, enhance, and protect the tree canopy of the Nation's Capital.

For my part, as I wrote in the earlier editions of *City of Trees*, I hope someday to bring my grandchildren to see the cherry trees. And I hope the ephemeral beauty of their blossoms will continue to inspire generations of residents and visitors. But in order to ensure that the Tidal Basin will endure as an arboreal refuge throughout this new century and beyond, we will have to come to terms with the looming crisis of global climate change. I believe that environmental awareness begins with an intimate love of nature. I hope that those of us who appreciate the trees of the nation's capital will become sensitive stewards, not only of this city but of the earth itself. Let George Washington, Thomas Jefferson, and the many visionary Washington tree-lovers who have preceded and followed them be our guides.

Acknowledgments

Many people have contributed to *City of Trees* in its three editions over a period of thirty years. Polly and I wish to thank our families and friends; our husbands, Jim Choukas-Bradley and Bill Nash; and our children, Sophie and Jesse Choukas-Bradley and Tyler Nash, all of whom supported us during our work on the latest edition of the book. We would also like to thank our loyal readers, who have shown up at book signings through the years carrying dog-eared copies that have spent many hours in the field.

For their contributions to the first two editions of *City of Trees*, the authors gratefully acknowledge the support and assistance of the American Forest Institute, the National Forest Products Association, and the following companies and associations of the forest products industry: International Paper Company, Crown Zellerbach Corporation, American Pulpwood Association, American Paper Institute, Union Camp Corporation, the Bendix Corporation, and Time, Inc.

The following individuals were invaluable to the creation of the first editions of the book: the Honorable Fred Schwengel, Jane Spivy Keough, James Choukas-Bradley, Roland Jefferson, Peter Mazzeo, Dr. Frederick Meyer, Horace Wester, Ralph Hodges, Joseph McGrath, Don-Lee Davidson, Sharon Connelly, David Kolkebeck, Al Hackl, David Uslan, and the senior staff of the American Forest Institute.

Others who contributed their time and energy: Mrs. Lyndon Baines Johnson, Senator Patrick Leahy, Senator Mark Hatfield, Dr. John L. Creech, Dr. Marc Cathey, Joann Klappauf, Robert Hickey, Dick Hammerschlag, Jim Patterson, Dean Norton,

R. Bernard and Eleanor Alexander, Michael Choukas Jr. and Nita Choukas, Eleanor Choukas, Michael A. Choukas, Hubert Bermont, Howell Begle, Nancy Clark Reynolds, Helen Neal, Theodore Dudley, Gene Eisenbeiss, Hans Johannsen, Nash Castro, Rex Scouten, Irvin Williams, Bill Rooney, James Buckler, Jack Mundy, Karen Solit, Don Smith, Elmer Jones, Robert Fisher, Kevin Murphy, Jeffrey Carson, Darwina Neal, Florian Thayne, Tom Beers, Perry Fisher, Paul Pincus, George Berklacey, Dorothy Provine, Peter Atkinson, Richard Howard, John Hall, H. P. Newson, Raphael Sagalyn, Cindy Weaver, Jakie Lewis, David Barrington, and the support staff at the American Forest Institute.

And we also wish to thank the Johns Hopkins University Press staff for devoting time and talent to the second edition of *City of Trees.*

For this, the third edition of *City of Trees,* our list of people to thank has grown. We extend our appreciation to the board of directors and staff at Casey Trees, including Barbara Shea, Mark Buscaino, Dan Smith, Barbara Deutsch, Holli Howard, and Robin Dublin.

For their help along the way, we also thank Wayne Amos, Dixie T. Barlow, Megan Barlow, Brian Barr, Dana Bender, Susan Bentz, Carole Bergmann, Peggy Bowers, Tina Brown, Marney Bruce, Kate Bucco, Kevin Conrad, Mary Kay Crow, Ryan Daniels, Bob Day, Robert DeFeo, Pat Durkin, Elizabeth Eby, David J. Ellis, Matthew Evans, Cliff Fairweather, Joan Feely, Neal Fitzpatrick, Cris Fleming, Sally Gagne, Deborah Gangloff, John Gibbs, Doris Greer, Gail Griffin, Charles Jacobs, Eric Korpon, Sophia Lynn, Jim Lyons, Stephanie Mason, William McLaughlin, Philip M. Normandy, Dean Norton, Dr. Richard Olsen, Lorne Peterson, Paul D. Polinsky, Dr. Margaret Pooler, Gail Ross, Susan A. Roth, Mary Pat Rowan, Deborah Shapley, Dr. James L. Sherald, Dr. Stanwyn Shetler, Kevin Tunison, Irvin Williams, Dr. Alan Whittemore, Carter L. Wormeley, Michael Xander, Annie Young, and Greg Zell.

Finally, we are grateful to Penny Kaiserlian and the staff at the University of Virginia Press for working so tirelessly and creatively to bring forth the current edition of the book. Special thanks go to project manager Ruth Steinberg, copyeditor Lynne Bonenberger, and designer Chris Harrison. Thank you also to George F. Thompson and the Center for American Places.

City *of* Trees

The City Is Born

How Washington Came to Be Known as the City of Trees

In 1790 President George Washington was granted the authority to oversee the selection of a site for a permanent national capital. The city was to be located on the Maryland–Virginia border, along the Potomac River. No individual could have been better suited to this task. The distinguished general and first president of the United States was also a land surveyor and farmer, who possessed a great sensitivity to the land. The site he chose, early in 1791, was just a few miles upriver from his estate at Mount Vernon, Virginia.

The eighteenth-century landscape where the city of Washington, D.C., now lies was laid out with picturesque orchards, and corn and tobacco fields set among the native woodlands. American Indians had cleared the land and planted crops along the Potomac centuries earlier, and they had become consummate traders. As Frederick Gutheim noted in his 1949 classic *The Potomac*: "The very name Potomac in the Algonkin tongue is a verbal noun meaning 'something brought,' and as a designation for a place, 'where something is brought,' or, more freely, 'trading place.' Living, as they did, on one of the great natural routes east and west through the mountains, north and south along the fall line, with a highly developed and specialized culture, it was inevitable that the natives of this section should be great traders."[1]

Although trade between the Indians of the region and early Europeans developed and flourished for decades, the seventeenth and early eighteenth centuries were a time of turmoil in the Potomac Valley, as the Indians were betrayed by the English colonists who befriended them and hostilities broke out with the more warlike tribes who traveled and hunted in the region. By the mid-eighteenth century, most Indians were gone from the area, pushed farther to the north and west or dead from European-borne disease.

As Gutheim observed, however, their legacy survived their tragic disappearance:

> The Indians of the Potomac valley had a powerful influence on white settlement and subsequent white culture. Indian forms of agriculture, construction, and language, and even forms of government and oratory, were silently absorbed into white settlements all over the Americas. In the Potomac we can see the introduction of specific plants (corn, tobacco, potatoes), new words (hominy, opossum, succotash, wigwam), a new diet. From the first white settlement a new civilization began to be born.[2]

By the 1790s, when George Washington chose the site for a permanent capital for the new nation, Georgetown had become a thriving tobacco port. Washington hired Major Pierre Charles L'Enfant, a European-born engineer who has been described as an "artist, adventurer, and spectacularly arrogant visionary,"[3] to design the Federal City. L'Enfant brought to the task an intimate knowledge of the great capitals of Europe. The Washington city plan benefited from his appreciation of the finest architectural elements of eighteenth-century Paris, London, and Rome. Broad avenues were laid out in every direction, radiating from the central axis of the Capitol. Stately government buildings would be surrounded by spacious grounds, and there would be parks aplenty throughout the city. Both George Washington and Pierre L'Enfant also appreciated the need to incorporate trees into the city plan. Every street, avenue, and federal building was to be generously graced by groves of trees.

While L'Enfant's splendid capital remains for the ages, his tenure as the city's designer met an untimely end. Disagreements between the temperamental engineer and the board of commissioners overseeing the city's development put the ever diplomatic George Washington in an uncomfortable position. For a time, the president managed to placate the commissioners and keep the rebellious L'Enfant in line. But the president's efforts were doomed. When Daniel Carroll, one of the area's wealthiest men, began erecting a house in the middle of where L'Enfant had envisioned New Jersey Avenue, L'Enfant sent his assistant to tear it down. When the assistant was arrested, L'Enfant himself attempted to raze the structure. Washington's fatherly scolding— "I must strictly enjoin you to touch no man's property without his consent"[4]—and numerous similar warnings did little to check L'Enfant's impetuous behavior. Eventually, he was fired.

L'Enfant later submitted a bill to Congress for $95,000, but he was paid less than $4,000 for designing the capital of the United States. The plan was completed by Andrew Ellicott, who originally had been commissioned to survey the land for the new city. Ellicott made minor adjustments to the L'Enfant map, then erased L'Enfant's name and signed his own. The map for the new city was known thereafter as the Ellicott map. One can't help but wonder what L'Enfant would think of the huge twentieth-century plaza in southwest Washington that sits so heavily on his delicate grid of streets, parks, and avenues, and so inappropriately bears his name.

Although the vision of the capital held by its founders would eventually become a reality, the early years of the city were bleak. During his administration, Thomas Jefferson was forced to bear witness to the widespread destruction of the area's trees, as property owners throughout the District cleared the beautiful stands of native timber from their land for profit and trees were felled by the poor for use as firewood. The staunchly democratic Jefferson even expressed a momentary wish that "in the possession of absolute power, I might enforce the preservation of these valuable groves."[5]

Despite his despair over the destruction of the city's native trees, Jefferson set to work planting new trees throughout the District. He sketched out a plan to plant Lombardy poplars along Pennsylvania Avenue from the Capitol to the White House, and then supervised its execution. This is the first planting of Washington street trees on record. Drawings and paintings that survive from the era depict the avenue lined with rows of Jefferson's delicate, columnar poplars.

The capital city experienced its darkest days following Jefferson's administration. Garbage and slops were freely dumped in the streets, the polluted marshlands along the Potomac posed a growing health threat, and the death rate was extremely high. Poverty was severe and crime rampant. In her book, *Washington: Village and Capital*, Constance McGlaughlin Green described the depressing landscape of the 1820s:

> The city L'Enfant had laid out on a scale to represent the genius of the new republic had in fact attained little aesthetic distinction. Partial execution of the plan left large areas untouched, which spoiled the effect.

Most of the Mall was a wasteland of swamps dotted with
clusters of sheds along the canal.

Vacant lots occupied much of the ["]city of magnificent dis-
tances,["] and the streets connecting one village with the others
that comprised the capital were little more than rutted paths.[6]

As depressing as Washington had become out-of-doors, it is
easy to understand why people flocked indoors during the 1840s
to view the botanical wonders housed in the new greenhouse adjacent to the Patent Office Building on F Street. Plants collected
in remote parts of the world by government-sponsored expeditions were displayed inside the popular greenhouse, which was
a precursor to the United States Botanic Garden now located at
the foot of Capitol Hill. Toward the end of that decade, interest
in beautifying the nation's capital was rekindled. In 1847, the
cornerstone for the romantic Smithsonian Castle was laid, and
the following year ground was broken for the Washington Monument. Unfortunately, this promising trend was destined to be cut
short by the Civil War.

An interesting interlude in the city's design began in the
1850s, when the government hired the eminent landscape
gardener Andrew Jackson Downing to take charge of the design
and planting of Washington's park system. Downing's ideas dif-
fered radically from L'Enfant's. Where L'Enfant had called for
open spaces and grand vistas, Downing sketched out plans for
romantic paths through groves of trees. Downing believed that
"the straight lines and broad avenues of the streets of Washington would be relieved and contrasted by the beauty of curved
lines and natural groups of trees."[7] It was just such a plan that was
carried out on the Mall. For many years, the expansive, green avenue we know today was planted with Downing's clumps of trees
amid curving walkways. Downing drowned in a steamboat ac-
cident in 1852 before he was able carry out most of the work he'd
been commissioned to do. In addition to the landscaping plan
for the Mall, many of his plans for the White House grounds, the
Ellipse, and Lafayette Park were executed during and after his
lifetime.

During the Civil War (1861–65), Washington was a grim city
indeed. The Mall was the site of horse and cattle corrals, a fetid
and nearly useless canal, and clusters of Union Army tents. The
marshlands along the Potomac grew more unhealthful by the
day, and worst of all, the skyline of the capital was dominated by

two disheartening sights: at one end of the Mall the unfinished Capitol dome, and at the other the uncompleted Washington Monument. After the war, in 1872, a railroad station and tracks were added to the Mall, moving the city even further away from the original vision of Washington, Jefferson, and L'Enfant. Nevertheless, it was a good year for the District of Columbia overall, because something began happening that was to turn Washington into one of the world's most beautiful cities. Alexander R. Shepherd began planting trees.

Alexander Shepherd (who was often called "Boss" Shepherd) was the second and last governor of the District of Columbia. A native Washingtonian, he had ambitious plans for improving the quality of life in the District. They included not only planting 60,000 trees, but also installing crucially needed sewers, and filling in the polluted canal on the Mall. Shepherd also tore up the railroad tracks at the foot of Capitol Hill and ran the District of Columbia into debt that was $10 million over the authorized allowable ceiling. Congress decided in 1874 that the District of Columbia would do better without a governor.

During his brief term in office, however, the energetic Shepherd turned Washington, D.C., into the world-famous City of Trees. He appointed three experienced horticulturists to serve as a "parking commission" to oversee the tree plantings throughout the city. During the next decade, under the commission's direction, the streets of Washington were amply lined with maples, poplars, lindens, sycamores, elms, ashes, and many other trees. These early plantings not only beautified the city; for the first time, they made Washington truly livable, providing relief from the summer heat, as well as a rather mysterious check on the spread of malaria.

An 1889 article in *Harper's Magazine* described a very different city from the one the world had grown accustomed to grumbling about: "The city of Washington, the capital of the nation, exceeds in beauty any city in the world. The grand conception of the plan of its broad streets and avenues paved with asphalt, smooth as marble, and its hundreds of palatial residences erected in the highest style of art, but above all, its magnificent trees, make it without a peer."[8] For the first time, Washington, D.C., was favorably compared to the great capitals of Europe. Visitors to Berlin claimed that its famous Unter den Linden, a linden-lined avenue, was a disappointment compared to Washington's Massachusetts Avenue and its miles of lindens. There was even talk that the trees of Washington surpassed those of Paris and London in beauty and variety.

Soon Washington was known the world over as the "City of Trees." Although Governor Shepherd was in office for only a brief time, his legacy has endured. In 1932, Erle Kauffman wrote:

> After [Shepherd] the vision was never lost. The Federal Government, the city fathers, tree loving citizens, even outsiders, labored tirelessly to repair the tragic results of those early depredations. Trees appeared on every street, the parks blossomed in new glory, and tiny seedlings took root on lawns and in backyards. At first the trees were confined to those native to the region, those easily accessible, but soon plants from other sections of the country, from other lands, were flowering in all their exotic beauty. From the Orient came the exquisite cherry trees, the ginkgo, the umbrella tree, the ailanthus—the Chinese Tree of Heaven—the paulownia and the Scholar tree. From the Holy Land came the cedar and locust, while Asia contributed spruce, thorn, and magnolia. Europe gave the hornbeam, willow elm, and holly.
>
> Today in Washington the visitor may find more than two thousand varieties of trees and shrubs, representing nearly two hundred distinct species. It holds, with the exception of a few arboretums, more different kinds of trees and shrubs than any city on earth.[9]

The twentieth century dawned auspiciously for the city of Washington. After a commission headed by Senator James McMillan visited the capitals of Europe, its members returned home with the conviction that the city should be returned to L'Enfant's original conception. Downing's arboretum would be removed, reestablishing the vista from the Capitol to the Washington Monument. The railroad station would be torn down and the Mall extended. At the same time, work already was under way to fill in the polluted tidal flats along the river, creating today's beautiful East and West Potomac Parks. The McMillan Commission selected the American elm to line the National Mall, citing the "architectural character of its columnar trunk and the delicate traceries formed by its wide-spreading branches."[10] Today, these rows of elms, stretching from the Capitol to the Washington Monument, are a magnificent example of a tastefully designed landscape. Then, in 1912, the beautiful Japanese flowering cherry trees, a gift from Japan, were laid out around the newly created Tidal Basin and along the shores of East Potomac Park. And in

1927 Congress authorized the creation of an arboretum in the capital.

The early street trees planted by Shepherd's parking commission had served as a useful experiment in the new science of urban silviculture. In time, it was learned that the fast-growing silver maple, planted in the 1870s for the fast shade it provided, was too brittle and prone to storm damage to be a practical city tree. Poplars, also widely planted by Shepherd's commission, turned out to be surface rooters that tore up the landscape with their shallow roots. And ash-leafed maples (or boxelders) were found to be particularly susceptible to insect pests. Other maples, oaks, plane trees, and ginkgoes proved to be better suited to the urban environment.

As the times changed, so did the problems associated with Washington's street trees. Hungry horses nibbling on the trees to which they were hitched—a serious problem in the nineteenth century—gave way to the far more destructive automobile. Underground gas leaks became an increasing problem as the city grew; and early in the twentieth century, ice cream manufacturers wreaked havoc on the city's trees simply by dumping briny water on their roots.

Even the pests changed with the times. During the twentieth century two devastating diseases were imported on foreign plant material. The chestnut blight virtually destroyed the American chestnut, and Dutch elm disease devastated urban landscapes throughout the country. However, by pooling their expertise, arborists employed by the National Park Service, the National Arboretum, and the District of Columbia have managed to save many of the historic and beautiful elms of Washington, and have made simultaneous strides in the science of urban forestry.

During the 1960s Lady Bird Johnson's Committee for a More Beautiful Capital set an example in Washington that inspired a drive to beautify cities across the country. This group of thirty public officials, private citizens, and urban designers revitalized parks throughout the city by planting thousands of trees and flowers and making extensive physical improvements. Commenting on the drive, Mrs. Johnson said: "To me, in sum, 'beautification' means our total concern for the physical and human quality of the world we pass on to our children."[11]

In recent years, the National Park Service's Center for Urban Ecology, located in Washington, has focused on the most common problems plaguing natural areas in today's urban environment. The center has studied and implemented soil protection and improvement programs in Washington's parks, and it has helped coordinate citywide efforts to manage tree diseases and pests.

The end of the twentieth century and the dawn of the twenty-first have brought new arboreal challenges, as well as promising innovations. Our trees have had to contend with new pests and diseases, including the woolly adelgid, a foreign insect that has savaged hemlock populations throughout the eastern United States, and a flowering dogwood blight that has sickened and killed many of these native and cultivated trees in the Washington area. Moreover, cuts in the city's budget during the latter years of the twentieth century, coupled with increased development, took a serious toll on Washington's street trees.

Fortunately, once again a new century dawned auspiciously for the City of Trees. Under the leadership of then mayor Anthony A. Williams, Washington increased its Urban Forestry Administration budget and the number of professional arborists on its staff. And when satellite images revealed that a significant loss of trees had occurred citywide between 1973 and 1999, Maryland philanthropist Betty Brown Casey took dramatic action. In May 2001 the nonprofit organization Casey Trees was formed with a $50 million grant from the Eugene B. Casey Foundation. Its mission: "To restore, enhance, and protect the tree canopy of the Nation's Capital."[12]

Working with the Urban Forestry Administration, the National Park Service, and civic groups throughout the region, Casey Trees has inventoried Washington's street trees, assisted with plantings and maintenance, and educated hundreds of volunteers through its Citizen Forester program. Each summer, Casey Trees employs teams of interns from local high schools to help care for the city's trees. According to communications director Dan Smith, the intern program has a strong environmental leadership component. Additional teams of college students, recent college graduates, and volunteers are organized from time to time to conduct tree inventories. Street trees, schoolyard trees, the condition of large trees, and the extent of Dutch elm disease have all been subjects of recent and ongoing inventories. Volunteers from city neighborhoods have joined the ambitious program of arboreal revitalization, a legacy already apparent along streets in every ward of the city. Once again, the citizens of the nation's capital have come to the rescue of their beloved trees.

With heightened appreciation for the cultural landscapes of Washington, the city's botanists, horticulturists, and arborists, and those of the National Park Service, the U.S. Capitol and Botanic Garden, and the Smithsonian Institution, are now pooling their expertise to make the wisest choices of trees for specific sites. Robert DeFeo, chief horticulturist for the National Park Service, explains that, today, aesthetics, historic precedence, and sustainability are all taken into consideration when trees are chosen for planting in the city's landscapes.

Washington's renewed efforts at tree protection dovetail with a growing global recognition of the importance of trees in the urban environment. Many scientific studies have shown that city trees cool and clean the air, reduce the incidence of childhood asthma and other lung diseases, increase property values, regulate storm-water runoff, and enhance the overall quality of life. In the ongoing effort to reduce greenhouse gases and mediate global climate change, trees play a critical role in decreasing carbon dioxide. The reasons for enhancing and protecting the tree canopy in the nation's capital, and in cities and towns throughout the country, could not be more compelling. (See page 403 for information about how you can contribute to the health and well-being of Washington's urban forest.)

Today, the beautiful City of Trees is a living tribute to humankind's ability to work in harmony with nature. These words from a 1915 volume of *National Geographic* still hold true: "Washington rests lightly on its people. In many of the world's larger cities a necessity for 'letting in the country upon the city' is being felt. Such a necessity does not exist in the National Capital, which has been built around the country, leaving many delightful strips within, where a mighty forest is growing in the midst of metropolitan life."[13]

This, then, is the City of Trees, the magnificent capital of the United States.

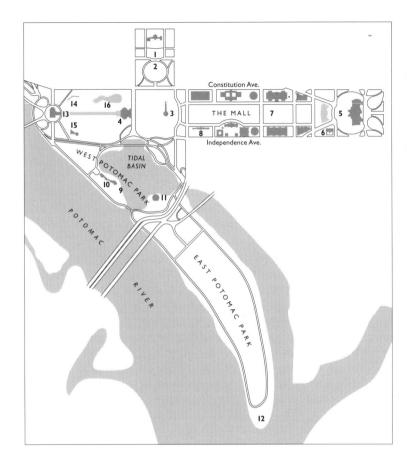

THE MALL AND VICINITY

1   White House Grounds
2   National Christmas Tree
3   Washington Monument
4   World War II Memorial
5   Capitol Hill
6   U.S. Botanic Garden
7   Smithsonian Museum and National
    Gallery of Art Grounds
8   U.S. Department of Agriculture
    Grounds

9   Japanese Flowering Cherry Trees
10 Franklin Delano Roosevelt
    Memorial
11 Jefferson Memorial
12 East Potomac Park (Hains Point)
13 Lincoln Memorial
14 Vietnam Veterans Memorial and
    Vietnam Women's Memorial
15 Korean War Veterans Memorial
16 Constitution Gardens

Part I

Site Guide
to the City of Trees

Part I of *City of Trees* is organized in two sections. The first
describes tree-viewing sites in the vicinity of the Mall, and the
second takes you to outlying areas of the District and beyond.
To learn more about the trees you see, and to identify unknown
species, consult Part II of this book, where you will find detailed,
illustrated descriptions of more than 300 types of native and
exotic trees. The index provides a quick and easy way to locate
illustrated descriptions of the trees that are mentioned in Part I.
Moreover, the sites discussed in Part I are keyed to the two maps
that follow: the first map profiles the Mall area, and the second
one shows outlying locations.

TREE VIEWING AROUND THE MALL

The White House Grounds:
Site of Presidential Tree Plantings

President William Howard Taft once wrote: "The view from the
White House windows plays an important part in the life of its
occupants. [The president] can look from the south windows of
the White House on a scene of rare beauty."[14]

Occupants of the most demanding, and often the loneliest,
office in the land have consistently drawn sustenance from the
lovely acres surrounding the White House. During the Cuban
Missile Crisis of 1962, John F. Kennedy described the White
House Rose Garden as the "brightest spot in the somber surroundings of the last few days."[15]

And those who have found solace in the White House surroundings also have a long-standing tradition of leaving the

grounds of the executive mansion even more beautiful than they found them. President Kennedy himself decided to redesign the famous garden just outside the Oval Office. Nearly every American president has picked up a spade to perform the simple and symbolic ritual of planting a tree at 1600 Pennsylvania Avenue. The present occupants of the White House know that spring has arrived when Kennedy's saucer magnolias bloom in the Rose Garden. And as the days grow warmer still, the white dogwoods planted by President Bill Clinton and First Lady Hillary Rodham Clinton unfurl their showy white blossoms. The first hot days of summer mean there will be warm evenings on the Truman balcony, with the fragrance of Andrew Jackson's southern magnolias in the air.

Individually, the trees of the White House grounds are living memorials to the people who have served in their country's highest office. Together, they form a graceful frame for the nation's first home.

History of the Grounds

When John and Abigail Adams moved into the newly constructed executive mansion in 1800, the site selected by George Washington bore little resemblance to the White House setting of today. The barren grounds were strewn with tools, rubble, and workmen's shacks. The first lady described the scene in a letter to her daughter: "We have not the least fence, yard or other convenience, without." With no private place outdoors to hang the family wash, Mrs. Adams was forced to string up a clothesline in what she called "the great unfinished audience room," known today as the East Room.[16]

But if the first woman to set up housekeeping at 1600 Pennsylvania Avenue found some aspects of her situation slightly primitive, she was able to rise above them to make this observation: "The President's House is in a beautiful situation in front of which is the Potomac with a view of Alexandr[i]a. The country around is romantic but a wild, a wilderness at present."[17]

When Thomas Jefferson succeeded John Adams to the presidency, he developed a landscaping plan for the mansion grounds with the assistance of architect Benjamin Latrobe. During his administration, Jefferson planted many seedling trees, though none survive today. In 1807, an English visitor to the White House, apparently unimpressed by the landscaping in progress, wrote: "The ground around [the White House], instead of being laid out in a suitable style, is in a condition so that in a dark night instead of finding your way to the house, you may, perchance, fall into a pit, or stumble over a heap of rubbish." This same British visitor was also unfavorably impressed by Jefferson's rustic wooden fence, the first enclosure ever erected around the executive mansion. According to the guest: "The fence around the house is of the meanest sort; a common post and rail enclosure. This parsimony destroys every sentiment of pleasure that arises in the mind, in viewing the residence of the President of a nation, and is a disgrace to the country."[18] While it is hard to imagine the third president concurring with his visitor's strong sentiments, Jefferson did later remove the wooden fence in favor of a low fieldstone wall.

James Madison's wife, Dolley, known as a charming and tactful hostess and first lady, is said to have taken an avid interest in the White House grounds. But in 1814, midway through Madison's two terms as president (1809–1817), the invading British set fire to the White House, and the president and first lady were forced to live elsewhere. Thanks to a heavy rain, the shell of the mansion remained intact, and the original architect, James Hoban, was able to salvage the presidential home. In 1817, James Monroe, the nation's fifth president, moved into the reconstructed White House.

Monroe's successor, John Quincy Adams, made the greatest improvements of any American president to the White House grounds. Adams spent many hours planting and tending the mansion's gardens and trees, an avocation that earned him his sobriquet, "The tree planting Mr. Adams."[19] Diary entries tell of the joy Adams derived from his horticultural endeavors, and they give a rough record of what grew on the White House grounds during the late 1820s: "forest and fruit-trees, shrubs, hedges, esculent vegetables, kitchen and medicinal herbs, hot-house plants, flowers and weeds, to the amount I conjecture, of at least one thousand."[20]

In an attempt to boost a national silk industry, Adams planted white mulberries on the grounds and nurtured silkworms on their leaves. His wife, Louisa, performed the delicate task of unreeling the slender silk filaments from the cocoons. Despite their efforts, the industry never got off the ground.

Martin Van Buren, who occupied the White House from 1837 until 1841, supervised additional changes to the grounds. During the Van Buren administration, fountains were installed and stone walls erected, and more flower gardens were added around the mansion. When Charles Dickens visited the White House in 1841, his British eye saw the "garden walks" as being "pretty and agreeable . . . though they have that uncomfortable air of having been made yesterday."[21]

In 1851, with Millard Fillmore in the White House, the prominent landscape architect Andrew Jackson Downing was commissioned to formally lay out the grounds. Only sketchy records of the Downing plan and its execution remain, but there is evidence that Downing recommended changing the angular outline of the south lawn to the curved perimeter we know today. Downing also sketched out a plan for a circular park, to be located south of the grounds. Downing met a tragic death by drowning just two years after he was commissioned to landscape the White House grounds and other parks throughout Washington. But his plan for a circular park south of the White House would eventually be carried out after the Civil War, during the administration of Ulysses S. Grant.

James Buchanan's major contribution to the White House grounds, a series of conservatories on the west lawn, became a prominent feature of the landscape for nearly half a century, until they were removed to make way for a new west wing in the early 1900s. It was Buchanan's niece and White House hostess, Harriet Lane, who convinced the fifteenth president to build the first of these greenhouses. Although the conservatories grew to unsightly proportions over the years, their lush interiors became a panacea for first families needing a break from the interminable round of official duties. Myriad potted plants, including orchids, camellias, and orange trees, were grown in the conservatories, providing the mansion with a constant supply of flowers and greenery.

During the Civil War, President Abraham Lincoln's view from the south windows of the White House was indisputably grim. Looking out over Union troops bivouacked on the lawn, the beleaguered commander in chief saw a badly polluted canal (where Constitution Avenue runs today) surrounded by fetid marshland. Beyond, cattle and horse corrals stretched all the way up to the unfinished Washington Monument. During the summer months, when the marshland was particularly unhealthy, the president stayed at the Soldiers' Home, several miles away. After the war, the canal and surrounding lowlands were filled in and the present-day Ellipse was created, guided by the plan worked out years earlier by Andrew Jackson Downing.

The Teddy Roosevelt era (1901–1909) saw the removal of the White House conservatories. Mrs. Roosevelt also redesigned the outdoor cutting gardens near the mansion, creating an old-fashioned colonial garden instead.

Woodrow Wilson's tenure in the White House saw two major changes to the grounds. The first was decidedly temporary. During World War I, the president installed a flock of sheep to keep the grass trim without wasting money or manpower. The second innovation has been longer-lasting: Ellen Wilson planted the first White House rose garden.

In 1935, Frederick Law Olmsted Jr., son of the eminent landscape architect Frederick Law Olmsted, was commissioned to devise a landscaping plan for the White House. He and his half brother, John Charles, headed up the Olmsted Brothers firm in Brookline, Massachusetts. Their proposal, made to President Franklin D. Roosevelt, displayed a landscape sensitivity reminiscent of the elder Olmsted's design for the Capitol grounds more than half a century earlier. In it, they sought to add dignity to the acres surrounding the White House, while simultaneously adapting them to the functional needs of the thirty-second president. The Olmsted Brothers advocated the creation of an open swath of land through the center of the south grounds. Today's residents of the White House not only enjoy an unobstructed view of the Washington Monument and Jefferson Memorial, but they also appreciate the convenience of being able to land a helicopter on the south lawn.

The Olmsted firm also recommended that trees and shrubs be planted along the perimeter of the grounds. The aesthetics of this arboreal frame for the executive mansion, meticulously maintained by today's White House gardeners, can best be appreciated from the south, where the graceful tree-lined curve of the south lawn meets the opposite curve of the Ellipse. An 82-acre area including the Ellipse and Lafayette Park, as well as the grounds around the mansion, the President's Park (as it is officially called) is cared for by a team of National Park Service horticulturists and gardeners. It was President John F. Kennedy who requested that the Park Service assume responsibility for the grounds.

Use of the White House Grounds

Gone are the egalitarian days of the nineteenth century when the public strolled freely under the White House trees. Today the south grounds of the White House are generally open to the public only for the spring and fall garden tours. And each year, during the Easter season, the children of Washington are invited to participate in an egg-rolling celebration on the south lawn, a tradition begun during the administration of Rutherford B. Hayes. Adults are admitted to the festivities only if they are accompanied by a child.

Since the turn of the twentieth century, the White House grounds have been host to a variety of presidential events, from formal receptions for visiting heads of state to picnics and concerts. True to character, it was the great outdoorsman, Teddy Roosevelt, who began the tradition of regularly holding parties outside the executive mansion walls.

Children living in the White House also have made use of the spacious grounds. The first Roosevelt's several rambunctious offspring rode their pony, Algonquin, on the grounds and walked on stilts through the gardens. In the 1960s, Caroline Kennedy trotted across the south lawn on Macaroni, and later, young Amy Carter preferred to survey her surroundings from a tree house nestled in the boughs of an Atlas cedar. Recognizing a child's need for secret space, especially in the White House, Lyndon Baines Johnson and Lady Bird Johnson created the Children's Garden on the south grounds. Sheltered year-round by American holly trees, the garden contains child-sized chairs and tables, a lily pond, azaleas, and other flowering plants. Handprints and footprints of presidential grandchildren are a recently added feature of this garden.

The Rose Garden

Ever since the early 1800s, when the first seed was sown at 1600 Pennsylvania Avenue, the gardens around the White House have been nearly as transitory as the parade of first families who have loved and tended them. One garden, however, has risen in the public imagination to become a lasting and powerful symbol of the presidency.

In 1913, First Lady Ellen Wilson, the first wife of Woodrow Wilson, planted roses near her husband's office in the West Wing of the White House. Inadvertently, she had chosen the site for America's most historic garden. In 1928, during the Calvin Coolidge administration, the *Washington Star* reported: "The opinion is that the President's chief interest lies in the White House rose gardens. The larger of these gardens is immediately east of the President's office and contains more than 300 bushes and a dozen or so rose trees. Virtually every known variety and specimen of rose may be found in this garden, and when it is in full bloom, it is a spot of rare beauty."[22] Each succeeding president has welcomed the opportunity to pause and catch his breath in the shelter of the Rose Garden. It was John F. Kennedy, however, who made the garden what it is today.

Shortly after Kennedy was inaugurated in 1961, he and Jacqueline Kennedy made a state visit to Europe, where they toured the royal gardens of Austria, France, and England. According to William Seale, author of *The White House Garden*, the trip sparked the president's desire to create something to equal the beauty of the gardens of the Palais de l'Élysée or Buckingham Palace; but having studied Thomas Jefferson's notes on gardening, Kennedy envisioned a garden that would be uniquely American.

The president invited his friend and able amateur horticulturist Rachel Lambert Mellon (wife of Paul Mellon, and often known as Bunny) to design a garden for a small piece of land, less than a quarter of an acre, between the Oval Office and the South Portico. With the assistance of Irvin M. Williams, superintendent of the White House grounds, and under the direct supervision of the president, Bunny Mellon worked out the plan for a new White House rose garden. A pink saucer magnolia would go in each corner of the plot; white Katherine crabapples would line the north and south sides; neat green osmanthus and boxwood hedges would surround the trees. And there were the flowers: tulips and hyacinths for early spring, a rainbow of annuals for summer, chrysanthemums for fall, and, of course, roses. Irvin Williams and the White House gardeners meticulously executed the design.

The president took a great interest in the way his garden was progressing. According to the architectural critic Wolf Von Eckardt: "He would always walk through it on his way to his office and back for lunch or dinner. Many times he would stop, and if Williams was in sight ask him one thing or another. As his garden grew, so did his knowledge of its plants and wonders. . . . It was the only thing he ever bragged about." Von Eckardt continued: "Often late at night he would walk out to clear his mind to seek inspiration. The garden had turned out just as he had hoped it would."[23]

Kennedy would use his lovely new garden as the site to bestow honorary citizenship upon Sir Winston Churchill. He would also greet many of his White House guests there, and no matter what the occasion, he took every opportunity to share his newfound knowledge of the trees, shrubs, and flowers with his visitors. Kennedy was assassinated in November 1963; he had only been able to enjoy his garden for two summers. Three days after his death, his young widow requested that a simple basket of flowers from the Rose Garden be placed beside his grave. Von Eckardt described its contents with the cadence and poignancy of a poem: "Roses still blooming, berries from the crabapples and a few flowers that had survived the first frost."[24]

The White House Rose Garden was a great comfort to Kennedy's successor, Lyndon Baines Johnson, under whose presidency the country was torn apart by the Vietnam War. And in the first outdoor White House wedding, Tricia Nixon, the daughter of President Richard M. Nixon, was married in the Rose Garden. The garden has become so closely associated with recent presidents who regularly use it to conduct ceremonial business, that more than one incumbent, cloistered in the White House during an election year, has been accused of practicing the so-called Rose Garden strategy.

Today, the garden remains under the constant scrutiny of a National Park Service team of horticulturists and gardeners, who weed the grass by hand and carefully tend the flowers, shrubs, and trees. As of 2007, Irvin Williams still serves as superintendent of the White House grounds.

The Jacqueline Kennedy Garden

John F. Kennedy and Jacqueline Kennedy had planned another White House garden, to be used by the first lady. Located next to the East Wing, on the opposite side of the South Portico from the Rose Garden, it was to be as convenient a retreat for the first lady as the Rose Garden was for the president.

When the Johnson family moved into the executive mansion, Lady Bird Johnson became determined to finish the garden exactly as the Kennedys had envisioned it. With the help of Bunny Mellon and the National Park Service White House crew, she set to work.

Beautifying her surroundings came as naturally to Lady Bird Johnson as breathing, and within months the garden was completed. In April 1965, Mrs. Johnson dedicated it to Jacqueline Kennedy. In a moving tribute to the former first lady, Mrs. Johnson said: "The Kennedys brought to the White House many striking qualities, but perhaps above all they brought the lilt of youth, an instinct for the lovely, an infinite quality of grace." Every detail of the garden, she went on, "reflects the unfailing taste of the gifted and gracious Jacqueline Kennedy."[25]

Sculpted hollies, a grape arbor, lindens, magnolias, and other trees and shrubs share the graceful plot with tasteful pockets of flowers. A simple plaque attached to a pillar bears a handwritten dedication to Mrs. Kennedy. The Jacqueline Kennedy Garden is a perfect companion to the Rose Garden. Together they form a moving memorial to the Kennedy years.

Trees Planted by Presidents

Nineteenth-Century Presidential Trees. There is a special poignancy about the presidential trees at the White House. In the words of former First Lady Rosalynn Carter, "They stand as personal expressions of faith in the future, not only of this place, but of our nation."[26] In a sadder sense, the White House trees speak to us of the transitory nature of human existence. They are our only living links with many of the individuals who achieved their country's highest office, and then served so briefly.

The greatest tree enthusiast among the presidents was George Washington, the only chief executive who never lived at the White House. While the first president probably never sowed a seed at 1600 Pennsylvania Avenue, he planted dozens of trees at his estate in Mount Vernon, Virginia. Several of them are still alive today.

Thomas Jefferson shared Washington's reverence for trees, and he lined Pennsylvania Avenue from the White House to the Capitol with Lombardy poplars. Although no trees planted by Jefferson survive on the White House grounds, his words lamenting the negligent felling of trees in the capital do: "I wish I was a despot that I might save the noble, the beautiful trees that are daily falling sacrifices to the cupidity of their owners, or the necessity of the poor. . . . The unnecessary felling of a tree, perhaps the growth of centuries, seems to me a crime little short of murder; it pains me to an unspeakable degree."[27]

For many decades, the oldest authenticated presidential planting on the White House grounds was the "John Quincy Adams Elm." Planted by the sixth president in 1826, this venerable American elm dominated the eastern "Jefferson Mound" on the south lawn. Watchful gardeners helped the historic tree escape the plague of Dutch elm disease and a lightning bolt that brought down one of its main limbs in the late 1960s. In 1991, however, the elm finally succumbed to old age; that same year, First Lady

Barbara Bush planted a replacement tree, propagated from the original tree. When the original elm's rings were counted, it proved to be 165 years old, authenticating its link to the Adams administration.

Andrew Jackson, the Tennessean who was the seventh president, carried the spirit of the frontier to the White House. He also carried with him tremendous grief. His cherished wife, Rachel, had recently died, following a bitter political campaign in which the circumstances surrounding their marriage—her second—had been questioned. Unbeknownst to the couple, Rachel's first husband had failed to finalize their divorce, so that the Jacksons had technically lived as adulterers for more than two years before they could be legally married. "Old Hickory" brought a pair of southern magnolias from the couple's Tennessee home, the Hermitage, so that he would have "something green" in Washington to remember Rachel by. These beautiful evergreen magnolias stand between the Rose Garden and the South Portico, delighting White House occupants and guests year after year with their lemon-scented blossoms.

In 1994, they might have been lost, when a small plane crashed into the White House south lawn. The crash killed the pilot and delivered a glancing blow to one of the Jackson magnolias. The tree suffered some damage to its bark, but it survived and has continued to thrive.

For many years Jackson's magnolias graced the $20 bill. On one side of the bill was an engraving of Andrew Jackson. On the other was the White House, with the two magnolias plainly visible to the left of the South Portico. In 1998, however, a new $20 bill was issued, showing the north, rather than the south, grounds of the White House. At the time, I wrote a story for the *Washington Post* titled "Jackson's Magnolias Lose Their Currency." (I can't take credit for the clever headline, which goes to the *Post*'s garden editor, Adrian Higgins.)

Many years earlier, in 1933, the *Washington Post Magazine* had written of Jackson: "Few people ever knew that 'Old Hickory' was one of the greatest tree lovers ever to occupy the White House. His old plantation home, the Hermitage, near Nashville, Tennessee, is one of the tree show places of the nation."[28] Sadly, in the spring of 1998, a tornado ripped through Nashville, uprooting more than twelve hundred trees at the Hermitage, including the historic magnolia next to Andrew Jackson's and his wife Rachel's gravesites. That particular magnolia may have been the parent of the White House trees. According to a Hermitage spokesperson, of all the trees lost during the storm, the magnolia is the one that Nashville residents miss most.

Another White House tree featured in the tragedy of a later administration. In 1881, just months after his inauguration, President James A. Garfield was struck down by an assassin's bullet. For more than two months, the nation anxiously followed Garfield's unsuccessful fight to survive. Legend has it that periodic bulletins about the president's health were placed on an elm tree outside the White House, and that this tree was known for years afterward as the "Bulletin Elm."[29]

Grover Cleveland, the only president to serve two non-consecutive terms, was also the only chief executive to marry in the White House. His young bride, Frances Folsom, just twenty-one years old at the time of their 1886 wedding, planted two delicate "blood-leaf," or "spider-leaf," Japanese maples on the White House south lawn. One of the trees, located to the west of the central fountain, is thriving today. The other was replaced by First Lady Rosalynn Carter.

While many of the presidential trees that were planted in the nineteenth century are no longer alive today, the handsome scarlet oak planted by President Benjamin Harrison in 1889 and located just inside the fence to the east of the eastern Pennsylvania Avenue gate, survives to this day.

Twentieth-Century Presidential Trees. Charles Henlock, the White House gardener during ten presidential administrations, from 1886 until 1931, told an amusing story after his retirement. During the presidency of William Howard Taft, Mrs. Taft requested that a hedge be planted along the west side of the White House, for privacy. When Taft's successor, Woodrow Wilson, deployed a flock of sheep to keep the White House lawns clipped during World War I, it seems the creatures weren't content with an all-grass diet. According to Henlock, "The best thing those sheep ever did was to eat up Mrs. Taft's hedge."[30]

Warren G. Harding's administration is memorialized by a beautiful southern magnolia, which stands between the East Wing of the White House and East Executive Park. (The 1922 planting was replaced in 1947.) Mrs. Harding spent many hours in the White House gardens in the company of the family dog, Laddie Boy. On a spring day in the early 1920s, a Washington newspaper reported: "Mrs. Harding and the faithful Laddie Boy have passed some pleasant hours in and out of [the gardens] gathering some blossoms for the sanctum of the second floor and admiring the stately procession of tulips. One of the ancient beliefs is that a dog is destructive to a flower garden, but to see the care with which the Airedale picks his steps following his mistress is to revise this opinion."[31]

President Herbert Hoover gave impetus to a national tree-planting movement in the early 1930s by planting an American elm in memory of George Washington on the White House north lawn. The tree is no longer extant, but two stately white oaks on the south lawn do survive from the Hoover administration.

When Franklin Delano Roosevelt took office in 1933, the *Washington Post Magazine* reported: "The tree-loving nature of Franklin D. Roosevelt has come to rest in a virtual Eden . . . where the personalities of America's most honored citizens are reflected in trees." The story continued, "For years the planting and management of trees have been his chief hobby on his Hyde Park estate in New York. As governor of New York he set in motion the necessary machinery for one of the greatest tree planting programs a state has ever undertaken."[32] Trees planted by FDR at the White House are alive and well today. His southern magnolia—now very large and full—is located just to the south of the Harding magnolia on East Executive Park, and his white oak thrives on the north lawn. Roosevelt also planted two little-leafed lindens on the south lawn in 1937, one of them to commemorate the coronation of King George VI.

Possibly the best proof of Roosevelt's tree-loving nature can be found in a *Post* news story that appeared following one of Washington's violent thunderstorms, during Roosevelt's first summer in office: "President Roosevelt, an ardent forest lover, showed himself equally interested in individual trees by his anxiety for the elms on the White House lawn yesterday. Early in the morning, at the request of the president, Mrs. Roosevelt telephoned the White House to learn if the White House trees had suffered in Wednesday's storm. He was pleased to learn that no serious damage had been done to them."[33]

Roosevelt's successor, Harry S. Truman, planted boxwoods on the north lawn of the White House directly in front of the North Portico. However, the most significant Truman arboreal innovation was the placement of a mature southern magnolia on the east side of the South Portico, one of three magnolias still there today. The story goes that toward the end of his administration,

Truman quipped: "I've been kept so busy I didn't even know I had a backyard. Now I'm going to get it ready for the next tenant!"[34] It was Truman's idea to move the magnolia from another part of the grounds to its present spot close to the portico, in order to balance the Andrew Jackson magnolias on the opposite side.

In a related story, it is said that after the magnolia had been put in place, Truman asked a friend to hand him a $20 bill (the same twenty that depicts Andrew Jackson's magnolias to the west of the South Portico but not Truman's tree to the east). Pointing from the south window of the White House, the president declared, "It's a counterfeit! See the trees in the engraving of the White House? They don't look like the ones out there, do they?"[35] Interestingly, although the Jackson magnolias are no longer featured on the current $20 bill, Truman's boxwoods are.

Every modern president has felt indebted to Harry Truman for his innovation to White House architecture, known today as the "Truman balcony." From this second-story perch behind the columns of the South Portico, the first family can enjoy the beautiful and historic view of the President's Park away from the scrutiny of the public and the press.

Offered the choice of an antique dinner bell or a silver bowl as a gift for his seventieth birthday, President Dwight D. Eisenhower said he would prefer to be given a red oak tree. Ike celebrated his birthday by planting the tree, a gift from the District of Columbia, on the White House lawn. The red oak, and a pin oak also planted by Eisenhower, both survive today. A third Eisenhower oak died during the 1990s.

In addition to the four saucer magnolias that President John F. Kennedy planted in the Rose Garden, which are still alive today, the thirty-fifth president also added a Pacific pride apple tree to the verdant south lawn of the White House. The tree stood just to the southeast of the Jacqueline Kennedy Garden during its lifetime. It suffered from fire blight, a bacterial disease, and was replaced by a Delicious variety apple tree. That tree's fruit never makes it to the White House table, however, because squirrels quickly devour the young apples.

It's no surprise that Lady Bird Johnson helped select the trees that would memorialize her husband's years in the White House. The first lady was disappointed to learn that the live oak, the poetic symbol of the Texas landscape, would be unable to endure many Washington winters. So she and LBJ decided on a compromise. In October 1964 the thirty-sixth president planted two oaks just outside the Oval Office: a willow oak and a Darlington (also known as laurel) oak, both similar in appearance to the live oak. During the simple tree-planting ceremony, President Johnson spoke these words: "I think it is fitting for an occupant of this house to plant trees—not for today, but for the future. . . . These trees will say 'there lived those who loved this land.'"[36] The willow oak has grown into a large tree, but the Darlington oak has since died.

On Arbor Day in 1968, Mrs. Johnson added another attractive feature to the White House landscape. With the help of a group of children from the District of Columbia, Lady Bird planted a lovely European fern-leaf beech just to the north of the West Wing. During the subsequent administration, First Lady Patricia Nixon added a second fern-leaf beech to the north lawn. The beeches are lovely year-round, but they are especially beautiful in late autumn when they show their golden fall foliage.

In the tradition of his predecessors, President Richard M. Nixon took a strong interest in the trees on the White House grounds. For the first time in history, a tree from the American West was added to the presidential collection, when Nixon planted a giant sequoia, the official tree of his home state of California, on the south lawn. Unfortunately, the original Nixon sequoia died, as did two replacement trees.

President Gerald R. Ford created a presidential triangle of trees when he added a white pine to the northeastern portion of the south lawn, just to the north of Eisenhower's seventieth-birthday red oak and Kennedy's Pacific pride apple tree. As noted previously, the apple has since succumbed to fire blight. The Ford pine declined, and was removed in 1999. First Lady Betty Ford planted a seedling of the John Quincy Adams American elm on the north lawn of the White House to commemorate the nation's bicentennial celebration in 1976. This descendant of what was once the oldest presidential tree is thriving today.

President Jimmy Carter took an avid interest in the trees at 1600 Pennsylvania Avenue. His request that the White House trees bear name labels was carried out by the National Park Service. The Carters brought a young red maple from Plains, Georgia, which the president planted on the north lawn. President Carter also planted a cedar of Lebanon on the grounds. And First Lady Rosalynn Carter planted a delicately weeping spider-leaf Japanese maple east of the south fountain, to serve as a companion for the tree to the west of the fountain planted by former First Lady Frances Cleveland. The foliage of this pair of maples is red throughout the season, in dramatic contrast to the brilliant green of the White House south lawn. All the Carter trees are alive today.

In the Reagan years, the White House grounds received extra bursts of color during fall and spring. In 1982, First Lady Nancy Reagan planted a pair of white saucer magnolias in the upper-central portion of the north lawn. In early spring their blossoms are clearly visible to passersby on Pennsylvania Avenue. Two years later, Ronald Reagan brightened up the northern West Wing grounds when he planted a young sugar maple, known for its vibrant autumn leaves. He also planted a willow oak near the Jacqueline Kennedy Garden in 1988.

With the help of Britain's Queen Elizabeth II, President George H. W. Bush planted a little-leafed linden, which replaced the tree of the same species that had been planted by Franklin Delano Roosevelt to honor the coronation of Queen Elizabeth's father, George VI. The first President Bush also planted a Patmore ash, a redbud, and a purple beech on the White House grounds. First Lady Barbara Bush planted a grafted tree propagated from the John Quincy Adams Elm in 1991, to replace the original American elm.

President William Jefferson Clinton planted yet another little-leafed linden, and he and First Lady Hillary Rodham Clinton planted a willow oak, an American elm, and several white flowering dogwoods.

Twenty-First Century Presidential Trees. President George W. Bush and First Lady Laura Bush have followed in the footsteps of their tree-planting predecessors. In October 2006 they planted a Jefferson cultivar of the American elm, to replace a large tree that had been lost during a deluge the previous June. The American elm that was lost is the one featured to the right of the White House on the current $20 bill. Earlier in his administration, in honor of Arbor Day 2005, President Bush planted an American chestnut. The president and Mrs. Bush also planted a cutleaf silver maple in 2001, and a little-leafed linden in 2003. The linden replaced one of two little-leafed lindens planted by Franklin Delano Roosevelt. The Roosevelt tree had blown down in a storm earlier that year.

Other Trees on the White House Grounds

Many other trees grace the White House lawns. They do not hold the distinction of having been planted by presidents, but they are beautiful nonetheless. Although the lawns are usually closed to the public, many of these trees are clearly visible through the fence. Those on the south lawn include ginkgoes, horse-chestnuts and buckeyes, Chinese chestnuts, Persian ironwoods (one of these is more than a hundred years old), maples, hollies, dogwoods, flowering crabapples, beeches, a yellowwood, and a large golden-rain-tree. The north lawn is shaded by many handsome, venerable trees, with oaks and American elms predominating.

The National Christmas Tree

The National Christmas Tree is a living Colorado blue spruce planted on the Ellipse, just south of the White House. Traditionally, the president lights the tree in a ceremony held about two weeks before Christmas. In 1978, the National Christmas Tree was transplanted from York, Pennsylvania, where it was growing in a private yard. It replaced two previous living Christmas trees, which were planted on the Ellipse in 1973 and 1977.

The Washington Monument

The summit of the Washington Monument provides the most dramatic view of the City of Trees. To the east, the elm-lined Mall stretches to the Capitol, flanked by the generously landscaped buildings of the Smithsonian. To the north, the White House is tucked in among numerous trees, many of them planted by U.S. presidents. And to the south, the world-famous Japanese flowering cherry trees encircle the Tidal Basin. The streets, avenues, and parks of the nation's capital are sumptuously adorned with green as far as the eye can see.

The Washington Monument itself is wreathed in cherry trees, a fitting though unwitting tribute to the legend associated with George Washington's boyhood. The memorial to the first president was forty years in the making—from 1848, when the cornerstone was laid, until 1888, when it was first opened to the public. A scarcity of funds, general controversy, and the Civil War held up construction. For almost a quarter of a century, the monument stood, completed to less than a third of its present height. A subtle change in the color of the marble marks the spot where construction was halted for so many years.

Ever since the late 1960s, the springtime beauty of the Tidal Basin has extended up the hill to the Washington Monument, where hundreds of young cherry trees were planted during the Johnson administration. The trees, mostly American-grown Akebono cherries, were a gift from the Japanese government. Their masses of pink blossoms against the marble monument and new green grass are a beautiful sight.

Many mature trees grow on the monument grounds, including two large white mulberries on the hill overlooking Independence Avenue and 17th Street. White pines, several species of maple and oak, lindens, horse-chestnuts, and two species of catalpa are among the trees shading the Independence Avenue and 15th Street sides of the grounds. American (and some Dutch) elms line the perimeter, and at the corner of 15th and Constitution is a small grove of European hedge maples.

The monument grounds are striking in late spring and early summer when the horse-chestnuts and catalpas are in bloom.

The World War II Memorial

In April 2004 a dramatic new memorial was dedicated on the Mall. The National World War II Memorial commemorates the sacrifices and achievements of the World War II generation. Made up of a large plaza surrounding a pool of water, and fifty-six commemorative pillars representing the states and territories and the District of Columbia, the new memorial is located between the Washington Monument and the Lincoln Memorial Reflecting Pool. Oak and wheat bronze wreathes displayed on the pillars symbolize the wartime contributions of the nation's farmers and industries. Four thousand gold stars on the Freedom Wall memorialize the 400,000 Americans who gave their lives during the war. Two large pavilions representing the Atlantic and Pacific Theaters emphasize the geographic scale of World War II.

Shortly after the World War II Memorial opened, it was my privilege to visit it in the company of my father-in-law, Dr. William Bradley. Many young people, recognizing him as a veteran of the war, approached him to pay spontaneous tribute.

The memorial setting is surrounded by elm trees. Sugar maples, yellowwoods, lindens, sweetbay magnolias, and other young trees have been planted on the memorial grounds.

Capitol Hill: One of the World's Finest Arboretums

More than 3,000 trees from four continents are planted on the U.S. Capitol, Supreme Court, and Library of Congress grounds, making the area known as Capitol Hill one of the finest arboretums in the world. Trees native to most parts of the United States, including many official state trees, stand side by side with Asian, European, and Northern African species. Visitors from the southern states will find several species of native American magnolias thriving here. Westerners may not recognize them yet, but three giant sequoias are growing up under the shadow of the Capitol dome. Europeans will see healthy specimens of familiar elms. And visitors from Asia will recognize many trees, including the ginkgo, jujube, and several Asian species of magnolia.

No matter what time of year you visit Capitol Hill, you will be struck by the beauty and diversity of its trees, shrubs, and herbaceous plants. Beginning with the Japanese flowering cherry trees and Asian magnolias in the early spring, and continuing through the summer months with the southern magnolias, golden-rain, and Japanese pagoda trees, the Hill is adorned by a steady procession of blossoms. During autumn, maples, oaks, and ginkgoes envelop the Capitol, Supreme Court, and Library of Congress with dramatic red, orange, yellow, and gold foliage. Even throughout the winter months, the trees of Capitol Hill are beautiful. The beeches are particularly striking with their smooth gray bark, and many evergreen trees and shrubs provide a handsome frame for the Capitol.

Capitol Hill's international tree collection is noteworthy historically as well as botanically. Throughout the years, members of the House and Senate, as well as representatives of state and national organizations, have planted trees commemorating people and events. Dozens of these living memorials grace the Capitol grounds.

The Capitol Building

The long, turbulent history of the Capitol building began in 1793, when George Washington laid the cornerstone on what was then known as Jenkins Hill. By 1800, Congress was in business there. In 1814, the newly completed House and Senate wings were burned by the British, along with much of the city of Washington. Later in the century, midway into construction of the impressive white cast-iron dome that is such a familiar landmark today, the Civil War broke out. Throughout the war, while the building was used as a combination barracks, hospital, and bakery for the Union Army, its unfinished dome dominated the city's horizon—a poignant reminder of the nation's uncertain future. President Lincoln, recognizing the powerful symbolism of the half-finished dome, ordered construction to proceed despite the division of the country. When the war drew to a close in 1865 and national unity was restored, the beautiful dome was nearly completed.

The Grounds

Major Pierre Charles L'Enfant, the man who designed the city of Washington, is said to have called the hill on which the Capitol now stands "a pedestal waiting for a monument." The physiographic aspects of the hill, pre-Capitol, have been described in considerably less lofty terms. Frederick Law Olmsted, the renowned landscape architect commissioned by Congress during the 1870s and 1880s to design and direct a major overhaul of the Capitol grounds, wrote in 1882: "When government, near the close of the last century, took possession of the site of the Capitol, it was a sterile place, partly overgrown with 'scrub oak.' The soil was described as an *exceedingly stiff* clay, becoming dust in dry and mortar in rainy weather."[37]

Although it is difficult to imagine the now lush and fertile Capitol grounds as a "sterile place," only scanty, short-lived improvements had been made to the site prior to Olmsted's time. During the first part of the nineteenth century, the western half of Capitol Hill, which is the most magnificent side of the grounds today, was largely ignored. Early Washingtonians believed that the city would grow up to the east, rather than the west, so that today's famous western front of the Capitol was thought of as the "rear" of the building. A creek, bordered by an alder swamp, flowed along the foot of Capitol Hill, where the U.S. Botanic Garden and Capitol Reflecting Pool now stand. According to Olmsted: "When this stream was in freshet it was not fordable, and members of Congress were often compelled to hitch their riding horses on the further side and cross it, first, on fallen trees, afterwards on a foot-bridge."[38]

Although some initial plantings had been made, the first notable landscaping efforts were undertaken during the late 1820s, under the direction of groundskeeper John Foy. Foy began the execution of a landscaping plan that Olmsted later described as "an enlarged form of the ordinary village door-yards of the time, flat rectangular 'grass plats,' bordered by rows of trees, flower-beds, and gravel walks, with a belt of close planting on the outside of it all." As Olmsted explained: "So long as the trees were saplings and the turf and flowers could be kept nicely, it was pretty and becoming. But as the trees grew they robbed and dried out the flower-beds, leaving hardly any thing to flourish in them but violets and periwinkle."[39]

As it became apparent that the city was going to develop to the west as well as the east, and interest began to focus on the "rear" side of the Capitol, groundskeeper James Maher, a successor to Foy, began planting trees at the foot of the Hill. Maher also added two circular groups of trees, which became known as the "Barbecue Groves," on the eastern side of the grounds—"one probably intended for Democratic, the other for Whig jollifications," according to Olmsted.[40] Although a few of the "barbecue" trees and other plantings made during the Foy and Maher years were still alive when Congress commissioned Olmsted to re-landscape the newly extended grounds in 1874, the architect was unimpressed by the arboreal picture he inherited. With few exceptions, he would order an entire re-grading of the grounds.

Olmsted Landscaping

The man who designed Central Park in New York City, as well as countless other parks and campuses throughout the country, exhibited his customary wisdom when he approached the challenge of landscaping the Capitol building. Olmsted considered it his first priority to ensure the "convenience of business of and with Congress and the Supreme Court." His second most important consideration, he said, was "that of supporting and presenting to advantage a great national monument." Olmsted wrote, "The ground is in design part of the Capitol, [and is] in all respects subsidiary to the central structure."[41]

With his priorities firmly established, Olmsted tackled what he considered his central landscaping problem: the conflict between the need to leave enough space to show the Capitol off to its best advantage and accommodate large numbers of people, and the desirability of providing enough shade to combat

Washington's summer heat and offset the "glaring whiteness" of the building. Olmsted solved the problem by stationing groves of trees in such a way that unobstructed views of the Capitol could be had from all sides. In some places, he planted only trees with low crowns, in order to create views of the dome "rising above banks of foliage from several miles distant."[42] Trees were chosen not with the idea of exhibiting unusual or exotic specimens, but "with a view of their growing together in groups in which their individual qualities would gradually merge harmoniously."[43]

Olmsted made an exception to this rule around his "summerhouse" on the northwestern part of the grounds. Appropriately, he surrounded this charming brick grotto with trees of a "somewhat quaint or exotic aspect,"[44] including the "cedrella" and "golden catalpa." The cedrela is there to this day. But in order that the all-important view should remain unobstructed, no large conifers, such as spruces, were planted on the grounds.

Despite his insistence that the particular be subsidiary to the whole, Olmsted was able to account for more than 200 species and varieties of trees and shrubs by the time he had finished replanting the Capitol grounds. To ensure that his thousands of new trees would have something more substantial than "dust" and "mortar" in which to grow, Olmsted went to extremes:

> The revised ground having been attained, the ground was thoroughly drained with collared, cylindrical tile, and trench-plowed and subsoiled to a depth of two feet or more from the present surface. . . . It was then ridged up and exposed to a winter's frost, dressed with oyster-shell lime, and with swamp muck previously treated with salt and lime, then plowed, harrowed, and rolled and plowed again. The old surface was laid upon this improved subsoil with a sufficient addition of the same poor soil drawn from without the ground to make the stratum one foot (loose) in depth. With this well pulverized, a compost of stable manure and prepared swamp muck was mixed.[45]

Olmsted's Legacy

Olmsted's painstaking efforts have reached fruition in the twentieth and twenty-first centuries. Many of the groves that were planted under his meticulous direction "merge harmoniously" today, providing a softly dramatic setting for the nation's most important building. In addition to the extensive plantings and quaint "summerhouse," the Olmsted legacy includes the gently curving walks and drives that lead to the Capitol from every direction, and the spectacular terrace on the western front of the building.

Tree Labeling on the Hill

Frederick Law Olmsted also began the tradition of tree labeling on the Capitol grounds, a practice that has survived to the present. In 1882, he wrote: "There being trees on the ground unknown to many visitors from distant parts of the country, upon a suggestion kindly made by Members of Congress, labels have been placed before a large number."[46]

While tree labels are a great help in identifying the many unusual woody plants on the grounds, it is also true that over the years many a tree has stoically borne the indignity of having the wrong name tacked to its trunk. One mislabeled tree gained national acclaim when it was officially declared the largest of its species in the United States. Having proudly worn a large "Mountain Maple" label for years, this imposter turned out to be a Cappadocian maple, native to the mountains of Asia and Eastern Europe.

Twentieth- and Twenty-First Century Improvements on the Grounds

The twentieth century's most dramatic change in the Capitol grounds occurred in the 1960s. During the Lady Bird Johnson years, when interest in beautification was at a peak, many flowering plants were added, including Japanese flowering cherry trees, flowering dogwoods, crabapples, and redbuds. In the early part of the twenty-first century, an underground Visitor Center was added to the east side of the grounds. As this book goes to press, the center is still under construction and much of the east side is fenced, restricting public access. At least 68 trees were sacrificed for the construction, but approximately 85 trees will replace them, including young tulip-trees (or tulip poplars), which have been planted in double rows along two parallel walkways. As new trees are planted in the vicinity of the Visitor Center and design elements are created and preserved, every effort is being made to honor the Olmsted landscaping plan.

Historic Trees of Capitol Hill: Past and Present

The Cameron Elm.   This American elm, for many decades the
most venerable tree on Capitol Hill, managed to survive the
twentieth-century threats of Dutch elm disease and urban pollution, as well as an even greater nineteenth-century threat:
Frederick Law Olmsted. Legend has it that Senator Simon D.
Cameron of Pennsylvania became so upset when he saw Olmsted's crew about to remove the elm during the re-landscaping
program of the 1870s that he rushed to the Senate floor and
made an impassioned speech on its behalf. Although no record of
such a speech has been found, documents housed in the Architect of the Capitol's office confirm that Olmsted's crew was about
to remove the tree and that Senator Cameron's influence saved
it. The real proof of the story was evident to any observant visitor
to the Capitol grounds for well over a century. Until recently, the
vase-shaped American elm—with a sidewalk winding politely
around it—dominated the rise next to the House of Representatives. In July 2004, however, this historic tree was removed,
after arborists identified a cavity in its trunk and it was deemed
a safety hazard. The tree is gone, but hopefully the story of its
triumph will live on.

The Humility Elm.   In 1978 the huge English elm that dominated
the northeast grounds between the Capitol and the Russell Senate Office Building fell victim to Dutch elm disease. On June 27
of that year, Senator Edward Kennedy gave this moving tribute
to the tree on the Senate floor: "Few if any trees anywhere were
better known or more loved by Members of the Senate. As we
walked to the Capitol from the Russell Building, we passed under
its giant limb, a cantilevered miracle of nature that stretched out
across the sidewalk and over the roadway. Often we would reach
up to touch the limb, or give it a warm slap of recognition and
appreciation for its enduring vigil. President Kennedy, when he
was a Senator, liked to call it the Humility Tree, because Senators
instinctively ducked or bowed their heads as they approached the
limb and passed beneath it. Its loss is a real one, deeply felt."[47]

The Washington Elm.   Until the late 1940s, this beautiful American elm stood near the eastern entrance to the Senate wing of
the Capitol. Two legends, widely circulated over the years, nei-
ther of which can be substantiated, connect this tree to the first
president. The first, and least likely of the two, holds that George

Washington planted the tree. The second, and more probable story, is that Washington stood under the shade of this tree while overseeing the construction of the Capitol.

Memorial Trees

Formal memorial tree-planting ceremonies on the Capitol grounds got their start in earnest in 1912, when one vice president (James S. Sherman), five senators, two representatives, and the Speaker of the House all spaded up the ground to plant their favorite trees. Since then, dozens of commemorative trees have been planted on the Capitol grounds, many of them by, or in honor of, members of Congress. Some of the trees were planted to commemorate specific events, such as Arbor Day. Others were planted in honor of national or state associations. Following are some of the most notable memorial trees:

The Sam Rayburn Oak.   On October 11, 1949, Speaker of the House Sam Rayburn of Texas planted a white oak on the southeastern section of the Capitol grounds. Throughout his many years in Washington, Rayburn or an associate frequently visited the tree to measure its growing circumference.

The Sullivan Brothers Crabapples.   Five flowering crabapples were planted on the northeastern section of the Capitol grounds to memorialize a tragic event in U.S. naval history: after the navy had given the five Sullivan brothers, of Waterloo, Iowa, special permission to serve on the same ship during World War II, they were all killed when the ship went down under fire in the Pacific.

The Cherokee Indian Giant Sequoia.   In 1966 the Cherokee Indian Nation commemorated the bicentennial of the birth of Sequoyah, the famous Cherokee leader and scholar, with a ceremonial planting of a giant sequoia on the northwest grounds. The original tree died later that year, but was replaced in 1969 with a tree grown from one of its cuttings.

The Senator Sam Ervin Dogwood.   In 1974, when Sam Ervin retired from the U.S. Senate, he planted a flowering dogwood, the official flower of his home state of North Carolina, on the northeast Capitol grounds.

U.S. Botanic Garden

The conservatory of the U.S. Botanic Garden at the foot of Capitol Hill houses plants from around the world, including many tropical species. The first Botanic Garden greenhouse dates to the 1840s, and the present-day conservatory has been located at its current site since 1933. In recent years, the conservatory has undergone extensive renovations, and innovative outdoor gardens have been created. Within the conservatory walls, visitors can contemplate cacti and succulents typical of desert landscapes; a tropical jungle within a 93-foot dome; and exhibits devoted to orchids, medicinal plants, plants typical of Old and New World oases, and a "garden primeval" featuring Jurassic-era cycads, tree ferns, and other ancient plants.

In fall 2006 the U.S. Botanic Garden dedicated its outdoor National Garden. The National Garden features a formal rose garden bordered by American hornbeams, a butterfly garden, the First Ladies' Water Garden, and a lawn terrace surrounded by pond cypresses. For tree enthusiasts, the most interesting aspect of the new National Garden is the Regional Garden, a showcase for plants that are indigenous to the Piedmont and Coastal Plain from New Jersey to North Carolina. A small stream bordered by a rock path serves as a divider between the Coastal Plain and Piedmont plant communities, each of which is planted in soil typical of its region. All the trees and shrubs planted in the Regional Garden are labeled, and among them one can find laurel oak, sourwood, hop-hornbeam, pawpaw, hop-tree, red buckeye, tupelo, Carolina silverbell, flowering dogwood, American holly and winterberry, laurelcherry, southern magnolia, and several species of viburnum, along with long-leaf, loblolly, and pitch pines.

Across Independence Avenue from the conservatory is the lovely Bartholdi Fountain, designed by Frederic Auguste Bartholdi, the sculptor who created the Statue of Liberty. A garden dating to 1932 and now known as Bartholdi Park surrounds the fountain. In recent years, the garden beds have been redesigned to reflect contemporary horticultural trends. An ancient jujube grows in Bartholdi Park, along with American and European smoke-trees, European hornbeam, river birch, pawpaw, callery pear, two-winged silverbell, serviceberry, trifoliate orange, common horse-chestnut, paperbark maple, dwarf pomegranate, Serbian spruce, and Hinoki false-cypress.

The U.S. Botanic Garden is administered by the office of the

Architect of the Capitol. Picnic tables and benches invite visitors to rest and contemplate their surroundings. Many historic trees have graced the grounds of this lovely spot, including, ironically, a hornbeam planted by Abraham Lincoln and a bald-cypress planted by his assassin, John Wilkes Booth.

Gardens of the Smithsonian Museums and the National Gallery of Art

The grounds of the Smithsonian museums and the National Gallery of Art, flanking the Mall, have long been handsomely landscaped. Since the earlier editions of *City of Trees*, tree-viewing and garden visits around the Mall have become even more rewarding, thanks to several horticultural innovations.

The **National Museum of the American Indian,** at 4th Street and Independence Avenue on the Mall, opened on September 21, 2004, with a procession of tens of thousands of North American Indian tribe members, joined by visitors from South America and other parts of the globe. Weeklong festivities on the Mall accompanied the opening of the magnificent golden-colored limestone-clad museum, which houses exhibits designed and maintained by American Indian tribes from across the continent. The museum is surrounded by wetland, woodland, and meadow habitats dedicated to native plants and the early medicinal and food crops grown by regional tribes. Native trees featured in the landscapes include oaks, river birch, bald-cypress, witch-hazel, red maple, sassafras, and tulip-tree.

The Independence Avenue side of the Smithsonian Castle is now the site of two new underground museums—the **National Museum of African Art** and the **Arthur M. Sackler Gallery**—as well as the location for the **Enid A. Haupt Garden**, created by S. Dillon Ripley, eighth secretary of the Smithsonian, and dedicated to philanthropist Enid Annenberg Haupt in 1987. The garden is a peaceful and resplendent refuge composed of Victorian, Asian, and African elements that reflect the history of the Smithsonian Institution and provide horticultural enhancement for the museums it frames. This spacious garden is home to many mature and young trees, including a magnificent weeping European beech, a pair of venerable ginkgoes, lindens, tupelos, weeping cherries, umbrella pine, Darlington oaks, katsura-trees, Japanese snowbell, saucer and southern magnolias, and crape-myrtle.

Adjacent to the Smithsonian Arts and Industries Building

is another charming and innovative garden, the **Mary Livings-ton Ripley Garden,** dedicated in 1988. Mary Ripley, Secretary Ripley's wife, founded the Smithsonian Institution Women's Committee. According to her daughter Sylvia Ripley, Mary was an accomplished horticulturist. "She and her co-workers raised the money to start a garden next to the Arts and Industries Building," Sylvia explained. "The design was quite clever, beginning narrow and low and then meandering out to a lovely open space with a fountain and benches, at once joyous and contemplative. My mother wanted handicapped people in wheelchairs to be able to see at their level, and she wanted people who are blind to be able to smell the fragrance of the flowers. . . . She had no idea that the garden was going to be dedicated to her."[48] The trees, shrubs, and herbaceous plants in this garden, as in many other places around the Mall and the Botanic Garden, are labeled. Trees here include native fringe-tree, American elms, paperbark and Japanese maples, witch-hazel hybrids, American arborvitae, golden Hinoki false-cypress, and goldthread false-cypress.

In recent years, the interdependence of trees and wildlife has become a source of concern and interest to local gardeners. On the opposite (northern) side of the Mall is another new Smithsonian garden—the **Butterfly Habitat Garden.** A collaborative effort, the original garden was created in 1995 with funds from the Smithsonian Women's Committee, and was expanded in 2000, thanks to a gift from the Garden Club of America. The garden is dedicated to the relationships between indigenous plants and butterflies. Many of our native flowering trees and shrubs serve as nectar plants for butterflies and, even more significantly, as host plants for the larvae of individual species. For example, the tulip-tree is host plant for the tiger swallowtail, the paw-paw for the zebra swallowtail, the spice-bush for the spice-bush swallowtail, and the black willow for the viceroy and mourning cloak.

A hop, skip, and a flutter from the butterfly garden is the 6.1-acre **National Gallery of Art Sculpture Garden,** which opened in 1999. Works by internationally known artists are on display in this delightful mini-arboretum. A large central fountain, ringed by lindens, serves as the setting for jazz concerts during the summer and as an ice-skating rink in winter. Noteworthy tree specimens in the sculpture garden include Kentucky coffee-tree, cedar of Lebanon and Atlas and Deodar cedars, a row of lamarkii serviceberries, umbrella pine, paperbark maple, several magnolia species, Japanese stewartia, fragrant snowbell, yellow buckeye, yellowwood, and white Texas redbud (struggling in Washington's climate but extant as of this writing).

U.S. Department of Agriculture

The U.S. Department of Agriculture building, also bordering the Mall, was once an arboretum containing many exotic trees and shrubs. It is still surrounded by magnificent woody plants, including many commemorative trees. A beautiful mature white oak was dedicated to First Lady Hillary Rodham Clinton in December 1999, and this quote of hers is featured on a plaque at the base of the tree: "As we enter the new millennium, we will not simply be celebrating a new year, we will be celebrating the enduring strength of our democracy, the renewal of our sense of citizenship, and the full flowering of the American mind and spirit."

Another large oak on the Department of Agriculture grounds—a bur, or mossycup, oak—is dedicated to the memory of civil rights leader Dr. Martin Luther King Jr. Also on the grounds is a redbud grown from seed collected at President Franklin Delano Roosevelt's "Little White House," near Warm Springs, Georgia, and dedicated in 2000 "as a Living Reminder in memory of the victims of the Holocaust." Other noteworthy trees include a bald-cypress commemorating "the many contributions Native Americans have made to American agriculture"; a Bradford pear planted in 1987 to replace one planted by Lady Bird Johnson in 1966; and a blue spruce planted in 1984 to honor the fortieth birthday of Smokey Bear, the national symbol of wildfire prevention awareness.

The Japanese Flowering Cherry Trees

For centuries, the flowering cherry, or sakura, has stood at the center of Japan's poetic consciousness, as a powerful symbol of the beautiful yet transient nature of life. Ancient legends tell how the cherry blossoms are awakened in spring by the "maiden who causes trees to bloom,"[49] or by fairies who visit the emperor at the Palace of Yoshino in the moonlight. Japanese paintings abound with delicate sakura blossoms. Poets throughout the ages have exalted the cherry tree and mourned the brief life of its blossoms, often in the same breath.

The world-famous Japanese cherry trees encircling the Tidal

Basin in Washington's West Potomac Park were a gift to the American people from the city of Tokyo. They are one of the world's most enduring living symbols of friendship between two nations.

History of the Cherry Trees

America's loveliest urban acres were the site of a polluted and health-threatening tidal marshland just a little over a century ago. By the late 1800s, the area that now comprises West and East Potomac Parks had become backed up with the city's wastes, and was also a breeding ground for malarial mosquitoes. In 1882, Congress approved an act to reclaim the tidal marshland along the Potomac. Today's beautiful Tidal Basin was thus created for practical rather than aesthetic reasons. Long before the cherry trees and the Jefferson Memorial were even imagined, the basin was carved out to catch the tides flowing up from the Potomac through the Washington Channel. The human-made channel (now bordered by East Potomac Park and the Maine Avenue waterfront) was filling up with mud and unhealthy debris. With the creation of the Tidal Basin and its southern outlet to the Potomac, the incoming tide could freely flow through the channel and eventually back into the Potomac River. This system still cleanses the channel of debris today, making the Tidal Basin a model combination of utility and beauty.

In 1909, the city of Tokyo sent a gift of 2,000 cherry trees to the United States for planting in Potomac Park. Unfortunately, this first shipment of trees—which arrived in Seattle on December 10 and was then loaded onto a train bound for the District of Columbia—proved to be infested with insects and diseases. With great dismay, the U.S. Department of Agriculture was forced to recommend that the trees be burned. The potentially embarrassing situation did not weaken the bond between Tokyo and Washington, however. Tokyo mayor Yukio Ozaki simply ordered that special precautions be taken to ensure a healthy second shipment of trees. In 1912, 3,020 trees bound for the nation's capital arrived in Seattle, and by March 27 the first cherry trees were planted at the Tidal Basin. First Lady Helen Herron ("Nellie") Taft planted the first flowering cherry tree; Viscountess Iwa Chinda, wife of the Japanese ambassador, planted the second. The two trees, located on the northwest side of the Tidal Basin, are still alive today.

Twelve selections of flowering cherries were included among

the 3,020 trees in the second gift shipment. Most of the trees planted around the Tidal Basin were specimens of the white or pale pink, single-blossomed Somei-Yoshino, usually known simply as Yoshino. The Yoshino cherry blooms very early in the spring. The later-blooming double-blossomed varieties were planted extensively in East Potomac Park. Among these trees was the deep pink Kwanzan, which is still popular in Washington today. Several specimens of the intriguing Gyoiko, with its pale green blossoms, were planted on the White House grounds.

Of the original twelve selections, nearly all but the Yoshino and Kwanzan had subsequently disappeared from the Washington landscape. During the latter part of the twentieth century, botanist Roland M. Jefferson of the National Arboretum conducted a worldwide survey of cultivated cherry trees, locating specimens of all but one of the original dozen, and propagating them. Jefferson also made grafted propagations of the old Yoshino cherries that had been planted by Mrs. Taft and Viscountess Chinda. Jefferson's work contributed to increased horticultural knowledge of the historic trees.

Today, Dr. Margaret Pooler, a geneticist at the National Arboretum, conducts flowering cherry research and propagation. Building on breeding work begun during the 1970s by her predecessor, Dr. Donald Egolf, Pooler and her colleagues have developed new flowering cherries (see page 287). They have also propagated new plants from the original 1912 trees. Some of these trees have replaced their elders at the Tidal Basin. According to Dr. Pooler, Roland Jefferson's earlier cherry research and his collection are contributing to present-day breeding efforts.

During the early 1920s, W. B. Clarke selected an unusually pink form of Yoshino from his collection in San Jose, California, for propagation. Clarke christened the tree Akebono, meaning "dawn." The Akebono, which is identical to the Yoshino except for its slightly deeper pink blossoms, is widely planted throughout Washington today. A few of Dr. Clarke's Akebono trees have replaced some of the dying Tidal Basin Yoshino cherries, but most have been replaced by young Yoshino cherries. Of the 2,971 Yoshino trees in Potomac Park today, only 125 are from the original 1912 planting. There are 104 Akebono trees in Potomac Park.

In 1999, five Usuzumi cherry trees were planted near the Potomac River, part of a gift from the people of Neo Mura Village in Japan. That same year, several beavers famously gnawed and felled four Japanese flowering cherries at the Tidal Basin. The beavers were caught and relocated amidst much media hoopla.

In recent years, the National Park Service has increased the diversity of America's favorite flowering trees. The springtime beauty of East and West Potomac Parks has been enhanced by several less common or rare Japanese flowering cherries. They include 112 Takesimensis, 44 Usuzumi, 20 Sargent, 14 Fugenzo, 21 fall-blooming or autumn-blooming, 3 Afterglow (a pinker form of the hybrid that gave rise to the Yoshino and Akebono), and a single specimen each of Okame and Shirofugen cherries. Still, according to Robert DeFeo, chief horticulturist for the National Park Service, the cultural landscape of the Tidal Basin, while encompassing additional Japanese flowering cherry varieties, continues to retain the integrity of the original early twentieth-century design concept.[50]

Despite every effort to give them the best possible care, a few Japanese flowering cherries are lost each year. In recent years, the National Capital Region Cherry Tree Replacement Fund was established to ensure timely replacement and maintenance of trees. Administered by the National Park Foundation and designed to augment congressional appropriations, the fund accepts private donations to its endowment. Endowment income goes directly to the trees.

The first Cherry Blossom Festival was held in 1935. Since that time, interest in the Washington flowering cherries has spread throughout the world. Today, many a Japanese visitor can be seen among the Tidal Basin visitors, proudly beaming his or her approval and trying to capture the elusive beauty of the blossoms in photographs.

In 1949, the first Cherry Blossom Princesses came to Washington. Each spring since then, the capital has been adorned not only by the cherry blossoms, but by the princesses, who represent every state and American territory.

In 1957, Japan gave the United States the "Mikimoto Pearl Crown," to be worn by the Cherry Blossom Queen, who is chosen each year by lot from among the group of princesses. When it was given to the United States, the crown was valued at $100,000.

Three years earlier, in 1954, Japanese ambassador Sadao Iguchi had presented the United States with a large ancient stone lantern to commemorate the 100th anniversary of the first treaty between Japan and the United States. The Treaty of Peace, Amity, and Commerce was signed by Commodore Matthew Perry in Yokohama on March 31, 1854. Today, the ceremonial lighting of the 8½-foot-high lantern—which is more than 350 years old—marks the official opening of the Cherry Blossom Festival.

In 1958, a second gift commemorating the 1854 treaty was presented to the United States by the mayor of Yokohama. This simple Japanese stone pagoda, which dates to the 1600s, now stands among the Tidal Basin cherry trees near the Franklin Delano Roosevelt Memorial.

The year 1965 saw yet another gift from the people of Japan. Thousands of American-grown Akebono cherries were given to the city of Washington. Many were planted on the grounds of the Washington Monument, providing an attractive frame for the marble obelisk. And, once again, the first lady of the United States and the wife of the Japanese ambassador (in this case, Lady Bird Johnson and Mrs. Ryuji Takeuchi) joined in planting two ceremonial cherry trees. The new trees are planted near the trees planted in 1912 by Mrs. Taft and Viscountess Chinda.

In 1981, the Japanese flowering cherries were featured in another gesture of international friendship. Cherry trees along the Arakawa River in Tokyo—the place where the historic Tidal Basin trees originated—had succumbed to the adverse effects of pollution. The National Arboretum's Roland Jefferson, working in conjunction with the National Park Service, selected budwood (propagating material) from healthy trees at the Tidal Basin and the National Arboretum for shipment to Japan. In Japan, the buds of the Washington trees were grafted onto Japanese-grown root stock. The trees arising from this union replaced some of the Japanese–grown cherries that once flourished along the Tokyo waterway. In February 1981, First Lady Nancy Reagan took part in a White House ceremony to commemorate the international exchange. Mrs. Reagan presented Japanese ambassador Yoshi Okawara with a young cherry tree propagated from the original Tidal Basin tree planted by Nellie Taft.

Today, thousands of people from all over the world converge on the shores of the Potomac for Washington's annual Cherry Blossom Festival. The weeklong rite of spring includes a parade and many other events. However, the main event does not always come off on schedule. Few could envy the National Park Service horticulturist who is given the task of predicting the appearance of the fickle blossoms. Even days before they bloom, the mysterious trees divulge few signs that they are about to flower. On average, the Yoshino and Akebono cherries bloom in the first few days of April, but they have bloomed as early as March 15, in 1990, and as late as April 18, in 1958!

A new book by Ann McClellan, *The Cherry Blossom Festival "Sakura Celebration,"* gives a comprehensive history of the Tidal Basin trees and the festival, as well as a glimpse of more than one thousand years of celebrating the blossoms in Japan. It bears this dedication: "To the Japanese Cherry Trees, whose ethereal and evanescent blooming lifts our spirits and makes us all poets."[51]

Back in 1934, Department of Agriculture botanist Paul Russell wrote: "For him who has visited Japan in the spring, as he walks under the flower-laden boughs in the old plantings near the Potomac River in Washington, D.C., there come memories of the gay kimono-clad crowds in the Japanese parks, the sound of geta (wooden sandals) on the gravel-covered walks, staccato talk and the vendors' cries."[52] Today, springtime in Japan might evoke a similar nostalgia in someone acquainted with the beauty of the Japanese flowering cherry trees in Washington.

The Franklin Delano Roosevelt Memorial

Franklin Delano Roosevelt's presidency spanned the Great Depression of the 1930s and America's involvement in World War II. Renowned for his New Deal programs designed to bring relief to the poor and economic recovery for the nation, as well as for his steely resolve during the war, Roosevelt is immortalized by his words: "We have nothing to fear but fear itself." His wife, Eleanor, was also an important twentieth-century figure and a champion of social justice and human rights. The two of them are remembered in a simple yet stunningly designed memorial, dedicated in 1997 and tucked in among the Japanese flowering cherries of the Tidal Basin. The memorial is comprised of a series of four outdoor rooms, each representing one of FDR's terms as president. These rooms, or galleries, are partially walled in South Dakota granite, with quotations carved in the stone walls. Larger-than-life statues of the thirty-second president and the first lady are featured, and a series of cascading waterfalls adds to the inspirational atmosphere.

The memorial is handsomely landscaped with trees, including the rare Japanese white pine and other pine species, red and Japanese maples, honey locust, zelkova, willow oak, and flowering crabapple. Adjacent to the memorial near the eastern entrance are three old blue ashes, a Midwestern species that is rarely planted in Washington. A large Japanese raisin tree, also rare, stands between the FDR Memorial and the Tidal Basin.

The Jefferson Memorial

One of America's most photographed sights is the white marble Jefferson Memorial framed by a pale pink cloud of cherry blossoms. While there is no doubt that the memorial looks its loveliest with the cherry trees in bloom, Washingtonians know another side of the Jefferson Memorial that is nearly as pleasing. Day and night throughout the year, the dark silhouettes of white pine trees against the white marble structure are a favorite sight from many of the city's commuter routes.

When the site for the Jefferson Memorial was proposed in the 1930s, friends of the flowering cherry trees protested vehemently. Some women who were particularly outraged by the plans to break ground in the middle of the cherries actually chained themselves to the trees! Finally, the furor died down (although a few trees were sacrificed), and the memorial was completed in 1942.

Thomas Jefferson was a serious architect, as anyone who has visited his lovely Charlottesville home, Monticello, or the University of Virginia campus knows. The Jefferson Memorial was designed in an architectural style reminiscent of that of the third president. Jefferson was also fond of trees, and the grounds around the memorial are liberally planted with them. In addition to the striking white pines that encircle the memorial, hollies, zelkovas, and American elms are among the woody plants that provide an arboreal frame for this beloved landmark.

East Potomac Park (Hains Point)

It has been said of East Potomac Park: "If Washington has a village green, this is it."[53] Throughout most of the year, residents of every part of the city can be found on this peaceful point of land, spending their leisure hours in the company of family and friends, pursuing their favorite sports, or simply enjoying a few moments of solitude. Joggers and cyclists crisscross past fishermen and family barbecues, while a perennial breeze keeps the willows in motion. Gulls, ducks, and geese share the golf course with golfers and the water with sailors during the warmer months. In the winter, the park is a refuge for wildlife, invaded only by the most dedicated joggers and fishermen, employees of the National Park Service, and a few straggling sightseers along Ohio Drive.

History of East Potomac Park

East Potomac Park is a promontory of nearly 330 acres stretching out in a southeasterly direction and culminating in Hains Point. The park is surrounded by the Washington Channel to the east and northeast, the Potomac River to the southwest, and the Tidal Basin to the northwest.

As incredible as it may seem, today's popular park was once a major health hazard. A little more than a century ago, East Potomac Park was a tidal marsh that had become badly polluted by the city's sewers. During the summer months, the marshes, or flats, along the Potomac were a breeding ground for malarial mosquitoes and other disease-carrying organisms. Peter C. Hains, the army engineer who directed much of the work of turning the Potomac marshes into parkland (and for whom Hains Point is named), wrote that sanitary conditions along the river had become so bad during the latter part of the nineteenth century that adjacent parts of the city "had become almost uninhabitable."[54]

An 1882 Act of Congress called for the reclamation of hundreds of acres of marshland along the Potomac. East Potomac Park was the first area to be transformed, under Colonel Hains's guidance, from polluted marsh to pleasant parkland. In 1913, with East and West Potomac Parks successfully created, the *Washington Star* reported: "Out of the slimy and reedy marshes of the Potomac River at Washington the government of the United States has created one of the most beautiful parks of the world."[55]

East Potomac Park enjoyed early popularity among Washingtonians and visitors to the nation's capital. Where joggers tread today, horseback riders moseyed under the cottonwoods and willows along the Potomac River and the newly created Washington Channel.

The Trees of East Potomac Park

The maritime atmosphere of East Potomac Park is doubly pleasing because of the presence of beautiful trees. Weeping willows

trail their delicate spring-green foliage all along the shoreline.
Ohio Drive is lined with Japanese flowering cherry trees, which
bloom at staggered times. Dozens of other native and exotic trees
adorn Washington's "village green."

The weeping willows predate the park itself. Legend says that
the park's original willows were propagated from trees brought to
the District of Columbia from Napoleon's gravesite at St. Helena.
While this legend may or may not be true, weeping willows are
not native, and they were on the scene before Colonel Hains.
Ulysses S. Grant III, grandson of the famous general and U.S.
president and director of the former Office of Public Buildings and Public Parks, wrote during the 1920s: "When . . . East
Potomac Park was still a salt water tidal flat, these old willows
marked the few high and dry places where one could safely walk
and stand."[56]

Nothing complements weeping willows more perfectly than
Japanese flowering cherry trees, and with these the park is well
endowed. Among the first to bloom are the delicate weeping
cherries, much like small weeping willows in silhouette. While
the weeping cherries are still in full flower, hundreds of Yoshino
and Akebono cherry trees (of the same hybrid planted around
the Tidal Basin) come into bloom. Many of the Yoshino and Akebono trees along both sides of Ohio Drive were planted by Lady
Bird Johnson's Committee for a More Beautiful Capital during
the 1960s. The former first lady planted one of the trees personally.

The most famous East Potomac Park cherries are the deep
pink, double-blossomed Kwanzans. These trees come into bloom
in mid- to late April, about two weeks later than the early, single-
blossomed cherry trees. When the original Japanese gift of cherry
trees was planted in 1912, several double-blossomed forms were
planted in East Potomac Park. Of these, only the Kwanzans
survived in any numbers. While they are not nearly as famous as
the Tidal Basin Yoshino cherries, the Kwanzans of East Potomac
Park—which have been replaced by young specimens in many
instances—are perhaps better loved by Washingtonians, who can
enjoy them in relative solitude after most of the tourists have
departed.

In recent years, rare Japanese cherries have been added to the
mix at East Potomac Park. Consult the National Park Service's
Cherry Blossom Trail Guide for locations of the Okame cherry,
the Afterglow cherries, the Takesimensis trees, and the "Hula

Skirt" tree—an individual weeping cherry that has upswept and then pendulous branches, suggesting a Hawaiian dancer's skirt. The guide also gives the location of a botanical mystery: several extremely old and gnarled cherries on the East Potomac Golf Course could be survivors from the original 1909 Tokyo gift of trees that had to be burned because of infestation by pests and diseases (see page 39). It's possible that this small grove of trees escaped destruction, and therefore the National Park Service has dubbed them "Survivors of the Burn." They are featured in the Witness Tree Protection Program of the National Park Service's Historic American Landscapes Survey, which identifies trees that have been living "witnesses" to history.

No observant park visitor will fail to notice the tall, tapered conifers planted on either side of Hains Point. Striking in both summer and winter, with or without the delicate needles that they shed in autumn, the bald-cypresses of East Potomac Park look right at home. And they very nearly are. While these residents of southern swamps are no longer indigenous to the Washington area, botanists theorize that much of Washington was once a cypress swamp. During construction of the Metro subway system, remains of bald-cypress trees dating back thousands of years were unearthed in Northwest Washington.

North of the bald-cypress groves, on the eastern side of the promontory, are some very old cottonwoods. The history of planting cottonwoods (or Carolina poplars, as they were once called) along the Potomac River dates back to the nineteenth century, when it was believed that these trees possessed "wonderful malaria-absorbing qualities." While it was not known precisely how, it was widely believed that stands of the Carolina poplars slowed the spread of the disease. The tree seemed especially suited for this purpose, perhaps only because it could survive in wet, mosquito-infested places. There is evidence that by 1890, following massive plantings of cottonwood and other trees along the Potomac and throughout Washington, the threat of malaria had lessened.

The headquarters of the U.S. Park Police and the National Capital Region of the National Park Service on the northwestern side of the park are surrounded by interesting trees. Delicate Japanese red pines and groves of European hornbeams and lindens are among the trees planted as landscaping (or camouflage!) for the collection of austere Park Service buildings.

Between the National Park Service buildings and the Tidal

Basin is the new George Mason Memorial, dedicated in 2002 to the Virginia patriot who was the author of the 1776 Virginia Declaration of Rights, precursor of the Declaration of Independence and the U.S. Bill of Rights. The memorial is surrounded by saucer and star magnolias.

Among the other noteworthy trees of East Potomac Park are a grove of Ohio buckeyes close to the point on the Potomac side; Austrian, Japanese black, and eastern white pines; London planes and American sycamores; river birches; zelkovas; and several oak species and hybrids.

The Lincoln Memorial

The white marble Lincoln Memorial honors President Abraham Lincoln, who steered the country through the Civil War and helped bring an end to slavery in the United States. Believed by many people to be the most beautiful monument in Washington, the Lincoln Memorial is especially attractive at night, when it seems to glow from within. The cornerstone for the memorial was laid in 1915, but not until 1922 was the completed structure dedicated.

The Lincoln Memorial is surrounded by a brilliantly conceived border of evergreens. Although from a distance the plants all appear to be shrubby, up close they comprise a delightful mini-forest that includes southern magnolias, American hollies, and other trees that are green throughout the year. A trip through this little woodland is especially delightful after a snowfall.

The original trees lining the Lincoln Memorial Reflecting Pool baffled botanists for decades. They were imported from Europe as clones of the English elm. However, they are more likely some form of Dutch elm, a hybrid group of trees. As the original plantings have died, they have been replaced with several Dutch elm cultivars (see pages 206–7).

War Veterans' Memorials and Constitution Gardens

Visitors to the memorials of recent twentieth-century wars, located on the Mall near the Lincoln Memorial, are greeted by many beautiful tree specimens, both mature and newly planted. Young zelkovas, little-leafed lindens, and red maples are planted around the **Korean War Veterans Memorial,** which captures the experience of military personnel in the field during the Korean War. That war, which was fought from 1950 until 1953, was one of the first major challenges for the newly formed United Nations. A large hackberry and mature white pines grow near the memorial. The hackberry has received special pampering and has been honored with its own protective wall.

The **Vietnam Veterans Memorial** honors those who fought in a war that bitterly divided the country during the 1960s and early 1970s. The memorial is a simple yet dramatically effective black granite wall chiseled with the names of the more than 58,000 Americans who died in the war or were listed as missing. It is located near groves of London plane, red maple, white pine, American beech, and sweetgum, among other trees. A large bronze sculpture of three servicemen stands nearby.

The nearby **Vietnam Women's Memorial** honors the 265,000 women who served during the Vietnam era, including 11,000 who saw active duty in Vietnam—many of them health care professionals. The Vietnam Women's Memorial is surrounded by young yellowwoods. Hedge, or field, maples, sweetgums, willow oaks, and southern red oaks grow near the memorial.

Just to the east of the memorials, a body of water in **Constitution Gardens** is surrounded by weeping willow, bald-cypress, flowering crabapples, honey locust, tulip-tree, and willow, pin, and red oaks.

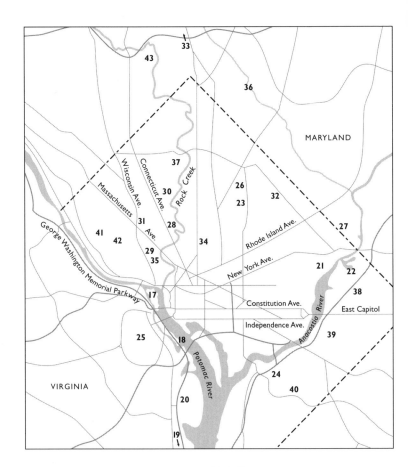

DISTRICT OF COLUMBIA AND BEYOND

Theodore Roosevelt Island

During the administration of President Theodore Roosevelt, five national parks, more than fifty bird and animal refuges, and the U.S. Forest Service were all created. Today's Theodore Roosevelt Island remains true to the spirit of this great wilderness adventurer and conservationist. Hikers on one of the island's woodland paths can easily imagine themselves somewhere in the wild. Yet the island is just a stone's throw away from the tumult of Washington.

Theodore Roosevelt Island, located midstream in the Potomac between two other presidential memorials—the Kennedy Center and the George Washington Memorial Parkway—has been known by several names in the past, including Anacostian, Analostan, Barbadoes, and My Lord's Island. For many years it was owned by the family of the Virginia patriot George Mason, and was generally called Mason's Island. During the latter part of the eighteenth century, George Mason's son, John, built an estate on the island, where he raised sheep, cotton, and other crops. The island changed hands several times before the Roosevelt Memorial Association purchased it in the early 1930s and turned it over to the federal government.

The Memorial Association hired the Olmsted Brothers firm (run by the son and stepson of Frederick Law Olmsted—Frederick Law Olmsted Jr. and John Charles Olmsted) to draw up a landscaping plan for the island. The Olmsted plan, which was carried out during the 1930s, called for the removal of all human-made structures on the island and the planting of thousands of trees and shrubs.

During the 1960s, federal funds were appropriated to construct a formal memorial to Theodore Roosevelt in the interior of the island. Today, this unique memorial is a haven for those who, in Roosevelt's words, "delight in the hardy life of the open." A giant bronze statue of the former president overlooks an expansive terrace surrounded by a picturesque moat. The moat is crossed by stone footbridges and lined with willow oaks. On a still day, when the reflection in the water of oaks and sky is interrupted only by families of ducks, the effect is truly hypnotic. The footpaths radiate outward from the terrace to all parts of the island. The trees under which hikers pass include mature oaks (there's a large specimen of the uncommon Shumard), hickories, black walnuts, maples, elms, ashes, and tulip-trees. Willows, boxelders, sycamores, and American hornbeams grow along the shorelines. Pawpaws and spice-bush also are part of the island's varied woody plant community.

Visitors can gain access to the Potomac Heritage National Scenic Trail at the northern end of the parking lot for Theodore Roosevelt Island. From there, it is a ten-mile hike through riverside woodlands to the I-495 American Legion Bridge.

Lyndon Baines Johnson Memorial Grove

Lyndon Baines Johnson, the thirty-sixth president, was a tireless promoter of his Great Society programs. Yet he once wrote: "I would have been content to be simply a conservation President. . . . My deepest attitudes and beliefs were shaped by a closeness to the land, and it was only natural for me to think of preserving it."[57] During the Johnson years, more than 3.5 million acres were added to America's national park system, including the famous Redwood National Park; the Wilderness Act, first of its kind in the world, was signed into law; and important laws were passed to control the growing problems of air and water pollution.

LBJ, as he was so often called, grew up in the hill country of central Texas. In the tradition of many American presidents, he possessed a deep understanding of the close relationship between the land and its people. For Lyndon Johnson and his wife, Lady Bird, social equality and environmental awareness were integral elements of a healthy society. In 1973, soon after his death, family friends began planning a memorial to the former president. It did not take them long to agree that a traditional monument was not in keeping with the spirit of LBJ. Instead, they decided upon a grove of trees.

The Lyndon Baines Johnson Memorial Grove would be located within Lady Bird Johnson Park on the Virginia side of the Potomac. A seventy-member committee was formed to work on the plan, which included a nationwide fund-raising drive. Meade Palmer, a Virginia landscape architect, was commissioned to design the grove. Seventeen acres would be laid out with peaceful walkways among plantings of white pine, flowering shrubs, and daffodils. A roughly hewn, 43-ton block of granite would be transported from a Texas quarry to serve in place of a traditional statue.

Ground was broken in September 1974, and less than two years later the grove was ready for formal dedication. More than a thousand people gathered under the young pine trees on an April day in 1976 for the official opening of the grove. President Gerald Ford spoke for all who knew the former president when he said: "It is entirely fitting that in this city of bronze and marble monuments we choose to remember Lyndon Johnson with a living memorial of pines."[58] Lady Bird Johnson, who "grew up listening to the wind in the pine trees of east Texas woods," spoke of the "joy in the outdoors" that she and Lyndon had shared together. "If I were to make one wish for today," she told the crowd, "that wish is that this bower of trees will forever set people dreaming."[59]

In 1977, a footbridge across the boundary channel was completed, creating a new access to the grove. From this western approach, one crosses the channel, a favorite haven for water birds, to the heart of the grove without having to contend with parkway traffic.

Today, the young white pines are thriving, and the spring procession of daffodils, dogwood, laurelcherry, viburnums, azaleas, and rhododendrons is spectacular. In addition, the National Park Service has added wildflowers to the grove flora. Surrounding the memorial plantings are many lovely old trees, including pears, cottonwoods, maples, and willows.

Lady Bird Johnson Park

On November 12, 1968, Secretary of the Interior Stewart Udall christened Columbia Island Lady Bird Johnson Park in honor of the first lady who inspired a drive to beautify cities and towns across the United States. Nowhere are her efforts more apparent than in Washington. The park lies directly across the Potomac from the city, providing a spectacular view of the Lincoln and Jefferson memorials and the Washington Monument. The Lyndon Baines Johnson Memorial Grove is located within the park.

The Lady Bird Johnson Park is beautiful year-round, but is in its glory in the spring. During the first lady's beautification drive of the mid-1960s, thousands of flowering plants were added to the island's acreage. Members of area garden clubs helped plant hundreds of thousands of daffodils along the river. A profusion of flowering dogwoods and other trees were also planted, and a biking and walking path was added to the shoreline.

The innovations of the 1960s enhanced what was already a pleasing spot. Many mature trees, including pears, willows, American elms, and willow oaks, bend in the wind along the riverside. Three of the trees in Lady Bird Johnson Park are part of the Witness Tree Protection Program of the National Park Service's Historic American Landscapes Survey: a large cotton-wood, a pear (which is scheduled for removal for the widening of Humpback Bridge), and an old flowering crabapple. The crabapple and the pear were both part of the planting for the historic highway now known as the George Washington Memorial Parkway.

George Washington's Mount Vernon

The tall, indomitable general who marched to war at the head of the Continental Army, defeated the British, and served as the first president had a gentle side. On a spring day in 1786, George Washington wrote from Mount Vernon: "The warmth of yesterday and this day, forwarded vegetation much; the buds of some trees, particularly the Weeping Willow and Maple, had displayed their leaves & blossoms and all others were swelled, and many ready to put forth. The apricot trees were beginning to blossom and the grass to shew its verdure."[60] While no man could have served his country better or loved it more, there is no question that George Washington's heart frequently strayed to his Virginia home. In 1775, as newly appointed commander in chief of the Continental Army, the general wrote to his wife, Martha, from Philadelphia: "I should enjoy more real happiness in one month with you at home than I have the most distant prospect of finding abroad, if my stay were to be seven times seven years."[61]

It's easy to see why George Washington loved Mount Vernon. In the president's own words, there were few homes that could be more "pleasantly situated." Spacious lawns and open fields overlook a graceful bend in the Potomac. Deer feed at twilight at the wood's edge. And everywhere, there are pleasing groves of trees.

"Trees were Washington's really great love in nature," wrote author Erle Kauffman in the 1930s.[62] Indeed, Washington's diaries abound with detailed descriptions of the trees and shrubs at Mount Vernon. Several trees planted by Washington himself are alive today after two centuries.

History of George Washington at Mount Vernon

The Mount Vernon property, lying along the Virginia side of the Potomac River between Little Hunting Creek and Dogue Creek, had been in the Washington family for years before George

Washington officially acquired it in 1754. During his childhood Washington's immediate family had resided at Mount Vernon for three years, and throughout his early life young George continued to visit relatives living at the estate.

Five years after it became his, in 1759, Washington married Martha Dandridge Custis, a widow and the mother of two children. The couple never had their own children, but Washington took pride in his stepchildren and their offspring. In 1781, following the death of Martha's son, John Parke Custis, Washington adopted John's two youngest children.

The years between 1759 and the outbreak of the Revolution in 1775 were peaceful ones for the Washingtons. George lived the life of a prosperous farmer, overseeing his estate and constantly devising ways to increase its productivity and beauty. He was interested in every detail of the workings of his farm, from growing wheat to grinding flour. During these years, Washington supervised the creation of two beautiful gardens, which today have been restored by the Mount Vernon Ladies' Association. Referred to as the "flower garden" and the "kitchen garden" in the first editions of *City of Trees,* they are now called the Upper Garden and Lower Garden, as they were in Washington's day.

Following the Revolution, and prior to becoming president, Washington once again took up the life of a farmer and horticulturist. To satisfy his ever-increasing desire for knowledge about the plant world, he built a greenhouse to protect his citrus trees and other warm-weather plants during the winter. He even created his own botanical garden, where he experimented with exotic seeds from places as far away as China.

It was during the hiatus between the Revolution and his presidency that Washington laid out the lovely serpentine road and walkways on the Bowling Green, the lawn in front of the main entrance to the mansion. For the most part, he chose native trees and shrubs to line the graceful curves of the road and outer edges of the lawn. Some of the original plantings in these "wildernesses" and "shrubberies," as he called them, are alive today.

Washington was no purist about planting trees indigenous to Virginia, however. In 1785 he wrote to a cousin, William Washington, of South Carolina: "I would thank you my Good Sir, for the Acorns, Nutts, or seeds of trees or plants not common in this Country; but which you think would grow here, especially of the flowering kind."[63] This request and numerous others brought trees from all over the country and the world to the home overlooking the Potomac. From the South came the southern magnolia and the live oak; from Europe and Asia, the horse-chestnut, weeping willow, and Lombardy poplar; and from New England, spruce and eastern hemlock, one of which survives today. The great French botanist André Michaux brought seeds, shrubs, and trees to Washington from France. And New York governor George Clinton sent linden (or lime) trees to Mount Vernon.

It is no secret that George Washington reluctantly assumed the responsibility of becoming the nation's first president. His country needed him, and once again he tore himself away from Mount Vernon to serve. But although Washington was compelled to reside in the temporary capitals of New York and Philadelphia for the eight years of his presidency, his heart was never far from home. And when, in 1790, the year after he took office, the president was entrusted with the responsibility of choosing the site for the permanent capital of the United States, he determined that the capital city would be located along the Potomac.

The business of choosing the location for the new "Federal City," and then supervising its design and construction, gave Washington a reason to visit Mount Vernon, just down the river from Georgetown. On one such visit, during the summer of 1792, he happily wrote: "The day and night we reached home, there fell a most delightful and refreshing rain, and the weather since has been as seasonable as the most sanguine farmer could wish."[64] The president went on to discuss the salubrious effect the rain would have on his Indian corn crop.

In May 1797, with his eight years as president over, George Washington described his bucolic plans for retirement: "To make and sell a little flour, to repair houses going fast to ruin, to build one for the security of my papers of a public nature, and to amuse myself with Agriculture and rural pursuits, will constitute employment for the years I have to remain on this terrestrial Globe. If . . . I could now and then meet friends I esteem, it would fill the measure . . . but, if ever this happens, it must be under my own vine and fig-tree, as I do not think it probable that I shall go beyond twenty miles from them."[65]

Though Washington had little time left on this earth, he lived his remaining days in precisely the manner he had wished—in the peaceful pursuit of happiness at Mount Vernon. He died on December 14, 1799, at the age of sixty-seven. He was survived by Martha, who lived until 1802. They are buried at Mount Vernon.

The Mount Vernon Ladies' Association

A South Carolina woman, Ann Pamela Cunningham, was the founder of the Mount Vernon Ladies' Association. She formed the organization after she learned that Washington's Mount Vernon estate had been offered for sale to both the United States and the Commonwealth of Virginia, and that both had turned it down. The new association raised the money to purchase the property by public subscription, and in 1858 it succeeded in buying it from one of Washington's heirs for $200,000. It was a felicitous day for George Washington's trees, gardens, and grounds when the Mount Vernon Ladies' Association became the proprietor of the estate.

In 1926, the association published a report on the trees at Mount Vernon, written by Charles Sprague Sargent, an eminent botanist and director of the Arnold Arboretum at Harvard University. Sargent had made a careful study, comparing the trees then growing on the grounds with plantings described in Washington's diaries. He concluded that forty-five trees planted by George Washington, or under his direction, were still living in 1926 (though he has since been proven wrong in a few cases). Several trees had been brought down just two years earlier by a tornado. In the report, Sargent wrote: "No trees planted by man have the human interest of the Mount Vernon trees. They belong to the nation and are one of its precious possessions. No care should be spared to preserve them, and as they pass away they should be replaced with trees of the same kinds, that Mount Vernon may be kept for all time as near as possible in the condition in which Washington left it."[66]

In recent years, the Mount Vernon Ladies' Association has treated Sargent's word as gospel. Every effort is made to preserve the health of the original plantings. When they do succumb to old age or storm damage, the original trees are replaced, whenever possible, with their offspring. Trees and shrubs planted at Mount Vernon today conform, for the most part, to those growing on the estate during Washington's time.

George Washington's Trees

On January 12, 1785, George Washington wrote in his diary: "Rode to my Mill Swamp . . . & to other places in search of the sort of Trees I shall want for my walks, groves, & Wildernesses." An entry recorded one week later read: "Employed until dinner in laying out my Serpentine road & shrubberies adjoining."[67]

During the next three years, Washington planted between 120 and 150 trees along the serpentine road and outer edges of the Bowling Green. When the first edition of *City of Trees* was published in 1981, it was believed that twelve of the original Bowling Green trees survived: two tulip-trees, three white ashes, five hollies, one hemlock, and one hybrid buckeye. A thirteenth tree, a white mulberry located near the entrance to the Bowling Green, was also traced to Washington's time. However, according to Dean Norton, Mount Vernon's longtime director of horticulture, core samples taken in recent years have debunked the authenticity of several of the Bowling Green trees, and it's now believed that only the hemlock, the tulip-trees, and the mulberry date to Washington's lifetime. "Dendrochronologists have found that the two tulip poplars [or tulip-trees] date to 'no later than 1796,' meaning they were in existence prior to 1796," Norton explained. "The mulberry only yielded a 5.5-inch core, but with the number of rings counted in the core it is extremely likely that the tree dates to Washington's time. He was trying to grow a white mulberry grove to introduce the silkworm for the silk industry."[68] Some of the Bowling Green trees that are no longer thought to be among George Washington's plantings are quite old nonetheless. Recent core samplings show that two of the towering white ashes date to 1819, and three of the largest American hollies go back to 1806, 1812, and 1863.

According to Norton, in addition to the four Bowling Green trees, there are at least two other trees near the mansion that date to Washington's time: "A narrow-leaved chestnut oak [also called chinquapin, or yellow oak (*Quercus muhlenbergii*)] can now be dated to 'no later than 1771,' and a beautiful white oak dates to 'no later than 1783.'"[69] These ancient oaks are located between the mansion and the Potomac River, in a newly restored area designed to look as it did in Washington's day, when it was a "deer park," or "hanging wood"—a semi-open, sloping woodland. Norton and his crew have removed several acres of dense undergrowth in the area, including many invasive woody plants, in recent restoration efforts. A visit to Mount Vernon would not be complete without a stop to view this charming wooded slope with its historic oaks and the wide tidal Potomac below it.

Moreover, as a result of recent core sampling, additional eighteenth-century trees have been discovered in the forests that surround the Mount Vernon historic area. These include white oaks, chestnut oaks, tulip-trees, and a pitch pine. One of the chestnut oaks dates to no later than 1673, according to Norton. Research on the trees that were living during Washington's lifetime is ongoing, he said.

Norton delights in the stories of specific trees, including the hemlock that Washington received in a whiskey barrel from Major General Benjamin Lincoln of Massachusetts. Norton believes the hemlock is probably one of the original Bowling Green trees still standing, and points to Washington's diary as proof. From a July 6, 1785, entry: "Received from Genl. Lincoln 3 young trees of the Spruce Pine and two of the Fir or Hemlock in half Barrels which seemed to be healthy and vegitating." And one week later: "Transplanted the Spruce & Fir (or Hemlock) from the Boxes in which they were sent to me by General Lincoln to the Walks by the Garden Gates."[70] As Norton points out, "The most exciting aspect of this story is that it is the only example Mount Vernon has of a specific tree with a planting location mentioned in George Washington's diaries [and] that dendrochronologists confirm dates to 1791–1796."[71]

Norton and his staff of more than twenty-three workers meticulously care for the Mount Vernon gardens and grounds. He says he feels honored to do so, and to be "maintaining it at the level that George Washington would have desired," adding, "I have history backing me up."[72]

Other Trees at Mount Vernon

In 2006, two new buildings opened at Mount Vernon: a museum and education center and an orientation center. Both structures were built largely underground in order to protect the view of Mount Vernon's rolling acreage. Large windows provide glimpses of the landscaping surrounding the new buildings and the fields and wooded walks beyond them.

In keeping with tradition, only trees growing at Mount Vernon during Washington's time were planted around the new buildings. These include sweetgum, tulip-tree, American beech, sycamore, hemlock, willow, scarlet and other oak species, hickories, hollies, fringe-tree, witch-hazel, serviceberry or shadbush, honey-locust, redbud, and flowering dogwood. Disease-resistant cultivated forms of the dogwood were used in response to the dogwood blight prevalent at the time of planting.

Returning visitors may miss the London planes that used to greet them along the lane leading to the Bowling Green. Most of these trees were suffering from anthracnose, so only a few healthy trees had to be removed for the new construction, according to Dean Norton. The planes postdated Washington, and although they provided an attractive border to the lane, they were not native, but a hybrid of the American sycamore and Oriental plane.

A peculiar story is connected with the two tall pecan trees that for many years crowned the hill leading from the Potomac River to the mansion. One of the pecans remains, but the other had to be removed following Hurricane Isabel in September 2003. These trees were reputed to have been a gift to George Washington from Thomas Jefferson, another horticulturally minded president. That legend was shattered, however, when a photograph taken in 1856 turned up. The picture shows a bare hillside where the remaining pecan stands today.

The black locust grove just north of the house has an interesting history. In 1776, General Washington wrote from New York instructing his grounds manager to plant "groves of Trees at each end of the dwelling House . . . to consist . . . at the North end, of locusts altogether."[73] The general's orders were carried out, and for many years a black locust grove has graced the northern grounds of the mansion. In 1934, the grove was restored according to Washington's 1776 specifications. These locusts are especially lovely in May, with their pendulous clusters of fragrant white blossoms.

The grounds of Mount Vernon are liberally adorned with southern magnolia trees. Washington planted several dozen of these flowering trees from a shipment he received from South Carolina in 1785. Although none has survived to the present day, in 1977 the Mount Vernon Ladies' Association planted southern magnolias in two of the original locations recorded in Washington's diary, just to the west of the mansion.

A magnificent blue Atlas cedar stands to the southeast of the house, on the hill overlooking the Potomac. Planted in 1874 in honor of Ann Pamela Cunningham, founder of the Mount Vernon Ladies' Association, this cedar, which stands in front of a white oak dating to Washington's time, is native to the Atlas Mountain region of northern Africa. In 1899, to commemorate the centenary of Washington's death, a delegation of Masons planted a closely related tree, the cedar of Lebanon, near his grave. This tree, too, is magnificent today.

Mid-April is undoubtedly the most spectacular time of year to visit Mount Vernon. The eighteenth-century flower gardens are in full bloom and trees everywhere are just beginning to show their softly electric spring greens. The loveliest sight of all is a magical arboreal combination that was known to George Washington: the simultaneous blooming of the redbud and the flowering dogwood. In his 1926 report on the trees of Mount Vernon, Charles Sprague Sargent noted: "That [Washington] appreciated the beauty which can be obtained by contrasting the white flowers of the Dogwood with the rose-colored flowers of the Redbud is shown by his planting, on March 1, 1785, 'a circle of Dogwood with a Redbud in the middle.'"[74]

Today, the dogwood and redbud trees grow in profusion at Mount Vernon, and along the memorial parkway connecting George Washington's home with the capital city named in his honor. The combination of snow-white and purplish pink blossoms is particularly beautiful during a soft spring rain. Appropriately, the loveliest dogwoods and redbuds of all grow close to Washington's gravesite, where the elegantly landscaped Mount Vernon estate and peaceful native woodland meet.

One final question remains about the trees in George Washington's life: Did he chop down that cherry tree? Many adults may know that the story was only a fable made up by Parson Weems. Or was it? In his diary entry for August 18, 1785, the first president of the United States confessed that he had (indeed!) "Cut down the two cherry trees in the Court yard."[75]

River Farm

River Farm is located along the George Washington Memorial Parkway several miles north of Mount Vernon. This historic 25-acre property, which was once owned and farmed by George Washington, serves as the national headquarters of the American Horticultural Society. A pleasing tapestry of gardens and semi-wild Potomac riverside meadow and woodland, River Farm is a good place to visit on the way to or from Mount Vernon, or as a separate destination. Tree enthusiasts will find specimens noteworthy because of their age, size, beauty, and botanic rarity.

A large osage-orange tree, estimated to be about two hundred years old, sprawls next to a brick wall in the "Garden Calm" near the central mansion. The tree is considered the second largest of this species in the country. A male tree, it does not produce the species' characteristic fruit.

Two large black walnut trees that may date to George Washington's time grow in the sloping meadow between the mansion and the Potomac River. Just north of the meadow is a small grove of Franklin trees, believed to be extinct in the wild. In late autumn, their leaf color is a vivid mix of scarlet and orange. Below the meadow and the Franklin grove, a woodland of native oaks, maples, tulip-tree, sassafras, holly, and sycamore borders the Potomac shoreline.

Other noteworthy trees at River Farm include dawn redwood, Kentucky coffee-tree, the rare dove tree, a fern-leafed European beech, and the native fringe-tree. Many of the trees at River Farm are labeled, so this is a good place for horticultural study— a fitting tribute to George Washington, one of the nation's first and foremost horticulturists.

George Washington Memorial Parkway

The scenic national parkway running along the Virginia side of the Potomac River from the Washington beltway to Mount Vernon passes through both Piedmont and Coastal Plain woodlands and crosses the fall line near Theodore Roosevelt Island. The springtime displays of redbud and flowering dogwood and the early leaves of tulip-trees and other native forest trees near the parkway are breathtaking. Fall foliage along this historic roadway is also noteworthy. Tulip-trees, tupelos, maples, and oaks contribute vivid color to the autumn landscape. During winter, Potomac River vistas are particularly striking, both above and below the fall line.

Any time of year, the views of the City of Trees and surroundings from the George Washington Memorial Parkway are memorable. The earliest completed leg of the parkway—from Memorial Bridge to George Washington's Mount Vernon home— was originally named the Mount Vernon Memorial Highway, and dates to 1932, the bicentennial of Washington's birth. The parkway also passes through Lady Bird Johnson Park and skirts the LBJ Memorial Grove. Turkey Run Park, one of the most diverse woodlands in the area; Theodore Roosevelt Island; and the Potomac Heritage National Scenic Trail are all accessed from the parkway as well. The Mount Vernon Trail, a paved bike and jogging path, runs alongside the parkway from Key Bridge to Mount Vernon.

There is a large willow oak at the Belle Haven parking lot south of Old Town Alexandria that is featured in the Witness

Tree Protection Program of the National Park Service's Historic American Landscapes Survey. The oak predates the parkway and was integrated into the original planting design of the 1930s. According to the National Park Service, the parkway tree crew refers to the tree as "Methuselah," a reference to the oldest person described in the Bible. The Dyke Marsh Wildlife Preserve nearby is a famous birding spot, memorialized in Louis J. Halle's nature classic, *Spring in Washington*. Another Witness Tree Protection Program tree, a pin oak, is located in Fort Hunt Park near Mount Vernon. The tree was planted to honor a royal visit to a model CCC (Civilian Conservation Corps) camp by England's King George VI and Queen Elizabeth in 1939. In the Wellington area, near River Farm (headquarters of the American Horticultural Society), there is a large grouping of native cedars that were saved and transplanted during the parkway's construction, with the intent to honor Virginia's historic rural countryside.

The National Arboretum

The cherry trees bloom but once a year, their blossoms soon scattered by the brisk spring wind. Even the most hardened urbanite must wish for more than that teasing glimpse of their stirring beauty. Washington has its pockets of beauty year round, of course, but does anything even remotely compare with the cherry trees? The answer is "Yes! . . . The National Arboretum."

Among the National Arboretum's many attractions are two that are nearly as awe-inspiring as the sight of Washington's cherry trees in bloom: Mount Hamilton and the National Bonsai and Penjing Museum collection. The first comes alive in April and May with an incredible display of azaleas and flowering dogwoods. The second is an experience to refresh the spirit throughout the year, with its miniature trees from Japan, China, and North America, some of which are hundreds of years old yet stand no higher than seedlings.

The National Arboretum is located in Northeast Washington, on 446 acres of varied terrain. The hills and vales of the Arboretum support an outstanding array of native and exotic trees and shrubs, with peaceful roads and footpaths winding through them. From the first spring wildflower in Fern Valley to the last blanket of snow on the groves of dwarf conifers, every part of the Arboretum is worth exploring, every season of the year.

Brief History and General Background

In the last part of the nineteenth century, Secretary of Agriculture James Wilson dreamed of a place in the nation's capital that would be "a perennial feast of botanical education."[76] Wilson and some of his contemporaries envisioned an extensive plant research center that would also rate among the great botanical gardens of the world. In 1901, the McMillan Commission (which later became the Commission of Fine Arts) gave impetus to the idea by recommending that a combination arboretum and botanical garden be created. It was not until 1927, however, that Congress approved the bill creating the present-day National Arboretum.

Two U.S. Department of Agriculture scientists, F. V. Coville and B. Y. Morrison, chose the Northeast Washington site and directed the planning for the new arboretum. In 1951, Morrison became the National Arboretum's first director.

While a more pleasant urban getaway can hardly be imagined, providing a place for public recreation is not the Arboretum's primary goal. Plant research and education are what the Arboretum is really all about. A large staff of scientists conducts breeding experiments to develop improved varieties of plants. The researchers also evaluate and classify cultivars developed elsewhere.

Within the administration building, an attractive glass-and-concrete structure surrounded by pools filled with colorful lilies, lotuses, and exotic fish, is the Arboretum's herbarium, where 650,000 pressed-plant specimens are kept on file. These specimens are an important resource, not only for the Arboretum staff, but for scientists from around the world, who come here to conduct research or who are loaned specimens from the collection. The Department of Agriculture, which administers the Arboretum, also makes use of this vast plant library. In keeping with the Arboretum's educational objectives, members of the staff regularly publish their research findings in government and professional publications. Lectures, films, and exhibits are open to the public.

The Azaleas

It's as simple as this: If you haven't seen the Arboretum's azaleas, you have no idea what you are missing. The widest wide-angle lens could not begin to capture the all-encompassing feeling one gets in the midst of the Mount Hamilton azaleas. The colors are out of an Impressionist painting: salmon, lilac, rose, orange, and scarlet. Brilliant white flowering dogwoods, including doublebracted forms, are intermingled with the colorful shrubs. Tall trees and wildflowers complete the scene, which seems to have sprung from a romantic fantasy.

The Arboretum azaleas actually have a far less ethereal origin. The majority of the shrubs (those above the roadway on Mount Hamilton) are the result of breeding experiments conducted by the first director of the Arboretum, B. Y. Morrison. Morrison's colorful array of selections are generally known as the Glenn Dale hybrids, after the place where they were developed. In addition to the thousands of specimens scattered across the hillside, a quaint brick-walled area called the Morrison Garden and its immediate surroundings are also planted with Glenn Dale hybrids. Below the roadway are lovely Ghent and Mollis hybrid azaleas, a gift to the United States from the Netherlands. Other types of azaleas and rhododendrons also adorn the slopes of Mount Hamilton.

The National Bonsai and Penjing Museum

For bonsai and penjing trees, as for other plants, leaves unfold in the spring, flowers bloom, and autumn foliage turns red or gold before falling. Only the conifers and camellias remain green throughout the winter. Nothing could sound more natural. But in the case of the National Bonsai and Penjing Museum collection, two factors elevate these simple phenomena to the level of the extraordinary. Bonsai and penjing plants exhibit all the characteristics of full-sized trees, but they stand only a few inches to a few feet tall; and some trees in the collection are well into their third and fourth centuries of existence. One feels the almost eerie presence of dozens of human generations embodied in these tiny trees—generations that have come and gone but that are linked to the present by a miniature forest, representing centuries of human care.

Philosophy aside, the bonsai and penjing trees are one of the most thrilling sights in the nation's capital. And along with their ancient pedigrees, the small trees are also noteworthy for making recent history. Like the famous cherry trees, the bonsai trees were a gift to the United States from Japan. Assembled from some of the finest private collections in that country by Japan's Nippon Bonsai Association, they were presented to the United States in honor of this country's bicentennial celebration. It is difficult to imagine a more generous gift from one nation to another.

Bonsai (which, translated, means "to plant in a shallow pot") is an ancient Japanese art that originated in China. Through careful, periodic pruning of a plant's roots and limbs over the course of its lifetime, a perfect, tiny tree is created that looks exactly as it would in nature, only in miniature. The exacting maintenance of the ancient trees at the National Arboretum is carried on today by bonsai specialists.

The miniature trees are housed in a meditative setting near the Arboretum's administration building. Thirty-four species were represented among the original trees. Tiny "shade" trees include ginkgoes, Japanese and trident maples, Japanese beeches, and hornbeams. The little azaleas, quince, flowering crabapples, and camellias are spectacular in spring with their oversized blossoms. And the miniature conifers, such as pines, junipers, spruces, and yews, nicely complement the collection year-round.

In recent years the bonsai collection has been expanded to include miniature trees from China (penjing), as well as North American bonsai. Four separate pavilions house the collections, with peaceful courtyards and "stroll gardens" connecting them. Visitors enter the museum through a grove of Cryptomeria, past a sign that reads: "Trees shaped by human hands. Nature's essence revealed in living sculptures. Enter the world of bonsai."

The Gotelli Dwarf and Slow-Growing Conifer Collection

The National Arboretum has another forest of trees in miniature, the Gotelli Dwarf and Slow-Growing Conifer Collection. Unlike the bonsai, which require periodic pruning to maintain their miniature size and shape, the trees in the dwarf conifer collection are naturally small for their species. Some are cultivars or naturally occurring varieties; others have been affected by mutations or adverse environmental conditions. Whatever the reasons, the collective result is a troll-sized forest in the middle of Northeast Washington. The collection is planted outdoors on a five-acre hillside in the northeastern part of the Arboretum. Donated by William T. Gotelli in 1962, the planting comprises 1,500 trees, including fir, cedar, pine, yew, spruce, and many others.

Fern Valley

One of my favorite city refuges is the National Arboretum's Fern Valley. A mature woodland with a stream running through it, Fern Valley is replete with native ferns, wildflowers, shrubs, and trees. Here, one can contemplate the beauty of our native flora, from the first spring beauty to the last fallen tulip-tree leaf. Many of the woody and herbaceous plants are labeled, and in some instances their herbal histories are given, making Fern Valley an ideal setting for botanical study.

Fern Valley encompasses a number of habitats, from streamside wetland to dry upland woods. Mature native trees of Fern Valley include huge American beeches and tulip-trees, tupelos, American holly, and several species of oak, hickory, and maple. Sweetbay magnolia and river birch are found in the wetland areas.

The National Grove of State Trees

In 1990, a 30-acre area of the Arboretum was dedicated as the National Grove of State Trees. Official trees of the states and the District of Columbia are planted here in small groves, and all of them were planted by volunteers. Picnic tables are located within the grove, making this an ideal spot to have lunch while you stroll among Iowa's bur oaks, Nebraska's cottonwoods, Oklahoma's redbuds, and Delaware's American hollies. Bring the family back throughout the years to watch the young trees flourish and mature.

Asian Collections

Another relatively new feature of the National Arboretum graces a steep hillside above the Anacostia River across from the Kenilworth Aquatic Gardens. The Asian Collections feature plants of China, Korea, and Japan. Pathways wind down the hillside and through the collections, toward the river. Here you will find trees so rare that they may grow nowhere else in the city. One of my favorite aspects of the collection is the "similar species factor": the Chinese tulip-tree (*Liriodendron chinense*), the Chinese tupelo (*Nyssa sinensis*), and the Chinese sweetgum (*Liquidambar acalycina*) all resemble the eastern North American species to which they are closely related.

The Dawn Redwood

The enchanting dawn redwood, or metasequoia, is often called a "living fossil." Until 1941, when it was found growing in a remote part of central China, the genus *Metasequoia* was known to the world's botanical community only in fossilized form, and was assumed to be extinct. The present range of the fifty-million-year-old genus seems to include only several small areas in Hupeh and Szechuan provinces. Nevertheless, the trees are doing well in cultivation in many parts of the world. The dawn redwood favors moist mountain ravines and is most abundant in Hupeh province's picturesque Shui-sha Valley.

In 1948, just two years after discovery of the dawn redwood was made known, young specimens were brought to the new National Arboretum. These trees are thriving today. The dawn redwood is planted in charming groves throughout the Arboretum. The grove on the lower slope of Mount Hamilton, with a tiny stream flowing through it, looks most at home, however. Like the native American bald-cypress of our own southern swamps, which it closely resembles in appearance, the dawn redwood is a deciduous conifer.

Betula uber

The dawn redwood is not the only tree on the National Arboretum grounds to have returned from the dead. Another "extinct" species is planted there, and this tree is a Virginia native and recent rediscovery. The story of *Betula uber*'s re-surfacing has all the elements of a good detective yarn. Even the Latin name of the tree sounds dark and mysterious.

The story begins in the summer of 1963 with a young botanist named Peter Mazzeo (for many years on the staff of the National Arboretum, and a tremendous help and support to the youthful authors of this volume in their efforts to complete the first edition, more than twenty-five years ago). While working as a ranger naturalist in Virginia's Shenandoah National Park, Mazzeo became intrigued by the legend of *Betula uber*—the mysterious birch that hadn't been seen in the Virginia woods since 1914. Some botanists believed the tree to be extinct, but Mazzeo had a strong feeling it was still growing somewhere in the Blue Ridge Mountains of southwestern Virginia—and that someday he would find it.

After joining the staff of the National Arboretum, Mazzeo began to search for *Betula uber* in earnest. The scant literature available on the rare tree mentioned only one locale where it had ever been sighted: Dickey Creek in Smyth County, Virginia. But Mazzeo's investigation of this southwestern Virginia creek, like the efforts of many botanists before him, yielded no sign of the elusive *Betula uber*.

Then, something happened. Among the *Betula uber* herbarium specimens loaned to Mazzeo by Harvard University's Arnold Arboretum, he found an undated specimen collected along a stream, near Dickey Creek, called Cressy Creek. No mention of this second *Betula uber* sighting had ever appeared in the literature. Mazzeo was excited. Harvard University, however, did not share the young botanist's enthusiasm. Mazzeo's paper about the new finding was turned down by the editors of *Rhodora,* the publication of the prestigious New England Botanical Club. The unpublished paper was returned with the comment, "No new material."

In 1975, the Smithsonian published a report on the endangered and threatened plants of the United States which listed *Betula uber* as "probably extinct." Before the year was out, that assessment would be challenged.

Meanwhile, the editors of *Castanea,* the journal of the Southern Appalachian Botanical Club, had accepted the *uber* paper for publication. The article was printed in the fall of 1974.

In the summer of the following year, 1975, while Peter Mazzeo and the Arboretum's Dr. Frederick Meyer were in the process of planning a trip to Smyth County, another botanical sleuth was on the trail of *Betula uber.* Douglas Ogle, a young biology teacher at Virginia Highlands Community College, had seen the *Castanea* article. He, too, was excited by the new Cressy Creek evidence.

On August 22nd, Ogle rediscovered *Betula uber* on the banks of Cressy Creek. Spotting the characteristic rounded leaves he had seen only in photographs, Ogle became so excited that he shinnied up the slender tree trunk to break off a leafing branch. Sure enough, it had to be *uber.*

When news of the discovery reached Peter Mazzeo back in Washington, he was thrilled. Together, the two men were credited with the *uber* find. Several other specimens were also found in the immediate vicinity along Cressy Creek. The re-found tree was christened with the common name, "Virginia round-leaf birch."

Although botanists now know where *Betula uber* is, they still don't know for sure what it is. According to Mazzeo, it could be a subspecies or a variety, rather than a true species. But however the botanists finally classify it (and Gleason and Cronquist currently classify it as a variant of *Betula lenta*—common names: black birch, sweet birch, cherry birch), there is no doubt that *Betula uber* is unique.

Several young specimens of the Virginia round-leaf birch are planted at the National Arboretum. There is a labeled tree next to one of the Fern Valley trails.

Other National Arboretum Collections

We have barely scratched the surface when it comes to the delightful attractions of the National Arboretum. Also not to be missed are the National Herb Garden, the Holly and Magnolia Collections, the Dogwood Collection, the Friendship Garden, the National Boxwood Collection, the National Capitol Columns, the Perennial Collections, and the Youth Garden. Information and maps are available in the main lobby of the National Arboretum administration building.

Kenilworth Aquatic Gardens

While the Kenilworth Aquatic Gardens are best known for water lilies and other aquatic plants, their colorful pools are surrounded by some very interesting trees. Appropriately, the bald-cypress of southern swamps stands guard over this aquatic park. Japanese raisin-trees, Carolina laurelcherries, and paperbark maple are among the unusual species planted at the gardens. In addition to specific plantings made along the entrance to the park and around the lily pools, many native trees grow along the Anacostia River and at the edges of the tidal marshes. These include red and silver maples, willows, tupelo, sycamore, black locust, river birch, American holly, black walnut, sweetgum, and tulip-tree.

The Anacostia once had thousands of adjacent acres of wetlands, where the Nacotchtank Indians hunted and fished. Wild rice thrived in the tidal marshes. During the 1900s, much of the wetland area was destroyed by dredging and filling. Efforts are being made to revitalize some of these lost wetlands, and the Kenilworth Aquatic Gardens boardwalk and the River Trail are good vantage points for viewing restored tidal marsh. Great egrets fish in the tidal flats, kingfishers zoom low over the water, osprey and bald eagles soar overhead, and turtles sun themselves on logs and rocks. Wild rice has been planted and is flourishing once again. Except for the far-off hum of the city, the marshlands feel decidedly non-urban.

The Kenilworth Aquatic Gardens are located along the eastern shore of the Anacostia River and are administered by the National Park Service. Groups of schoolchildren can often be seen at the gardens as they learn about plants, aquatic animals, and wetland ecology. For information about the colorful history of the gardens, consult *A City of Gardens* by Barbara H. Seeber.

The Soldiers' Home (Armed Forces Retirement Home)

Some of the oldest and most beautiful trees in the District of Columbia are located on the hundreds of rolling acres of what was once called the Soldiers' and Airmen's Home, and is now officially known as the Armed Forces Retirement Home. Located in Northwest Washington, the Soldiers' Home, as it is still most often called, accommodates former members of the military who have either served the requisite number of years or have been disabled in the line of duty. It is the oldest soldiers' home in the country.

During the nineteenth century, a stucco house known as President Lincoln's Cottage, or simply the Lincoln Cottage (formerly, the Anderson Cottage), served as a "summer White House" for President Lincoln. Lincoln and his immediate family resided on the Soldiers' Home property during the Civil War summers from 1862 to 1864. It was one of the first places Lincoln visited after he became president, and he had been horseback riding on this high, wooded hill on the day before his assassination. Presidents Buchanan, Hayes, and Arthur also summered at the Soldiers' Home. In February of 2008, the Lincoln Cottage and the 2.3 acres surrounding it were opened to the public. The official title of the site, which has been restored and renovated by the National Trust for Historic Preservation, is the President Lincoln and Soldiers' Home National Monument.

It is around the historic Lincoln Cottage that many of the most beautiful trees at the Soldiers' Home can be found. Undoubtedly, the most striking tree is an ancient osage-orange. Ginkgo trees, southern magnolias, and old American hollies also grace the grounds of the Lincoln Cottage and adjacent areas, and nearby is a grove of Siberian elms. A mammoth copper beech, once believed to date to Lincoln's time, proved to be too young: its rings were analyzed after it came down, shortly after the turn of the twenty-first century.

A large tree-like osmanthus stands in front of the Sherman Building, putting forth fragrant blossoms in the late fall. To the east and down a gentle hill is a handsome grove of shingle oaks.

One of the most unusual trees at the Soldiers' Home is a variegated tulip-tree planted near Grant Hall. In the spring and early summer, the leaves of this tree have whitish or pale yellow margins.

To the south, the complex that includes the Forwood and Lagarde buildings is ringed with many old native and exotic trees. The Japanese maples there are particularly beautiful.

The residents in the trees at the Soldiers' Home are as interesting as the trees themselves. Black squirrels scamper from limb to limb, along with their more common gray-brown companions. These nimble critters have plenty of time to play, since the retired soldiers keep them fattened up with generous handouts. Their favorite trees are easily identified by the telltale peanut shells that litter the ground below.

Pastoral duck ponds grace the landscape in the southwestern section of the grounds. Bald-cypresses grow along the shoreline. From the Soldiers' Home property there is a sweeping view of the city, spanning the Capitol building, the Washington Monument, and Washington National Cathedral. Rock Creek Cemetery, also a haven for historic trees, is nearby.

Frederick Douglass National Historic Site (Cedar Hill)

Cedar Hill, the colonial-style home of the renowned nineteenth-century abolitionist and women's rights advocate, is situated atop a tree-shaded rise in Anacostia, overlooking the city of Washington. Although the original red-cedars for which the Frederick Douglass Home is named are no longer alive, the National Park Service has planted new red-cedars around the home site.

Born a slave in Tuckahoe, Maryland, in 1817, Frederick Douglass was a forceful lecturer and writer who befriended not only the oppressed, but many of the leaders of his time, including President Lincoln and Queen Victoria. Douglass moved to Cedar Hill in 1877 and lived there until his death in 1895. In 1962, concern for the continued preservation of Cedar Hill resulted in an Act of Congress, which was signed into law by President Kennedy. The home is now under the care of the National Park Service, and is officially known as the Frederick Douglass National Historic Site. In recent years, the home has undergone historic renovation.

Most of the mature trees on the grounds are native species. Large tulip-trees, white ashes, black locusts, hickories, and several species of oaks surround the house. Good-sized southern magnolias and hackberries also adorn the crest of the hill. A large white oak near the front porch dates to the time of Douglass's residence at Cedar Hill and is featured in the Witness Tree Protection Program of the National Park Service's Historic American Landscapes Survey. One of the southern magnolias—which may date to the Douglass era and is located just southeast of the house—also is in the Witness Tree Protection Program. In addition to the red-cedars, the National Park Service has planted young oaks, tulip-trees, and other native trees in an attempt to simulate the setting of Douglass's day.

St. Elizabeths Hospital—West Campus

The extensive western grounds of the area that has long been occupied by St. Elizabeths Hospital (a residential mental-health facility dating to 1852) at 2700 Martin Luther King Jr. Avenue in Anacostia are replete with beautiful trees, including hundreds of grand old specimens. The federal facility is spread out on a tract of land that overlooks the Anacostia River and provides a magnificent view of the city. The trees at St. Elizabeths have traditionally included American hollies, white and Himalayan pines, deodar cedars, American and English elms, southern and umbrella magnolias, white oaks, silverbells, and Kentucky coffee-trees. At this writing, much of the federally owned section of the property formerly occupied by St. Elizabeths has been closed and the government is considering potential uses of the property, including the relocation there of the Department of Homeland Security.

Historic Cemeteries

Old gravestones are not the only historic landmarks found in Washington's cemeteries. The area's graveyards are among the finest places for old and historic trees, and they are also liberally endowed with flowering trees such as magnolias and dogwoods. Here, we mention cemeteries with trees of yesterday and today that are tied to the nation's history.

Arlington National Cemetery

One of the most pampered trees of all time stands next to the grave of President John F. Kennedy in Arlington National Cemetery, where First Lady Jacqueline Kennedy and the couple's two infant children are also buried. This ancient post oak is more than two hundred years old. According to a story by Janine Gug-lielmino, which ran in *American Forests* magazine in the spring of 2001: "When the president visited Arlington Cemetery [in 1963] after daughter Caroline raved about her visit there, JFK told his brother Bobby it was so peaceful at this site, he could spend 'forever' there." Sadly, that comment "influenced the selection of his burial place before the year was out."[77]

In 1965, the architect employed to design the permanent gravesite of the former president expressed his concern that the tree, which has been known for many years as the Arlington Oak, would be unable to withstand the shock of construction going on around it. So, at a cost of several thousand dollars, an elaborate aeration, drainage, and soil improvement plan was developed by National Park Service plant pathologist Horace Wester. Today the Arlington Oak is healthy and vigorous, and each year thousands of people pass beneath its boughs to pay homage to the former president and first lady.

Before the Union Army claimed the land that is now Arling-ton Cemetery, the property was owned by several generations of prominent Virginians. George Washington's stepson, John Parke Custis (son of Martha Custis Washington), purchased the land in 1778. In turn, his son, George Washington Parke Custis (who had become George Washington's ward following John's death), built the beautiful Greek Revival mansion on the hill. And to increase the confusing entanglement of famous Virginia families, George Washington Parke Custis's daughter, Mary Ann Randolph Custis (his only child to reach maturity), married Robert E. Lee. And so it was the Lee family who owned the property at the outbreak of the Civil War.

The elegant house that overlooks the cemetery, long known as the Custis-Lee Mansion, is called simply Arlington House today. It stands in the shade of one of Washington's most outstanding trees: a huge deodar cedar with massive branches and feathery evergreen foliage. The second-largest known tree of its species in Virginia, it was the official state champion, before part of its crown was lost during a storm. This deodar cedar is one of the trees featured in the Witness Tree Protection Program of the National Park Service's Historic American Landscapes Survey.

In front of the mansion is a ginkgo tree of magnificent propor-tions. Beneath its branches many small ginkgo seedlings periodi-cally spring up, revealing that the parent tree is a female, and producer of the (in)famously odorous fruit.

A little-known landmark of the hill on which Arlington House stands is the permanent gravesite of Major Pierre Charles L'Enfant, designer of the city of Washington. L'Enfant's remains were moved to the present site overlooking the city from another cemetery.

Arlington National Cemetery is shaded by many beautiful trees. Ancient native oaks are interspersed with exotic conifers and numerous flowering trees and shrubs.

Rock Creek Cemetery

The man who lined Washington's streets with thousands of trees in the 1870s is buried in Rock Creek Cemetery, near the Soldiers' Home in Northwest Washington. It was largely because of the efforts of District of Columbia governor Alexander Shepherd that Washington became known as the City of Trees. When I visited the Shepherd mausoleum on a late autumn afternoon while re-searching this edition of *City of Trees*, the steps were fittingly and poetically adorned with fallen, brightly hued sweetgum leaves and the winged seeds of tulip-trees.

Many well-known Americans and their relatives are buried in Rock Creek Cemetery, including the novelist Upton Sinclair; Alice Roosevelt Longworth, the daughter of President Theodore Roosevelt; and Edgar Allan Poe's sister Rosalie. There is a famous nineteenth-century Augustus Saint-Gaudens sculpture, commis-sioned by the author and historian Henry Adams (grandson of President John Quincy Adams) to honor his wife, Marian, who committed suicide. The sculpture has drawn visitors for over a century, including Mark Twain, in 1906, and First Lady Eleanor Roosevelt, who stopped by often for comfort and inspiration.

Rock Creek Cemetery was the home of the famous Glebe Oak, but sadly the tree is one of many ancient and historic trees that have died within the past few years. According to legend, the white oak was alive in the early 1700s, when the first church was built in what is now the District of Columbia. It was called the Glebe Oak because the area that is now Rock Creek Cemetery was once known as a "glebe"—a parish-owned tract of land used to raise money for the church. The old oak stood next to Saint Paul's Church, which was built just prior to the Revolution to replace the original chapel built in 1712. The present-day church has undergone major restorations since 1775.

There are many other striking trees in Rock Creek Cemetery. Tall incense cedars from the West Coast grow in the vicinity of the church, as do many mature oaks of several species. Also, an absolutely beautiful fern-leaf Japanese maple is planted on the church grounds.

Fort Lincoln Cemetery

Until the 1990s, Fort Lincoln Cemetery, just across the District line in Maryland, was the site of a sprawling tree known as the Lincoln Oak. The old white oak had been showing its age for many years; several of its limbs had already been amputated prior to the first edition of *City of Trees*. But still the ancient tree held on. The Lincoln Oak stood next to one of the oldest structures in Maryland, the Old Spring House, built in 1683. During the Civil War, President Lincoln is said to have drunk from the spring at the house and to have conferred with his commanders under the oak that came to bear his name. The waters of the spring continue to flow. But alas, in 1994 a lightning bolt dealt the final blow to the Lincoln Oak. The remaining stump has been encased in concrete, and a plaque placed at the site, reads: "This gnarled and ringed stump, attesting to its age, is all that remains of the majestic oak tree that once shaded the Old Spring House. Steeped in history, it was put to rest by the forces of nature. Its passing will never be forgotten and its existence will be remembered forever as a sentinel over these historic grounds."

The National Zoo

Although their competition is formidable, the trees at the National Zoo are worth at least a small portion of the attention that is lavished upon the animals. For instance, the exotic cats on lion-tiger hill sleep in the shade of equally exotic Himalayan pines.

In recent years, many of the National Zoo's trees have been labeled, so this is a good place for botanical, as well as zoological, study. Along the Olmsted Walk leading past the elephant house and the small mammal and great ape houses, you'll find many noteworthy tree species, including European and red horse-chestnut, green and white ash, sugar maple, Turkish hazel, yellowwood, and golden catalpa. Some handsome oaks grow at the zoo, including overcup and chinquapin oaks. Native magnolias include cucumber, bigleaf, and sweetbay. Even the parking lots at the National Zoo are handsomely landscaped. So take a hint from a couple of animal lovers. The National Zoo is one of the best tree places in town!

Storybook Garden Settings

Almost every structure in Washington, from the tiniest town-house to the most lavish ambassador's residence, has its garden. And the gardens of the District of Columbia are particularly pleasing, benefiting as they do from a potpourri of influences: a touch of the Deep South, a large slice of Europe, an abundance of Oriental flowering trees. Dumbarton Oaks and other garden settings mentioned here are stand-outs.

Dumbarton Oaks

The Dumbarton Oaks estate in Georgetown is one of North America's most renowned landscaped settings. Its quaintly terraced hillside, laid out in seventeenth- and eighteenth-century European style, flows downward into a sea of flowering trees and shrubs. Dumbarton Oaks seems to be part of another world. Yet the gardens are largely the work of two twentieth-century women.

History of the Gardens. In 1702, the land where Dumbarton Oaks is now situated was granted to Ninian Beall, who was born at Dumbarton on the Clyde in Scotland. Beall named his new home the "Rock of Dumbarton." The estate changed hands and names several times before it was purchased as "The Oaks" by the diplomat Robert Woods Bliss and his wife, Mildred, in 1920. Combining the estate's oldest and newest names, the Blisses christened it "Dumbarton Oaks."

While traveling the world as a young woman, Mildred Bliss had developed a vision of a garden of her own, inspired by the historic landscapes of France, Italy, and England but also honoring the sylvan simplicity of her early years in New England. In 1922, she was fortunate enough to find the perfect person to help execute that vision—the brilliant and accomplished landscape architect Beatrix Farrand, niece of the novelist Edith Wharton, whom Mildred Bliss knew and admired. Farrand, too, was well acquainted with the finest gardens of Europe.

Together, the women planned the romantic gardens for which Dumbarton Oaks has become famous. Both believed that a garden should be a place to live in, so they planned a series of small gardens, each with its own atmosphere. Many have likened these garden spaces to the rooms of a house. Mature trees were respected and integrated into the individual garden designs, but trees and shrubs were only a part of the plan. Intricate stone carvings, fountains, romantic benches, quaint stone walls, and iron gates were carefully conceived to give the garden its rich, intimate atmosphere.

Farrand and Bliss had a challenging setting to work with. Dumbarton Oaks commands the highest spot in Georgetown, and the "backyard" of the Georgian mansion slopes rather steeply into a Rock Creek Park ravine. In order to link the woodland below with the imposing appearance of the brick mansion, Farrand and Bliss planned a series of terraced gardens, progressing gradually from formality to informality. On the crest of the hill, close to the mansion, the Green Garden, the Beech Terrace, and the Urn Terrace are neatly surrounded by brick walls. However, as one progresses down the hill, the vista opens up and plantings are no longer confined within rectangular spaces. The landscape culminates in an orgiastic display of springtime abandon, a golden hillside of forsythia bordered by a storybook grove of pink and white Japanese flowering cherry trees. Below the flowering cherries and forsythia lies Dumbarton Oaks Park, a "wild garden," or cultivated wood, that serves as a transition between the formal landscape of the Dumbarton Oaks estate and Rock Creek Park.

Beatrix Farrand's clients included Rockefellers, Roosevelts, and Mrs. Woodrow Wilson. Her abilities were even recognized by the Western world's gardening elite, the British, who invited her to re-create the grounds of Dartington Hall in Devonshire. But it was her work at Dumbarton Oaks that she described, before her death in 1960, as "the most deeply felt and the best of a fifty years' practice."[78] With a few exceptions, today's Dumbarton Oaks gardens look very much as Beatrix Farrand and Mildred Bliss planned them.

The Blisses gave Dumbarton Oaks to Harvard University in 1940, but Mildred Bliss continued to work on her beloved gardens into the 1960s with the help of landscape professionals, including the architect Ruth Havey, an associate of Beatrix Farrand. Four years after Dumbarton Oaks was donated to Harvard, this romantic setting was the scene of the international conference that led to the establishment of the United Nations. Today, the Dumbarton Oaks Research Library and Collection (begun with the collection of books and artworks donated to Harvard by the Blisses) is an internationally acclaimed center for scholarship in Byzantine Studies, Pre-Columbian Art, and Landscape Studies. The house and collections are open to the public. The gardens and grounds are accessible from the entrance near the corner of 32nd and R Streets, N.W., and are open to the public in the afternoon.

The Trees at Dumbarton Oaks. Selecting trees at Dumbarton Oaks for special mention is like trying to find the brightest stars in the sky. Each tree is beautiful, both in its own right and as an integral part of the landscape. So much perfection inspires the eye but boggles the mind.

The estate is entered from R Street to the south. An expansive lawn is surrounded by tall trees, many of them evergreen. Most notable on the south lawn are two Yulan magnolias directly in front of the little orangery to the east of the mansion. In early spring, this pair of rare Asian trees dons beautiful cream-white blossoms. According to former head gardener Don Smith, Mrs. Bliss nicknamed the older of the two magnolias "The Bride." Gail Griffin, the current director of gardens, told me that the younger tree has been given the moniker "The Bridesmaid." Also on the grounds of the south lawn are two huge katsura trees. The bigger of the two is probably the largest katsura in the area. Nearby is a venerable though delicate Japanese maple.

Directly in back of the orangery, on the crest of the northern slope, is the Green Garden, once home to three of Dumbarton Oaks' old oaks. The largest was a black oak, and the other two were red oaks. Unfortunately, only one of the red oaks remains, but there are many mature oaks throughout the Dumbarton Oaks gardens, and in adjacent Montrose Park and Dumbarton Oaks Park.

A handsome American beech dominates the Beech Terrace east of the Green Garden. In the early spring, colorful scilla, glory of the snow, and crocus blooms appear between the tree's exposed silvery roots.

Two delicate kobus magnolias, uncommon in the Washington area, light up the Urn Terrace in spring with their star-like white blossoms. The Urn Terrace overlooks the Rose Garden, a major attraction during the summer months.

A pleasant boxwood walk leads down the hill past the exotic pebble garden (a post-Farrand innovation), passing under many pleasant trees. A striking feature of the mid-level northern slope is the Ellipse (also added after Farrand's time). This garden space contains a central fountain surrounded by a European-looking elliptical planting of closely clipped hornbeams. The Prunus

Walk nearby is lined with rare double cherry-plums (*Prunus* ×
blireana), which produce deep pink blossoms and reddish purple
leaves. The flowering plums were replaced during 2006 and,
according to Gail Griffin, they bloomed during their first spring.
The Prunus Walk leads downward to Dumbarton Oaks' most
romantic grove, on a slope known as Cherry Hill. In the spring,
several varieties of Japanese flowering cherry trees produce a
delicate pink-and-white canopy over the newly green hillside.
One could easily imagine a wedding here, although choosing
a date to coincide with the elusive blossoms would be a daring
gamble.

While the cherry trees are in bloom, adjacent Forsythia Hill is
a sea of golden blossoms. Looking downward from the higher ter-
races or across from Cherry Hill, the view of this wild forsythia
garden is an experience never to be forgotten. The stone path
winding through the weeping branches is pleasantly reminiscent of the fabled Yellow Brick Road in the Land of Oz. Nearby
is a rare Yulan magnolia known as Purple Eye, because of the
purplish blush at the base of its petals and petal-like sepals. Later
in the spring, the flowering crabapples on Crabapple Hill, just
above Forsythia Hill, are beautiful. And the North Vista is lined
with stately conifers, pink weeping cherries, and other attractive
trees.

Finally, a tree that can't go unmentioned is the massive copper
beech located near Lovers' Lane Pool in the easternmost section
of the grounds. During the spring, wildflowers pop up between
the large, sprawling roots of this tree.

Montrose Park and Dumbarton Oaks Park. While it would be
nice to linger at Dumbarton Oaks forever, it's time to bid it adieu.
Not, however, without brief stops at neighboring Montrose Park
and Dumbarton Oaks Park. The ancient, white oak–studded
acres of Montrose Park perfectly complement the elaborately
landscaped estate next door, radiating the same romantic aura of
past centuries. An ancient tulip-tree in the park holds the record
as the District's champion of the species. This tree, and a large
swamp white oak, are featured in the Witness Tree Protection
Program of the National Park Service's Historic American Landscapes Survey.

Down the hill from Montrose Park and the Dumbarton Oaks
gardens is the charming, semi-wild Dumbarton Oaks Park. A
thicket of rhododendron borders a small stream crossed by a

stone bridge and a series of small dams. Trees in the park include sugar maples (which were dropping brilliant orange and yellow leaves when I visited in autumn), American beech, tulip-tree, flowering dogwood, oaks, and hickories. Spicebush grows in the rich, moist woods. During spring, the park comes alive with wildflowers, bulbs, and flowering woody plants. The National Park Service recently completed a historic landscape report on Dumbarton Oaks Park, which is receiving new recognition and appreciation as an "in-between" landscape, partly cultivated and partly wild, and as an integral part of the world-renowned Dumbarton Oaks garden.

Tudor Place

In recent years, another historic Georgetown estate near Dumbarton Oaks and Montrose Park has been opened to the public. Tudor Place, once the home of George Washington's step-granddaughter, Martha Custis Peter, and her husband, Thomas Peter, is a National Historic Landmark. The Peters purchased the property in 1805 with money Martha inherited from George Washington. Overlooking Georgetown and the Potomac water-front, the Tudor Place gardens and grounds reflect two hundred years of horticultural history and six generations of the Peter family, who resided there until 1984. The grounds feature an original boxwood hedge.

Visitors to the 5½-acre property will quickly notice several large old trees. On the southern side of the grounds are some ancient white oaks, an old and massive tulip-tree (designated the District's Millennium Tree, and in size, just shy of the District champion tulip-tree in nearby Montrose Park), and a pecan planted in 1875, which holds the District's current record as champion of that species. A huge scarlet oak, planted in 1932 to commemorate the bicentennial of George Washington's birth, is located on the northern side of the grounds. A white oak dating to the eighteenth century stands nearby.

Other significant tree species at Tudor Place include kobus magnolia, Japanese snowbell, yellow buckeye, Kentucky coffee-tree, fullmoon maple, European smoke-tree, West Coast incense cedar, silver Atlas cedar, and Nordmann fir. The Tudor Place gardens and grounds are located on 31st Street, N.W., above Q Street, and are open to the public from 10 to 4 Tuesday through Saturday and from noon to 4 on Sunday (closed during January).

Hillwood Estate, Museum & Gardens

Another historic mansion overlooking Rock Creek Park also
has extensive, elaborately landscaped grounds. The home of the
late Marjorie Merriweather Post (daughter of the founder of the
Post cereal company) is surrounded by many lovely gardens that
blend, as do the gardens at Dumbarton Oaks, into a single romantic whole. The late heiress took great interest in the gardens
and grounds. She even created a cemetery for her pets, complete
with engraved headstones. Among the highlights of Hillwood Estate is a picturesque Japanese garden. Japanese maples, Cryptomeria, and other trees shade the miniature bridges that cross the
garden's hillside stream. The trees of Hillwood include stately old
American elms and an abundance of conifers: dawn redwoods,
spruces, hemlocks, arborvitae, and many others. The grounds
are replete with flowering shrubs, including roses, azaleas, and
rhododendrons. Hillwood is located on Linnean Avenue, N.W.
Reservations are recommended.

The Bishop's Garden of the Washington National Cathedral and the Olmsted Woods

The Bishop's Garden of the Washington National Cathedral
is a favorite sanctuary for many Washingtonians. Through an
arched door in a medieval-style stone wall, one enters a tunnel of
boxwood and American holly. The winding path passes under the
boughs of an immense silver Atlas cedar, and then descends to an
open rose and herb garden. The Bishop's Garden is tucked into
a gentle slope at the base of the cathedral, providing an outdoor
setting for prayer, meditation, quiet conversation, and horticultural study. The roses are large, multi-hued, and fragrant, and the
plantings of medicinal and culinary herbs add texture, pungent
aromas, and a sense of history to the landscape.

Many noteworthy trees grace the garden and its surroundings,
including southern magnolia, 'Betty' and 'Elizabeth' magnolias,
ginkgo, weeping cherry and fall-blooming cherry, yellowwood,
Voss's laburnum, the rare medlar, golden-rain-tree, bald-cypress,
dawn redwood, Himalayan pine, and incense-cedar. Next to the
sculpture of the Prodigal Son (for which my husband's father and
great-grandfather served as sculptor's models) is a winter hazel
(*Corylopsis sinensis*) that blooms in early spring. The garden is a
delightful place to visit year-round. The roses bloom into very
late autumn, and Lenten roses, snowdrops, and crocuses bloom a
few weeks after the last rose succumbs to the cold.

The historic Glastonbury thorn, described on page 298, grows nearby, and the Olmsted Woods—a serene native woodland with recently developed trails and other features—lies just down the hill from the Bishop's Garden. Mature oaks, red maple, American beech, and American holly grow in the Olmsted Woods.

Other Storybook Garden Settings of the Washington, D.C., Area

Franciscan Monastery (1400 Quincy Street, N.E.)

Meridian Hill Park (16th and W Streets, N.W.)

Brookside Gardens (1500 Glenallan Avenue, Wheaton, Maryland)

Green Spring Gardens Park (4603 Green Spring Road, Alexandria, Virginia)

Meadowlark Gardens Regional Park (9750 Meadowlark Gardens Court, Vienna, Virginia)

The Presidents' Tree and Its Replacement

Although "Hieroglyphics Tree" would have been a more descriptive name, the American beech that stood at the corner of Sligo Creek Parkway and Maple Avenue in Takoma Park was officially named the Presidents' Tree. It was honored with its own private fence and an impressive plaque. Sadly, it is among the many historic trees that have met their demise since the earlier editions of *City of Trees*.

The story goes that back in the 1860s, a farmer named Samuel Fenton carved the names of all the presidents from Washington to Andrew Johnson on the bark of the tree. He also included the name of "Lieutenant General" Ulysses S. Grant, who later became president.

In 1948, the Maryland–National Capital Park and Planning Commission officially declared the tree a Civil War Memorial and erected an iron fence around it to protect it from modern-day beech-bark carvers. A plaque explaining its history was added in 1960. Although by the end of the twentieth century it took a good deal of imagination to decipher the writings engraved on the tree, this American beech was another one of the great living memorials of the Washington area.

The tree died of old age in the early 1990s, yet it continued to stand until 1997, when it was blown over during a summer thunderstorm. A few years later, local residents spruced up the iron gate—which was damaged when the tree fell—and planted a replacement tree within it.

Rock Creek Park and Other Wooded Parkland Within the District of Columbia

Rock Creek Park

Rock Creek Park is the wild, wooded heart of Washington, D.C. Every Washingtonian should applaud the Act of Congress that established Rock Creek Park in 1890, and the many visionary individuals who have supported this parkland through the decades. Comprised of 1,754 acres, D.C.'s Rock Creek Park is one of the largest urban wooded parks in the country. It is more than twice the size of New York City's Central Park.

Rock Creek Park is a delightful destination for picnics, hikes, bicycle and horseback rides, and nature study. On weekends and holidays, a large stretch of Beach Drive, which runs through the heart of the park along the scenic rocky creek, is closed to motorized vehicles, and cyclists, walkers, runners, and skaters take over the wooded roadway. A network of hiking trails winds through the wooded slopes and along Rock Creek and its tributaries.

Because the park has been protected for more than a century, its forests have matured, and many of the District's tallest woodland trees grow within its boundaries. In the upland woods, tulip-trees, white ashes, American beeches, and white, chestnut, red, southern red, black, and other oak species reach great heights. Along the creek, hornbeam or ironwood, green ash, river birch, sycamore, red and silver maple, boxelder, bladdernut, elms, pawpaw, and spicebush grow. Sugar maple, tupelo, black walnut, butternut, hop-hornbeam, hickories, American holly, common witch-hazel, scrub or Virginia pine, and other pines also grow in the park. During spring, the creek is lined with wildflowers.

Invasive plants and storm water runoff are among the threats to the integrity of Rock Creek Park. National Park Service staff and citizen volunteer groups are working to alleviate the stresses threatening the Rock Creek watershed.

Other District of Columbia Wooded Parkland

Consult a map of the District of Columbia and its surroundings and you will note large patches of green parkland. In Northeast Washington, the **Watts Branch Watershed** cuts a green swath through the street grid, encompassing the newly named **Marvin Gaye Park.** Sweetgum, willow oak, and sycamore are among the trees growing along Watts Branch. In Southeast Washington, **Anacostia Park** stretches along the east side of the Anacostia, providing striking views of the river and the city. Weeping willows, black locusts, and flowering crabapples (some of which were here during Washington's crabapple festival days—see page 290) grow along the river. Red oaks, red maples, sugar maples, and many other young trees are planted along the Anacostia Riverwalk Trail. Efforts are under way to clean up the Anacostia River, which has been severely compromised by storm water runoff and other threats.

For many Washingtonians, a favorite place in Southeast Washington is **Fort Dupont Park**. In the picnic area near Minnesota and Massachusetts Avenues are many mature native trees, including tulip-tree, silver maple, black locust, and red, southern red, white, and chestnut oak. The expansive park encompasses native woodlands, with chestnut oak and mountain laurel growing in the uplands, and sycamore, boxelder, and American beech in the wooded stream valley. Willow oak and sweetgum grow along the roadside.

Fort Stanton Park, site of the Smithsonian Anacostia Community Museum, is also home to native trees (including white oak, tulip-tree, and black locust), as well as some exotics planted near the museum. The Southwest Washington waterfront comprises beautiful open space with stately shade trees and flowering cherries.

In addition to Rock Creek Park, Northwest Washington is home to many other wooded parks, including several along Rock Creek tributaries. **Battery Kemble Run** and **Foundry Branch,** two north–south creeks flowing toward the Potomac and the C&O Canal have trails running alongside them through wooded parkland. The **Glover Archbold Trail** runs for more than 2½ miles along Foundry Branch through Glover Archbold Park. The tall native trees and native shrubs growing along the trail include tulip-tree, sycamore, American beech, American holly, and spicebush.

Wooded Parkland Beyond the District of Columbia

I asked a group of Washington-area botanists and naturalists to describe some of their favorite places for tree study beyond the city limits but within easy access of Washington. Some of their recommendations follow.

Dr. Stanwyn Shetler is botanist emeritus at the Smithsonian Institution and a longtime teacher for the Natural History Field Studies Program co-sponsored by the Audubon Naturalist Society and the USDA Graduate School. Among his favorites:

"**Algonkian Regional Park,** a bottomland park along the Potomac River just inside Loudoun County, has a good selection of trees, including common bottomland species. Of special interest to me is the wooded area at the mouth of Sugarland Run, which I long ago dubbed 'Woodpecker Flats,' because over time I have seen all the local woodpeckers there. Here you will find one of Virginia's largest Shumard oaks (118 feet high, crown spreading 95 feet, dbh—diameter at breast height—of over 4 feet) and a beautiful big American elm. Also, bitternut hickory is very common here. For particulars on the Shumard oak and other Loudoun trees, go to the Web site of the Virginia Big Tree Program: www.fw.vt.edu/4h/bigtree/. A large Shumard oak can also be found on **Theodore Roosevelt Island**."

Dr. Shetler also recommended **Great Falls Park,** in McLean, Virginia: "This is a favorite spot for trees. . . . By going around the edges of the parking lot, walking along the path past the overlooks, and along the road to the Swamp Nature Trail, you can make a nice list of oaks, including the post oak (flats near overlook area) and swamp white oak (far end of parking lot)."

Also, **Scott's Run Nature Preserve,** just beyond the beltway on the Virginia side of the Potomac: "I always take my class here to see native hemlock, black (sweet) birch, chestnut oak, and shortleaf pine. Unfortunately, the great hemlock monarchs along the creek that were here for so many years are dying out, but at least one big one is most impressive. . . . There are some impressive beeches in this park."[79] I would add that Scott's Run is also home to sugar, red, and silver maples, white ash, cottonwood, hop-hornbeam, American basswood, bladdernut, and the native fringe-tree.

In Maryland, Dr. Shetler recommended the **Carderock** area of the **C&O Canal** (across the Potomac from Scott's Run), where swamp chestnut oak (*Quercus michauxii*) and mockernut hickory are among the resident tree species. Down the Potomac toward D.C. (inside the beltway), parking at Lock 10 and walking up the towpath to the Lock 12 area, Dr. Shetler noted that there is a large chinquapin or yellow oak (*Quercus muehlenbergii*).

Carole Bergmann is the forest ecologist for Montgomery County Parks, a longtime teacher for the Natural History Field Studies Program, and an Audubon Naturalist Society field trip leader. She also recommended visiting the C&O Canal, including **Great Falls, Maryland,** for tree viewing and study. It is "a fabulous place to go and see huge sycamores, and more silver maple and boxelder than you can imagine. Large cottonwood, ash, paw-paw, and the less common to our area hackberry (*Celtis occidentalis*), yellow or chinquapin oak, post oak, and hop-tree or wafer-ash."

Bergmann also lauded **Blockhouse Point Conservation Park,** which is adjacent to the C&O Canal and accessed from River Road, as "the best example of high-quality contiguous upland forest in the Montgomery County park system, in my opinion—650 acres of forest with hardly any non-native invasives to speak of compared with other properties . . . [with] many large trees, mostly mixed oaks, chestnut oaks, tulip-trees," and other species not common in Washington-area woodlands.[80] A dramatic cliff-top vantage point yields a view of the Potomac River stretching for many miles to the northwest and southeast.

John Parrish is vice president of the Maryland Native Plant Society. In a recent address to the society he also spoke about the beauty of Blockhouse Point, noting that the cucumber magnolia, table mountain pine, and the county champion shagbark hickory are found there.

Both Carole Bergmann and John Parrish recommended visiting Montgomery County's **Northwest Branch Stream Valley Park,** especially the spectacular gorge near Route 29. There is a great diversity of trees along Northwest Branch, including the uncommon table mountain pine. President Theodore Roosevelt was especially fond of this spot, as he wrote in a letter to his son Ted in June 1904:

> Dear Ted,
>   Mother and I had a most lovely ride the other day, way up beyond Sligo Creek to what is called North-west Branch, at Burnt Mills, where is a beautiful gorge, deep and narrow, with great

boulders and even cliffs. Excepting Great Falls, it is the most beautiful place around here. Mother scrambled among the cliffs in her riding habit, very pretty and interesting. The roads were good and some of the scenery really beautiful. We were gone four hours, half an hour being occupied with the scrambling in the gorge.[81]

I'm sure I am not alone in enjoying the image of the president and first lady "scrambling" across the rocks in a dramatic gorge so close to the nation's capital.

Botanist Cris Fleming is president of the Maryland Native Plant Society, an instructor in the Natural History Field Studies Program of the Audubon Naturalist Society and the USDA Graduate School, and a co-author of *Finding Wildflowers in the Washington–Baltimore Area*. She suggested visiting **Turkey Run Park,** between the Potomac River and the George Washington Memorial Parkway in Virginia, to see notable native trees. American basswood, sugar maple, and butternut grow at Turkey Run. According to Fleming: "Turkey Run has the largest recorded trees of several species found on the Virginia side of the Potomac Gorge. Several are thought to be over two hundred years old, including specimens of silver maple, tulip-tree, white oak, beech, chestnut oak, and American basswood."[82]

As someone who has lived at its base for more than twenty years and written two books about it, I must recommend **Sugarloaf Mountain,** about 35 miles northwest of Washington and the only real mountain in the Maryland Piedmont. Here you'll find upland forests of chestnut oak, hickories, red maple, tupelo, American chestnut (which eventually succumbs to the blight and dies back), and white, red, and black oak. On the summit of the mountain are picturesque groves of table mountain pine, black (sweet or cherry) birch, and blackjack oak. American beeches grow along Mount Ephraim Road on the western side of the mountain.

Stephanie Mason is the senior naturalist for the Audubon Naturalist Society of the Central Atlantic States. She noted that in addition to the many Piedmont woodlands with which our region is still blessed, Washingtonians also have ready access to Coastal Plain habitat. She suggested visiting **Piscataway Park,** on the Maryland side of the Potomac across from Mount Vernon, where a large willow oak, persimmons, silver maple, tupelo, and pumpkin ash can be found. She also recommended the adjacent

National Colonial Farm, and in Virginia, **Huntley Meadows Park, Mason Neck National Wildlife Refuge,** and **Mason Neck State Park.** Coastal Plain tree communities include oak-pine forests and species not commonly found growing naturally in the Piedmont, such as sweetgum.

Audubon Naturalist Society Sanctuaries

The Audubon Naturalist Society of the Central Atlantic States harbors many venerable trees within its verdant sanctuaries. ANS is dedicated to natural history education and environmental protection in the mid-Atlantic region. Classes and workshops are offered at Woodend Sanctuary in Chevy Chase, Maryland, and at Rust Sanctuary in Leesburg, Virginia. For many years, ANS has sponsored educational field trips to natural areas throughout the region.

The 40-acre **Woodend Sanctuary** encompasses a Georgian Revival mansion designed by John Russell Pope (designer of the Jefferson Memorial, Constitution Hall, and the National Gallery of Art). The mansion crests a gentle slope and is surrounded by several large native trees, including a tulip-tree, a tupelo, and an American beech. Three Montgomery County champion trees grow at Woodend: an American basswood next to the sanctuary shop, an English oak, and a Japanese maple. A large black walnut is located to the right of the Woodend drive along the approach to the mansion, and a Franklin tree (believed extinct in the wild) and a massive Atlas cedar—one of Montgomery County's largest—grow near the garden shed. Tulip-tree, white ash, and American beech are among the woodland trees growing along the sanctuary's walking trails.

At the 68-acre **Rust Nature Sanctuary** in Leesburg, there is a stand of large white oaks. A gnarled old red maple in a Rust wetland has been dubbed the "Hobbit Tree." A white pine planta-tion at Rust is transitioning to hardwood, according to manager-naturalist Cliff Fairweather. There is a mature oak-hickory forest at the sanctuary and an area of riparian woods around the pond. A few chestnut oaks grow in the vicinity of a small quartzite outcrop.

Part II

Botanical Guide
to the City of Trees

Identifying trees is great detective work, especially in a city
with more than three hundred species from all over the world.
Washington, D.C.'s outstanding tree collection has evolved from
a centuries-old tradition of planting and caring for trees, an
avocation that traces back to the Founding Fathers. The mild
climate of the city—which is located on the geologic boundary
of the Atlantic Coastal Plain and the Piedmont—has made it possible for a vast number of trees that could not survive in cooler
or hotter climates to flourish here. In recent years, Washington's
climate has grown warmer and its winters milder. If this trend
continues, it could affect the range of species able to grow in and
around the city.

Part II of *City of Trees* is an illustrated botanical guide to Washington's hundreds of native and exotic trees. With the exception
of the trees found in the National Arboretum, which harbors
many woody and herbaceous plants encountered nowhere else
in the area, Part II describes nearly every mature tree commonly
grown in the District. Nurseries are constantly offering new species, varieties, and cultivars, so some young specimens may not
be covered in this edition. And there is always the possibility—
one that has fueled tree enthusiasts in the District for decades—
that *your* backyard may cloister a tree so rare that it is found
nowhere else in the city.

City of Trees is primarily a guide to cultivated trees (trees
planted for shade and ornament), but this third edition focuses
increased attention on native woodland trees. Although specifi-
cally about the trees of the District of Columbia, it should also
prove useful for identifying trees in cities and towns throughout
the temperate zones of eastern and central North America, as

well as parts of Europe and Asia. Many of the trees planted in
Washington, D.C., are also grown in Boston, New York, Philadelphia, London, Paris, and Tokyo.

How to Identify Trees Using *City of Trees*

"Is it really a tree?" The query is not as simple-minded as it
sounds. Both trees and shrubs are woody plants (with stems and
limbs containing wood). Although there is no scientific distinction between a tree and a shrub, trees tend to grow taller than
twenty feet at maturity and are usually single-trunked, while
shrubs reach an approximate height of fifteen to twenty feet or
less and are usually multi-trunked. *City of Trees* is almost exclusively a guide to trees, although we have included a few large
shrubs that are particularly showy. Some woody plants, such as
the common witch-hazel, can take the form of a shrub or small
tree.

WOODY PLANTS

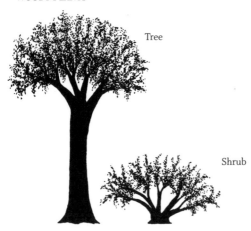

Tree

Shrub

Once you have established that your woody plant is a tree, you
must then decide whether it is a conifer or a broad-leaved tree.

The Conifers

Conifers are gymnosperms, a word adapted from the Greek,
meaning "naked seeds." Conifer seeds are not enclosed in an
ovary. Most conifers produce cones (although in our cultivated

city flora, there are a few conifers that do not). The cones contain the tree's seeds, which are usually scattered by the wind. Conifer foliage is needle-like or scale-like, with the exception of the ginkgo, or maidenhair, tree.

CONIFER CONES AND FOLIAGE

Scale-like foliage   Needle-like foliage

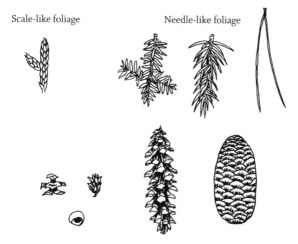

If your tree is a conifer, you should turn to the "Illustrated Descriptions of Conifers" on page 97. The introductory text there will give further instructions on how to use the "Key to the Conifer Genera," which immediately follows the text and which is grouped according to plant families.

The Broad-Leaved Genera

If your tree is not a conifer, it belongs to one of the broad-leaved genera. Most broad-leaved trees belong to the angiosperms. Unlike the seeds of the gymnosperms, angiosperm seeds are contained in ovaries. The fruit produced by the broad-leaved trees may be fleshy (apples, pears) or dry (acorns, chestnuts, and maple samaras).

The leaves of broad-leaved trees may be deciduous (falling in autumn) or evergreen. Most broad-leaved trees in our area are deciduous, but some, such as the American holly and the southern magnolia, retain their leaves throughout the year.

The introductory text to the "Illustrated Descriptions of Broad-Leaved Trees" on page 147 will give you instructions

Broad-Leaved Tree Fruit

Fleshy Fruit　　　　　　　　　　　*Dry Fruit*

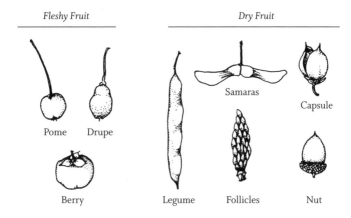

Pome　　Drupe

Berry

Samaras

Capsule

Legume　　Follicles　　Nut

on how to use the "Key to the Broad-Leaved Genera," which immediately follows it, and which is grouped according to leaf structure.

Once you have consulted the appropriate key and have identified your tree as a maple or an oak, for example, you can turn to the appropriate text pages to determine the species and learn about the tree.

How to Use the Descriptive Text and Illustrations

In many cases, the illustrations that accompany the tree descriptions will tell you what your tree is. In most cases, however, you will need to use the text and illustrations together in order to be sure of the species. Two rules of thumb will help you in your detective work. First, always gather as much information about the tree as you can (leaves, flowers, fruit, bark, etc.). The more clues you have, the easier your work will be. Second, never jump to conclusions. You will find that Washington's trees are crafty. That old oak in the backyard that you thought was a native may in fact be an Asian or European species that was planted years ago.

In some cases, we have augmented the text with botanical keys to individual species. To use these keys, simply keep in mind that you must make one of two choices, given consecutively. For instance:

1a) Flowers yellow.........................Yellow Catalpa (*Catalpa ovata*)

1b) Flowers white

    2a) Leaf with a foul odor when crushed.................................
    .... Common Catalpa (*Catalpa bignonioides*)

    2b) Leaf with no foul odor when crushed ....
    .... Northern Catalpa (*Catalpa speciosa*)

If you choose 1a, your tree is a yellow catalpa. If you choose 1b, you have more choices to make. So you proceed to 2, where you must decide between 2a and 2b.

If there had been more than one species that fit the description of 2a, "Leaf with a foul odor when crushed," you would have been given a third set of choices. Choose between each pair of options until you are no longer given a choice, and your tree is identified for you.

Tools You Will Need to Identify Trees

Sometimes the only difference between two trees is the absence or presence of tiny hairs on the leaf blade or stalk that are visible only with a hand lens. Small hand lenses are available at good hardware stores or nature centers. Binoculars are also helpful, since many trees bear fruit only on their higher branches.

Some trees are difficult to identify without the presence of flowers and/or fruit. Therefore, you may want to start your own little herbarium or plant library. The only materials required are newspapers, two rectangular pieces of cardboard, and some rawhide, rope, or string. Simply place your leaves or flowers inside the pages of a newspaper and record the place and date of collection and any other information you would like to remember on the newspaper. Fold the paper, place it between two pieces of cardboard, and then tie the whole bundle tightly. You may want to place your plant specimen under some books for a few days while it dries. Plant specimens preserved in this manner will last for years. If you have collected leaves in late summer and the tree blooms during early spring before the leaves are out, your herbarium will enable you to examine the leaves and flowers together. Fruit and cones may also be collected and tagged, and kept in egg cartons. Some fruits will last a long time; others will have to be discarded. You may also want to keep a field notebook and/or sketch pad to record your arboreal observations throughout the year during your travels in and around the city.

The most essential tool to acquire is a basic botanical vocabulary. We have kept this guide as simple as we can without
sacrificing vital information. But you may come across words
you have never seen before. When you do, consult the illustrated
glossary on pages 379–94. Don't be intimidated by words
such as "glabrous" or "lanceolate." Once you learn a handful
of new words, you will notice that they are used over and over
again, and they will quickly become an integral part of your
vocabulary.

We hope you enjoy using *City of Trees* as much as we have
enjoyed creating it. Keep in mind that the locations given for
each tree are only examples. With a little perseverance, you will
undoubtedly discover your own rare and beautiful specimens.

A Note on Scale: All botanical illustrations are reproduced at 50
percent of their actual size. For some compound leaves, where
size prohibited printing to scale in their entirety, only a portion
of the leaf has been reproduced.

See page 403 for a special message from Casey Trees about
planting and caring for trees in the city. When planting trees in
your own yard, please choose native trees or trees that have no
history of invasiveness. Invasive woody and herbaceous plants
threaten native plant populations.

Illustrated Descriptions of Conifers

The "Key to the Conifer Genera" that introduces this section is organized according to a scientific classification system that recognizes similarities among plant families, genera (the plural of genus), and species within their larger divisions, classes, and orders. Classifying living organisms in a systematic manner based on similar and dissimilar characteristics is known as taxonomy. Modern plant classification is an evolving science, but it embodies many of the elements introduced by Carl Linnaeus, an eighteenth-century Swedish naturalist and botanist.

The Pine family (*Pinaceae*), for example, is further broken down into many genera, which include pines (*Pinus*), hemlocks (*Tsuga*), spruces (*Picea*), firs (*Abies*), cedars (*Cedrus*), and larches (*Larix*). Then each genus is further subdivided into individual species. The spruce genus, for example, includes the species blue spruce (*Picea pungens*) and Norway spruce (*Picea abies*).

In this key, you will find five families included among the gymnosperms: Ginkgo (*Ginkgoaceae*), Yew (*Taxaceae*), Pine (*Pinaceae*), Taxodium (*Taxodiaceae*), and Cypress (*Cupressaceae*). Because the only species in the Ginkgo family (*Ginkgo biloba*) is a broad-leaved conifer, we have also included it in the "Key to the Broad-Leaved Genera" (see pages 150–68).

The "Key to the Conifer Genera" is meant to guide you to the genus of your individual species. Therefore, you should not look for an illustration that is identical to your particular specimen. Rather, look for general characteristics. If your tree has long needles that are grouped in bundles of fives, it is a pine (*Pinus*). It may or may not be the species pictured in the key. However, the key will direct you to the page or pages where the combination of text and illustrations will help you single out the individual species.

Although the key is meant mostly as a visual aid, pay attention to the abbreviated text that accompanies the illustrations. For instance, within the Pine family, under "The Spruces *Picea*," the text tells you: "Needles more or less four-sided. Cones pendulous." These characteristics are important, especially in distinguishing the spruces from the similar firs (*Abies*), which have flat needles and erect cones.

Key to the Conifer Genera
Gymnosperms

Ginkgo Family *Ginkgoaceae*

Leaves fan-shaped, deciduous (falling in autumn).

Ginkgo (Maidenhair Tree)
Ginkgo biloba
Page 103

Ginkgo
Ginkgo biloba

Yew Family *Taxaceae*

Leaves needle-like. Fruit berry-like.

The Yews
Taxus
Pages 144–45

English Yew
Taxus baccata

Pine Family *Pinaceae*

Leaves needle-like.

---

1. Leaves evergreen

The Pines
Pinus
Pages 105–16

Eastern White Pine
Pinus strobus

Japanese Red Pine
Pinus densiflora

Douglas-Fir
Pseudotsuga menziesii
Page 129

Douglas-Fir
Pseudotsuga menziesii

The Hemlocks
Tsuga
Pages 128–29

Eastern Hemlock
Tsuga canadensis

The Spruces *Picea*
Pages 124–27

Needles more or less
four-sided. Cones
pendulous.

Blue Spruce
Picea pungens

Norway Spruce
Picea abies

The Firs *Abies* Pages 121–24

Needles usually flat. Cones erect.

Momi Fir
Abies firma

White (Colorado) Fir
Abies concolor

Nordmann Fir
Abies nordmanniana

The Cedars
Cedrus
Pages 117–20

Atlas Cedar
Cedrus atlantica

---

2. Leaves deciduous (shedding in autumn)

Larch
Larix
Page 130

European Larch
Larix decidua

Golden Larch
Pseudolarix
Page 131

Golden Larch
Pseudolarix kaempferi

Taxodium Family *Taxodiaceae*

Leaves needle-like or scale-like.

1. Leaves evergreen

Umbrella-Pine
Sciadopitys verticillata
Page 137

Umbrella-Pine
Sciadopitys verticillata

Cryptomeria (Japanese Cedar)
Cryptomeria japonica
Page 131

Cryptomeria
Cryptomeria japonica

Chinese Fir
Cunninghamia lanceolata
Page 135

Chinese Fir
Cunninghamia lanceolata

Giant Sequoia
Sequoiadendron giganteum
Page 136

Giant Sequoia
Sequoiadendron giganteum

2. Leaves deciduous (shedding in autumn)

Dawn Redwood
Metasequoia glyptostroboides
Page 134

Leaves opposite.
Cone stalked.

Dawn Redwood
Metasequoia glyptostroboides

Bald-Cypress
Taxodium distichum
Page 132

Leaves alternate or sub-opposite. Cone sessile (no stalk) or with a very short stalk.

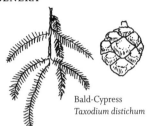

Bald-Cypress
Taxodium distichum

Cypress Family *Cupressaceae*

Leaves usually scale-like and pressed against the branchlets.

Chamaecyparis
Chamaecyparis
Pages 140–41

Sawara Cypress
Chamaecyparis pisifera

Eastern Red-Cedar (Juniper)
Juniperus
Pages 142–43

Eastern Red-Cedar
Juniperus virginiana

Eastern White Cedar (Arborvitae)
Thuja occidentalis
Page 139

Eastern White Cedar
Thuja occidentalis

Oriental Arborvitae
Platycladus orientalis
Page 139

Oriental Arborvitae
Platycladus orientalis

Incense-Cedar
Calocedrus decurrens
Page 143

Incense-Cedar
Calocedrus decurrens

Leyland Cypress
× *Cupressocyparis leylandii*
Page 142

Leyland Cypress
× *Cupressocyparis leylandii*

The Ginkgo Family

Ginkgo (Maidenhair Tree)

Ginkgo biloba L. • Ginkgo Family *Ginkgoaceae*

The enchanting ginkgo tree, one of Washington's most striking Asian ornamentals, may be the oldest living tree species on earth. It has remained almost unchanged since dinosaurs roamed the planet 125 million years ago. Resistance to disease and immunity to insect pests—attributes that helped the ginkgo outlast the dinosaurs—also make it ideally suited for the rigors of urban life. *Ginkgo biloba,* long a stalwart herbal remedy in Asia, has enjoyed a popularity surge in Europe and North America in recent years as the crushed leaves are sold as an antidote to memory loss associated with aging.

NATIVE RANGE   Eastern China, long cultivated in Japan. (The genus *Ginkgo* was once represented in many parts of the world, including the western hemisphere. *Ginkgo biloba* is the only species in the genus still extant.)

LEAVES   Simple, alternate, deciduous. 1 to 3 inches (2.5–7.5 cm) long, 2 to 4 inches (5–10 cm) wide. Unique: fan-shaped, leathery, with numerous thin parallel veins that give the leaf a ribbed look. May be unlobed or with one or more deep or shallow sinuses. Margin smooth on the sides, wavy across the top. Clustered on short spur shoots. Petiole 1 to 3 inches (2.5–7.5 cm) long. Autumn color: brilliant yellow in late October or early November. Washington's most spectacular fall tree. (The shape of the leaf has suggested many things to many cultures. An old Chinese name for the tree, *ya chio,* means "duck's foot." The ginkgo gained the modern common name, maidenhair tree, because the leaf resembles the maidenhair fern.)

FLOWERS   Male and female flowers on separate trees. Male flowers yellow, in thick hanging clusters, with the new spring leaves. Female flower looks like a small acorn on a long stalk.

FRUIT   On female trees only. Round or ovoid, pulpy, about an inch (2.5 cm) long. Smooth and green, becoming yellow and wrinkled; containing an edible seed kernel within a hard shell. In late fall the fruit rots on the ground, emitting an infamously foul odor. Although the edible seed kernel is considered a healthful delicacy in China, the idea of ingesting any part of a ginkgo fruit is anathema to most North Americans. However, Asian-American residents of the District collect the fruit along Washington streets each fall. To avoid the odor emitted by the fruit of female trees, nurseries take great pains to propagate male trees only. However, it is hard to tell the sex of a young ginkgo tree. Because only older ginkgoes produce fruit, innocuous "male" trees have been known to surprise their owners even after decades of fruit-lessness.

BARK AND TWIGS   Bark deeply furrowed and prominently ridged on mature trees. Twigs conspicuous in winter with their alternate woody spur shoots, up to an inch (2.5 cm) long. Winter bud at the end of each shoot.

GROWTH HABIT   Slow-growing but ultimately tall, rather sparsely branched tree. On young trees, branches are upright or bent slightly inward. Crown spreads out with age.

LOCATIONS
- 5th Street, N.W., Chinatown
- R Street, N.W. (across from Montrose Park)
- Corcoran Street, N.W., and Kingman Place, N.W.
- Duddington Place and Ivy Street, S.E.
- 13th Street, S.E.
- K Street, N.W. (Georgetown waterfront)
- Adams Morgan streets, including 18th Street, N.W.
- U.S. Capitol and Library of Congress grounds
- U.S. Department of Agriculture, the Mall
- Farragut Square (named D.C. 2006 Champion Ginkgo by Casey Trees)
- Maret School

FEMALE TREE LOCATIONS
- Scott Circle (16th Street and Massachusetts Avenue, N.W.)
- Crescent Place, N.W.
- Arlington National Cemetery in front of the Custis-Lee Mansion (Arlington House)

The Pine Family

The Pines   *Pinus* L. • Pine Family *Pinaceae*

The pines are the largest and most important genus of conifers in the northern hemisphere. About a hundred species are distributed from the Arctic Circle to Central America, northern Africa, and southeastern Asia. Some species have been introduced elsewhere. Pines are widely harvested for timber and frequently planted for shade and beauty.

FOLIAGE   Evergreen; needle-like. Mature needles are borne in fascicled bundles of from two to five needles (rarely one or more than five), enclosed at their bases in small sheaths that in some species soon fall off.

CONES   Male and female cones are produced on the same tree. The small male cones are usually orange, yellow, or red. The females develop into the mature cones, made up of many woody scales that open to release small, sometimes winged seeds.

In this book, the various species that make up part of the larger pine genus are divided into three groups. The first is the soft or white group, containing pines with needles in bundles of fives. The second group contains pines with needles in bundles of twos; and the third, bundles of threes. In a category of its own is the shortleaf pine (*Pinus echinata*), the state tree of Arkansas, with needles in bundles of twos and threes.

The Soft Pines

The soft, or white, pine group is characterized by needles usually in bundles of fives, with often pendulous, usually thin-scaled and thornless cones. The eastern white pine (*Pinus strobus*) is by far the most commonly planted white pine in Washington. However, several other species are in cultivation here.

Needles in Bundles of Fives

Eastern White Pine

Pinus strobus L. • Pine Family *Pinaceae*

STATE TREE OF MAINE AND MICHIGAN

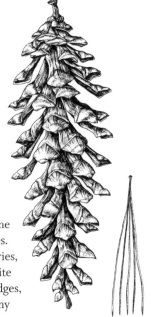

The soft, subtle beauty of the eastern
white pine perfectly complements
Washington's stone monuments.
Eastern white pines encircle the
Jefferson Memorial and stand near
the Washington Monument and the
Lincoln Memorial. The Lyndon Baines
Johnson Memorial Grove is a stand of
white pines. The eastern white pine is one
of America's most important timber trees.
In the eighteenth and nineteenth centuries,
native stands of tall, straight eastern white
pines were used to build ship masts, bridges,
and homes. The tree is important to many
birds and mammals for food (seeds, foliage,
bark, and twigs) and shelter.

NATIVE RANGE   Newfoundland to Manitoba; south to Maryland,
western North Carolina, northern Georgia, eastern Tennessee,
and Iowa.

FOLIAGE   Evergreen. Needles slender, 2 to 5 inches (5–12.5 cm)
long, in bundles of fives.

CONES   3 to 10 inches (7.5–25.3 cm) long, slender, pendulous,
slightly tapered. Scales are spineless.

BARK   Dark purple-gray, deeply fissured, with broad scaly ridges.

GROWTH HABIT   Tall tree with few horizontal limbs. Older
trunks are often bare of branches until fairly high up.

SIMILAR SPECIES   Himalayan pine (*Pinus wallichiana*). The
eastern white pine is far more commonly planted than any other
pine with needles in bundles of fives.

LOCATIONS
• West Potomac Park and Jefferson Memorial (including Casey
  Trees' D.C. 2006 Champion White Pine)
• Lyndon Baines Johnson Memorial Grove

- White House grounds (tree planted by Gerald Ford)
- U.S. Capitol grounds
- Potomac Parkway near Lincoln Memorial
- Washington Monument and the Mall
- National Gallery of Art
- Franciscan Monastery
- Vice President's Residence
- National Zoo
- Vietnam Veterans Memorial
- Common throughout the city

Himalayan Pine (Bhutan Pine)

Pinus wallichiana A. B. Jacks (*Pinus griffithii* McClelland) •
Pine Family *Pinaceae*

The Himalayan pine played an important role in the early evolution of *City of Trees*. The tree is so similar to the eastern white pine that it keys out perfectly to *Pinus strobus* in native field guides. It was one of our first encounters with a rare exotic that could easily be mistaken for a native tree, a common occurrence in Washington and one of the primary reasons for creating this book.

NATIVE RANGE   Himalayan Mountains west to Afghanistan.

FOLIAGE   Evergreen. Needles slightly longer than eastern white pine, 4 to 8 inches (10–20 cm) long, in bundles of fives. Grayish green. Mature needles droop.

CONES   Similar to white pine, but usually longer and more resinous.

BARK   Orange-gray, cracked into small plates.

GROWTH HABIT   Pyramidal tree with slightly drooping branches.

SIMILAR SPECIES   Eastern white pine (*Pinus strobus*). The Himalayan pine's best distinguishing characteristics are its drooping needles and branches and its orange-gray bark.

LOCATIONS
- National Zoo (lion and tiger area)
- National Arboretum
- Maryland Avenue, N.E., at 9th and E Streets
- Some private yards throughout the city
- Town of Washington Grove, Maryland

Other Rare White Pines with Needles in Bundles of Fives

At least three other members of the soft or white pine group are planted in Washington, but they are very rare. Several specimens of the Japanese white pine (*Pinus parviflora* Siebold & Zucc.) are planted at the attractively landscaped Franklin Delano Roosevelt Memorial. The Japanese white pine is a small, gracefully shaped tree, with blue-green to green 2 to 2½ inch (5–7 cm) curved, often twisted needles, 2 to 2½ inches (5–7 cm) long, in bundles of fives. Its cones are egg-shaped to almost round, 1½ to 3 inches (4–7.5 cm) long, with thick, leathery, reddish brown scales.

LOCATION
• Franklin Delano Roosevelt Memorial

The limber pine (*Pinus flexilis* James), which is native to mountainous regions of the western states and Canada, has needles 1½ to 3½ inches (3.8–9 cm) long, in crowded and often twisted bundles of fives. Cones have very thick scales for the white pine group, and are reddish yellow in color, 2¾ to 6 inches (7–15 cm) long.

Limber Pine
Pinus flexilis

LOCATIONS
• Soldiers' Home
• National Arboretum

The Swiss stone pine (*Pinus cembra* L.) is not commonly planted in Washington. Native to the Alps and Carpathians of Europe and Asia, this handsome tree has needles in bundles of fives, 2 to 5 inches (5–12.5 cm) long, are green on one side and blue-white striped on the other. The cones are egg-shaped or nearly round and 2 to 3¼ inches (5–8 cm) long.

LOCATIONS
• Uncommon in Washington

Needles in Bundles of Twos

Austrian Pine

Pinus nigra Arnold • Pine Family *Pinaceae*

The Austrian pine is widely cultivated in Washington.

NATIVE RANGE   Austria south to Italy and Greece.

FOLIAGE Evergreen. Needles 4 to 6 inches (10–15 cm) long, in bundles of twos; very stiff, either straight or slightly curved.

CONES Yellowish, reddish, or grayish brown. Egg-shaped, 2 to 4 inches (5–10 cm) long.

BARK Gray or pinkish gray, deeply cracked and scaly.

GROWTH HABIT Pyramidal or flat-topped crown. Most Washington specimens have short trunks and many level or slightly ascending branches.

SIMILAR SPECIES Very difficult to distinguish from the Japanese black pine (*Pinus thunbergii*). Among D.C. trees, growth habit seems to be the characteristic that differs most greatly between the two. The Austrian pine is usually single-trunked and upright, while the Japanese black pine's trunk tends to lean slightly and fork into two or more main limbs. However, this is not true of all specimens.

LOCATIONS
• East Potomac Park
• Public buildings and private homes throughout the city

Japanese Black Pine

Pinus thunbergii Parl. • Pine Family *Pinaceae*

This tree is commonly planted here.

NATIVE RANGE Japan.

FOLIAGE AND CONES Evergreen. Needles very similar to Austrian pine (*Pinus nigra*) but slightly shorter: 2¼ to 4½ inches (5.5–11.3 cm) long. Cones 1½ to 2½ inches (3.8–6.3 cm) long.

BARK Dark gray, fissured.

GROWTH HABIT Mature trees in D.C. tend to lean slightly and fork into two or more divergent main limbs. Crown often irregular, somewhat jagged in appearance.

SIMILAR SPECIES Even botanists have a hard time telling apart the Japanese black pine and the Austrian pine (*Pinus nigra*). The leaning, forked trunk of the Japanese black pine and its irregular crown are its best distinguishing characteristics. However, trees do not assume this growth habit in some settings. The best location to see the two similar trees growing side by side is East Potomac Park.

LOCATIONS
- East Potomac Park
- Hillwood Estate (Japanese garden)
- Public buildings and private yards throughout the city

Red Pine (Norway Pine)

Pinus resinosa Ait. • Pine Family *Pinaceae*

STATE TREE OF MINNESOTA

Three young specimens of the red pine were planted on the lawn of the Vice President's Residence by Walter Mondale in 1979. The trees came from a nursery in Mondale's home state of Minnesota; however, they were not able to survive in Washington's climate.

NATIVE HABITAT AND RANGE   Sandy or rocky soils; Nova Scotia to Manitoba; south to New Jersey, Pennsylvania, West Virginia, northern Illinois, and Minnesota.

FOLIAGE   Evergreen. Needles in bundles of twos, 4 to 7 inches (10–17.8 cm) long. Straight, slender, dark yellowish green or dark green.

CONES   Egg-shaped or somewhat elongated, 1½ to 2½ inches (3.8–6.3 cm) long, reddish brown. When the cone falls, it often leaves a few scales on the tree.

BARK   Reddish brown, fissured, and scaly.

GROWTH HABIT   Medium-sized tree with a broad, rounded, or pyramidal crown. Spreading branches are sometimes slightly pendulous.

DISTINGUISHING CHARACTERISTICS   The long needles set the red pine apart from other locally planted pines with needles in bundles of twos.

LOCATIONS
- National Arboretum
- Some public buildings and private yards

Japanese Red Pine

Pinus densiflora Sieb. & Zucc. •
Pine Family *Pinaceae*

A very handsome Japanese tree.

NATIVE RANGE   Japan.

FOLIAGE   Evergreen. Needles 2¾ to 4¾ inches (7–12 cm) long, in bundles of twos.

CONES   Delicate egg-shaped or oblong cones are ¾ to 2 inches (2–5 cm) long.

BARK   Orange-brown or reddish, thin and scaly. Older bark near the base may become gray and fissured into plates.

GROWTH HABIT   Usually small- to medium-sized in Washington gardens, but can grow quite tall. The tree sometimes leans, and it usually has horizontal or nearly horizontal branches. Crown is broad and flat-topped or rounded.

DISTINGUISHING CHARACTERISTICS   Size of cones combined with orange-brown or reddish young bark separates the Japanese red pine from other species.

LOCATIONS
• National Park Service Headquarters, East Potomac Park
• U.S. Capitol grounds

Scrub Pine (Virginia Pine, Jersey Pine)

Pinus virginiana Mill. •
Pine Family *Pinaceae*

A native tree and the most common pine in Rock Creek Park. Not often cultivated as an ornamental, but prevalent in regional woodlands and abandoned fields. Chipmunks, squirrels, and birds eat the seeds, and deer browse the young trees.

NATIVE HABITAT AND RANGE   A variety of habitats, but most common in dry sandy or clay soils; southern New York to South Carolina and Mississippi; west to Tennessee, Kentucky, and southern Indiana.

FOLIAGE   Evergreen. Needles 1½ to 3 inches (3.8–7.5 cm) long, in bundles of twos. Stout, slightly twisted, grayish green.

CONES   Egg-shaped, 1½ to 3 inches (3.8–7.5 cm) long; scales thin, with slender spines.

GROWTH HABIT   Small- to medium-sized tree with an irregular, rather scraggly crown.

SIMILAR SPECIES   The Canadian and northern U.S. Jack pine (*Pinus banksiana* Lamb.), which is rarely cultivated and not included in this guide, has slightly shorter needles. Jack pine cones have very small spines or no spines on their scales. The table mountain pine (*Pinus pungens* Lamb.), also not included, is an Appalachian Mountain species that grows on the summit of nearby Sugarloaf Mountain, at Blockhouse Point on the Potomac, and in the Blue Ridge. It has cones with longer, stouter spines.

LOCATIONS
• National Zoo
• National Arboretum
• Rock Creek Park and other regional woodland parks
• Hillwood Estate
• Some public grounds and private yards throughout the city

Scots Pine (Scotch Pine)

Pinus sylvestris L. • Pine Family *Pinaceae*

An important European timber tree and popular ornamental and Christmas tree. Not widely cultivated in Washington.

NATIVE RANGE   Europe to Siberia, occasionally escapes from cultivation in the U.S.

FOLIAGE   Evergreen. Short, bluish green, twisted needles are 1 to 3 inches (2.5–7.5 cm) long, in bundles of twos.

CONES   Egg-shaped, 1 to 2½ inches (2.5–6.3 cm) long.

BARK   Reddish brown or orange-brown, scaly.

LOCATIONS
• Some public buildings and private yards

Needles in Bundles of Threes

Loblolly Pine

Pinus taeda L. • Pine Family *Pinaceae*

A beautiful southern pine, with a tall, straight trunk and cinnamon-colored bark. Its seeds are a critical food source for birds and mammals, including the endangered Delmarva fox squirrel, which lives in the Chincoteague National Wildlife Refuge.

NATIVE HABITAT AND RANGE   Usually growing in moist, sandy soils of the Coastal Plain, Piedmont, and Mississippi River Valley; southern New Jersey to Florida, west to eastern Texas, Arkansas, and western Tennessee.

FOLIAGE   Evergreen. Needles slender, 4½ to 10 inches (11.4–25.5 cm) long, in bundles of threes (rarely twos).

CONES   Conic when closed, egg-shaped when open, 2½ to 6½ inches (6.3–16.5 cm) long. Scales armed with short, stout, sharp spines.

BARK   Cinnamon-colored, broken into thick scales on mature trees.

GROWTH HABIT   Medium to tall tree with a long, clear trunk and dense, rounded crown.

SIMILAR SPECIES   Shortleaf pine (*Pinus echinata*) has shorter needles in bundles of twos and threes, and cones armed with smaller spines.

LOCATIONS
• National Arboretum
• Rock Creek Park
• National Garden of the U.S. Botanic Garden
• Meadowbrook Stables, Chevy Chase, Maryland
• Common on the Eastern Shore and Chincoteague and Assateague Islands

Pitch Pine

Pinus rigida Mill. • Pine Family *Pinaceae*

A native pine that is not often cultivated.

Native Habitat and Range　Dry, sandy, or rocky soils; Maine and southern Ontario south to northern Georgia.

Foliage　Evergreen. Stiff, stout, usually twisted needles, 3 to 5 inches (7.5–12.5 cm) long, in bundles of threes.

Cones　Egg-shaped, 1½ to 3½ inches (3.8–9 cm) long. Scales armed with short, stiff spines.

Bark　Reddish brown; mature bark deeply furrowed and broken into scaly plates.

Growth Habit　Medium-sized tree with an irregular crown.

Similar Species　Shortleaf pine (*Pinus echinata*) has straight, not twisted, needles in bundles of twos and threes.

Locations
• National Arboretum
• National Garden of the U.S. Botanic Garden
• Rock Creek Park and other regional woodlands
• George Washington Memorial Parkway
• Mount Vernon
• Town of Washington Grove, Maryland

Lace-Bark Pine

Pinus bungeana Zucc. ex Endl. • Pine Family *Pinaceae*

Named for its ornamental bark, the lace-bark pine has gained popularity as a cultivated tree since the first edition of *City of Trees* was published.

Native Range　China.

Foliage　Evergreen. Dark yellow-green needles, 2 to 4 inches (5–10 cm) long, in bundles of threes.

Cones　Egg-shaped, 1½ to 3 inches (3.8–7.5 cm) long; scales are thick and armed with sharp spines.

Bark　Truly beautiful, and more like a plane tree than a pine. Thin gray and olive-green outer bark flakes away to reveal cream, green, yellow, and pale purple patches.

Growth Habit   Somewhat shrubby, especially when young. Usually multi-trunked, with a rounded, pyramidal, or flat-topped crown and, at maturity, broadly spreading branches.

Distinguishing Characteristics   The bark is a giveaway, although it takes a few years to mature.

Locations
• National Arboretum
• Smithsonian National Museum of Natural History
• Public gardens and private yards throughout the region

Longleaf Pine

Pinus palustris Mill. • Pine Family *Pinaceae*

State Tree of Alabama and North Carolina

A lovely southern pine with long needles. Rare as a cultivated tree in Washington.

Native Habitat and Range   Sandy soils, mostly of the southern Coastal Plain (also Piedmont) from southeastern Virginia to Florida, west to eastern Texas.

Foliage   Evergreen. Needles 8 to 18 inches (20–45.5 cm) long, in bundles of threes.

Cones   Conic when closed, egg-shaped when open, 4 to 10 inches (10–25.3 cm) long. Large scales armed with short, thin, incurved spines.

Bark   Orange-brown or grayish brown, rough and scaly.

Distinguishing Characteristics   No other pine commonly cultivated in Washington has such long needles.

Locations
• Arlington National Cemetery, in front of the Custis-Lee Mansion (Arlington House)
• National Garden of the U.S. Botanic Garden
• National Arboretum

Needles in Bundles of Twos and Threes

Shortleaf Pine (Yellow Pine)

Pinus echinata Mill. • Pine Family *Pinaceae*

STATE TREE OF ARKANSAS

An important timber tree, sometimes cultivated for ornament. Native to the area, but not common.

NATIVE HABITAT AND RANGE   Dry, sandy, or rocky soils; southern New York to northern Florida, west to eastern Texas, Oklahoma, and southern Missouri.

FOLIAGE   Evergreen. Needles 3 to 5 inches (7.5–12.5 cm) long, in bundles of twos and sometimes threes.

CONES   Oblong-conic when closed, egg-shaped when open, 1½ to 3 inches (3.8–7.5 cm) long. Thin scales are armed with small, sharp spines.

BARK   Reddish brown and scaly on mature trees.

SIMILAR SPECIES   Red pine (*Pinus resinosa*) has needles in twos and cone scales without spines. Loblolly pine (*Pinus taeda*) has longer needles (usually in threes) and cone scales armed with stout spines. Pitch pine (*Pinus rigida*) has needles in threes that are usually twisted.

LOCATIONS
• U.S. Capitol grounds
• National Arboretum
• Public parks and private yards throughout the city
• Potomac, Maryland

The True Cedars

Cedrus Trew. • Pine Family *Pinaceae*

While the name cedar is applied to several trees in our native flora, none of the true cedars is native to this continent. The genus is made up of four closely related species, three of which are in cultivation in Washington. All three are magnificent trees. The cedars are the only evergreen conifers that bear their foliage on short spur shoots on mature branchlets. Like the spruces, the cedars bear erect cones.

KEY TO THE CEDARS COMMONLY CULTIVATED IN WASHINGTON, D.C.

Note: This key will not apply to pendulous cedar cultivars, which have grown in popularity since the first editions of City of Trees.

1a) New shoot gently drooping............Deodar Cedar (*C. deodara*)

1b) Newest shoot stiff and level or ascending (except in pendulous forms, and all forms may droop with age)

    2a) Foliage usually bluish green to bright blue-white (rarely green in Washington-grown forms); needles ⅓ to 1 inch (1–2.5 cm) long. Branches both ascending and level (unless a pendulous form)............... Atlas Cedar (*C. atlantica*)

    2b) Foliage dark green, grayish green, or bluish green; needles usually 1 to 1¼ inches (2.5–3 cm) long. Upper branches level and layered....Cedar of Lebanon (*C. libani*)

Atlas Cedar (Silver Atlas Cedar, Atlantic Cedar)

Cedrus atlantica (Endl.) G. Manetti ex Carrière, *Cedrus atlantica* 'Glauca' • Pine Family *Pinaceae*

A very impressive tree, with somewhat helter-skelter ascending and level branches. The bright blue-white color of the form most often planted here is breathtaking, especially after a snowfall.

Native Range   Atlas Mountains of Algeria and Morocco.

Foliage   Evergreen. Needles stiff, pointed, about ⅓ to 1 inch (1–2.5 cm) long. Color varies from blue-green or blue-gray to blue-white (in the cultivar 'Glauca'), less often green. Newest shoots are stiff and usually slightly ascending or level (except in pendulous forms, and all forms may droop with age). Needles on older growth borne in clusters on spur shoots.

Cones   Erect, egg-shaped or barrel-shaped; greenish, tinged purple when young, becoming purplish brown at maturity. 2 to 3½ inches (5–9 cm) long, often slightly concave at apex.

Bark and Branchlets   Bark gray, smooth when young, becoming fissured and scaly with age. Branchlets often with short pubescence (visible with a hand lens) and small, ovoid winter buds.

Growth Habit   Distinctive combination of ascending, level, and slightly drooping branches; crown pyramidal.

Other Forms   Pendulous forms of the Atlas cedar include 'Glauca Pendula.'

Similar Species   The rare cedar of Lebanon (*Cedrus libani*) has mostly level branches, usually greener foliage, and needles that are 1 inch (2.5–3 cm) long or longer. The deodar cedar has new shoots that arch downward.

Locations
• White House grounds
• Rock Creek Cemetery
• Hillwood Estate
• Franciscan Monastery
• National Arboretum
• Washington National Cathedral
• National Gallery of Art Sculpture Garden
• Parks, gardens, and grounds citywide

Deodar Cedar

Cedrus deodara (Roxb. ex D. Don) G. Don • Pine Family *Pinaceae*

The true cedars are Washington's most striking cultivated conifers. Their tall, dark silhouettes give great depth to the landscape. The deodar cedar is the most commonly planted of the three species growing here. A magnificent specimen of this tree stands in back of the Custis-Lee Mansion (Arlington House) in Arlington National Cemetery.

NATIVE RANGE Himalayan Mountains from Afghanistan to Nepal.

FOLIAGE Evergreen. Needles ¾ to 2 inches (2–5 cm) long, stiff, sharply pointed, usually triangular in cross-section; gray-green or green. New shoots arch gently downward. Needles on older growth borne in clusters on short spur shoots.

CONES Erect, barrel-shaped or egg-shaped; somewhat bluish when young, becoming reddish brown toward maturity. 2½ to 4 inches (6.3–10 cm) long. Cones take two to three years to mature.

BARK AND BRANCHLETS Bark grayish green and smooth on young trees, becoming dark gray or brown and fissured and scaly with age. Young branchlets densely pubescent. Winter buds tiny, ovoid, and pointed.

GROWTH HABIT Perhaps the most graceful of the large conifers planted here. The crown is pyramidal (except on a few old trees such as the one behind the Custis-Lee Mansion). The branches are large, dramatically sweeping, and sparsely set, creating an impressive profile.

SIMILAR SPECIES The best way to distinguish the deodar cedar from the other true cedars in Washington (excluding pendulous forms) is by the new shoot, which arches gently downward. Newest growth on the cedar of Lebanon (*Cedrus libani*) and the Atlas cedar (*Cedrus atlantica*) is level or ascending (except in pendulous cultivars—and older growth on both species may droop). [See illustrations for the similar Atlas cedar (*Cedrus atlantica*)]

LOCATIONS
• Arlington National Cemetery
• Dumbarton Oaks
• National Arboretum
• Hillwood Estate
• White House grounds
• National Zoo
• Folger Park
• National Gallery of Art Sculpture Garden
• Common throughout the city

Cedar of Lebanon

Cedrus libani A. Rich. • Pine Family *Pinaceae*

The cedar of Lebanon is the famous tree of the Holy Land that provided the wood for King Solomon's temple, according to legend. This tree is rare in Washington, despite the widespread belief that it is commonly cultivated here.

NATIVE RANGE   Asia Minor, Syria.

SIMILAR SPECIES   The cedar of Lebanon closely resembles the other true cedars that are commonly planted in the area. It can be distinguished from the deodar cedar (*Cedrus deodara*) by its stiff new shoots, level or ascending. (While the new growth on the cedar of Lebanon may nod toward the very tip of the branchlet, on the deodar the entire new shoot gently droops.) It is more difficult to tell the cedar of Lebanon and the Atlas cedar (*Cedrus atlantica*) apart. The blue-white form of the latter species (*C. atlantica* 'Glauca') is readily distinguishable. When the foliage is grayish green or bluish green, compare the following characteristics:

CEDAR OF LEBANON
Needles on older growth up to 1¼ inches (3 cm) long
Upper branches level and layered; crown often develops a
   tabletop effect

ATLAS CEDAR
Needles on older growth usually less than 1 inch (2.5 cm) long
Branches ascending and level (except in pendulous forms);
   crown usually pyramidal

[See illustrations for the similar Atlas cedar (*Cedrus atlantica*)]

LOCATIONS
• White House grounds (tree planted by Jimmy Carter)
• Outdoor Nursery School, Chevy Chase, Maryland (Turkish
  form of the tree with slightly shorter needles)
• National Gallery of Art Sculpture Garden
• George Washington's gravesite, Mount Vernon

The Firs

Abies Mill. • Pine Family *Pinaceae*

Firs are the "Christmas tree genus." Their pleasantly aromatic foliage stays on the tree longer than most other evergreen needles, and their lovely shapes conjure up images of snow-covered forests. The genus is characterized by erect cones and usually flat needles that often are grooved above and frequently have two pale parallel bands below. Many wildlife species depend on the food and shelter provided by the fir species.

Nordmann Fir (Caucasian Fir)

Abies nordmanniana (Steven) Spach. •
Pine Family *Pinaceae*

This handsome fir is frequently planted in Washington.

NATIVE RANGE   Caucasus, Asia Minor.

FOLIAGE   Evergreen. Needles stiff, ½ to 1½ inches (1.3–3.8 cm) long. Lustrous above and grooved down the middle; two parallel white bands below. The blunt tip is notched. Needles radiate from sides and top of branchlet, and most point gently and evenly forward.

CONES   Tall, erect, cylindric, usually on upper branches only. Pale green at first, becoming dark reddish brown. 4½ to 7½ inches (11.4–19 cm) long.

BARK AND BRANCHLETS   Bark grayish brown, sometimes becoming fissured with age. Branchlets reddish or grayish brown, pubescent or nearly glabrous. Winter buds reddish brown, ovoid, not resinous.

GROWTH HABIT   Attractive narrow pyramidal silhouette.

SIMILAR SPECIES   This fir is the most commonly planted true fir in Washington. The rare Greek fir (*Abies cephalonica*) has needles that are not notched at the tips.

LOCATIONS
• Along Independence Avenue near the Washington Monument
• Lafayette Park
• Montrose Park
• Soldiers' Home
• National Zoo

• Common in parks and private yards throughout the city
• Agricultural History Farm Park, Derwood, Maryland

Momi Fir

Abies firma Sieb. & Zucc. • Pine Family *Pinaceae*

A rare tree, planted in a few parks and private yards.

NATIVE RANGE   Japan.

FOLIAGE   Evergreen. Needles thick, stiff, ¾ to 1½ inches (2–4 cm) long. Usually notched at the tip; shallowly grooved above, with two gray parallel bands below. Needles arranged on each side of the branchlet like the teeth of a comb (or sometimes with needles also radiating from the top of the branchlet).

CONES   Erect, cylindric, 3 to 6 inches (7.5–15.2 cm) long. Yellowish green when young, becoming brown at maturity.

BARK AND BRANCHLETS   Bark dark pinkish gray, often becoming scaly and fissured with age. Branchlets light grayish or reddish brown with (usually pubescent) grooves. Winter buds ovoid, reddish brown, slightly resinous.

GROWTH HABIT   Pyramidal tree with nearly horizontal branches.

SIMILAR SPECIES   The white or Colorado fir (*Abies concolor*) has slightly longer needles that are irregularly arranged on the branchlet and usually curved.

LOCATION
• National Arboretum

White Fir (Colorado Fir)

Abies concolor (Gordon & Glend.) Lindl. ex Hildebr. • Pine Family *Pinaceae*

This handsome fir is not commonly planted in Washington's public parks, but is a rather popular backyard tree.

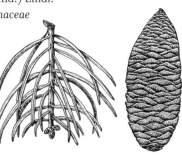

NATIVE HABITAT AND RANGE Mountains; Colorado west to California, south to southern Arizona, New Mexico, and northern Mexico.

FOLIAGE Evergreen. Needles long, thin, often curved forward or upswept; irregularly arranged on branchlet. 1¼ to 2½ inches (3–6 cm) long, dull blue-green or yellow-green above, with two slightly paler bands beneath. Tip pointed, rounded, or rarely with a tiny notch. Foliage emits a strong smell of lemon and balsam when crushed.

CONES Erect, cylindric, 2¾ to 6 inches (7–15 cm) long. Greenish or purplish when young, becoming brown at maturity.

BARK AND BRANCHLETS Bark gray and smooth on young trees; often grows scaly and fissured with age, remaining gray or becoming reddish brown. Branchlets yellowish or greenish brown, glabrous or slightly pubescent. Winter buds rounded, resinous.

GROWTH HABIT Pyramidal; crown may grow rounded with age.

SIMILAR SPECIES Momi fir (*Abies firma*) has needles that are thick, stiff, and regularly arranged.

LOCATIONS
• Washington Monument grounds
• Hillwood Estate
• Soldiers' Home

Greek Fir

Abies cephalonica Loud. • Pine Family *Pinaceae*

A beautiful but extremely rare tree.

NATIVE RANGE Greece and southeastern Europe.

FOLIAGE Evergreen. Needles stiff, ½ to 1¼ inches (1.3–3.2 cm) long; upper needles usually shorter than those on the sides of the twig. Tips pointed, sometimes sharply so. Two parallel white bands below. Needles radiate from all parts of branchlet; most point forward.

CONES Erect, cylindric; greenish brown when young, brown at maturity. 4½ to 7 inches (11.4–17.8 cm) long.

BARK AND BRANCHLETS Bark grayish brown, sometimes becoming fissured with age. Branchlets reddish brown, glabrous. Needles have bases that look like small suction cups and leave large scars on the twig when they fall. Winter buds ovoid, reddish brown, resinous.

Growth Habit   Pyramidal at first, but may become flat-topped with age. Older trees have heavy, low-sweeping branches.

Similar Species   Commonly planted Nordmann fir has needles with notched tips.

Locations
• Rarely planted in Washington

Other Firs (Members of the Genus *Abies*) Planted in the Washington Area

A specimen of the handsome Fraser fir [*Abies fraseri* (Pursh) Poir.], native only to the high southern Appalachians, once grew in Fern Valley at the National Arboretum. The Fraser fir potentially could be found growing in Washington. Several other rare species of fir are planted at the Arboretum.

The Spruces

Picea A. Dietr. • Pine Family *Pinaceae*

The two spruces most commonly cultivated in Washington are the Norway (*Picea abies*) and the blue or Colorado blue (*Picea pungens*). The spruce genus is characterized by usually four-sided needles and pendulous cones, distinguishing them from the firs, which have flat needles and erect cones. Spruces provide food and shelter for many wildlife species.

Key to Spruces Commonly Cultivated in Washington, D.C.

1a) Branchlets drooping, giving the tree a weeping look.

    2a) Needles ½ to 1 inch (1.2–2.5 cm) long; cones 4 to 7 inches (10–18 cm) long........Norway Spruce (*Picea abies*)

    2b) Needles ½ inch (1.2 cm) long or less; cones 4 inches (10 cm) long or less.............Oriental Spruce (*Picea orientalis*)

1b) Branchlets not drooping or only slightly so.

    3a) Foliage silvery blue or gray.................. Blue Spruce or Colorado Blue Spruce (*Picea pungens*) (Note: young weeping cultivars exist)

    3b) Foliage green or bluish green....... See "Other Spruces Cultivated in the Washington Area"

Norway Spruce

Picea abies (L.) H. Karst. • Pine Family *Pinaceae*

A tall tree with weeping branchlets and long, pendulous cones. Widely planted in temperate North America, including the Washington area.

Native Range   Central and northern Europe.

Foliage   Evergreen. Needles four-sided, dark green, ½ to 1 inch (1.2–2.5 cm) long.

Cones   4 to 7 inches (10–18 cm) long, pendulous, green when young, ripening to reddish brown. Cone scales stiff, broadly wedge-shaped.

Branchlets   Drooping, usually glabrous.

Growth Habit   Tall, conical tree with weeping branchlets.

Similar Species   The less commonly cultivated Oriental spruce (*Picea orientalis*) has shorter needles and smaller cones.

Locations
• National Zoo
• Tidal Basin
• Arlington National Cemetery
• Franciscan Monastery
• Ingraham Street, N.W. (Casey Trees'
   2006 D.C. Champion Norway Spruce)
• Hillwood Estate
• Washington National Cathedral
• Sandy Spring Woodlawn Manor
• Strong Mansion, Sugarloaf Mountain, Maryland

Oriental Spruce

Picea orientalis (L.) Link. • Pine Family *Pinaceae*

Native Range   Caucasus and Asia Minor.

Foliage, Cones, Branchlets
Similar to preceding species, but far less commonly cultivated. Needles are shorter and cones smaller than Norway spruce (*Picea abies*). Drooping branchlets are minutely pubescent (visible with a hand lens).

LOCATIONS
- Franciscan Monastery
- Organization of American States headquarters
- National Zoo
- National Arboretum
- Strong Mansion, Sugarloaf Mountain, Maryland

Blue Spruce (Colorado Blue Spruce)

Picea pungens Engelm. • Pine
Family *Pinaceae*

STATE TREE OF COLORADO
AND UTAH

Many forms of the blue spruce,
including the cultivar 'Glauca,'
are widely planted throughout the
United States and Europe. Several
weeping forms have been propagated in recent years. Blue spruce
foliage ranges from silvery blue to
bluish green.

NATIVE HABITAT AND RANGE   Usually in moist soils; higher
elevations of the Rocky Mountains, New Mexico to Wyoming
and Idaho.

FOLIAGE   Evergreen. ½ to 1¼ inches (1.2–3.2 cm) long. Grayish,
greenish blue, or silvery blue needles are four-sided, sharp-
pointed, curved, and very stiff.

CONES   2 to 4½ inches (5–11.5 cm) long, pendulous, green
when young, then reddish brown. Cone scales stiff, with irregularly toothed margins.

DISTINGUISHING CHARACTERISTICS   Foliage color distinguishes
the blue spruce from other spruces planted in Washington.

LOCATIONS
- U.S. Botanic Garden
- Soldiers' Home
- Rock Creek Cemetery
- National Arboretum
- U.S. Department of Agriculture, the Mall (commemorative
  trees including one dedicated to fortieth birthday of Smokey
  Bear)
- Public and private grounds throughout the city

Other Spruces Cultivated in the Washington Area

White Spruce

Picea glauca (Moench) Voss. • Pine Family *Pinaceae*

NATIVE HABITAT AND RANGE   Usually in rich, moist soils; much of Canada, northern U.S. in New England, Midwest, Plains, and Alaska.

FOLIAGE   Evergreen. ⅔ to ¾ inch (2 cm or less) long. Green or bluish green needles are four-sided and bluntly pointed.

CONES   Slender, pendulous, 1½ to 3 inches (3.8–7.7 cm) long. Scales thin, flexible, with rounded margins.

GROWTH HABIT   Evenly conical crown.

LOCATIONS
• Hillwood Estate
• Montrose Park
• National Zoo

Serbian Spruce

Picea omorika (Pancic) Purkyne • Pine Family *Pinaceae*

A rare European spruce, carried by some nurseries.

NATIVE RANGE   Western Serbia, eastern Bosnia.

FOLIAGE AND CONES   Evergreen needles are blunt-tipped or abruptly pointed, slightly flattened, and marked with two broad white bands below. Cones are small, less than 2½ inches (6 cm) long.

GROWTH HABIT   Very narrow, steeple-like crown.

LOCATIONS
• National Arboretum
• Some private yards

Tigertail Spruce

Picea polita (Sieb. & Zucc.) Carrière • Pine Family *Pinaceae*

NATIVE RANGE   Japan.

FOLIAGE   Evergreen. Stiff, sharply pointed needles are curved forward, very stout, and painful to the touch.

LOCATIONS
• Rarely planted in Washington

The Hemlocks

Eastern Hemlock

Tsuga canadensis (L.) Carrière •
Pine Family *Pinaceae*

<small>STATE TREE OF PENNSYLVANIA</small>

A delicately foliaged evergreen indigenous to the
cool, moist woodlands of the eastern U.S. and southeastern Canada. Its seeds, bark, and young shoots are an important food source for birds, deer, and other animals during the
winter months, while its sweeping branches serve as an excellent
storm shelter. There is nothing quite so peaceful (for human,
bird, or beast) as a hemlock grove during a quiet snowfall. Tragi-
cally, many hemlock groves are dying or have died due to the
invasion of an Asian insect called the woolly adelgid (*Adelges
tsugae*).

<small>NATIVE HABITAT AND RANGE</small>   Moist soils of rocky ravines,
valleys, hillsides, and ridges.; southeastern Canada, and northeastern U.S. in the Appalachians south to Georgia, west to the
Great Lakes.

<small>FOLIAGE</small>   Evergreen. Needles flat, ⅓ to ¾ inch (1–2 cm) long.
Rounded or just barely notched at the tip; usually slightly verti-
cally grooved above, with two pale parallel bands below.
Arranged on a horizontal plane.

<small>CONES</small>   Small, delicate, pendulous. ½ to 1 inch (1.2–2.5 cm)
long, with thin, light brown scales. Ovoid, on a short stalk.

<small>BARK</small>   Reddish brown, separating into large, thin, peeling scales.
Becoming deeply furrowed with age.

<small>GROWTH HABIT</small>   Medium-sized or large tree with a pyramidal
crown, tapered trunk, and long, sweeping branches.

<small>SIMILAR SPECIES</small>   Cones, almost always present, are distinctive
of the genus. See Carolina hemlock (*Tsuga caroliniana*), which is
less commonly planted in Washington.

<small>LOCATIONS</small>
• Dumbarton Oaks
• Franciscan Monastery
• National Zoo
• Hillwood Estate

Carolina Hemlock

Tsuga caroliniana Engelm. • Pine Family *Pinaceae*

A beautiful hemlock, infrequently planted in Washington. The Carolina hemlock is native only to the southern Appalachians in Virginia, Tennessee, the Carolinas, and Georgia, where it grows next to stream beds and along the lower slopes of the Blue Ridge. Distinguished from the Eastern hemlock by its needles, which are arranged all the way around the branchlet, rather than on a horizontal plane, and by its cones, which are slightly longer (1 to 1½ inches [2.5–3.8 cm]), with longer stalks.

LOCATIONS
• Uncommon in Washington in private yards and on public grounds
• National Institutes of Health, Bethesda, Maryland (2007 Montgomery County Champion Carolina Hemlock)

Other Pine Family Species Cultivated in the Washington Area

Douglas-Fir

Pseudotsuga menziesii (Mirb.) Franco.
[*Pseudotsuga taxifolia* (Poir.) Britt.] •
Pine Family *Pinaceae*

STATE TREE OF OREGON

The cones and seeds of this western tree are a significant food source for mammals and birds. Douglas-fir is an important timber tree, providing wood for bridges, beams, railroad ties, and many other uses.

NATIVE HABITAT AND RANGE   Abundant in many habitats; British Columbia and California to Colorado and Mexico.

FOLIAGE   Evergreen. Needles ¾ to 2 inches (2–5 cm) long. Flat, straight, or slightly curved; vertically grooved above, with pale vertical bands below. Apex blunt or rounded.

CONES   Very distinctive. Pendulous, 2 to 4 inches (5–10 cm) long, with thin, three-pronged bracts hanging below the scales.

GROWTH HABIT   Trees in cultivation here rarely attain the stature or form of the large specimens in their native habitat. Trees found in Washington usually have conical crowns with ascending upper branches.

SIMILAR SPECIES   Could be confused with fir, spruce, or hemlock. Best distinguished by its cones.

LOCATIONS
• National Arboretum
• Hillwood Estate
• St. Rose of Lima Church, Gaithersburg, Maryland

European Larch

Larix decidua Mill. • Pine Family *Pinaceae*

Closely related to the tamarack or Eastern larch [*Larix laricina* (Du Roi) K. Koch], not included in this guide, which is indigenous to the northeastern U.S., much of Canada, and Alaska. The European larch turns gold before shedding its leaves in autumn. The tree is better adapted to a climate cooler than Washington's.

NATIVE RANGE   Northern, central, and eastern Europe.

FOLIAGE   Deciduous. Clusters of bright green needles, ¾ to 1¼ inches (2–3 cm) long, at the end of lateral shoots.

CONES   ¾ to 1¾ inches (2–4.5 cm) long, with somewhat wavy scales.

BARK   Gray or pinkish gray, ridged and scaly.

GROWTH HABIT   Pyramidal crown, growing irregular with age.

SIMILAR SPECIES   See golden larch (*Pseudolarix amabilis*). While it is conceivable that some other members of the genus *Larix* may be planted in some private yards, the European larch is the one most likely to be encountered.

LOCATIONS
• A few public buildings and private yards, but not as common as it once was.

Golden Larch

Pseudolarix amabilis (J. Nels.)
Rehd., [*Pseudolarix kaempferi*
(Lamb.) Gordon] •
Pine Family *Pinaceae*

A rarely planted conifer
that resembles the Euro-
pean larch (*Larix decidua*)
and turns bright orange-bronze
before shedding its leaves in autumn.

NATIVE RANGE   Eastern China.

FOLIAGE   Deciduous. Needles coarser
and larger than European larch, borne
on long, curved spur shoots that are thickest at the tip (where
needles are joined).

CONES   1¾ to 3 inches (4.5–7.5 cm) long, with thick, triangular
scales. Resemble a small artichoke.

SIMILAR SPECIES   European larch (*Larix decidua*).

LOCATIONS
• Some private homes and public buildings throughout the city

The Taxodium Family

Cryptomeria (Japanese Cedar)

Cryptomeria japonica D. Don • Taxodium Family *Taxodiaceae*

Cryptomeria is one of Japan's most highly
valued trees. It is an important timber
tree as well as a favorite ornamental.

NATIVE RANGE   Japan, China.

FOLIAGE   Evergreen. Needles bright
green, ¼ to ¾ inch (6 mm–2 cm) long.
Widest at the base, tapering to a sharp
point and curving inward toward the
branchlet. Flattened and ridged on both
sides.

Cones   Round or nearly round, ½ to 1 inch (1.3–2.5 cm) in diameter; remaining on the tree after splitting to release seeds. Wedge-shaped scales bear small, curved spines.

Bark and Branchlets   Bark reddish brown, peeling in long, thin strips. Branchlets and tiny winter buds concealed under the needles.

Growth Habit   Trunk straight and tapering, crown narrowly pyramidal.

Similar Species   No tree commonly planted in Washington, D.C., is apt to be confused with Cryptomeria.

Locations
• Meridian Hill Park
• Franciscan Monastery
• Hillwood Estate
• National Arboretum
• Common throughout the city

Bald-Cypress (Swamp Cypress)

Taxodium distichum (L.) Rich. • Taxodium Family *Taxodiaceae.* (Some taxonomists place this tree in the Cypress Family *Cupressaceae.*)

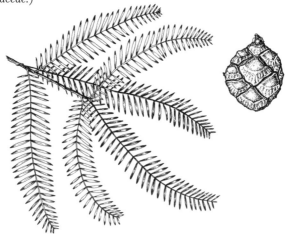

State Tree of Louisiana

The bald-cypress is the Spanish moss–draped tree of southern swamps and stream banks that produces knees, the peculiar woody root projections that protrude above the water. Although the bald-cypress is no longer native to the Washington area, botanists have found evidence that much of the region was once a cypress swamp like the ones common in the Deep South.

NATIVE HABITAT AND RANGE Swamps, edges of ponds and lakes, riversides and streamsides; primarily the Coastal Plain from southern Maryland and Delaware to Florida, west to Texas and north in the Mississippi River Valley to southern Illinois and Indiana.

FOLIAGE Deciduous. Delicate yellow-green needles are alternately arranged on slender shoots. Each needle ¼ to ¾ inch (6 mm–2 cm) long. Alternately arranged shoots vary in length from 2 to several inches (5 cm or more). Foliage turns dull orange-brown in autumn before falling.

CONES Round or ovoid, pale green at first, becoming purplish brown. ⅔ to 1 inch (1.5–2.5 cm) in diameter. Scales peltately attached (attached at the center rather than the base of the cone). Short-stalked or nearly sessile.

BARK AND BRANCHLETS Bark reddish brown or grayish brown, separating into thin shreds and shallow vertical fissures. Branchlets reddish brown, with small, rounded winter buds.

GROWTH HABIT Tall tree with tapered trunk and nearly horizontal branches. Base is usually fluted. Crown pyramidal, but often becoming flat-topped with age.

SIMILAR SPECIES See pond cypress (*Taxodium ascendens*). Very similar to dawn redwood (*Metasequoia glyptostroboides*), which has oppositely arranged foliage and cones on long stalks.

LOCATIONS
• Hains Point, East Potomac Park
• Smithsonian National Museum of the American Indian, wetlands
• U.S. Department of Agriculture, the Mall (tree commemorates American Indian contributions to agriculture)
• Lafayette Park
• Kenilworth Aquatic Gardens
• The Mall
• East side of the Ellipse (including Casey Trees' 2006 D.C. Champion Bald-Cypress)
• 16th Street, N.W., Meridian Hill Park
• U.S. Capitol grounds
• National Arboretum

Pond Cypress

Taxodium ascendens Brongn., [*Taxodium distichum* var. *imbricarium* (Nutt.) Croom], [*Taxodium distichum* var. *nutans* (Ait.) Sweet] • Taxodium Family *Taxodiaceae.* (Some taxonomists place this tree in the Cypress Family *Cupressaceae*)

The pond cypress, which some botanists consider to be a variety of the bald-cypress, differs from that tree in the following minor ways.

NATIVE HABITAT AND RANGE   Similar habitat, but often in more upland areas; Virginia to Florida and Louisiana.

FOLIAGE   Needles usually pressed flat against the branchlets or strongly incurved, often appearing scale-like.

BARK   Grayish brown, thick and furrowed.

LOCATIONS
• U.S. Department of Agriculture, the Mall
• Dupont Circle
• National Garden of the U.S. Botanic Garden
• National Arboretum

Dawn Redwood (Metasequoia)

Metasequoia glyptostroboides Hu. & Cheng • Taxodium Family *Taxodiaceae*

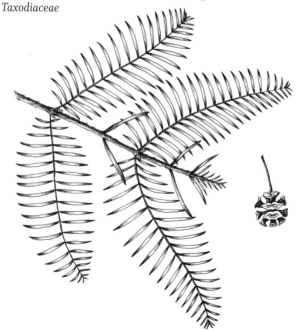

The dawn redwood is often called a living fossil because it was believed to be extinct for many years. For information about the twentieth-century discovery of living specimens of this ancient tree, see page 67. The dawn redwood, like the bald-cypress and the larches, is a deciduous conifer.

NATIVE RANGE Szechuan and Hupeh provinces, China.

FOLIAGE Deciduous. Thin, flat, delicate needles are arranged oppositely. Each needle ½ to 1½ inches (1–4 cm) long, soft spring green. Needles on thin, oppositely arranged shoots that are 3 to 6 inches (7.5–15 cm) long. Autumn color: bright orange-brown.

CONES Round or cylindric, green at first, becoming brown, ½ to 1 inch (1.3–2.5 cm) long, hanging on a stalk 1 to 2½ inches (2.5–6.3 cm) long. Scales peltately attached (attached at the center rather than the base of the cone).

BARK AND BRANCHLETS Bark reddish brown or grayish brown, cracked and peeling in thin strips. Branchlets also have peeling bark. Winter buds small, pale, ovoid.

GROWTH HABIT Tapered trunk, ascending branches, and pyramidal crown. Crown may grow somewhat rounded with age.

SIMILAR SPECIES Very similar to the bald-cypress (*Taxodium distichum*). The needles and shoots of the bald-cypress are alternately arranged (although they can appear to be nearly opposite). Bald-cypress cones are sessile or very short-stalked.

LOCATIONS
- National Arboretum
- Smithsonian National Museum of Natural History
- Hillwood Estate
- Reno Road, N.W. (Casey Trees' 2006 D.C. Champion Dawn Redwood)
- U.S. Capitol grounds

Chinese Fir (China-Fir)

Cunninghamia lanceolata (Lamb.) Hook • Taxodium Family *Taxodiaceae*

In China, the Chinese fir is valued for its fragrant, durable wood as well as its appearance.

NATIVE RANGE China.

FOLIAGE   Evergreen. 1¼ to 2¾ inches (3–7 cm) long. Needles thick, widest toward the base, gradually tapering to a sharp point. Thickly set and usually slightly curved downward. Flat, bright green, with two parallel bands below. Dead foliage often remains on the tree.

CONES   Round or ovoid, 1 to 2 inches (2.5–5 cm) long, Wedge-shaped scales end in sharp, often curved spines.

BARK AND BRANCHLETS   Bark reddish brown and peeling. Branchlets greenish, mostly covered by the clasping bases of the needles. Buds squatly rounded, covered with leaf-like scales.

GROWTH HABIT   Pyramidal tree with a few more or less pendulous branches.

SIMILAR SPECIES   Not apt to be confused with any other species, but in the absence of cones bears a slight resemblance to the true firs (*Abies*). Chinese fir needles are longer and more sharply pointed than those of the true firs commonly planted here. Also, the presence of dead foliage is a common characteristic of the Chinese fir.

LOCATIONS
• U.S. Capitol grounds
• Franciscan Monastery
• Hillwood Estate
• National Arboretum
• Some public grounds and private yards throughout the city and suburbs

Giant Sequoia (Big Tree, Sierra Redwood, Wellingtonia)

Sequoiadendron giganteum (Lindl.) Buchholz • Taxodium Family *Taxodiaceae*. (Some taxonomists place this tree in the Cypress Family *Cupressaceae*.)

STATE TREE OF CALIFORNIA (one of two official state trees)

Although they've got a little more growing to do before they tower over the skyline, bona fide giant sequoias are thriving in Washington. Native to a small mountain area in California, the giant sequoias are the most massive and among the oldest living things on earth. The closely related coastal redwood [*Sequoia sempervirens* (D. Don) Endl.] of

the California and Oregon coast has not been able to live for long in Washington. While the giant sequoia is considered the most massive overall, the coastal redwood is probably the tallest tree in the world. The state of California, apparently unable to decide between the two arboreal giants, adopted both the redwood and the giant sequoia as its official trees. Since earlier editions of *City of Trees* were published, the giant sequoias at Dumbarton Oaks and the White House have died and been removed.

NATIVE HABITAT   Well-drained, moist soils of the western slopes of the Sierra Nevada in California.

FOLIAGE   Evergreen. Scale-like, sharply pointed leaves are thickly and spirally arranged on branchlet. Each leaf ¼ to ½ inch (5–12 mm) long, either closely pressed against branchlet or spreading outward. Bluish or grayish green.

CONES   Ovoid, pendulous; green at first, becoming dark brown. 2 to 3½ inches (5–9 cm) long, with peltately attached scales (attached at middle rather than base).

BARK AND BRANCHLETS   Cinnamon-colored bark is very thick, deeply furrowed, and spongy. Slender branchlets are leaf-clad. Winter buds are small and naked.

GROWTH HABIT   Some of the tallest trees on record are giant sequoias. The tree has large, spreading branches; lower ones droop, then sweep up. Usually forms a pyramidal crown, although some of the specimens in Washington are rather round-topped.

DISTINGUISHING CHARACTERISTICS   Combination of bark and foliage separates the giant sequoia from other conifers planted in the area.

LOCATIONS
• U.S. Capitol grounds
• National Arboretum

Umbrella-Pine

Sciadopitys verticillata (Thunb.) Sieb. & Zucc. • Taxodium Family *Taxodiaceae*

A beautiful tree, rarely grown in Washington. Named for its whorled umbrella-shaped clusters of needles, which slightly resemble the foliage of the true pines.

NATIVE RANGE   Japan.

FOLIAGE   Evergreen. Deep shiny green clusters of eight to thirty flat needles arranged in whorls. Needles 3 to 5½ inches (7.5–12.5 cm) long, grooved on both sides, with a bright yellow-green band below. Small, scale-like foliage is scattered on the branchlet; the tips of these scales form the pronounced knobs from which the whorls of needles arise.

CONES   Ovoid, 2 to 4 inches (5–10 cm) long; green, then ripening brown. Loosely attached scales often break off when handled.

BARK   Reddish or grayish brown, peeling away in coarse strips.

DISTINGUISHING CHARACTERISTICS   The whorled clusters of grooved, shiny green needles are unique.

LOCATIONS
• National Zoo
• National Arboretum
• National Gallery of Art Sculpture Garden
• Smithsonian Castle: Enid A. Haupt Garden

The Araucaria Family

Monkey-Puzzle Tree (Chilean Pine)

Araucaria araucana (Molina) K. Koch • Araucaria Family *Araucariaceae*

A striking, unforgettable tree with sparse, upswept branches, closely covered with deep green foliage. Rare in the Washington, D.C., area.

NATIVE RANGE   Chile, Argentina.

FOLIAGE   Evergreen. ¾ to 2 inches (2–5 cm) long, densely covering the branches. Spirally arranged. Stiff, ovate-triangular, and spiny-pointed at apex.

LOCATIONS
• Georgetown near Dumbarton Oaks
• Bethesda, Maryland

The Cypress Family

Eastern White Cedar (Aborvitae)

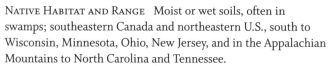

Thuja occidentalis L. • Cypress Family *Cupressaceae*

NATIVE HABITAT AND RANGE   Moist or wet soils, often in swamps; southeastern Canada and northeastern U.S., south to Wisconsin, Minnesota, Ohio, New Jersey, and in the Appalachian Mountains to North Carolina and Tennessee.

FOLIAGE   Evergreen. Small, yellowish green, scale-like leaves in flattened sprays. Each scale lance-shaped, less than ¼ inch (5 mm) long, closely pressed against the branchlet. Scales hugging the middle of the branchlet are glandular.

CONES   Tulip-shaped, about ½ inch (1.2 cm) long, with scales attached at the base. Eight to twelve cone scales are thin, light brown (green when young), somewhat leathery. Seeds (attached to scales) with two narrow wings.

BARK   Thin, reddish brown, shallowly ridged and fissured, with long peeling scales.

GROWTH HABIT   Narrowly pyramidal crown, with short branches and a tapered trunk.

SIMILAR SPECIES   Oriental arborvitae (*Platycladus orientalis*).

LOCATIONS
• Hillwood Estate
• Smithsonian Arts and Industries Building: Mary Livingston Ripley Garden
• National Arboretum
• Private yards

Oriental Arborvitae

Platycladus orientalis (L.) Franco, (*Thuja orientalis* L.), [*Biota orientalis* (L.) Endl.] • Cypress Family *Cupressaceae*

NATIVE RANGE   China, Korea.

CONES   Distinguished from the Eastern white cedar (*Thuja occidentalis*) by its bluish or bluish green cones with their thick scales and wingless seeds.

LOCATIONS
• National Arboretum
• Private yards

Sawara Cypress (Sawara False-Cypress)

Chamaecyparis pisifera (Sieb. & Zucc.) Endl. • Cypress
Family *Cupressaceae*

The Sawara cypress is the member of the genus *Chamaecyparis*
most frequently planted in our area. The most popular form of
this tree is the cultivar 'Squarrosa,' with its pale bluish foliage.

Native Range   Japan.

Foliage   Evergreen. Scale-like; each tiny scale finely pointed
and slightly curved at the tip. Inside bases of scales are white.

Cones   Small, round, brown ¼ inch (6–8 mm) in diameter. Ten
to twelve scales attached at the center (peltate), with a fine point
protruding from each scale's slightly depressed center.

Bark   Fairly smooth, thin, reddish brown, peeling in strips.

Growth Habit   Small tree with a narrow pyramidal shape.

Other Forms   Many forms of the Sawara cypress are in cultivation. The most common in Washington is 'Squarrosa,' with its
soft bluish or gray-green foliage that is mostly needle-like rather
than scale-like. 'Filifera,' another popular form, has drooping,
thread-like branchlets.

Similar Species   Compare features with other *Chamaecyparis*
species.

Locations
• Franciscan Monastery
• Hillwood Estate
• Soldiers' Home
• Smithsonian Arts and Industries Building: Mary Livingston
  Ripley Garden
• National Zoo
• Rock Creek Cemetery
• National Arboretum

Other Members of the Genus Chamaecyparis *Planted in Washington*

Hinoki Cypress (Hinoki False-Cypress)

Chamaecyparis obtusa (Sieb. & Zucc.) Endl. • Cypress Family
Cupressaceae

Native Range   Japan.

Foliage and Cones   Best distinguished from the Sawara cypress (*Chamaecyparis pisifera*) by its foliage. Scales are blunt or rounded at the tip, rather than pointed (or with a minute point). Cones are bright green when young, then orange-brown.

Locations
• Franciscan Monastery
• U.S. Botanic Garden: Bartholdi Park
• National Arboretum

Lawson Cypress (Lawson False-Cypress, Port Orford Cedar)

Chamaecyparis lawsoniana (Murray) Parl. • Cypress Family *Cupressaceae*

Native Range   Southwestern Oregon, northwestern California.

Distinguishing Characteristics   The Lawson cypress is similar in appearance to the two preceding species, but it has thick, furrowed bark and conspicuous glands on the backs of the scale-like leaves. In spring, this species bears small, bright red, male cones. Lawson cypress branches droop in fan-like patterns.

Locations
• Franciscan Monastery
• National Arboretum

Atlantic White-Cedar

Chamaecyparis thyoides (L.) B.S.P. • Cypress Family *Cupressaceae*

The Atlantic white-cedar is a tree of Maryland's Coastal Plain. Although we didn't include it in earlier editions of *City of Trees,* we mention it here because the nursery trade has taken interest in propagating cultivated varieties of the tree.

Native Habitat and Range   Swamps and bogs, mainly on the Coastal Plain; southern Maine to Florida and Mississippi.

Foliage and Cones   Leaves tiny, scale-like, dark bluish green or green, usually glandular. Cones round, with four to six scales.

Locations
• Fern Valley, National Arboretum
• Private yards around the city
• Eastern Shore

Leyland Cypress

× *Cupressocyparis leylandii* (Dallim. & A. B.
Jackson) Dallim • Cypress Family *Cupressaceae*

The Leyland cypress arose as a naturally occurring cross between
two genera, an unusual phenomenon. The tree is a hybrid of the
Nootka cypress [*Chamaecyparis nootkatensis* (D. Don) Spach.]
and the Monterey cypress (*Cupressus macrocarpa* Hartw. ex
Gordon), both indigenous to the West Coast. Similar in appearance to the *Chamaecyparis* species previously described, but the
scale-like leaves are not so flattened and may be triangular in
cross-section. The cultivar 'Haggerston Grey,' with gray-green
foliage, is frequently planted.

LOCATIONS
• National Arboretum
• Franciscan Monastery
• Private yards

Eastern Red-Cedar (Virginia Juniper)

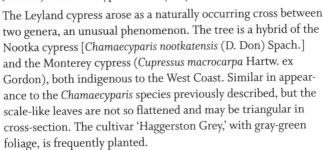

Juniperus virginiana L. • Cypress Family *Cupressaceae*

The Eastern red-cedar yields the fragrant wood used to construct
the familiar cedar chest. An abundant tree of the eastern United
States, it is not a true cedar but a member of the juniper genus.
The berry-like cones of the *Juniperus* genus are eaten by a variety
of birds and also used to flavor gin. The tree serves as a larval
host plant for the juniper hairstreak butterfly.

NATIVE HABITAT AND RANGE   Found in many habitats, and
one of the first trees to appear in abandoned fields; Maine and
southern Quebec to North Dakota, south to Georgia, northwestern Florida, and Texas.

FOLIAGE   Evergreen. Of two types (dimorphic): tiny, bluish
green, scale-like leaves are oppositely arranged, closely pressed
against the four-sided branchlet, and overlapping; needle-like
leaves are often present on the same tree, sharply pointed, arranged oppositely or sometimes in threes, about ¼ inch (less
than 1 cm) long.

CONES   Small, round, berry-like, about ¼ inch (less than 1 cm)
in diameter. Light green, bluish, then dark blue, with a whitish
bloom.

BARK   Reddish brown, shredding into long, thin strips.

GROWTH HABIT   Small to medium-sized tree, usually with a narrow pyramidal or columnar shape. (Some specimens more spreading.)

SIMILAR SPECIES   Rare Chinese juniper (*Juniperus chinensis*). Also, common juniper (*Juniperus communis* L.) grows near the entrance to Fern Valley at the National Arboretum and in the adjacent meadow. Its leaves are in whorls of threes. Although common juniper can become a tree, most specimens planted in the Washington area are shrubby and sometimes prostrate. This widely distributed woody plant grows in Europe, Asia, Canada, and the northern U.S. Its indigenous occurrence south of Pennsylvania is spotty.

LOCATIONS
• Franciscan Monastery
• Hillwood Estate
• Common in area cemeteries, along private drives, and in abandoned fields

Chinese Juniper

Juniperus chinensis L. • Cypress Family *Cupressaceae*

The Chinese juniper, native to China, Mongolia, and Japan, is usually planted in the Washington area in shrub-like form. Dwarf and prostrate forms are in cultivation here. When encountered as a tree, it's best distinguished from the Eastern red-cedar (*Juniperus virginiana*) by the cone, which is slightly larger and brownish when ripe, with a thick bloom.

LOCATIONS
• National Arboretum
• Private yards

Incense-Cedar

Calocedrus decurrens (Torr.) Florin, (*Libocedrus decurrens* Torr.) • Cypress Family *Cupressaceae*

A gorgeous western conifer, rarely planted in the Washington area.

NATIVE HABITAT AND RANGE   Mountains; Oregon, California, western Nevada, and Baja California.

FOLIAGE Evergreen. Tiny, flattened, scale-like leaves are whorled in fours and closely pressed against the branchlet. The side leaves overlap the middle two. Each leaf comes to a fine, sharp point.

CONES Small, oblong, yellowish brown, leathery cones ripen in summer and autumn, splitting open to release seeds. Each cone ¾ to 1½ inches (2–4 cm) long.

BARK AND BRANCHLETS Bark reddish brown, furrowed and very scaly. Flattened branchlets are covered by scale-like foliage. Tiny naked winter buds are inconspicuous.

GROWTH HABIT Although the branches of mature incense-cedars may be quite spreading in their native western habitats, the trees planted in Washington have narrow, columnar habits. The local specimens are strikingly tall for columnar trees.

SIMILAR SPECIES Could be confused with other members of the cypress family from a distance.

LOCATIONS
• Rock Creek Cemetery
• National Zoo
• Washington National Cathedral

The Yew Family

The Yews *Taxus* L.

Yews are planted throughout Washington. The most commonly grown is the English yew (*Taxus baccata*). The Irish yew (*Taxus baccata* 'Fastigiata'), an upright form of the English yew with a broadly columnar crown, is planted in cemeteries and church-yards here and in the British Isles. Asian species are also grown in some private collections here, but yews rarely attain tree stature in Washington, and therefore we treat only the commonly grown species.

English Yew (Common Yew)

Taxus baccata L. • Yew Family *Taxaceae*

NATIVE RANGE Europe, northern Africa, Asia Minor.

FOLIAGE Evergreen. Needles arranged in a comb-like pattern, each ½ to 1½ inches (1–4 cm) long, dark green above, with two pale parallel bands below.

SEEDS   A hard seed surrounded by a bright red, berry-like aril that is about ½ inch (1–1.5 cm) across and open at one end. Seed is visible through opening.

BARK   Reddish brown, very thin and flaky, peeling into long strips.

GROWTH HABIT   Large shrub or small tree with a broad, rambling crown. (The Irish yew has many upright branches that form a jagged, tabletopped crown.)

ENGLISH YEW LOCATIONS
• U.S. Capitol grounds
• Dumbarton Oaks
• Public buildings and private homes throughout the city

IRISH YEW LOCATIONS
• Rock Creek Cemetery and other area cemeteries

Japanese Nutmeg

Torreya nucifera (L.) Sieb. & Zucc. • Yew Family *Taxaceae*

Extremely rare in Washington.

NATIVE RANGE   Japan.

FOLIAGE   Evergreen. Needles dark shiny green above, with two pale parallel bands below, ¾ to 1½ inches (2–4 cm) long, tapered to a sharp point. Arranged in a regular, comb-shaped pattern.

SEEDS   Green with purplish streaks, plum-shaped, about an inch (2–2.5 cm) long.

GROWTH HABIT   Small tree with widely spreading branches.

LOCATION
• Dumbarton Oaks

Florida Torreya (Stinking Cedar)

Torreya taxifolia Arn. • Yew Family *Taxaceae*

This member of the *Torreya* genus is even less frequently planted in Washington than the previous species. It's an endangered plant, limited to ravines of the Apalachicola River in the Florida panhandle and adjacent Georgia. Its needles are 1 to 1½ inches (2.5–4.5 cm) long and malodorous when bruised (please don't). Two or three specimens of Florida torreya are planted in the National Arboretum's Fern Valley.

Illustrated Descriptions of Broad-Leaved Trees

The "Key to the Broad-Leaved Genera" that introduces this section is organized according to a scientific classification system that recognizes similarities among plant families, genera, and species within their larger divisions, classes, and orders. As with the conifers, once you have established that your tree is a broad-leaved tree, or angiosperm, you must determine which category it belongs in. In the case of the angiosperms, there are four possibilities:

A. Trees with opposite, simple leaves
B. Trees with opposite, compound leaves
C. Trees with alternate, compound leaves
D. Trees with alternate, simple leaves

A simple leaf is one that is not divided into individual leaflets. Oaks and most maples bear simple leaves. A compound leaf is divided into leaflets that may be arranged in a pinnate, palmate, or trifoliate pattern. Leaves are arranged along the branchlet either opposite one another or alternately. Leaves that are arranged in a whorled, or sub-opposite, pattern are also considered to be opposite. In deciding which one of the four categories (A, B, C, or D) your tree belongs in, make sure you have correctly determined whether your leaves are simple or compound. From midsummer through autumn, locate the axillary bud, which occurs just above the point where the leafstalk (petiole) is attached to the branchlet. The point where leafstalk meets branchlet is where a single leaf begins. Note that for a compound leaf there is no axillary bud at the base of each individual leaflet.

Simple Leaves

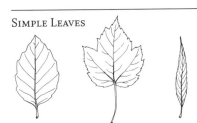

Compound Leaves

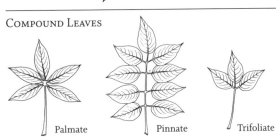

Palmate   Pinnate   Trifoliate

Opposite and Alternate Leaf Patterns

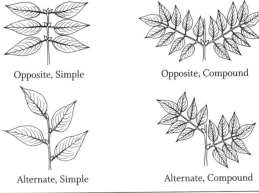

Opposite, Simple   Opposite, Compound

Alternate, Simple   Alternate, Compound

Opposite Leaves

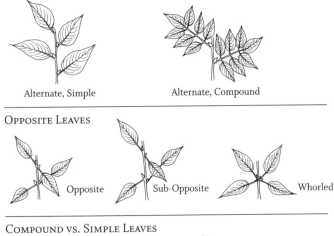

Opposite   Sub-Opposite   Whorled

Compound vs. Simple Leaves

Two Compound Leaves   Four Simple Leaves

Axillary Buds

When you have determined which of the categories your tree belongs to, turn to the appropriate section of the key. The pictures and abbreviated text will tell you the genus (Oak, Maple, Beech, etc.) to which the tree belongs. Then turn to the page number listed next to the drawings to find out what species the tree is (Chestnut Oak, Norway Maple, European Beech, etc.)

Identification of broad-leaved trees can be a little difficult. Most botanical guides contain complicated numerical keys, which can be intimidating to anyone without a scientific background. We believe our illustrated key makes the identification of these trees as simple as possible. Take some time to study the key, and soon you should be making snap identifications.

Key to the Broad-Leaved Genera

Angiosperms

A. Trees and shrubs with opposite, simple leaves

Paulownia (Royal Paulownia, Empress Tree, Princess Tree)
Paulownia tomentosa
Page 369

Paulownia
Paulownia tomentosa

The Catalpas *Catalpa* Pages 371–76

Leaves often whorled.

Yellow Catalpa
(Golden Catalpa)
Catalpa ovata

Northern Catalpa
(Western Catalpa,
Catawba-Tree,
Cigar Tree)
Catalpa speciosa

The Maples *Acer* Pages 321–39

Mostly full-sized trees. A few species are shrubby.

Sugar Maple
Acer saccharum

Trident Maple
Acer buergerianum

Fern-Leafed Japanese
Maple *Acer palmatum*
'Dissectum'

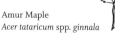

Amur Maple
Acer tataricum spp. *ginnala*

Japanese Maple *Acer palmatum*

Katsura *Cercidiphyllum*
Page 189

Katsura-Tree
Cercidiphyllum japonicum

Crape-Myrtle
Lagerstroemia
Page 312

Shrub or small tree.

Crape-Myrtle
Lagerstroemia indica

Fringe-Tree
Chionanthus
Pages 365–66

Shrub or small
tree.

Fringe-Tree
*Chionanthus
virginicus*

Osmanthus
Osmanthus
Page 365

Shrub. Leaves
evergreen.

Osmanthus
*Osmanthus
heterophyllus*

Viburnum *Viburnum* Pages 367–69

A large group of shrubs and small trees.
Leaves may also resemble those of the maples.

Viburnum
Viburnum

Euonymous
Euonymous
Pages 358–59

Shrub.

Winged
Euonymous
Euonymous alatus

Portion of
typically "winged"
branchlet

The Dogwoods (including
the Cornelian Cherry)
Cornus
Pages 349–54

Cornelian Cherry
Cornus mas (shrub)

Flowering Dogwood
Cornus florida

Lilac *Syringa* Page 366

Shrub.

Common Lilac
Syringa vulgaris

Box *Buxus* Page 283

Shrub or small tree.

Common Box
Buxus sempervirens

B. Trees with opposite, compound leaves

Boxelder
(Ash-Leaved Maple)
Acer negundo
Page 328

Boxelder *Acer negundo*

Paperbark Maple
Acer griseum
Page 339

Paperbark Maple
Acer griseum

Bladdernut
Staphylea trifolia
Page 320

Small tree or large shrub.

Bladdernut
Staphylea trifolia

Cork-Tree
Phellodendron
Page 316

Amur Cork-Tree
Phellodendron amurense

The Ashes
Fraxinus
Pages 360–64

White Ash
Fraxinus americana

European Ash
Fraxinus excelsior

**The Horse-Chestnuts
and Buckeyes**
Aesculus
Pages 342–49

Common Horse-Chestnut
Aesculus hippocastanum

Fruit of Sweet or
Yellow Buckeye
Aesculus flava

Chaste-Tree
Vitex agnus-castus
Page 376

Chaste-Tree
Vitex agnus-castus

C. Trees with alternate, compound leaves

**Japanese Pagoda Tree
(Chinese Scholar Tree)**
Sophora japonica
Page 310

Yellow-green or creamy
flowers. Midsummer.

Japanese Pagoda Tree
Sophora japonica

Black Locust
Robinia pseudoacacia
Page 308

White flowers. Spring.

Black Locust
Robinia pseudoacacia

Yellowwood
Cladrastis kentukea
(*Cladrastis lutea*)
Page 303

White flowers. Spring.

Yellowwood
Cladrastis kentukea
(*Cladrastis lutea*)

**Laburnum
(Golden Chain Tree)**
Laburnum
Pages 311–12

Yellow flowers. Spring.

Voss's Laburnum
Laburnum × watereri

Mimosa (Silk-Tree)
Albizia julibrissin
Page 300

Pink (rarely, white) flowers.
Summer.

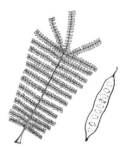

Mimosa
Albizia julibrissin

Honey-Locust
Gleditsia triacanthos
Page 304

Yellow flowers.
Spring.

Honey-Locust
Gleditsia triacanthos

Kentucky Coffee-Tree
Gymnocladus dioicus
Page 306

Greenish white flowers
(not particularly
showy). Spring.

Kentucky Coffee-Tree
Gymnocladus dioicus

**Rowan Tree
(European Mountain-Ash)**
Sorbus
Page 299

Rowan Tree
Sorbus aucuparia

Golden-Rain-Tree
Koelreuteria paniculata
Page 340

Golden-Rain-Tree
Koelreuteria paniculata

Trifoliate Orange
Poncirus trifoliata
Page 317

Winged petiole.

Trifoliate Orange
Poncirus trifoliata

Common Hop-Tree
Ptelea trifoliata
Page 318

Common Hop-Tree
Ptelea trifoliata

**Ailanthus
(Tree of Heaven)**
Ailanthus altissima
Page 314

Common.

Ailanthus
Ailanthus altissima

**Cedrela (Chinese Cedar,
Chinese Toon)**
Toona sinensis
(*Cedrela sinensis*)
Page 319

Rare.

Cedrela
Toona sinensis
(*Cedrela sinensis*)

The Walnuts and the Butternut
Juglans
Pages 261–63

One species has leaflets
with smooth margins.

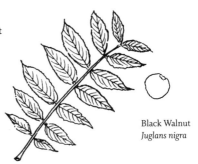

Black Walnut
Juglans nigra

The Hickories and the Pecan
Carya   Pages 257–60

Pignut Hickory *Carya glabra*

Pecan *Carya illinoensis*

Devil's Walkingstick
Aralia spinosa
Page 356

Leaves (not illustrated) are large, bipinnately compound. A small tree or large shrub,
best identified by its prickly branches.

Branchlet of Devil's
Walkingstick
Aralia spinosa

D. Trees with alternate, simple leaves

Trees with alternate, simple leaves are divided into the following categories:

D-1. Common flowering trees of Washington, D.C.
D-2. Common shade and street trees of Washington, D.C.
D-3. Rare trees
D-4. Common trees of native woodlands that are infrequently cultivated in
  formally landscaped areas of Washington, D.C.
D-5. Large shrubs or small trees

D-1. Common flowering trees of Washington, D.C.

The Magnolias *Magnolia* Pages 169–82

*Flowers before the leaves or with the young
leaves in early spring (Asian species).*

Star Magnolia
Magnolia stellata

Saucer Magnolia
Magnolia × soulangeana

*Flowers appear after the leaves are out in spring
and summer (native North American species).*

Southern Magnolia
Magnolia grandiflora

Leaf evergreen.

*Leaves deciduous (all other magnolia
species in the Washington area).*

Bigleaf Magnolia
Magnolia macrophylla
Base of leaf.

Cucumber Magnolia
Magnolia acuminata

Umbrella Magnolia
Magnolia tripetala

**The Flowering Cherries, Peaches,
and Plums** *Prunus* Pages 283–90

A very difficult genus. Common species
and hybrids best identified with the aid
of color close-ups.

Yoshino Cherry
Prunus × yedoensis

The Flowering Crabapples
Malus
Pages 290–92

Fruit of the Hopa Crab
Malus × 'Hopa'

Japanese Flowering Crab
Malus floribunda

The Pears
Pyrus
Pages 292–94

Bradford Pear
Pyrus calleryana
'Bradford'

Fruit of the
Callery Pear
Pyrus calleryana

The Hawthorns
Crataegus
Pages 297–99

English May
Crataegus laevigata

Hybrid Cockspur Thorn
Crataegus × *lavallei*

**Serviceberry (Shadbush, Shadblow,
or Juneberry)**
Amelanchier
Pages 296–97

Serviceberry
Amelanchier

The first native tree to bloom in area woodlands.
Flowers are creamy white or pale pink. Common
in the wild; increasingly common in cultivation.

The Redbuds
Cercis
Pages 301–3

Redbud
Cercis canadensis

Smoke-Trees
Cotinus
Pages 313–14

European Smoke-Tree
Cotinus coggygria

D-2. Common shade and street trees of Washington, D.C.

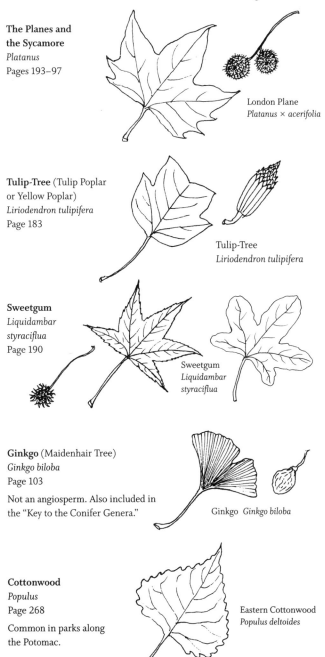

**The Planes and
the Sycamore**
Platanus
Pages 193–97

London Plane
Platanus × acerifolia

Tulip-Tree (Tulip Poplar
or Yellow Poplar)
Liriodendron tulipifera
Page 183

Tulip-Tree
Liriodendron tulipifera

Sweetgum
*Liquidambar
styraciflua*
Page 190

Sweetgum
*Liquidambar
styraciflua*

Ginkgo (Maidenhair Tree)
Ginkgo biloba
Page 103

Not an angiosperm. Also included in
the "Key to the Conifer Genera."

Ginkgo *Ginkgo biloba*

Cottonwood
Populus
Page 268

Common in parks along
the Potomac.

Eastern Cottonwood
Populus deltoides

The Willows
Salix
Pages 266–67

Weeping Willow
Salix babylonica

The Beeches *Fagus* Pages 218–20

Leaves green, purplish, reddish, or coppery.

American Beech
Fagus grandifolia

European Beech
Fagus sylvatica (including
Copper [Purple] Beech)

Fern-Leaf (Cut-Leaf)
Beech *Fagus sylvatica*
'Asplenifolia'

The Oaks *Quercus* Pages 224–50

White Oak
Quercus alba

Scarlet Oak
Quercus coccinea

Chestnut Oak
Quercus montana
(*Quercus prinus*)

Blackjack Oak
Quercus marilandica

Willow Oak
Quercus phellos

Saw-Toothed Oak
Quercus acutissima

The Chestnuts *Castanea*
Pages 221–24

Chinese Chestnut
Castanea mollissima

The Hackberries *Celtis*
Pages 212–13

Leaf base usually unequal. Bark
smooth, gray, with "warts." Ripe
fruit red.

Hackberry
Celtis occidentalis

Osage-Orange *Maclura pomifera*
Page 216

Bark orange, scaly. Fruit yellow-
green.

Osage-Orange
Maclura pomifera

The Mulberries *Morus*
Pages 213–14

Leaves often lobed. Fruit white,
pink, red, purple, or almost black.

White Mulberry
Morus alba

Paper Mulberry
Broussonetia papyrifera
Page 215

Leaves often lobed and may be
arranged oppositely. Fruit
round, orange-red.

Paper Mulberry
Broussonetia papyrifera

The Hollies *Ilex*
Pages 357–58

(Osmanthus has similar leaves,
but arranged oppositely.)

American Holly
Ilex opaca

The Lindens (Limes)
Tilia
Pages 275–81

Fragrant yellow or
white flowers in late
spring, early summer.
Margin usually un-
equal at the base.

American Linden
Tilia americana

European Linden
Tilia × europaea

The Elms *Ulmus* Pages 198–209

Leaf margin usually sharply and doubly toothed. Margin usually unequal at the base. Fruit is a small, papery samara.

Chinese Elm
Ulmus parvifolia

American Elm
Ulmus americana

Scotch Elm
Ulmus glabra

Zelkova *Zelkova serrata*
Page 209

Commonly planted in Washington. Margin
singly toothed. Equal or nearly equal base.
(Other zelkovas, rarely grown, are included
under "D-3. Rare Trees.")

Zelkova
Zelkova serrata

**The Hornbeams (also known as Ironwood,
Musclewood, or Blue-Beech)**
Carpinus Pages 254–55

Bark smooth, muscular-looking.

European Hornbeam
Carpinus betulus

The Birches *Betula* Pages 251–54

Bark white, reddish brown, or gray; smooth or peeling.

European White Birch
Betula pendula (bark white)

River Birch *Betula nigra*

Bark reddish brown, coarsely
scaly. Common along Rock
Creek.

Eastern Hop-Hornbeam
Ostrya virginiana
Page 255

Bark in narrow peeling strips.

Eastern Hop-Hornbeam
Ostrya virginiana

The Alders
Alnus
Pages 250–51

Fruit woody, cone-like.

Black (European) Alder
Alnus glutinosa

D-3. Rare trees

Common Jujube
Zizyphus jujuba
Page 360

Three main veins radiate up from base. Base usually unequal.

Common Jujube
Zizyphus jujuba

Japanese Raisin-Tree
Hovenia dulcis
Page 359

Sweet, edible, raisin-flavored fruit.

Japanese
Raisin-Tree
Hovenia dulcis

Franklin Tree
Franklinia alatamaha
Page 263

Blooms in late summer and autumn.

Franklin Tree
Franklinia alatamaha

Dove (Handkerchief) Tree
Davidia involucrata
Page 355

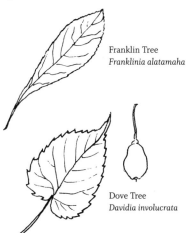

Dove Tree
Davidia involucrata

Idesia *Idesia polycarpa*
Page 265

Fruits (not illustrated) are reddish
brown berries in long, pendulous
clusters.

Idesia
Idesia polycarpa

Persian Ironwood *Parrotia persica*
Page 192

Bark smooth, flaky; pinkish or
grayish brown. Short, wide trunk
divides into many limbs.

Persian Ironwood
Parrotia persica

Silverbell *Halesia*
Page 273

Small, bell-shaped flowers
in spring.

Carolina Silverbell
Halesia carolina

Snowbell (Storax) *Styrax*
Pages 271–73

Hanging clusters of fragrant flowers
(sometimes hidden by the leaves)
appear in spring.

Japanese Snowbell
Styrax japonica

Fragrant Snowbell (Big-Leaf Storax)
Styrax obassia

Chinese Kaki Persimmon *Diospyros kaki*
Page 275

Chinese Kaki
Persimmon
Diospyros kaki

Fruit of the
wild form of
the tree

Japanese Stewartia (Deciduous Camellia)
Stewartia pseudocamellia
Page 264

A small tree with orange-brown bark
and white flowers in summer.

Japanese Stewartia
Stewartia pseudocamellia

Zelkovas *Zelkova* (rare species)
Pages 210–11

Leaves singly toothed.

Caucasian Elm
Zelkova carpinifolia

Cut-Leaf Zelkova
Zelkova × verschaffeltii

The Poplars *Populus*
Pages 269–70

Lombardy Poplar
Populus nigra
'Italica'

White Poplar
Populus alba

**Chinese Parasol Tree
(Phoenix-Tree)**
Firmiana simplex
Page 281

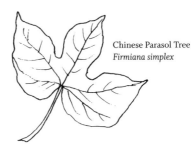

Chinese Parasol Tree
Firmiana simplex

Chinese Quince
Pseudocydonia sinensis Page 295

A small tree with a fluted trunk, mottled
bark, and fragrant yellow fruit. Leaves
(not illustrated) elliptic-ovate, two to four
inches (5–10 cm) long, finely toothed.

Fruit of the
Chinese Quince
Pseudocydonia sinensis

Medlar
Mespilus germanica
Page 294

Medlar
Mespilus germanica

D-4. Common trees of native woodlands that are infrequently cultivated in Washington, D.C.

These trees are planted in Washington, but are more apt to be found growing in private yards and in the wild than along streets or in formally landscaped areas.

Common Persimmon
Diospyros virginiana
Page 274

Common Persimmon
Diospyros virginiana

Tupelo (Black Tupelo, Black-Gum, Sour-Gum)
Nyssa sylvatica
Page 354

Leaves turn scarlet in early autumn.

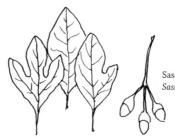

Tupelo
Nyssa sylvatica

Sassafras
Sassafras albidum
Page 187

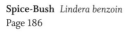

Sassafras
Sassafras albidum

D-5. Large shrubs or small trees

These species are included because of their showy flowers, fruit, or foliage.

Sourwood (Sorrel-Tree)
Oxydendrum arboreum
Page 270

A small tree. Leaves turn scarlet and wine in the fall.

Sourwood
Oxydendrum arboreum

Spice-Bush *Lindera benzoin*
Page 186

Flowers pale yellow in spring. A common woodland shrub or small tree.

Spice-Bush
Lindera benzoin

Pawpaw
Asimina triloba
Page 185

A small tree or tall shrub. Common along the Potomac and Rock Creek.

Pawpaw
Asimina triloba

Rose-of-Sharon
Hibiscus syriacus
Page 281

Common. Flowers pink, red, purple, white, or a combination of colors. Very showy. Summer to autumn.

Rose-of-Sharon
Hibiscus syriacus

The Tamarisks
Tamarix
Page 266

Delicate, feathery foliage. Wispy pink flowers.

Tamarisk
Tamarix

Chinese Photinia
Photinia serrulata
Page 294

A large shrub or small tree. Leaves shiny, evergreen. Flowers white, in upright clusters. Fruit bright red.

Chinese Photinia
Photinia serrulata

The Filberts (Hazelnuts)
Corylus
Pages 256–57

Tall shrubs or small trees with purple, reddish, or green leaves. Fruit (not illustrated) is an edible nut.

European Filbert
Corylus avellana

The Witch-Hazels
Hamamelis
Pages 191–93

Large shrubs or small trees
with pale yellow flowers in late
autumn or early spring.

Common Witch-Hazel
Hamamelis virginiana

Common Fig
Ficus carica
Page 217

Common Fig
Ficus carica

The Dogwoods
Cornus
Pages 349–54

Leaves opposite.

Flowering Dogwood
Cornus florida

The Magnolias

Magnolia L. • Magnolia Family *Magnoliaceae*

Magnolias have brought flowering beauty to the City of Trees for many years. Trees native to the southeastern United States and Asia grace Washington's parks, public buildings, and private residences. In recent years, new magnolia hybrids and cultivars have been introduced through the nursery trade, making magnolia identification a more complicated endeavor than it was when we researched our first edition of this book.

Native Magnolias

Leaves evergreen

Southern Magnolia
(Evergreen or Bullbay Magnolia)

Magnolia grandiflora L. • Magnolia Family *Magnoliaceae*

STATE TREE OF MISSISSIPPI

Although this tree is as southern as a mint julep, it has been planted in places as far from home as Europe, Asia, Africa, and South America, making it one of North America's most important native ornamentals. The rest of the world is finding out what residents of the Deep South have always known: there is nothing like the lemony fragrance of southern magnolia blossoms on a spring or early-summer evening.

NATIVE HABITAT AND RANGE Rich woods and bottomlands; southern coastal states from southeastern Virginia to Florida, west to Texas.

LEAVES Simple, alternate, evergreen. 5 to 8 inches (12.5–20.2 cm) long, with sharply or bluntly pointed apex and wedge-shaped base. Margin smooth or slightly wavy. Thick, leathery, glossy green above, paler and usually rusty-pubescent below. Petiole stout, pubescent, about an inch (2.5 cm) long.

FLOWERS Large, white, cup-shaped flowers, 6 to 8 inches (15.1–20.2 cm) wide. Strong, sweet, lemony fragrance. Six or more petals and three petal-like sepals are thick, stiff, and obovate. Early to midsummer, with a few as late as autumn. (See color close-up.)

FRUIT Upright, egg-shaped aggregate of follicles, 2¾ to 4 inches (7–10 cm) high. Bright red in late summer and early fall, becoming brown by mid-autumn. Densely pubescent. Fruit follicles open to release individual red seeds hanging on long white threads.

BARK AND TWIGS Bark gray or light brown, broken into small scales on older trees. Twigs stout, pubescent, with densely woolly winter terminal bud, 1 to 1½ inches (2.5–3.8 cm) long. Stipular scars encircle twig.

GROWTH HABIT Long, straight trunk, with many branches forming a tall, pyramidal crown (although some cultivars are shrubby).

OTHER FORMS There are more than a hundred cultivars of southern magnolia. We planted one called 'Little Gem' in a small space in our yard because it will not grow as large as most southern magnolias. It bloomed the first year, to our great delight.

SIMILAR SPECIES Not likely to be confused with any other species, but see sweetbay magnolia (*Magnolia virginiana*).

LOCATIONS
• White House grounds
• Old Executive Office Building grounds, along Pennsylvania Avenue and 17th Street, N.W.
• Lincoln Memorial
• Federal Triangle, Constitution Avenue, N.W.
• U.S. Capitol grounds

- Washington National Cathedral
- British Embassy
- Franciscan Monastery
- Cedar Hill, Frederick Douglass National Historic Site
- Mount Vernon
- Widely planted throughout the city in private yards and public parks, and on the grounds of government office buildings, museums, and schools

Leaves deciduous or nearly evergreen

Sweetbay Magnolia

Magnolia virginiana L. • Magnolia Family *Magnoliaceae*

A small tree with sweet-smelling blossoms. Deciduous in the northern part of its range, evergreen in the south.

NATIVE HABITAT AND RANGE   Swamps and moist woodlands; coastal Massachusetts to New Jersey and Pennsylvania, south to Florida and west through Gulf Coast states (farther north in some river valleys) to Texas.

LEAVES   Simple, alternate, deciduous or nearly evergreen. 3½ to 6½ inches (9–16.5 cm) long. Elliptic-lanceolate. Margin smooth. Apex bluntly pointed or rounded; base broadly wedge-shaped or (rarely) rounded. Somewhat leathery. Glossy green above, whitish (glaucous) below; may be silky when young. Petiole becoming glabrous, ½ to 1 inch (1.2–2.5 cm) long.

FLOWERS   White or yellow-white, fragrant. Cup-shaped, with from nine to twelve obovate petals and shorter, thinner, petal-like sepals. Flower 2 to 3 inches (5–7.5 cm) across. Late spring and early summer. (See color close-up.)

FRUIT   Erect, oblong, cone-like aggregate of follicles; dark red, 1½ to 3 inches (3.8–7.5 cm) high.

BARK AND TWIGS   Bark gray, fairly smooth. Twigs glabrous, brown or greenish, with encircling stipular scars. Pith chambered. Winter buds greenish, pubescent; terminal bud conspicuous.

GROWTH HABIT   Large shrub or small tree.

SIMILAR SPECIES   See southern magnolia (*Magnolia grandiflora*).

LOCATIONS
- U.S. Capitol grounds
- National Arboretum
- Parks, gardens, and private homes
- In the wild, along streams, and in swampy areas of the Coastal Plain

Leaves deciduous

Cucumber Magnolia
(Cucumber Tree)

Magnolia acuminata L. • Magnolia Family *Magnoliaceae*

Named for its fruit, which resembles a tiny cucumber. The cucumber magnolia grows in rich Piedmont and mountain woodlands to the north, west, and south of Washington. It is the most widespread and hardiest of all native species of magnolias, according to author and National Arboretum director Thomas S. Elias (*The Complete Trees of North America*).

NATIVE HABITAT AND RANGE
Rich woods; western New York to southern Illinois, south to Georgia, Louisiana, and southeastern Oklahoma.

LEAVES   Simple, alternate, deciduous. 4 to 10 inches (10–25.2 cm) long. Broadly elliptic or ovate. Gradually or abruptly pointed apex; wedge-shaped or rounded base. Margin smooth or slightly wavy. Thin-textured. Yellow-green above, paler below and usually finely pubescent. Petiole 1 to 1½ inches (2.5–3.8 cm) long.

FLOWERS   Yellow-green, erect, bell-shaped. 2 to 4 inches (5–10 cm) high. Not as showy as most magnolias. After the leaves in early May.

FRUIT   Small, erect "cucumber"; brilliant pink to deep red. 1 to 3 inches (2.5–7.5 cm) high. Fruit follicles split to release scarlet seeds on thin white threads. Late summer and early fall.

BARK AND TWIGS   Bark brown, furrowed and scaly. Twigs brown, glabrous, with whitish pubescent winter terminal bud.

GROWTH HABIT   Medium to large-sized tree with long, straight trunk and pyramidal crown.

SIMILAR SPECIES   Bigleaf magnolia (*Magnolia macrophylla*) has much longer leaves. Umbrella magnolia (*Magnolia tripetala*) also has longer leaves that are narrowly wedge-shaped at the base. [See page 182 for description of 'Elizabeth'—a yellow-flowered hybrid of the native cucumber magnolia and the exotic Yulan magnolia (*Magnolia denudata*).]

LOCATIONS
• U.S. Capitol grounds
• National Zoo
• National Arboretum
• Some private homes in the city
• Muddy Branch Park, Montgomery County, Maryland

Umbrella Magnolia

Magnolia tripetala L. • Magnolia Family *Magnoliaceae*

The umbrella-like clusters of leaves at the end of its branches give this tree its common name.

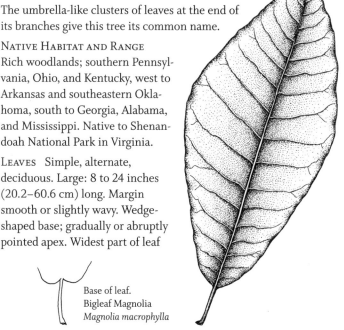

NATIVE HABITAT AND RANGE
Rich woodlands; southern Pennsylvania, Ohio, and Kentucky, west to Arkansas and southeastern Oklahoma, south to Georgia, Alabama, and Mississippi. Native to Shenandoah National Park in Virginia.

LEAVES   Simple, alternate, deciduous. Large: 8 to 24 inches (20.2–60.6 cm) long. Margin smooth or slightly wavy. Wedge-shaped base; gradually or abruptly pointed apex. Widest part of leaf

Base of leaf.
Bigleaf Magnolia
Magnolia macrophylla

above the middle. Usually somewhat pubescent below. Petiole ¾ to 1½ inches (2–3.8 cm) long.

FLOWERS   White or yellow-white. Six to nine narrow petals, each 3 to 5 inches (7.5–12.6 cm) long. Three outer petal-like sepals hang down. Late April to early May. (See color close-up.)

FRUIT   Erect, red, cone-like aggregate of follicles, 2¾ to 4 inches (7–10 cm) high, cylindrical. Follicles split to release scarlet seeds.

BARK AND TWIGS   Bark brown, smooth. Twigs stout, glabrous. Terminal winter bud glabrous, purplish. Stipular scars encircle twig.

GROWTH HABIT   Small to medium-sized tree, tropical-looking with its umbrella-like clusters of large leaves.

SIMILAR SPECIES   Bigleaf magnolia (*Magnolia macrophylla*) has larger leaves, with ear-like bases. (See other differences in flowers, bark, etc.) The pawpaw (*Asimina triloba*) has pubescent twigs with no encircling stipular scars and dissimilar flowers and fruit.

LOCATIONS
• U.S. Capitol grounds
• National Zoo
• National Arboretum
• Some parks and private yards
• Rock Creek Park (probably an escape but possibly native, according to Smithsonian checklist by Shetler and Orli)

Bigleaf Magnolia

Magnolia macrophylla Michx. • Magnolia Family *Magnoliaceae*

The largest-leafed native tree in temperate North America, the bigleaf magnolia bears giant, exotic-looking white flowers.

NATIVE HABITAT AND RANGE   Rich Appalachian woods; southern Ohio, southwestern Virginia, Kentucky, and Arkansas, south to Louisiana, Alabama, and Georgia.

LEAVES   Simple, alternate, deciduous. Huge: 12 to 36 inches (30–90 cm) long. Pointed or rounded apex; ear- or heart-shaped base. Thin-textured. Silvery soft-pubescent below. Petiole 1½ to 4 inches (3.8–10 cm) long, soft-pubescent.

FLOWERS   Giant, open, cup-shaped flowers. Usually six creamy white petals; inner petals with purple inside near the base. Up to 12 inches (30 cm) across. Sepals slightly shorter than petals. Fragrant. May and early June. (See color close-up.)

Fruit Upright, round or egg-shaped aggregate of follicles. Rose-colored, pubescent, 2½ to 4½ inches (6.3–11.4 cm) high. Follicles split to release orange-scarlet seeds on white threads.

Bark and Twigs Bark yellowish (gray on young trees), smooth. Twigs greenish, velvety, with white pubescent terminal buds in winter. Stipular scars encircle twig.

Growth Habit Never attains great height. Tropical-looking, with giant leaves and yellowish bark.

Similar Species Umbrella magnolia (*Magnolia tripetala*) has leaves that approach bigleaf size and are wedge-shaped at the base. Ashe or Ashe's magnolia (*M. ashei* Weatherby) is a rarely planted magnolia whose leaves are cordate at the base and whitened below, but slightly shorter than bigleaf magnolia. Ashe magnolia is planted at the National Arboretum near Fern Valley. It is a multi-trunked small tree or shrub whose native range is limited to Florida, where it is listed as endangered. Near the Fern Valley specimen is another southern species, pyramid magnolia (*Magnolia pyramidata* Bartr. ex Pursh), with leaves that are cordate at the base and broadened above the middle (kite-shaped). The leaves, while large, are smaller than the bigleaf and the Ashe and not so whitened below. Pyramid magnolia is indigenous to the Deep South from South Carolina and Florida to Texas. Mountain or Fraser magnolia (*M. fraseri* Walter) is another native magnolia with largish leaves that are cordate at the base. It grows in the mountains of West Virginia and southward.

Locations
• National Arboretum
• National Zoo
• Soldiers' Home
• Rock Creek Cemetery
• Some private yards

Asian Magnolias

Leaves deciduous; flowers bloom before and/or with the young leaves; petals thin, delicately reflexed

Star Magnolia

Magnolia stellata (Sieb. & Zucc.) Maxim., (*Magnolia kobus* var. *stellata* [Sieb. & Zucc.] Blackburn) • Magnolia Family *Magnoliaceae*

One of the authors' favorite harbingers of spring in the City of Trees. The delicate, fragrant flowers of the star magnolia open before the cherry blossoms.

NATIVE RANGE   Japan.

LEAVES   Simple, alternate, deciduous. 1½ to 4½ inches (3.8–11.4 cm) long. Bluntly pointed or rounded apex, gradually tapering to wedge-shaped base. Margin smooth. Glabrous above, may have some pubescence below. Petioles short, ½ inch (1.2 cm) or less.

FLOWERS   White or pale pink, profuse, fragrant. Twelve or more narrow, white or pink petals and petal-like sepals open wide, suggesting a star. Petals are not as wide as most magnolias. Before the leaves in March or early April; leaves usually appear during blooming time. (See color close-up.)

FRUIT   Reddish, twisted, somewhat carrot-shaped aggregate of follicles, 2 to 4 inches (5–10 cm) long.

BARK AND TWIGS   Bark pale gray, smooth or slightly roughened, with lenticels. Twigs pubescent, with conspicuous, very fuzzy terminal buds in winter. Stipular scars encircle twig.

GROWTH HABIT   Shrub or small tree.

OTHER FORMS   Many cultivars of the star magnolia have been planted in the Washington area, including 'Rosea,' which has petals suffused with pink. 'Rubra,' a rare purple form, is planted at the National Arboretum.

SIMILAR SPECIES   The kobus magnolia (*Magnolia kobus*) is very similar, but its flowers have fewer petals (six to nine). Most other white-flowering magnolias commonly planted in Washington have more or less cup-shaped flowers with stiff, thick petals. [But see also hybrid magnolia (*Magnolia* × *loebneri*).]

LOCATIONS
- U.S. Capitol and Library of Congress grounds
- Parkland near Jefferson Memorial
- National Arboretum
- District of Columbia cemeteries
- Brookside Gardens
- Common throughout the city

Kobus Magnolia (Northern or Japanese Magnolia)

Magnolia kobus DC. • Magnolia Family *Magnoliaceae*

Similar to the star magnolia (*Magnolia stellata*) but attaining greater height. Less common than the star magnolia in Washington.

NATIVE RANGE   Japan.

LEAVES   Simple, alternate, deciduous. 2¼ to 6½ inches (5.8–16.5 cm) long. Base wedge-shaped; blade widens toward apex, then ends in an abrupt point. Margin smooth. Dark green. Some pubescence on veins below. Petiole about ½ inch (1–1.5 cm) long.

FLOWERS   Six to nine petals; white with a faint purple line toward the base outside. Petals thin, narrow, and delicately reflexed. (Short sepals soon fall off [caducous].) Flower about 4 inches (10 cm) across. Late March and early April, before and then with the young leaves. (See color close-up.)

FRUIT   Pink, cylindric aggregate of follicles, 2 to 4 inches (5–10 cm) long. Follicles split to release red seeds on thin threads.

BARK AND TWIGS   Bark gray, smooth, with lenticels, becoming somewhat roughened with age. Twigs glabrous. Terminal buds gray, fuzzy, conspicuous in winter. Stipular scars encircle twig.

GROWTH HABIT   Shrubby or small to medium-sized tree with a broadly pyramidal crown.

SIMILAR SPECIES   Star magnolia (*Magnolia stellata*) has similar flowers, but with twelve or more petals and petal-like sepals. See also hybrid magnolia (*M.* × *loebneri*).

LOCATIONS
- Dumbarton Oaks
- National Arboretum Magnolia Collection
- Brookside Gardens
- Parks and private yards throughout the city and suburbs

Hybrid Magnolia

Magnolia × *loebneri* Kache. • Magnolia Family *Magnoliaceae*

A cultivated cross between the star and kobus magnolias. Several selections are grown in Washington, including 'Leonard Messel,' 'Merrill,' 'Spring Snow,' and 'Star Bright.' These magnolias all have the delicately reflexed flowers characteristic of both parents. Color ranges from white through shades of pink to purple.

LOCATIONS
• National Arboretum
• Some public and private gardens

Leaves deciduous; flowers bloom before and/or with the young leaves; petals thick, flowers cup-shaped or tulip-shaped

Saucer Magnolia

Magnolia × *soulangeana* Soul.-Bod., (*Magnolia denudata* × *Magnolia liliflora*) • Magnolia Family *Magnoliaceae*

A cross between the Yulan (*Magnolia denudata*) and lily (*M. liliflora*) magnolias. The saucer magnolia is more widely planted in Washington than either of its parents or any other Asian magnolia. Its flowers, which usually are pink or pink and white, open early, before the leaves. One of the city's most popular ornamentals.

LEAVES Simple, alternate, deciduous. 3½ to 9 inches (9–22.8 cm) long. Wedge-shaped base, gradually widening toward apex, then ending in an abrupt (blunt or sharp) point. Margin smooth. Usually some pubescence below, especially on the veins. Petiole ¼ to 1 inch (0.6–2.5 cm) long, usually pubescent.

FLOWERS Color varies from white to deep purple, but the most common forms are pale pink outside, with a darker rose blush toward the base, and white inside. Degree of fragrance varies. Six thick petals and three petal-like sepals that are half as long or nearly as long as petals. Petals and sepals more or less rounded at the top. Cup-like flower, but may open quite wide when mature. (See "Other Forms" for more flower descriptions.) March and April (may put forth a few flowers again during summer and early fall). (See color close-up.)

FRUIT Bright red, often twisted, somewhat carrot-like aggregate of follicles, 2 to 4 inches (5–10 cm) long.

BARK AND TWIGS Bark gray or brown, smooth or slightly roughened, with lenticels. Twigs reddish brown, with lenticels. Large, fuzzy, white or pale green terminal buds in winter. Stipular scars encircle twig.

GROWTH HABIT Large, full shrub or small spreading tree.

OTHER FORMS Many forms of the saucer magnolia are planted in Washington, and newly cultivated specimens are constantly being introduced. The cultivar 'Lennei' blooms slightly later and has petals that are purple outside, white inside, and very broad at the apex. Several forms of saucer magnolia have creamy white flowers barely suffused with pink.

SIMILAR SPECIES The typical pink-flowering forms are distinct. White-flowering trees may be confused with Yulan magnolia (*M. denudata*). The darker-hued 'Lennei' and other purplish forms could be confused with lily magnolia (*M. liliflora*). See lily magnolia for comparison.

LOCATIONS
• White House grounds
• Rawlins Park
• National Gallery of Art
• U.S. Capitol grounds
• Organization of American States headquarters
• Brookside Gardens
• Very popular throughout the city and suburbs

Yulan Magnolia

Magnolia denudata Desrouss., [*M. heptapeta* (Buc'hoz) Dandy] • Magnolia Family *Magnoliaceae*

A popular Chinese garden tree for centuries, but rare today in the U.S. Scarcity is partially due to propagation problems encountered by nurseries here, along with the tree's tendency to bloom early and succumb to frost. Also, most Americans probably are unwilling to wait the several years it takes for this tree to put forth its first flowers.

NATIVE HABITAT AND RANGE   Woodlands; central China.

LEAVES   Simple, alternate, deciduous. 3½ to 6 inches (9–15 cm) long. Wedge-shaped or rounded base, very wide toward apex, then ending in an abrupt point. Margin smooth. Deep even green. Pubescent below, especially along the veins. Petiole pubescent, about ½ to 1 inch (1.2–2.5 cm) long.

FLOWERS   Gorgeous large, white, cup-shaped flowers. Nine thick "petals" (actually six petals and three sepals) are white outside, very pale yellow inside toward the base. Fragrant. 4½ to 6½ inches (11.4–16.5 cm) across. Before the leaves in late March and early April. (See color close-up.)

FRUIT   Brownish, cylindric aggregate of follicles, 3 to 5 inches (7.5–12.5 cm) long.

BARK AND TWIGS   Young bark gray, smooth, with lenticels. Older bark dark gray-brown, scaly. Twigs reddish brown, pubescent, with large, fuzzy, pale terminal buds in winter. Stipular scars encircle twig.

GROWTH HABIT   Small to medium-sized tree with long, spreading branches.

SIMILAR SPECIES   May be confused with white-flowering forms of saucer magnolia (*M.* × *soulangeana*), but those are usually slightly suffused with pink. Other white-flowering magnolias that bloom before the leaves (star and kobus) have thinner, narrower petals and flowers that are less cup-shaped.

LOCATIONS
• Dumbarton Oaks
• National Arboretum Magnolia Collection
• Rare in Washington, D.C.

Lily Magnolia

Magnolia liliflora Desrouss., [*M. quinquepeta* (Buc'hoz) Dandy] • Magnolia Family *Magnoliaceae*

NATIVE RANGE   China, widely cultivated in Japan.

FLOWERS   A shrub with deep purple or wine-red flowers. Flowers large, tulip-shaped, with six petals and three small, green, lance-shaped sepals that soon fall. Flower color paler inside. Mid-April.

SIMILAR SPECIES   Saucer magnolia cultivar 'Lennei' (*Magnolia* × *soulangeana* 'Lennei'). 'Lennei' has nine "petals" (six petals and three sepals), which are white inside and very broad and rounded at the apex.

LOCATIONS
• U.S. Capitol grounds
• National Arboretum Magnolia Collection

Oyama Magnolia

Magnolia sieboldii K. Koch • Magnolia Family *Magnoliaceae*

This magnolia grows in the Mary Livingston Ripley Garden next to the Smithsonian Arts and Industries Building. It is native to Japan, China, and Korea.

Newer Native and Asian Magnolias

Some newer cultivated magnolias planted in Washington during recent years:

'Elizabeth'

Magnolia acuminata × M. denudata • Magnolia Family *Magnoliaceae*

'Elizabeth' is a hybrid of the native cucumber magnolia and the Chinese Yulan magnolia. Its flowers are yellow in early spring, before and with the young leaves.

LOCATIONS
• Washington National Cathedral, near the Bishop's Garden
• Private yards

The "Little Girl" Hybrids

Magnolia liliflora × M. stellata • Magnolia Family *Magnoliaceae*

These cultivated magnolias arose from hybrids developed at the National Arboretum to bloom later than the earliest magnolias and thus avoid damaging frosts. The star magnolia was crossed with the later-blooming lily magnolia. The growth habits are shrubby, and the cup-shaped blossoms are reddish purple, purple, or deep pink, at least on the outside, with hues varying from deep to pale. The rather colloquial group name, "Little Girl" hybrids, refers to the girls' names given to each cultivar, such as 'Ann,' 'Betty,' 'Jane,' 'Judy,' etc.

LOCATIONS
• National Arboretum
• 'Betty' is planted at the Washington National Cathedral, near the Bishop's Garden
• Parks and private yards

Other Magnolias

Magnolia hybridization is a dynamic field, and scientists are continually working on new forms designed to dazzle the eye and escape spring frosts.

Tulip-Tree (Tulip Poplar or Yellow Poplar)

Liriodendron tulipifera L., Magnolia Family *Magnoliaceae*

STATE TREE OF INDIANA,
KENTUCKY, AND TENNESSEE

An important timber tree,
and one of the tallest
broad-leaved trees in
the East. American In-
dians used the straight
trunks to make dugout
canoes. Bees use the
flowers for nectar, and
many birds and mammals
feed on the winged seeds (samaras). The tree serves as a larval
host plant for the eastern tiger swallowtail
butterfly. Our native tulip-tree and the
Chinese tulip-tree are the only living trees
in the world in the genus *Liriodendron*.

NATIVE HABITAT AND RANGE   Rich woods,
coves, abandoned fields; southern New
England to Michigan and Illinois, south to
Florida and Louisiana.

LEAVES   Simple, alternate, deciduous. 3½
to 6 inches (9–15 cm) long, 4 to 6½ inches
(10–16.5 cm) wide. Four-lobed, or sometimes
with an extra pair of lobes at the base. Top two lobes
separated by a widely and shallowly V-shaped sinus. Margin
smooth (apart from lobing). Leaf nearly flat across the bottom.
Usually glabrous. Petiole slender, 3 to 6 inches (7.5–15 cm) long.
Large stipules. The first native tree to leaf out in spring. Early
color: bright yellow-green. Autumn color: yellow, early in the
season.

FLOWERS   Petals are greenish at the top, with a broad orange
band near the base. Many yellow stamens arranged around
a yellowish cone-like center. 1½ to 2 inches (4–5 cm) high,
tulip-shaped, with six petals and three down-curved sepals.
The flowers are quite showy, but because the tree is tall and the

flowers are usually borne high above the ground, many people miss them. Late April to May. (See color close-up.)

FRUIT   Brown, erect, cone-like aggregate of winged seeds (samaras), 2½ to 3 inches (6.5–7.5 cm) high. In fall and winter the samaras break free and fly to the ground. The central cone-like axis often remains on the tree through winter and is a good diagnostic feature.

BARK AND TWIGS   Bark light brown or gray, becoming evenly and shallowly vertically furrowed with age. Twigs reddish brown, with rounded leaf scars. Stipular scars encircle twig. Winter buds flattened, shaped like ducks' bills.

GROWTH HABIT   Tall, handsome tree with a long straight trunk and oblong crown. Visible from far away in winter because of its stature and the many candle-like remains of the fall fruit.

OTHER FORMS   There are several cultivars of the tulip-tree, including *Liriodendron tulipifera* 'Aureomarginatum,' a rare form with pale yellow leaf margins early in the season.

DISTINGUISHING CHARACTERISTICS   Unmistakable year-round: in spring with its brilliant early foliage and showy flowers; in summer with its unique leaves; and in fall and winter with its candle-like fruit.

SIMILAR SPECIES   Apart from the rarely cultivated Asian species, none in Washington.

LOCATIONS
- U.S. Capitol grounds
- Mount Vernon
- Montrose Park (Casey Trees' 2006 Champion Tree)
- Vice President's Residence
- National Arboretum
- National Zoo
- Soldiers' Home
- Rock Creek Park, Capital Crescent Trail, Glover Archbold Park, and native woodlands throughout the region
- Manor Oaks subdivision, Brookeville, Maryland
- Sandy Spring Friends Meetinghouse Cemetery, Sandy Spring, Maryland

Star Magnolia   *Magnolia stellata*

Kobus Magnolia   *Magnolia kobus*

Saucer Magnolia   *Magnolia × soulangeana*

Yulan Magnolia   *Magnolia denudata*

Umbrella Magnolia   *Magnolia tripetala*

Bigleaf Magnolia   *Magnolia macrophylla*

Southern Magnolia   *Magnolia grandiflora*

Sweetbay Magnolia   *Magnolia virginiana*

Tulip-Tree   *Liriodendron tulipifera*

Witch-Hazel   *Hamamelis*

Red Maple   *Acer rubrum*

Fringe-Tree   *Chionanthus virginicus*

Pawpaw   *Asimina triloba*

Yoshino Cherry   *Prunus × yedoensis*

Weeping Cherry (single-blossomed)   *Prunus subhirtella pendula*

Kwanzan Cherry   *Prunus serrulata*   'Kwanzan'

Flowering Pear   *Pyrus*

Serviceberry (Shadbush)   *Amelanchier*

Flowering Crabapple   *Malus*

Carolina Silverbell   *Halesia carolina*

Japanese Snowbell   *Styrax japonicus*

Franklin Tree   *Franklinia alatamaha*

Dove Tree (Handkerchief Tree)   *Davidia involucrata*

Tamarisk   *Tamarix*

Cornelian Cherry   *Cornus mas*

Flowering Dogwood   *Cornus florida*

Stellar Dogwood   *Cornus* × *rutgersensis*

Kousa Dogwood   *Cornus kousa*

Redbud   *Cercis canadensis*

Black Locust   *Robinia pseudoacacia*

Yellowwood   *Cladrastis kentukea*

Japanese Pagoda Tree   *Sophora japonica*

Mimosa (Silk-Tree)   *Albizia julibrissin*

Golden-Rain-Tree   *Koelreuteria paniculata*

Paulownia   *Paulownia tomentosa*

Catalpa   *Catalpa*

Blackhaw   *Viburnum prunifolium*

European Smoke-Tree   *Cotinus coggygria*

Crape-Myrtle   *Lagerstroemia indica*

Chaste-Tree   *Vitex agnus-castus*

Red Horse-Chestnut   *Aesculus × carnea*

White Oak, autumn branching

Azaleas and Dogwoods at the National Arboretum

Yoshino Cherry at the Library of Congress

Street Trees (Ginkgo and American Elm)

Pawpaw

Asimina triloba (L.) Dunal • Custard-Apple Family *Annonaceae*

The pawpaw is the only member of the largely tropical custard-apple family that is indigenous to northeastern North America. It serves as the principal larval host plant for the zebra swallowtail butterfly. The butterfly can often be seen flitting near pawpaw groves along the Potomac River.

NATIVE HABITAT AND RANGE Moist woods, streamsides, and riversides; scattered distribution in southern Ontario and eastern U.S. from New York to Florida, west to Nebraska and Texas.

LEAVES Simple, alternate, deciduous. 6 to 12 inches (15–30 cm) long, with a smooth margin, abruptly pointed apex, and wedge-shaped base. Leaves are tropical-looking.

FLOWERS Purple, maroon, or brownish, just before the leaves in spring. Slightly drooping and somewhat bell-like, with two layers of three petals (six in all). (See color close-up.)

FRUIT Greenish yellow banana-like berry, 2 to 5 inches (5–12.7 cm) long. Edible, delicious; favored by humans, bears, raccoons, opossums, and wild turkeys. (I learned from Tony Fleming, a Washington-area geologist currently living in Indiana, that pawpaw is called "Indiana banana" in his adopted state.)

TWIGS Brown, slender, pubescent when young, with reddish brown winter buds. Flower buds are roundish, with reddish hairs. Leaf buds are long and narrow.

GROWTH HABIT Small tree or tall shrub.

SIMILAR SPECIES Easily confused with the umbrella magnolia (*Magnolia tripetala*).

In the absence of flowers or fruit, distinguish the two by twigs. Umbrella magnolia twigs are stout and glabrous, with encircling stipular scars and glabrous winter buds.

LOCATIONS
- Theodore Roosevelt Island
- U.S. Botanic Garden: National Garden and Bartholdi Park
- Smithsonian National Museum of Natural History
- Rock Creek Park
- Potomac River and C&O Canal
- Billy Goat Trail, near Great Falls, Maryland
- Sugarloaf Mountain, Maryland (lower slopes)
- Cultivated in some private yards

Spice-Bush

Lindera benzoin (L.) Blume • Laurel Family *Lauraceae*

Although spice-bush is a shrub, it can reach a height of more than 16 feet (5 m). Its twigs, leaves, and fruit exude a pleasant spicy fragrance when crushed and have been used as a medicinal tea and allspice substitute. Spice-bush is a larval host plant for the spice-bush swallowtail butterfly. It blooms in early spring along local rivers and streams, a cheering sight for the winter-weary.

NATIVE HABITAT AND RANGE   Rich moist woods, streamsides, riversides, and springs; southwestern Maine to southern Ontario, Iowa, and southeastern Kansas, south to Florida and Texas.

LEAVES   Simple, alternate, deciduous. 2 to 6 inches (5–15.2 cm) long. Obovate or oblong-obovate. Base wedge-shaped, narrowed to a short petiole; apex abruptly or gradually pointed. Margin smooth. Glabrous or barely pubescent below.

FLOWERS   Yellow. Tiny individual flowers in dense, rather showy clusters. Early spring, before the leaves.

FRUIT   Small, red, berry-like drupe in autumn (green at first).

TWIGS   Slender, glabrous, brown, with a spicy odor when crushed.

SIMILAR SPECIES   Sassafras (*Sassafras albidum*) also has spicy leaves and twigs, but its leaves are often two- or three-lobed, its fruit is dark blue, and its twigs are greenish and glaucous.

Dogwood (*Cornus*) twigs and leaves have no spicy odor when crushed, and most dogwoods have opposite leaves.

LOCATIONS
- Rock Creek Park
- Potomac River and C&O Canal
- Anacostia River
- Glover Archbold Park
- Theodore Roosevelt Island
- Capital Crescent Trail

Sassafras

Sassafras albidum (Nutt.) Nees • Laurel Family *Lauraceae*

A tree with variable leaves, often unlobed, two-lobed, and three-lobed all on the same tree. Sassafras leaves, twigs, and bark have a pleasant spicy fragrance when crushed. Bark and roots are the source of oil of sassafras, which is used in soaps. Sassafras tea, made from the roots of the tree, has fallen into some disfavor in recent years following the discovery that a component of oil of sassafras may be carcinogenic. This has not dissuaded many of those who swear by sassafras root-bark tea as a spring tonic and blood purifier. Sassafras fruit is eaten by squirrels and songbirds. The tree is one of the larval host plants for the spice-bush swallowtail butterfly.

In 1882, the eminent landscape architect Frederick Law Olmsted, who was in Washington working on the Capitol grounds, wrote: "The Sassafras which, rarely seen except as a shrub in the far north, is here a stout and lofty tree, richly furnished, very sportive in its form of foliage, and often exceeding all other deciduous trees in picturesqueness."

NATIVE HABITAT AND RANGE   Woods, thickets, roadsides, and fields; southern Maine, New Hampshire, and Vermont to northern Florida, west to southeastern Iowa, eastern Kansas, Oklahoma, and Texas.

LEAVES   Simple, alternate, deciduous. 3 to 7½ inches (7.5–19 cm) long. Three major leaf shapes, often all on the same tree: ovate, mitten-like, and three-lobed. Margin smooth, base wedge-shaped. Glabrous or velvety-pubescent beneath, glaucous. Petiole ⅔ to 1⅔ inches (1.5–4.2 cm) long. Autumn color: orange and red.

FLOWERS   Yellowish green. Male and female usually on separate trees. Spring, with the young leaves.

FRUIT   Small, dark blue, berry-like drupe, about ⅓ inch (1 cm) long, on a red or orange stalk, 1½ to 2 inches (3.8–5 cm) long. Late summer and fall.

BARK AND TWIGS   Bark brown or reddish brown and furrowed. Twigs greenish, glaucous, with a spicy odor when broken. Leaf scar with only one bundle scar. Terminal bud present.

GROWTH HABIT   Small to medium-sized tree with a flat or pyramidal crown.

SIMILAR SPECIES   Spice-bush (*Lindera benzoin*) also has spicy-smelling twigs and leaves, but its leaves are never lobed, its fruit is red, and its mature twigs are brown.

LOCATIONS
• Fern Valley, National Arboretum
• Kenilworth Aquatic Gardens
• Rock Creek Park
• C&O Canal, between Georgetown and Great Falls, Maryland
• Arlington National Cemetery
• Private yards in the District

Katsura-Tree

Cercidiphyllum japonicum Sieb. & Zucc. • Katsura-Tree
Family *Cercidiphyllaceae*

Long believed to be monotypic, one of the few trees in the world that is the sole species in its family and genus. In recent years, some authorities have recognized a Japanese variety of Katsura-tree as a second distinct species, giving it the name *Cercidiphyllum magnificum*. According to Michael A. Dirr's *Manual of Woody Landscape Plants,* this separate species (still considered a variety of *C. japonicum* by some authorities) is smaller in stature and has a native range restricted to Japan.

NATIVE RANGE   China, Japan.

LEAVES   Simple, opposite or sub-opposite, deciduous. 2 to 4 inches (5–10 cm) long, 1½ to 3½ inches (3.8–9 cm) wide. Heart-shaped. Palmately veined. Wavy-toothed margin, rounded or bluntly pointed apex, cordate base. Green or bluish green above, pale and slightly glaucous beneath, glabrous. Petiole thin, 1 to 1¾ inches (2.5–4.5 cm) long. Autumn color: brilliant yellow or orange-yellow.

FLOWERS   Male and female on separate trees (dioecious). Small, reddish clusters of stamens (male tree) and red or purple styles (female tree), no petals. Spring, before the leaves.

FRUIT   Small, erect pods on female trees containing thin, winged seeds. Summer to fall.

BARK AND TWIGS   Bark gray, shallowly fissured, may become shaggy with age. Twigs glabrous, with opposite, pointed, brown winter buds on short spur shoots; conspicuous in winter.

GROWTH HABIT   Upright when young. May become multi-trunked with age.

SIMILAR SPECIES   Redbuds (*Cercis canadensis* and *C. chinensis*) have larger, alternate leaves with smooth margins.

LOCATIONS
• Dumbarton Oaks
• Smithsonian Castle: Enid A. Haupt Garden
• U.S. Capitol grounds
• Town of Chevy Chase, Maryland

Sweetgum (Redgum)

Liquidambar styraciflua L. • Witch-Hazel Family
Hamamelidaceae

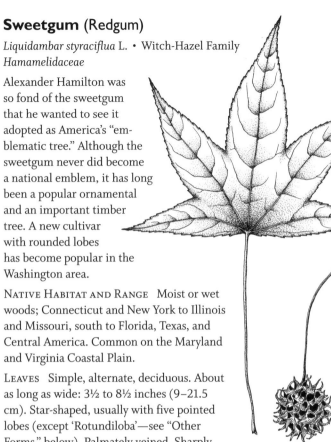

Alexander Hamilton was so fond of the sweetgum that he wanted to see it adopted as America's "emblematic tree." Although the sweetgum never did become a national emblem, it has long been a popular ornamental and an important timber tree. A new cultivar with rounded lobes has become popular in the Washington area.

NATIVE HABITAT AND RANGE   Moist or wet woods; Connecticut and New York to Illinois and Missouri, south to Florida, Texas, and Central America. Common on the Maryland and Virginia Coastal Plain.

LEAVES   Simple, alternate, deciduous. About as long as wide: 3½ to 8½ inches (9–21.5 cm). Star-shaped, usually with five pointed lobes (except 'Rotundiloba'—see "Other Forms," below). Palmately veined. Sharply toothed. Glabrous, but for tufts of hairs in vein axils below. Petiole slender, anywhere from 2 to 7 inches (5–17.7 cm) long. Autumn color: showy, variable, often with several colors on the same tree.

FLOWERS   Male and female on the same tree (monoecious). Inconspicuous yellow-green round heads. Spring, with the leaves.

FRUIT   A striking prickly sphere on a long, slender stalk, containing many beaked, two-seeded capsules. Sphere 1 to 1½ inches (2.5–3.8 cm) in diameter. Often remains on tree through winter, falling from late autumn to early spring. Used for ornamental purposes.

BARK AND TWIGS   Bark gray-brown, thick and furrowed. Twigs often with corky wings.

GROWTH HABIT   Large tree with a tall, full crown.

OTHER FORMS   'Rotundiloba'—a fairly new cultivar—has round-lobed leaves with toothless margins, very unlike the wild, native form of the tree.

SIMILAR SPECIES   Maples (*Acer* species) have opposite leaves and dissimilar fruit. (Although sweetgum leaves are alternate, they may be very closely crowded together.) Plane trees (*Platanus* species) have light-colored peeling bark.

LOCATIONS
- U.S. Capitol grounds
- Constitution Gardens
- National Zoo
- West Potomac Park
- Vietnam Veterans Memorial
- Hillwood Estate
- 12th Street, N.W., near the Mall (round-lobed form)
- Town of Chevy Chase, Maryland (round-lobed form)
- A common native tree, especially on the Coastal Plain

Sweetgum
'Rotundiloba'

The Witch-Hazels

Hamamelis spp. • Witch-Hazel Family *Hamamelidaceae*

Witch-hazels are native to eastern North America and Asia. They bloom in late autumn or late winter to early spring. The flowers of these small trees or shrubs are usually yellow (sometimes reddish), with delicate, ribbon-like petals. (See color close-up.) While some Asian witch-hazels are cultivated in Washington, they rarely attain tree stature and receive only brief mention here. They include Japanese Witch-Hazel (*Hamamelis japonica* Sieb. & Zucc.), Chinese Witch-Hazel (*Hamamelis mollis* Oliv.), and *Hamamelis* × *intermedia* Rehd., a large group of named hybrids of the two. 'Arnold Promise' and 'Aurora' are two of the named hybrids planted at Brookside Gardens in Wheaton, Maryland. The common witch-hazel of Washington-area woodlands blooms in fall. Vernal Witch-Hazel (*Hamamelis vernalis* Sarg.), another native North American witch-hazel that is sometimes cultivated in Washington, blooms from late winter to early spring and is indigenous from Missouri to Louisiana and Oklahoma.

Common Witch-Hazel

Hamamelis virginiana L. • Witch-Hazel Family *Hamamelidaceae*

The branchlets of common witch-hazel were
traditionally favored by water diviners.
Witch-hazel's astringent properties contribute to the well-known liniment, and
American Indians treated sore throats,
colds, and other medical conditions
with witch-hazel tea.

Native Habitat and Range   Woods
and streamsides; eastern United States
and extreme southeastern Canada.

Leaves   Simple, alternate, deciduous.
2 to 6 inches (5–15 cm) long. Leaf blade
is broadly obovate, oblong, or ovate, with a
scallop-toothed margin and unequal base.

Flowers   Pale to bright yellow with four small, spreading,
ribbon-like petals. Each petal ½ to 1 inch long. Flowers borne
in small axillary clusters as the leaves turn gold in autumn and
remain for a time after the leaves have dropped. October to
January.

Fruit   A short, thick, two-beaked capsule that becomes woody
and splits at the top to release seeds. Capsules take about a year
to mature and may remain on the tree for years.

Growth Habit   Large, multi-trunked shrub or small tree with a
broad, rounded crown.

Locations
• National Arboretum
• City gardens
• Potomac River and C&O Canal
• Rock Creek Park and other regional parks
• Sugarloaf Mountain, Maryland

Persian Ironwood (Persian Parrotia)

Parrotia persica C. A. Mey • Witch-Hazel Family *Hamamelidaceae*

Two beautiful specimens of this rare tree stand on the east and
west sides of the White House south lawn.

Native Range   Northern Iran to Caucasus Mountains.

LEAVES   Simple, alternate, deciduous. 2 to 5 inches (5–12.5 cm) long. Oblong-obovate or ovate, with about six to nine pairs of deeply impressed veins. Margin wavy, or with a few coarse teeth above the middle. Petiole short.

BARK   Pinkish or grayish brown, smooth, breaking off in thin flakes to expose paler patches.

GROWTH HABIT   Variable. Trees in Washington have short, wide trunks dividing into many limbs. Although very large, White House specimens look shrubby.

LOCATIONS
• White House, south lawn
• National Arboretum

London Plane Tree

Platanus × *acerifolia* (Ait.) Willd., (*Platanus* × *hybrida* Brot.), (*P. orientalis* × *P. occidentalis*) • Plane Tree Family *Platanaceae*

Widely planted in Washington, New York, Philadelphia, London, Paris, and other cities in the U.S. and Europe. Commonly mistaken for its parents, the American sycamore (*Platanus occidentalis*) and the oriental plane (*Platanus orientalis*). The London plane is the most frequently planted of the three, due to its resistance to disease, drought, and air pollution. According to Michael A. Dirr, author of *Manual of Woody Landscape Plants*: "London Planetree was once touted as a 'Super' tree by many people and was soon overplanted; many diseases have caught up with it and its use should be tempered."[83] Characteristics of the London plane vary a great deal, because it is actually a group of hybrids. Trees planted in the U.S. often closely resemble the American sycamore, while those in Europe tend to display more characteristics of the oriental plane.

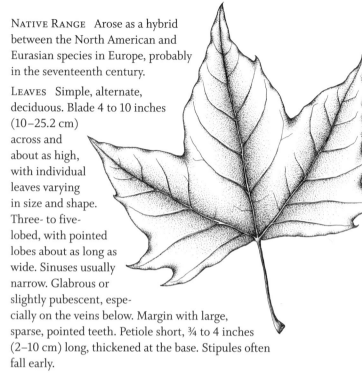

NATIVE RANGE Arose as a hybrid between the North American and Eurasian species in Europe, probably in the seventeenth century.

LEAVES Simple, alternate, deciduous. Blade 4 to 10 inches (10–25.2 cm) across and about as high, with individual leaves varying in size and shape. Three- to five-lobed, with pointed lobes about as long as wide. Sinuses usually narrow. Glabrous or slightly pubescent, especially on the veins below. Margin with large, sparse, pointed teeth. Petiole short, ¾ to 4 inches (2–10 cm) long, thickened at the base. Stipules often fall early.

FLOWERS Males and females in separate round heads on the same tree (monoecious). Late spring.

FRUIT Heads round, brown, bristly, about an inch (2.5 cm) in diameter, hanging on long stalks in pairs or singly (sometimes in threes, especially on younger cultivars). Remaining on the tree until early spring, when individual seeds are scattered by the wind.

BARK AND TWIGS Bark distinctive: creamy white, pale green, or very pale tan on mature trees, often with patches of reddish brown or gray older bark flaking off in jigsaw puzzle–like patterns. Twigs with winter buds hidden by thickened petiole bases in autumn. In winter, leaf scars nearly encircle buds and stipular scars encircle twig. Bud ovoid, covered by a single scale. Terminal bud lacking.

GROWTH HABIT Large tree with a long trunk and tall crown. Very striking in winter with its creamy bark and hanging fruit.

SIMILAR SPECIES Very similar to the American sycamore or plane tree (*Platanus occidentalis*). Leaves of the American sycamore—a tree common along area rivers and streams—usually have shorter, broader lobes. The older bark on the sycamore tends not to peel off as extensively as on the London plane, especially toward the base of the tree, so that the London plane's trunk often looks smoother. American sycamore inner bark tends to be whiter; London plane bark is cream, pale green, or very pale tan. However, the best way to distinguish the two trees is to examine the fruit balls. American sycamore fruits hang singly; London plane fruits hang singly, in pairs, and in threes. Therefore, if a tree has any hanging pairs of fruit (see illustration), it is likely a London plane. The oriental plane (*Platanus orientalis*), frequently mistaken for the London plane, is rare in Washington. It has fruits hanging in pairs and in groups of three or more.

LOCATIONS
• Streets and parks throughout the city and suburbs

Oriental Plane Tree

Platanus orientalis L. • Plane Tree
Family *Platanaceae*

Native to southeastern Europe and western Asia, the oriental plane tree was one of the first trees to be cultivated for shade and orna-ment. The literature of ancient Greece is replete with references to "the shady plane." The oriental plane has frequently been confused with the London plane, and the extent of its cultivation in the U.S. has consequently been overestimated. The tree actually is rare in Washington and other East Coast cities.

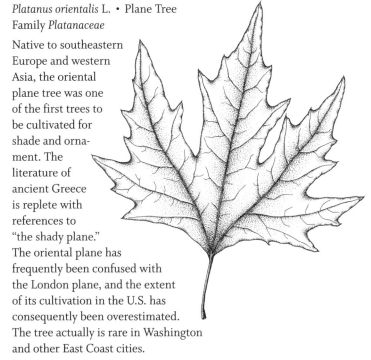

NATIVE RANGE   Southern Europe and western Asia.

Leaves   Similar to London plane (*Platanus* × *acerifolia*), but sinuses are more deeply cut. (See illustrations.)

Fruit   Also similar to London plane, but often with three or more round, bristly fruit balls per stalk.

Locations
• National Arboretum
• University of Maryland campus

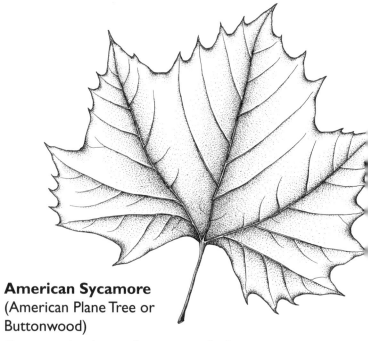

American Sycamore
(American Plane Tree or
Buttonwood)

Platanus occidentalis L. • Plane Tree Family *Platanaceae*

One of the largest trees of the eastern U.S. Common in the wild, but not planted in cities as frequently as the London plane, which has greater resistance to disease, drought, and pollution. The naturally occurring American sycamores along the Potomac River and Rock Creek are especially striking in winter, with their pale branches reflected in the water. American sycamore wood is often used to make butcher blocks.

Native Habitat and Range   Usually moist or wet alluvial soils, common along streams and in river bottoms; southern Maine to southern Ontario and Minnesota, south to Texas and Florida.

Leaves   Simple, alternate, deciduous. Blade 4 to 10 inches (10–25.2 cm) wide and about as long or slightly shorter. Three- to five-lobed, with shallow sinuses and lobes broader than long. Pubescent along the veins below. Margin covered with large, coarse, pointed teeth. Stipules leaf-like and conspicuous. Petiole 1 to 4 inches (2.5–10 cm) long.

Flowers   Males and females on the same tree (monoecious) in round, separate heads. Spring, after the leaves.

Fruit   Round, brown, fruiting head, about an inch (2.5 cm) in diameter. Each fruiting head hangs singly on a long stalk through winter. The heads break up in early spring, and individual seeds are dispersed by wind and water.

Bark and Twigs   Reddish brown and gray outer bark peels off in a jigsaw puzzle–like pattern, revealing white or very pale yellow bark underneath. Outer bark near the base of the tree thicker and breaking into smaller scales. Twigs reddish brown, with conical buds covered by single yellow-brown scale. Stipular scars encircle twig. End buds false.

Growth Habit   Large tree, with a long trunk and spreading crown. American sycamore limbs often stretch out over the water.

Similar Species   See London plane (*Platanus × acerifolia*) "Similar Species."

Locations
- Rock Creek Park
- Capital Crescent Trail
- Anacostia River
- Potomac River and C&O Canal
- Area rivers and streams throughout the region
- Parks and private yards citywide
- Some city streets

The Elms

Elms Native to North America

American Elm (White Elm)

Ulmus americana L. • Elm Family *Ulmaceae*

STATE TREE OF MASSACHUSETTS
AND NORTH DAKOTA

The most architecturally perfect
of all elms, and one of America's
favorite shade trees. Until recently,
the American elm lined the main
streets of cities, towns, and villages
throughout much of the United States.
Unfortunately, Dutch elm disease (a fungus
of European origin carried by the elm-bark
beetle) wreaked havoc on the traditional elm-
lined avenue. However, arborists working for the
National Park Service, the National Arboretum, and the District
of Columbia have helped the American elm stand its ground
in Washington. Working in partnership with the city and the
National Park Service, Casey Trees has planted many young
specimens of the disease-resistant Princeton elm cultivar along
city streets, including Pennsylvania Avenue in front of the White
House. While scientists hold little hope of finding a cure for
Dutch elm disease, they have managed to save many of the city's
historic trees. Meanwhile, new disease-resistant forms of the
American elm continue to be tested here and elsewhere.

One of the city's most historic elms is the Jackson Elm, approximately two hundred years old according to recent estimates. The
tree is located near Dupont Circle in an alley between Q and
Corcoran Streets, N.W., behind a house once owned by Andrew
Jackson.

NATIVE HABITAT AND RANGE   Moist, rich soils, including floodplains; eastern U.S. and southeastern Canada from Newfoundland to Florida, west to Saskatchewan and Texas.

LEAVES   Simple, alternate, deciduous. 2 to 6 inches (5–15 cm)
long. Oblong-ovate or obovate. Sharply and doubly toothed

margin, long-pointed apex, and unequal base. Dark green and smooth or slightly rough above, paler below and pubescent or glabrous. Petiole ¼ to ½ inch (0.6–1.2 cm) long.

FLOWERS   Tiny, reddish, on pendulous stalks. Early spring, before the leaves.

FRUIT   Flattened, papery samara, deeply notched at apex, containing a central seed. Margin hairy. About ½ inch (1.2 cm) long. An important food source for migrating birds in spring.

BARK AND TWIGS   Bark gray, thick, with vertical ridges and fissures. Twigs reddish brown. Winter buds scaly, ¼ inch (0.6 cm) long or more, red or mahogany.

GROWTH HABIT   Very distinctive vase-shaped growth habit with long, graceful, more or less pendulous limbs.

DISTINGUISHING CHARACTERISTICS   Growth habit separates the American elm from other elm species.

LOCATIONS
• The Mall
• U.S. Capitol grounds
• White House grounds
• West Potomac Park and Jefferson Memorial
• 18th Street, N.E., between South Dakota and Montana Avenues
• New Hampshire Avenue, N.W.
• East Capitol Street
• North Carolina Avenue, N.E.
• Madison Place, N.W.
• Alcova Heights (2007–2008 Arlington County Champion American Elm)
• Streets, parks, building grounds, and private yards throughout the city
• Potomac River, Rock Creek Park, and other woodland parks

Other Forms of the American Elm

Princeton Elm

Ulmus americana 'Princeton' • Elm Family *Ulmaceae*

An attractive and at least partially disease-resistant form of the American elm. Casey Trees and its volunteers have planted hundreds of Princeton elms in Washington to replace American elms that have died. The elm was developed at the Princeton Nursery in New Jersey during the 1920s. Its star has risen in recent years due to its resistance to disease and its classic form.

LOCATIONS
• Pennsylvania Avenue, N.W., in front of the White House
• Barracks Row (8th Street, S.E.) on Capitol Hill
• Streets, parks, and public spaces throughout the city

Jefferson Elm

Ulmus americana 'Jefferson' • Elm Family *Ulmaceae*

The original Jefferson elm, from which trees have been cloned, is approximately seventy years old. It grows on the Mall near the Freer Gallery (next to the Smithsonian Castle). The original Jefferson elm has a classically vase-shaped crown and leaves that are early to emerge and late to drop. Clones of the Jefferson elm, selected by Dr. James L. Sherald and tested by the National Park Service and the National Arboretum, have exhibited high levels of tolerance to Dutch elm disease, good drought resistance, and ease of propagation. The original tree is so handsome and vigorous, it is easy to distinguish from many yards away.

LOCATIONS
• The Mall (original tree)
• Franklin Delano Roosevelt Memorial
• Hains Point, East Potomac Park

Other cultivars of the American elm that are planted in Washington include 'Augustine Ascending,' 'Horace Wester' or 'Washington,' 'New Harmony,' and 'Valley Forge.'

Slippery Elm (Red Elm)

Ulmus rubra Muhl. (*U. fulva* Michx.) • Elm Family *Ulmaceae*

A native species of rich eastern North American woods, infrequently cultivated. Similar to the American elm (*Ulmus americana*), but with flowers usually stalkless, fruit pubescent on the seed but not along the margin, and densely pubescent reddish winter buds, especially at the tips. The leaves of the American elm may be slightly roughened above, but the slippery elm has rough, sandpaper-like leaves. The inner bark, with its mucilaginous coating (thus the name slippery elm), was made into a tea used in folk medicine for sore throats and other internal ailments and as an external treatment for wounds, burns, and ulcers.

LOCATIONS
• Area woodlands

Winged Elm (Wahoo or Cork Elm)

Ulmus alata Michx. • Elm Family *Ulmaceae*

The common names winged elm and cork elm refer to the opposite corky wings that usually develop on the twigs of this tree.

NATIVE HABITAT AND RANGE   Variable habitats with moist or dry soils. Virginia to Florida; west to southern Illinois and Indiana; and Missouri, Oklahoma, and Texas.

LEAVES   Simple, alternate, deciduous. 1 to 2½ inches (2.5–6.3 cm) long, coarsely double-toothed. Smooth or slightly roughened above, pubescent below. Petiole very short.

FRUIT   Single-seeded samara, ⅓ inch (less than 1 cm) long, narrowly ovate-elliptic, with two incurved beaks at apex. Fringed at the margin and usually pubescent overall. Spring.

LOCATIONS
• Uncommon in Washington

Cedar Elm

Ulmus crassifolia Nutt. • Elm Family *Ulmaceae*

Similar to the Chinese elm (*Ulmus parvifolia*), and a good example of the close relationship between the flora of the southeastern U.S. and that of parts of China and Japan. The cedar elm differs from the more commonly cultivated Chinese elm in having sandpaper-like leaves, pubescent and less abundant fruit, and light gray, vertically furrowed and scaly bark.

NATIVE HABITAT AND RANGE   Bottomlands, streamsides, and riversides; Arkansas and Mississippi west to Louisiana, Oklahoma, and Texas.

LOCATIONS
• Extremely rare in Washington

Cultivated Elms Not Native to North America

Chinese Elm (Lace-Bark Elm)

Ulmus parvifolia Jacq. • Elm Family *Ulmaceae*

A fall-blooming elm with pale brown and orange bark. Resistant to both Dutch elm disease and the elm-leaf beetle, Chinese elms have been planted throughout the city and suburbs as street trees. Many botanists have become concerned about the tree's invasiveness.

NATIVE RANGE   China, Korea, Japan.

LEAVES   Simple, alternate, deciduous. Small for an elm, ¾ to 2 inches (2–5 cm) long, ½ to ¾ inch (1.2–2 cm) wide. Singly or just barely doubly toothed. Ovate-lanceolate, obovate, or elliptic. Base unequal or nearly equal; apex sharply or bluntly pointed. Shiny green and smooth above, paler below and pubescent when young. Petiole thin, pubescent, about ¼ inch (0.5 cm) long. Nearly evergreen in the southern part of its native range and in warmer parts of the U.S.

FLOWERS   Small, greenish axillary clusters. Late summer and early fall.

FRUIT   Elliptic-ovate, single-seeded samara less than ½ inch (1 cm) long, glabrous. Apex notched. Fall, remaining on the tree until late November or December.

BARK AND TWIGS   Ornamental bark with lacy brown and orange scales. Twigs slender, reddish brown, pubescent, with small, reddish brown buds.

GROWTH HABIT   Graceful, somewhat vase-shaped crown with long, pendulous branches.

SIMILAR SPECIES   The rare fall-blooming cedar elm (*Ulmus crassifolia*) has leaves that are somewhat sandpapery above, very pubescent fruit, and gray, furrowed bark. Siberian elm (*Ulmus pumila*) blooms in spring and has larger, usually long-pointed leaves. It lacks the lacy bark of the Chinese elm.

LOCATIONS
• Library of Congress, southwest grounds
• Dumbarton Oaks

- National Arboretum
- Fessenden Street, N.W., between Wisconsin Avenue and Reno Road
- Duke Street, Old Town Alexandria
- A common street tree in the city and suburbs

Siberian Elm

Ulmus pumila L. • Elm Family *Ulmaceae*

This Asian tree occasionally escapes from cultivation and may be naturalizing in the wild, where it has become invasive in parts of the U.S.

NATIVE RANGE Eastern Siberia, northern China, Manchuria, Korea.

LEAVES Simple, alternate, deciduous. 1 to 3¼ inches (2.5–8.2 cm) long. Elliptic to elliptic-lanceolate. Singly or slightly doubly toothed. Usually long-pointed, equal or nearly equal at the base. Smooth above, glabrous or nearly so below, except when young. Petiole glabrous, ¼ to ½ inch (0.5–1.3 cm) long.

FLOWERS Greenish, short-stalked, in axillary clusters. Spring.

FRUIT Small, nearly round samara, ⅓ to ⅔ inch (1–1.5 cm) long. Single seed just above the middle. Notch closed at apex.

BARK AND TWIGS Bark gray or grayish brown, rough and furrowed. Twigs light brown or gray, soon glabrous, with rounded, red-brown pubescent winter buds.

SIMILAR SPECIES Chinese elm (*Ulmus parvifolia*) has smaller leaves with more abruptly pointed apices and orange-brown, scaly bark. The Chinese elm blooms and fruits in fall.

LOCATIONS
- Soldiers' Home
- Oakridge Avenue, Chevy Chase, Maryland
- Private yards in the city and suburbs

Smooth-Leaved Elm

Ulmus carpinifolia Gleditsch. • Elm Family
Ulmaceae

NATIVE RANGE   Europe, northern Africa,
western Asia.

LEAVES   Simple, alternate, deciduous. 2 to 3½
inches (5–9 cm) long. Elliptic, ovate, or obovate.
Doubly toothed margin. Base very unequal, apex
long-pointed. Bright shiny green and smooth above,
pubescent below in the vein axils and along the midrib. Petiole
pubescent, ¼ to ½ inch (6–12 mm) long.

FLOWERS   Dense red clusters. Stigmas white. Early spring.

FRUIT   Single-seeded samara with a wedge-shaped base and
rounded apex. Seed located near the closed notch at apex.

BARK AND TWIGS   Bark gray or gray-brown with deep, vertical
fissures and ridges. Twigs slender, soon glabrous, light brown.
Winter buds dark red with light brown tips, pubescent.

GROWTH HABIT   Main limbs upright, with arching branches
forming a rounded, usually fairly narrow crown.

OTHER FORMS   *Ulmus carpinifolia* 'Wredei' (golden elm) is a rare
form with golden leaves. *U. carpinifolia* 'Sarniensis' (Jersey elm)
has a narrowly conical form.

SIMILAR SPECIES   English elm (*Ulmus procera*) and American
elm (*Ulmus americana*) have leaves that usually are rough to the
touch above, although American elm leaves may be smooth or
nearly so. See Dutch and Belgian elms (*Ulmus* × *hollandica*).

LOCATIONS
• U.S. Capitol grounds
• Montrose Park
• George Washington Memorial Parkway, south of Alexandria
  near Belle Haven ('Sarniensis')
• Quite rare in Washington

English Elm

Ulmus procera Salisb., (*Ulmus minor* Mill.) • Elm Family *Ulmaceae*

A large elm that looks much like an oak from a distance. A huge English elm that dominated the southeast corner of the U.S. Capitol grounds for many decades was removed during construction of the Capitol Visitor Center during the early part of the twenty-first century. Until 1978, another English elm of the same age and stature stood at the northeast corner of the grounds. It was dubbed the Humility Elm by John F. Kennedy because it forced tall pedestrians who passed under a low-hanging limb (including U.S. senators) to duck their heads.

NATIVE RANGE   Great Britain.

LEAVES   Simple, alternate, deciduous. 1⅔ to 4 inches (4–10 cm) long. Ovate or rounded. Sharply and doubly toothed, with unequal base and abruptly pointed apex. Dark green and rough above, softly pubescent along the veins below. Petiole pubescent, about ¼ inch (4–6 mm) long.

FLOWERS   Dark red, short-stalked. Early spring, before the leaves.

FRUIT   Rounded, notched samara, about ½ inch (1.2 cm) across. Single seed located close to the notch. Notch closed at apex.

BARK AND TWIGS   Bark dark brown, fissured, often cracked into squarish plates. Twigs slender, reddish brown, pubescent. Winter buds darker red-brown, slightly pubescent.

GROWTH HABIT   Straight, massive trunk reaching well into the crown. Healthy trees resemble oaks with their long, full crowns.

SIMILAR SPECIES   Similar to the smooth-leaved elm (*Ulmus carpinifolia*) and some forms of the Dutch elm (*Ulmus × hollandica*). Smooth-leaved elm has leaves that are smooth above. Dutch elm leaves are smooth above or just barely roughened.

LOCATIONS
• Capitol Hill
• Independence Avenue
• Uncommon in Washington
• Goshen Elm, Gaithersburg, Maryland (Maryland's Millennium Tree)

Dutch Elm Group (Dutch, Belgian, Huntingdon, Commelin, and Buisman Elms)

Ulmus × *hollandica* Mill. (*U. glabra* × *U. carpinifolia*) • Elm Family *Ulmaceae*

A large, confusing group of hybrids that are a cross between the Scotch elm (*Ulmus glabra*) and the smooth-leaved elm (*Ulmus carpinifolia*).

LEAVES   Simple, alternate, deciduous. 3 to 6 inches (7.5–15 cm) long. Broadly elliptic or elliptic-ovate. Very unequal at base, often with one side slightly curled forward. Apex abruptly pointed or long-pointed. Coarsely doubly or triply toothed. Smooth or barely roughened above, pubescent below along veins, which stand out prominently. Petiole pubescent, may be slightly pink, less than ½ inch (1 cm) long.

FLOWERS   Red, short-stalked, in dense clusters. Early spring.

FRUIT   Single-seeded, notched samara, with seed touching the notch. Elliptic-obovate, ¾ to 1 inch (2–2.5 cm) long.

BARK AND TWIGS   Bark light and dark gray, vertically furrowed. Young limbs light gray, smooth, with brown and darker gray cracks and ridges. Twigs stout, medium brown, soon glabrous. Winter buds red-brown, shiny, egg-shaped.

GROWTH HABIT   Crown usually rounded (not vase-like). Branches and trunk usually meet at V-shaped angle. Habit varies with different forms of hybrid.

SIMILAR SPECIES   Leaves are larger and wider than smooth-leaved elm (*Ulmus carpinifolia*). English elm (*U. procera*) and Scotch elm (*U. glabra*) have leaves that are rough to the touch. American elm (*U. americana*) leaves are slightly rough to the touch or smooth. Zelkovas (*Zelkova* spp.) have singly toothed leaves.

LOCATIONS
• U.S. Capitol grounds
• The Mall

- Tidal Basin
- Large trees lining the Lincoln Memorial Reflecting Pool (original trees of uncertain origin; replacement trees include U. × hollandica 'Groeneveld,' 'Commelin,' 'Vegeta,' 'Urban,' and 'Homestead.' The latter two are cultivars of especially complex lineage, according to Dr. James L. Sherald, director of the Center for Urban Ecology and chief of natural resources and science for the National Capital Region. See descriptions of 'Commelin' and 'Vegeta.')
- Experimental forms of the Dutch elm planted throughout the city.

Other Trees in the Dutch Elm Group

Belgian Elm

Ulmus × *hollandica* 'Belgica'

This form originated in Belgium and is widely planted in Europe. Leaf narrowly elliptic with a very short petiole.

LOCATIONS
- Rarely planted in Washington

Huntingdon or Chichester Elm

Ulmus × *hollandica* 'Vegeta'

LOCATIONS
- Washington Monument grounds
- Lincoln Memorial Reflecting Pool

Commelin Elm

Ulmus × *hollandica* 'Commelin'

This form has a very upright, narrow crown and smaller leaves.

LOCATIONS
- Tidal Basin
- Lincoln Memorial Reflecting Pool

Buisman Elm

Ulmus × hollandica 'Buisman'

Resistant to Dutch elm disease, but of poor, unattractive habit.

LOCATION
• East Potomac Golf Course

Japanese Elm

Ulmus davidiana var. *japonica* (Rehd.) Nakai [*Ulmus japonica* (Rehd.) Sarg.] • Elm Family *Ulmaceae*

An elm native to Japan and northeast Asia that has so far shown good resistance to Dutch elm disease and the elm-leaf beetle.

LEAVES   Simple, alternate, deciduous. 3 to 4¾ inches (7.5–12 cm) long. Doubly toothed, long-pointed. Sandpaper-like and pubescent above, pubescent below.

FRUIT   Open-notched samara with the seed touching the notch.

LOCATIONS
• Uncommon in Washington

Scotch Elm (Wych Elm)

Ulmus glabra Huds. • Elm Family *Ulmaceae*

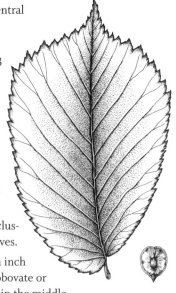

NATIVE RANGE   Northern and central Europe, western Asia.

LEAVES   Simple, alternate, deciduous. Large: up to 7 inches (18 cm) long. Sharply and doubly toothed. Very unequal base, widening slightly toward apex, then ending in an abrupt point. Many leaves have the suggestion of lobing toward the apex. Sandpaper-like above, pubescent below, on a very short, pubescent petiole.

FLOWERS   Purplish red, densely clustered. Early spring, before the leaves.

FRUIT   Large for an elm: up to an inch (2.5 cm) long. Slightly notched, obovate or elliptic samara with a single seed in the middle.

BARK AND TWIGS   Bark smooth for many years, eventually becoming cracked and ridged. Twigs reddish brown with pubescent, red-brown buds.

GROWTH HABIT   Crown broad with arching, nearly horizontal branches.

DISTINGUISHING CHARACTERISTICS   Leaf size and shape separate the Scotch elm from other elms planted in and around the city.

LOCATIONS
• U.S. Capitol grounds
• Fort McNair
• Some private yards and public parks, where it may escape from cultivation

OTHER FORMS   Camperdown Elm (*Ulmus glabra* 'Camperdown'). Dramatically weeping form, with branches reaching almost to the ground.

LOCATIONS
• White House grounds
• Thomas Circle

Zelkova (Japanese Zelkova, Keaki)

Zelkova serrata (Thunb.) Mak. • Elm Family *Ulmaceae*

This tree has been widely planted in the Washington area as a substitute for the American elm in the wake of Dutch elm disease.

NATIVE RANGE   Japan, Korea, Taiwan, Manchuria.

LEAVES   Simple, alternate, deciduous. 2¼ to 4¾ inches (5.5–12 cm) long. Lanceolate-ovate, with long-pointed apex, variable base (rounded, wedge-shaped, straight, or heart-shaped), and up to sixteen pairs of veins. Elm-like, but with sharply pointed single teeth and an equal or nearly equal base. Glabrous or nearly so. Petiole about ¼ to ⅔ inch (0.5–1.5 cm) long. Leaves stay on tree until late fall or early winter.

FLOWERS AND FRUIT   Flowers small, inconspicuous. Greenish females in the leaf axils toward the tips of new branchlets; males clustered in leaf axils toward new branchlet bases. Spring, with the leaves. Fruit is a tiny greenish drupe, ⅛ inch (3–6 mm) long.

BARK AND TWIGS   Bark on young trees gray, smooth, with pinkish horizontal stripes and orange-brown lenticels. Mature trees have attractive orange, brown, and gray scaly bark. Twigs slender, glabrous, reddish brown, and somewhat zigzagged, with small, ovoid, red-brown winter buds.

GROWTH HABIT   Broad, rounded crown with widely spreading branches. Young tree trunks straight, slightly enlarged at base. Older trees have very large trunks and limbs radiating outward not far from the ground.

SIMILAR SPECIES   This zelkova differs from the true elms in having leaves that are always singly toothed and equal or nearly equal at the base, distinctive bark and habit, and fruit that is not a samara. See Caucasian elm (*Zelkova carpinifolia*).

LOCATIONS
• G Street, S.W. (Casey Trees' 2006 D.C. Champion Zelkova)
• U.S. Capitol grounds
• Garfield Park
• Orren Street, N.E.
• Jefferson Memorial
• Franklin Delano Roosevelt Memorial
• Korean War Veterans Memorial
• Hains Point, East Potomac Park
• Independence Avenue, near the Mall
• Streets and parks throughout the city and suburbs

Caucasian Elm (Caucasian Zelkova, Elm Zelkova)

Zelkova carpinifolia (Pall.) K. Koch.   •   Elm Family *Ulmaceae*

The Caucasian elm or Caucasian zelkova is native to the Caucasus Mountains and Caspian Sea coast. It is rare in Washington.

LEAVES   Simple, alternate, deciduous. 1¾ to 4 inches (4.5–10 cm) long. Usually no more than twelve pairs of veins. Similar to Japanese zelkova, but without long-pointed (acuminate) apex (see illustrations), and with fatter, less sharply pointed teeth. Whitish hairs along the veins below. Petiole pubescent.

BARK   Smooth greenish or pinkish gray, scaly, revealing orange underneath.

GROWTH HABIT Strikingly unique: trunk fluted, with many limbs arising from the same level, not far from the ground, to form a large, egg-shaped crown.

LOCATIONS
• The Mall, near the U.S. Capitol Reflecting Pool
• East Potomac Golf Course

Cut-Leaf Zelkova

Zelkova × *verschaffeltii* (Dipp.) Nichols. • Elm Family *Ulmaceae*

A hybrid tree that is extremely rare in Washington. Small leaves, 1¼ to 2½ inches (3–6 cm) long, have five to nine pairs of large, pointed, slightly outcurved teeth. Rough above, pubescent below. Bark is similar to Caucasian elm (*Zelkova carpinifolia*). Twigs and tiny winter buds are reddish brown and pubescent. Large shrub or small tree.

SIMILAR SPECIES Far more common cut-leaf or fern-leaf beech (*Fagus sylvatica* 'Heterophylla') reaches greater heights and has gray, even bark and long, pointed winter buds.

LOCATIONS
• Glenn Dale, Maryland
• Rare in Washington

Schneider's Zelkova

Zelkova schneideriana Hand.-Mazz. • Elm Family *Ulmaceae*

Native to eastern China. Very rare here. Leaves are 1½ to 3½ inches (4–9 cm) long, with fat, incurved teeth and long-pointed apices; softly pubescent below, on a pubescent petiole. Twigs and small winter buds are reddish brown and pubescent.

SIMILAR SPECIES The common Japanese zelkova (*Zelkova serrata*) has glabrous leaves. The rare Caucasian elm (*Z. carpinifolia*) has leaves without long-pointed apices.

LOCATIONS
• Glenn Dale, Maryland
• Rare in Washington

Hackberry (Northern Hackberry or Sugarberry)

Celtis occidentalis L. • Elm Family *Ulmaceae*

Like the beeches, the hackberries have pale gray bark. Hackberry bark is usually marked with conspicuous wart-like protuberances. This tree serves as the larval host plant for several butterfly species: the hackberry emperor, tawny emperor, eastern comma, question mark, mourning cloak, and American snout. Many birds consume the tasty fruit.

NATIVE HABITAT AND RANGE   Usually in moist, rich soils in a variety of habitats, including slopes and bottomlands; southern Quebec to southern Manitoba, south to Georgia, Mississippi, Arkansas, and Oklahoma.

LEAVES   Simple, alternate, deciduous. 2 to 5 inches (5–12.5 cm) long. Ovate. Usually unequal at base, sharply toothed (except near base), and long-pointed. Sometimes sandpaper-like above, but may also be glabrous.

FRUIT   Small, edible, orange-red to purple, berry-like drupe.

GROWTH HABIT   Straight trunk; spreading, sometimes pendulous branches; and a full, rounded crown.

SIMILAR SPECIES   Two other species of hackberry trees are planted in Washington: the Mississippi hackberry (*Celtis laevigata*) and the exotic Chinese hackberry (*C. sinensis*). Brief descriptions of their differing characteristics follow. A shrubby species known as dwarf hackberry (*C. tenuifolia*) is native to the region.

LOCATIONS
• Cedar Hill, Frederick Douglass National Historic Site
• Rock Creek Park and other regional wild places
• Parks, private homes, and public buildings citywide

Mississippi Hackberry (Southern Hackberry, Sugarberry)

Celtis laevigata Willd. • Elm Family *Ulmaceae*

NATIVE HABITAT AND RANGE   Moist and wet soils; southeastern and south-central U.S. and Mexico, north to southern Illinois, Indiana, and Virginia.

LEAVES   Narrower and thinner than the other species planted in Washington. Oblong-lanceolate. Margins entire or with a few teeth.

FRUIT   Small, round, edible, orange-red or yellow drupe.

LOCATIONS
• The Mall
• Rare in Washington

Chinese Hackberry

Celtis sinensis Pers. • Elm Family *Ulmaceae*

The Chinese hackberry has dark-green leaves that are thick, almost leathery in texture. The leaf margin of the species is usually toothed only toward the apex. The dark orange drupe contains a ribbed, pitted stone.

NATIVE RANGE   China, Korea, Japan.

LOCATIONS
• Garfield Park
• A few city parks

White Mulberry

Morus alba L. • Mulberry Family *Moraceae*

This is the tree that nourishes the silkworm. The white mulberry has long been cultivated in Washington, but it readily escapes from cultivation and can become a problematic invasive. The town of Chevy Chase, Maryland, has listed the tree on its undesirable list due to its weak wood and the potential hazards associated with it.

NATIVE RANGE   China. Widely naturalized in Asia, Europe, and America.

LEAVES   Simple, alternate, deciduous. 2 to 4 inches (5–10 cm) long. Ovate. Variably lobed or unlobed. Coarsely toothed, often with bluntly pointed teeth. Base rounded or cordate, sometimes slightly oblique (not even). Usually smooth above, glabrous below or pubescent only along the veins.

FRUIT   The familiar mulberry shape. ⅓ to 1 inch (1–2.5 cm) long; white, pinkish, or purple.

OTHER FORMS   Many forms of the white mulberry are in cultivation in Washington. Particularly striking is the weeping form (*Morus alba* 'Pendula'), with long, slender, vertically hanging branches.

SIMILAR SPECIES   The other mulberry species cultivated in Washington and the paper mulberry (*Broussonetia papyrifera*) have leaves that are pubescent below.

LOCATIONS
• Washington Monument (two magnificent old trees)
• National Zoo
• Soldiers' Home
• Common throughout the D.C. area, both in cultivation and as an escape

Red Mulberry

Morus rubra L. • Mulberry Family *Moraceae*

The native red mulberry has leaves that are similar to the exotic white mulberry (*Morus alba*). However, red mulberry leaves are usually at least slightly rough above and pubescent below. The red mulberry leaf is not nearly as rough above as the paper mulberry (*Broussonetia papyrifera*); the paper mulberry can also be distinguished by its roughly pubescent twigs. Red mulberry fruit is purple and sweet.

NATIVE HABITAT AND RANGE   Rich woods, common on floodplains; New England to Minnesota, south to Florida and Texas.

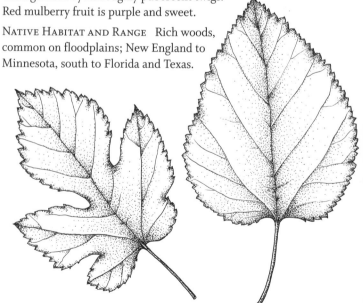

LOCATIONS
- National Arboretum
- Kenilworth Aquatic Gardens
- Common throughout the city
- Rock Creek Park, Potomac and Anacostia Rivers
- Powhatan Springs Park (2007–2008 Arlington County Champion Red Mulberry)

Paper Mulberry

Broussonetia papyrifera (L. Vent.) •
Mulberry Family *Moraceae*

The bark of this tree is used to make paper in Japan.

NATIVE RANGE China, Japan. Naturalized in the eastern U.S. and invasive in places.

LEAVES Simple, alternate, deciduous. Occasionally leaves are arranged oppositely. 3 to 8 inches (7.5–20 cm) long. Heart-shaped or with a rounded base. Lobed or unlobed, with coarse, outwardly pointed teeth. Rough above, grayish green, soft- and velvety-pubescent below. Petiole pubescent.

FLOWERS AND FRUIT Male catkins and round female flower clusters on separate trees. Fruit ripens round and orange-red on female trees.

BARK AND TWIGS Bark gray, smooth. Twigs stout, roughly pubescent.

SIMILAR SPECIES Red and white mulberries (*Morus* spp.).

LOCATIONS
- National Zoo
- C&O Canal, Georgetown
- Common throughout the city, and naturalized in area woodlands

Osage-Orange ("Bodarc," Hedge-Apple)

Maclura pomifera (Raf.) C. K. Schneid. • Mulberry Family *Moraceae*

Native to the home of the Osage Indians, who used the wood to make archery bows. The French name that consequently arose, "bois d'arc" (bow wood), became "bodarc" or "bodock" in parts of the south-central U.S. This name is still used today. The tree yields a yellow dye.

NATIVE HABITAT AND RANGE   Lowlands, including rich bottomlands; northern Texas, southwestern Arkansas, southeastern Oklahoma. Now naturalized in parts of the East.

LEAVES   Simple, alternate, deciduous. 2 to 6 inches (5–15 cm) long. Ovate. Margin smooth. May be wedge-shaped, rounded, or slightly cordate at base. Long-pointed apex. Shiny green above, paler below and glabrous at maturity. Petiole 1 to 2½ inches (2.5–5.5 cm) long. Autumn color: clear light yellow.

FLOWERS   Small, greenish, clustered. Males and females on separate trees. Late spring.

FRUIT   Female trees only. Large, round, yellow-green. Surface finely convoluted, like that of a brain. Vaguely resembles an orange, hence the name of the tree. May reach grapefruit size. Contains a bitter milky juice.

BARK AND TWIGS   Bark a distinctive dark orange-brown, irregularly ridged and furrowed. Sap milky. Twigs with stout thorns, ½ to ¾ inch (1–2 cm) long. Winter buds small, rounded, depressed; terminal bud absent.

GROWTH HABIT   Few branches forming an irregular crown.

SIMILAR SPECIES   From a distance it may be mistaken for a mulberry (*Morus* spp.). However, the combination of smooth-margined leaves, orange-brown bark, and unusual fruit set the osage-orange apart.

LOCATIONS
- Soldiers' Home (huge, ancient tree next to the Lincoln Cottage)
- Montrose Park
- U.S. Capitol grounds
- Maret School
- Seneca Creek State Park, Maryland

Common Fig

Ficus carica L. • Mulberry Family
Moraceae

This fig has long
been cultivated in
Europe and North
America for its fruit.
Most other members
of the genus *Ficus* are
hardy only in or near the
tropics.

NATIVE RANGE   Western
Asia, eastern Mediterra-
nean.

LEAVES   Simple, alternate, and,
unlike most members of the genus, deciduous. 4 to 8 inches (10–20 cm) long,
3½ to 7½ inches (9–19 cm) wide. Three
to five narrow lobes separated by deep
sinuses. Margin with large, rounded or
bluntly pointed teeth. Yellow-white veins
prominent, palmately arranged. Rough to
the touch above and below. Petiole 2 to 4
inches (5–10 cm) long.

FLOWERS   Borne inside a fleshy receptacle that later develops
into the fruit.

FRUIT   The familiar fig. Pear-shaped; greenish or brownish
purple when ripe in fall.

GROWTH HABIT   Spreading shrub or small tree.

LOCATIONS
- Dumbarton Oaks
- Gardens and backyards throughout the city and suburbs

American Beech

Fagus grandifolia Ehrh. • Beech Family *Fagaceae*

A magnificent native forest and shade tree.

NATIVE HABITAT AND RANGE   Rich woodland soils; New Brunswick to southern Ontario, south to northern Florida, eastern Texas, and Mexico.

LEAVES   Simple, alternate, deciduous. 2 to 4½ inches (5–11.5 cm) long. Ovate-elliptic. Nine or more pairs of veins, very straight, pinnately arranged. One sharp tooth at each point where vein meets leaf margin. Apex pointed. Base rounded or wedge-shaped, may be unequal. Sometimes slightly pubescent below, especially when young. Petiole glabrous or barely pubescent, less than ½ inch (0.5–1 cm) long. Wheat-colored leaves often remain on tree during winter.

FLOWERS   Male and female on the same tree (monoecious). Males yellowish, numerous, in hanging round clusters; two to four females in a spike at end of twig. Spring, with the leaves.

FRUIT   Two or three edible, triangular nuts, each ¾ inch (2 cm) or less long, enclosed by a prickly husk. In fall, the husk opens and releases the nuts, which are a favorite food of squirrels, raccoons, black bears, ruffed grouses, and wild turkeys.

BARK AND TWIGS   Bark pale gray, smooth (the favorite tree of lovers and other carvers of initials). Twigs slender, with long, pointed, distinctive reddish brown buds.

GROWTH HABIT   Straight trunk with many limbs forming a full, rounded crown. A striking winter tree with its silvery limbs, handsome form, and persistent wheat-colored leaves.

SIMILAR SPECIES   Very similar to the European beech (*Fagus sylvatica*). The best way to distinguish the two is to count the leaf veins (see "Leaves" for each species). The only other mature trees with similar bark commonly planted in Washington are the hackberries (*Celtis* spp.) and yellowwood (*Cladrastis kentukea*). Hackberry bark is warty in places. Yellowwood has pinnately compound leaves and naked winter buds.

LOCATIONS
• U.S. Capitol grounds
• Dumbarton Oaks

- Montrose Park
- 4000 Cathedral Avenue, N.W. (Casey Trees' 2006 D.C. Champion American Beech)
- Meridian Hill Park
- Capital Crescent Trail
- Sligo Creek Parkway, Takoma Park, Maryland
- Rock Creek Park
- Wheaton Regional Park
- Sugarloaf Mountain, Maryland
- Gulf Branch Park (2007–2008 Arlington County Champion American Beech)
- Common throughout the city, suburbs, and local woodlands

European Beech

Fagus sylvatica L. • Beech Family *Fagaceae*

The European beech is widely planted in Washington. Three different forms of the tree are also popular here: copper (or purple) beech, fern-leaf (or cut-leaf) beech, and weeping beech. (See "Other Forms of the European Beech," below.)

NATIVE RANGE   Europe.

LEAVES   Simple, alternate, deciduous. 2 to 4½ inches (5–11.5 cm) long. Ovate-elliptic. Eight or fewer pairs of veins. Margin wavy, or with one blunt tooth at each point where vein meets margin. Base usually wedge-shaped and often slightly unequal; apex bluntly or sharply pointed. Buff pubescence below, especially in vein axils. Petiole pubescent, ½ inch (1.5 cm) or more long. Autumn color: yellow, orange, late in the season [after the American beech (*Fagus grandifolia*) has lost its leaves].

FLOWERS   Male and female flowers on the same tree (monoecious). Males in hanging, pale yellow, rounded clusters; females fewer, on short stalks. Spring, with the leaves.

FRUIT   Edible, triangular nut, enclosed by a prickly husk about 1 inch (2.5 cm) long. Husks open, releasing the nuts, which are popular with squirrels and other wildlife.

BARK AND TWIGS   Bark gray, smooth or slightly roughened. Twigs with striking winter buds: long and narrow, scaly, reddish brown at base, light yellow-brown toward the sharply pointed tip.

GROWTH HABIT   Large tree with a very rounded crown and short trunk.

SIMILAR SPECIES   The American beech (*F. grandifolia*) has leaves with nine or more pairs of veins, paler bark, and slightly smaller fruit husks.

LOCATIONS
• Along the Potomac Parkway between the Lincoln Memorial and the Kennedy Center
• The Ellipse

Other Forms of the European Beech

Copper Beech (Purple Beech)

Fagus sylvatica f. *purpurea* (Ait.) Schneid.

Leaves coppery green or deep purple.

LOCATIONS
• Folger Park
• Dumbarton Oaks (large tree near amphitheatre)
• Rock Creek Cemetery
• Soldiers' Home
• Smithsonian National Museum of Natural History

Fern-Leaf Beech (Cut-Leaf Beech)

Fagus sylvatica 'Heterophylla' or 'Asplenifolia'

Leaves narrow, deeply cut, like small oak leaves.

LOCATIONS
• White House grounds (trees on Pennsylvania Avenue side planted by Lady Bird Johnson and Patricia Nixon)
• Library of Congress grounds (memorial tree)

Weeping Beech

Fagus sylvatica f. *pendula* (Loud.) Schelle

Branches pendulous. Tree may be tall and narrow, or full and rounded.

LOCATIONS
• Private yards throughout the city and suburbs

Chinese Chestnut

Castanea mollissima Bl. • Beech Family *Fagaceae*

The Chinese chestnut holds an ignominious distinction: it was the probable source of the Asian fungus responsible for the tragic chestnut blight. During the twentieth century, the blight destroyed the magnificent stands of American chestnuts (*Castanea dentata*) that once dominated forests throughout the eastern United States. Ironically, the Chinese chestnut itself is immune to the blight and is therefore planted extensively in the Washington area. However, it is a poor substitute in stature for the good old American chestnut.

NATIVE RANGE   China, Korea.

LEAVES   Simple, alternate, deciduous. 3 to 7 inches (7.5–17.8 cm) long. Oblong-lanceolate or oblong-elliptic. Rounded, squared, or wedge-shaped base; gradually or abruptly pointed apex. Margin has coarse, sharply pointed teeth. Dark glossy green above, whitish or pale green below and often softly pubescent.

FLOWERS   Male flowers in showy yellow or cream-colored catkins, 4 to 9 inches (10–22.8 cm) long. Late spring and early summer.

FRUIT   Painfully prickly bur, 1 to 2½ inches (2.5–6.3 cm) across; splits to release one to three edible chestnuts. Each nut less than 1 inch (2.5 cm) across, chestnut brown, with a pale scar across the base. Early autumn.

BARK AND TWIGS   Bark furrowed. Twigs pubescent, sometimes with long, spreading hairs.

GROWTH HABIT   Small tree with widely spreading branches.

SIMILAR SPECIES   The American chestnut (*Castanea dentata*) only occasionally reaches tree proportions, because of the blight. The only common ornamental in Washington that the Chinese chestnut is apt to be confused with is the saw-toothed oak (*Quercus acutissima*). The oak has a similar leaf, but each of its teeth ends in a long bristle-tip. During autumn the trees can be readily distinguished by their fruit.

LOCATIONS
• Lincoln Park
• Parks, streets, public buildings, and private homes

American Chestnut

Castanea dentata Borkh. • Beech Family *Fagaceae*

Although foreign trees and other non-native plants have enhanced the beauty of towns and cities throughout the country, exotic plants can harbor pests and diseases for which our domestic flora have no immunity. During the twentieth century, the elm-bark beetle arrived uninvited from Europe (probably on a shipment of elm logs), bringing the disease that was to denude American elm–lined avenues throughout the country. But even before Dutch elm disease began its relentless trail of destruction, an even more insidious foreign blight nearly destroyed the American chestnut, one of the most beautiful and important deciduous trees of the eastern United States. Victim of an Asian fungus probably imported on seedlings of Chinese and Japanese chestnuts, the American chestnut was a dominant tree of eastern forests for centuries. It now is rarely able to survive for more than a few years.

In 2003, I wrote in the *Washington Post*:

> A century ago, arboreal giants crowned the hills and mountains west of Washington. Lofty American chestnuts, up to 110 feet tall and five or more feet in diameter, towered over neighboring trees throughout the Appalachians. There were an estimated 4 billion American chestnut trees from Alabama to Maine, and they not only defined the forest but the lives of our ancestors.
>
> When the chestnut trees bloomed in early summer, the Appalachians appeared dusted with snow. During autumn, a nutritious crop of nuts rained down, to the delight of animals—domestic and wild—and the people who gathered and stored them for winter.
>
> Chestnuts also served as a lucrative cash crop. Street vendors sold them freshly roasted on city blocks throughout the East, a tradition that would provide the opening lyrics for a popular Christmas song. The rot-resistant wood of these tall, straight trees was a favorite choice for homes, fences, railroad ties, telegraph poles and furniture.[84]

The chestnut blight began killing trees in the northeastern states soon after the turn of the twentieth century. The fungus *Cryphonectria parasitica* (formerly known as *Endothia parasitica*) attacks the bark of the American chestnut, creating a spreading canker that eventually encircles the tree, cutting off the flow of nutrients. The blight spreads rapidly; by the middle of the century, it had killed virtually every mature chestnut in the East.

Although science has found no cure for the disease, the story of the American chestnut is not over. The roots of the tree are not destroyed by the fungus, and they persist in sending up new sprouts, year after year, although these eventually succumb to the blight. Two major organizations in the U.S. are trying to bring back the American chestnut, one by propagating the most disease-resistant native trees, and the other through a promising program of back-cross breeding in which the Chinese chestnut is crossed with the American chestnut to give it blight resistance. Subsequent generations are American-bred exclusively. It is hoped that the progeny of this experimental breeding program will have the stature of the American chestnut and the blight resistance of the Chinese tree.

NATIVE HABITAT AND RANGE   Piedmont and mountains; Maine, New York, and southeastern Michigan to Georgia and northeastern Mississippi.

LEAVES   Simple, alternate, deciduous. 5 to 9 inches (12.6–22.8 cm) long. Oblong-lanceolate to oblong-elliptic. Margin sharply toothed. Base wedge-shaped, apex abruptly or gradually pointed. Yellow-green above and below, glabrous. May have tiny glands below when young.

FLOWERS   Males in yellowish green or cream-colored catkins, 4 to 10 inches (10–25.3 cm) long. Late spring and early summer.

FRUIT   Two to three edible nuts, ½ to 1 inch (1.3–2.5 cm) long, contained in a sharply spiny bur.

GROWTH HABIT   Tall tree with a broad, open crown. Blighted plants are rarely more than shrubs or small trees, but a few manage to grow fairly tall.

SIMILAR SPECIES   The Chinese chestnut (*Castanea mollissima*) is the chestnut most commonly planted in Washington since the advent of the blight. Its leaves are whitish or pale green below and often softly pubescent. The chinquapin [*Castanea pumila* (L.) Mill.], which is not included in this guide, is a native shrub (occasionally a small tree) with leaves that are whitish and pubescent below, with short, coarse teeth. The rare Japanese chestnut (*Castanea crenata* Sieb. & Zucc.), also not included, has leaves that are usually pubescent below, at least along the veins.

LOCATIONS
- Smithsonian National Museum of Natural History (two trees planted in 2006 on the spring equinox)
- U.S. Department of Agriculture, the Mall (dedicated to Secretary Ann M. Veneman on the U.S. Forest Service Centennial, spring 2005)
- Glencarlyn Park (2007–2008 Arlington County Champion American Chestnut)
- Regional parks (young trees that usually succumb to the blight)
- Sugarloaf Mountain, Maryland (wild trees and cultivated specimens that are part of experimental plantings)

The White Oak Group

Leaves with lobes that are not bristle-tipped, and acorns maturing at the end of one growing season. (Compare to Red and Black Oak Group, page 237.) Oaks serve as larval host plants for Horace's, juvenal, and sleepy duskywing butterflies.

White Oaks Native to North America

White Oak

Quercus alba L. • Beech Family *Fagaceae*

STATE TREE OF CONNECTICUT, MARYLAND, AND ILLINOIS

The white oak has long been a friend to humankind, both as a shade tree and as an important source of hardwood. The acorns of this and other white oak species are edible after boiling to remove tannin. A protein-rich meal traditionally was made from the crushed, ground acorns and used in baked goods. The acorns are an important food source for wildlife, including white-tailed deer, squirrels, raccoons, wild turkeys, and quails. White oak wood is used in the construction of flooring, furniture, barrels, and ships. Some of Washington's ancient white oaks are older than the city itself, dating back to the eighteenth century.

NATIVE HABITAT AND RANGE   A variety of habitats including upland woods; grows best in deep, rich, well-drained soils. Eastern U.S. and southeastern Canada from Maine and southern Quebec to Minnesota, south to eastern Texas and northern Florida.

LEAVES   Simple, alternate, deciduous. 3½ to 9 inches (9–22.8 cm) long. Some leaves have narrow lobes separated by sinuses cut almost to the midrib; others have wider lobes and sinuses cut only about halfway to the midrib. Five to nine rounded lobes; lobes point forward and sometimes have one or more large, rounded teeth. Base wedge-shaped or slightly rounded. Pubescent at first, soon becoming glabrous; very pale and sometimes slightly glaucous below. Petiole ¼ to 1 inch (0.5–2.5 cm) long. Autumn color: deep wine-red some years. Dry leaves often remain on the tree through winter.

FRUIT   Acorn, maturing during the first year. Sessile or short-stalked. ½ to 1 inch (1.3–2.5 cm) long, enclosed for about one-quarter of its length by a bowl-shaped cup covered with thickened scales.

BARK AND TWIGS   Bark pale ash-gray, with shaggy vertical scales, sometimes slightly furrowed. Twigs reddish brown or gray, glabrous or nearly so when mature (greenish or reddish and may be hairy when young), with scaly, reddish brown, ovoid or nearly round winter buds.

GROWTH HABIT   Large tree with a full, rounded crown. Woodland trees tall and straight; trees grown in the open may have a short, wide trunk and broadly spreading limbs.

SIMILAR SPECIES   May be confused with other trees in the white oak group. (See illustrations.)

LOCATIONS
- Montrose Park and Dumbarton Oaks
- Tudor Place, Georgetown
- Arlington National Cemetery
- Meridian Hill Park
- Cleveland Park
- Logan Circle
- Franciscan Monastery
- Hains Point, East Potomac Park
- U.S. Capitol grounds
- Rock Creek Park and Carter Barron Amphitheatre
- Capital Crescent Trail
- Parks, cemeteries, private yards, and public building grounds throughout the city and suburbs

HISTORIC WHITE OAK LOCATIONS
- Northampton Street, N.W. (Casey Trees' 2006 D.C. Champion Tree of all species)
- Glebe Oak, Rock Creek Cemetery (historic tree gone)
- Lincoln Oak, Fort Lincoln Cemetery (historic tree gone)
- Cedar Hill, Frederick Douglass National Historic Site
- Presidential trees, the White House
- U.S. Department of Agriculture, the Mall (tree dedicated to Hillary Rodham Clinton, December 15, 1999)
- Ancient white oak, Vice President's Residence (historic tree gone)
- Capitol grounds memorial trees, including white oak planted by Speaker of the House Sam Rayburn and young seedling of the famous Wye Oak of Wye Mills, Maryland, killed during a storm on June 6, 2002
- Rockville Pike and Beach Drive, between Bethesda and Rockville, Maryland (historic Linden Oak)

Bur Oak (Mossycup Oak)

Quercus macrocarpa Michx. •
Beech Family *Fagaceae*

A tall, handsome tree with
large, mossy-cupped acorns.

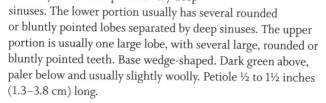

NATIVE HABITAT AND
RANGE A variety of
habitats, including bottomlands; scattered distribution
throughout the East Coast
states from Maine to Vir-
ginia; southeastern Canada,
Pennsylvania, Kentucky, Tennessee, and parts of Alabama; west
to Texas, Nebraska, the Dakotas, and
eastern Saskatchewan.

LEAVES Simple, alternate, deciduous. 4 to 10 inches (10–25 cm)
long. Shape varies considerably. Leaf
usually divided at the middle or just
below by one or two pairs of very deep
sinuses. The lower portion usually has several rounded
or bluntly pointed lobes separated by deep sinuses. The upper
portion is usually one large lobe, with several large, rounded or
bluntly pointed teeth. Base wedge-shaped. Dark green above,
paler below and usually slightly woolly. Petiole ½ to 1½ inches
(1.3–3.8 cm) long.

FRUIT Large acorn, maturing in one year. Sessile or short-
stalked. Broadly ovoid, ¾ to 2 inches (2–5 cm) long, enclosed for
one- to two-thirds of its length by a thick, bowl-shaped cup, with
the lower scales forming a distinctive fringed margin.

BARK AND TWIGS Bark grayish brown, thick, deeply furrowed
and scaly. Twigs stout, gray or yellowish brown, often developing
corky wings. Winter buds pubescent.

GROWTH HABIT Medium-sized to tall tree with large limbs
forming a broad, rounded crown.

SIMILAR SPECIES The fruit is distinctive; in its absence, however, the tree may be confused with other members of the white
oak group. (See illustrations.)

LOCATIONS
- Hains Point, East Potomac Park
- U.S. Department of Agriculture, the Mall (large mature tree dedicated to Martin Luther King Jr., January 14, 1983)
- Meridian Hill Park
- Montrose Park
- U.S. Capitol Reflecting Pool (Casey Trees' 2006 D.C. Champion Bur Oak and Witness Tree Protection Program specimen)
- U.S. Capitol grounds
- Soldiers' Home
- Fairly commonly planted throughout the city

Post Oak

Quercus stellata Wangenh. •
Beech Family *Fagaceae*

A small to large tree that grows in native woodlands but is infrequently cultivated. A historic post oak stands next to John F. Kennedy's gravesite in Arlington National Cemetery.

NATIVE HABITAT AND RANGE   A variety of habitats, including dry upland woods and rocky outcrops; extreme southern New England and New York, south to central Florida, west to Texas, Oklahoma, and southern Iowa.

LEAVES   Simple, alternate, deciduous. 3 to 7 inches (7.5–17.8 cm) long. Shape varies, but leaf usually has five rounded major lobes and a few large, rounded teeth. The pairs of lobes on either side of the end lobe are the longest, giving the leaf a vaguely cross-like look. Base wedge-shaped. Dark green above, paler below and usually pubescent.

FRUIT   Reddish brown acorn, maturing in one year. Sessile or short-stalked. ½ to ¾ inch (1.3 to 2 cm) long, enclosed for one-third to one-half of its length by a bowl-shaped cup.

BARK   Grayish brown, furrowed.

LOCATIONS
- Arlington National Cemetery (historic Kennedy tree)
- National Arboretum

- Regional woodlands
- Parks, cemeteries, private homes, and some public buildings throughout the city and suburbs
- Town of Chevy Chase, Maryland (2005 Montgomery County Champion Post Oak)
- North 11th Street, Arlington (Virginia State Champion Post Oak)

Overcup Oak

Quercus lyrata Walter • Beech Family *Fagaceae*

NATIVE HABITAT AND RANGE   Coastal Plain swamps and wet woods; New Jersey to northern Florida and eastern Texas, north in the Mississippi River drainage area to southern Illinois and Indiana.

LEAVES   Simple, alternate, deciduous. 3 to 8 inches (7.5–20.2 cm) long. Variably and irregularly lobed, with rounded or pointed lobes and teeth. The lowest pair(s) of lobes is usually small and triangular and separated from the upper lobes by deep, often squarish sinuses. The pairs of lobes on either side of the terminal one are usually widest, giving the leaf a top-heavy appearance. The terminal lobe itself is frequently three-lobed. Glabrous and dark green above, felty-pubescent or glabrous below.

FRUIT   The tree's common name refers to the acorn cup, which almost entirely encloses the sessile or short-stalked acorn, ½ to 1 inch (1.3–2.5 cm) long.

SIMILAR SPECIES   May be confused with post (*Quercus stellata*) and bur (*Q. macrocarpa*) oaks. (See illustrations.)

LOCATIONS
- National Gallery of Art
- Soldiers' Home
- Some parks, private homes, and public buildings
- C&O Canal Bear Island (2007 Maryland State Champion Overcup Oak)

Swamp White Oak

Quercus bicolor Willd. • Beech Family
Fagaceae

NATIVE HABITAT AND RANGE   Wet
soils, floodplains; Quebec to Minnesota, south to North Carolina
and Arkansas.

LEAVES   Simple, alternate,
deciduous. 4 to 9 inches (10–23
cm) long, 2 to 4 inches (5–10
cm) wide. Shape variable:
unlobed, with large, rounded or
bluntly pointed teeth; or with a few
shallow, irregular, bluntly pointed or
rounded lobes. Leaf gradually narrows
to wedge-shaped or rounded base. Dark
green above, paler below with felt-like
pubescence.

FRUIT   Acorn, maturing in one year. ¾ to 1¼ inches (2–3.2 cm)
long, on a long stalk, 1 to 4 inches (2.5–10 cm) in length. Enclosed for about one-third of its length by a thick, scaly, slightly
fringed cup.

BARK   Furrowed, with scaly ridges. Scales sometimes curl back.

SIMILAR SPECIES   May be confused with other trees in the white
oak group. However, the English oak (*Quercus robur*) is the only
other oak with such long acorn stalks commonly planted locally.
(See illustrations.)

LOCATIONS
• U.S. Capitol grounds
• Meridian Hill Park
• Montrose Park (Witness Tree Protection Program specimen)
• Garfield Park
• Other parks, public buildings, and private yards citywide
• Northwest Branch Stream Valley Park (Montgomery County
  2007 Champion Swamp White Oak)
• Bluemont Park (2007–2008 Arlington County Champion
  Swamp White Oak)

Chestnut Oak

Quercus montana Willd. (*Quercus prinus* L.) • Beech Family *Fagaceae*

A native oak that is common in the Washington area, both in cultivation and in the wild.

NATIVE HABITAT AND RANGE   Rocky, sandy, or rich woodlands. Common in the Appalachians and Piedmont, but also on the Coastal Plain except in the southern part of its range; Maine to southern Illinois, south to northern Georgia, Alabama, and Mississippi.

LEAVES   Simple, alternate, deciduous. 4 to 9 inches (10–22.8 cm) long. Somewhat leathery, usually widest above the middle, with large, rounded or bluntly pointed teeth or shallow lobes. Base wedge-shaped or rounded, apex bluntly pointed. Dark green or yellowish green above, paler and usually finely pubescent below. Petiole ½ to 1½ inches (1.3–3.8 cm) long.

FRUIT   Acorn maturing in one year. Short-stalked, ¾ to 1½ inches (2–3.8 cm) long. Enclosed for one-quarter to one-half of its length by a thin, bowl-shaped cup, with scales pressed close to cup except at their tips.

BARK AND TWIGS   Bark on mature trees dark, thick, with chunky broken ridges and valleys. Twigs reddish or orange-brown with reddish or orange-brown winter buds.

GROWTH HABIT   Medium-sized to large tree with a broad, open crown.

SIMILAR SPECIES   Very similar to the basket or swamp chestnut oak (*Quercus michauxii*), uncommon in Washington.

LOCATIONS
• Vice President's Residence
• Cedar Hill, Frederick Douglass National Historic Site

- Soldiers' Home
- 1300 Lawrence Street, N.E.
- Fern Valley, National Arboretum
- Potomac River
- Rock Creek Park and other regional woodland parks
- Common throughout the city and outlying areas
- Bluemont Park (2007–2008 Arlington County Champion Chestnut Oak)
- Sugarloaf Mountain, Maryland

Basket Oak (Swamp Chestnut Oak)

Quercus michauxii Nutt. (*Quercus prinus* L.) • Beech Family
Fagaceae

This tree is uncommonly planted in the District of Columbia, although it is native to the nearby Coastal Plain.

NATIVE HABITAT AND RANGE   Bottomlands and near streams, swamps, and ponds; Coastal Plain and southern Piedmont, New Jersey to Florida, west to eastern Texas, north in the Mississippi River Valley to southern Illinois and Indiana.

LEAVES   Very much like the chestnut oak, but usually with larger, more deeply cut teeth that often are abruptly pointed or mucronate.

FRUIT   Acorn cup with wedge-shaped scales attached only at the base.

Chestnut Oak
leaf margin

Basket Oak
leaf margin

LOCATIONS
- Tidal Basin (eastern side, near highway)
- C&O Canal (2007 Montgomery County Co-champion Basket Oak)
- Blockhouse Point Conservation Park (2007 Montgomery County Co-champion Basket Oak) and other Washington-area parks (especially in moist areas)

Chinquapin Oak (Yellow Oak)

Quercus muehlenbergii Engelm. • Beech Family
Fagaceae

NATIVE HABITAT AND RANGE   Upland,
chiefly alkaline soils; northwestern Vermont to northwestern Florida (excluding
the Coastal Plain), west to Texas and
eastern Nebraska.

LEAVES   Simple, alternate, deciduous.
3 to 7 inches (7.5–17.8 cm) long. Margin
with large, pointed, gland-tipped teeth that
often are slightly incurved. Lustrous dark
green or yellow-green above, paler and pubescent below. Petiole ¾ to 1½ inches (2–3.8 cm)
long.

FRUIT   Sessile or short-stalked acorn, maturing in
one year. Ovoid or nearly round, ½ to ¾ inch (1.3–2 cm) long,
enclosed for about one-half of its length by a pubescent cup.

BARK   Pale gray, thin, shallowly and irregularly furrowed or
scaly.

SIMILAR SPECIES   The far more common chestnut oak (*Quercus
montana*) has slightly larger leaves with rounded or bluntly
pointed teeth and thick, dark, deeply furrowed bark. The uncommon basket oak (*Q. michauxii*) also has larger leaves. (See
illustrations.)

LOCATIONS
• The Mall, near the U.S. Capitol Reflecting Pool
• National Zoo
• Theodore Roosevelt Island
• Not common in and near Washington

Live Oak

Quercus virginiana Mill. • Beech Family *Fagaceae*

STATE TREE OF GEORGIA

Although not really hardy this far north, some sheltered specimens of the live oak do manage to survive Washington's winters.
This massive, broadly spreading evergreen is often draped with

Spanish moss in the Deep South, where it is beloved as a shade and street tree. The live oak was Lady Bird Johnson's favorite tree.

NATIVE HABITAT AND RANGE   Sandy soils, rich woods, and stream banks; southern Coastal Plain, southeastern Virginia to Florida and Texas, inland in Texas and Mexico.

LEAVES   Simple, alternate, evergreen. 1½ to 5 inches (3.8–12.6 cm) long. Elliptic to oblong-obovate. Margin smooth, wavy, or rarely toothed; slightly rolled back. Apex rounded or bluntly pointed. Base rounded or wedge-shaped. Leathery, lustrous dark green above, paler with grayish or whitish pubescence below.

FRUIT   Dark brown acorn, maturing in one year. ¾ to 1 inch (2–2.5 cm) long, enclosed for one-quarter to one-half of its length by a reddish brown, pubescent, bowl-shaped cup.

GROWTH HABIT   Broad trunk usually divides near the base into several large, widely spreading branches.

SIMILAR SPECIES   Compton's Oak (*Quercus* × *comptoniae*) is a hybrid of the live oak and the overcup oak (*Q. lyrata*).

LOCATIONS
• National Arboretum
• Rare in Washington

Compton's Oak

Quercus × *comptoniae* Sarg. (*Quercus lyrata* × *Quercus virginiana*) • Beech Family *Fagaceae*

Compton's oak is a hybrid of two southeastern species: the live oak and the overcup oak. This rare tree has the spreading form of the former, combined with the greater winter hardiness of the latter.

LEAVES   Simple, alternate, deciduous. Persisting until early winter. Oblanceolate, with wavy margin or rounded lobes.

FRUIT   Similar to live oak acorn.

LOCATION
• East Potomac Golf Course

White Oaks Not Native to North America

English Oak

Quercus robur L. • Beech Family *Fagaceae*

This exotic oak is similar to our native white oak (*Quercus alba*), but can be distinguished from the North American tree by its less deeply lobed leaves and long-stalked acorns. A columnar form of the English oak (*Quercus robur* 'Fastigiata') lines parts of 16th Street, N.W., from Meridian Hill to Lafayette Park. The tree was chosen for this location because its compact form allowed for a long, unobstructed view of the 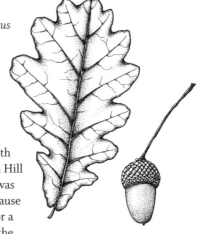 White House. Unfortunately, during the past few decades, many of the 16th Street trees have lost their compact form as they have aged.

NATIVE RANGE   Europe, western Asia, northern Africa.

LEAVES   Simple, alternate, deciduous. 2 to 6 inches (5–15 cm) long. Six to fourteen rounded lobes are very shallow or cut about halfway to the midrib. Lobe margins smooth, wavy, or sometimes with a few rounded, shallow teeth. Narrow base often slightly cordate. Dull dark green above, paler below and glabrous. Petiole short, less than ½ inch (1 cm) long.

FRUIT   Chestnut-brown acorn, maturing during the first year. Oblong-ovoid or ovoid. ⅔ to 1½ inches (1.5–4 cm) long. Often in pairs, on a long stalk 1¼ to 3½ inches (3–8 cm) in length. Enclosed for one-third or less of its length by a light-colored, bowl-shaped cup.

BARK AND TWIGS   Bark gray, narrowly furrowed. Twigs gray-brown with scaly, brown, pointed ovoid winter buds.

GROWTH HABIT Thick, rather short trunk; broad, open crown with stout, wide-spreading branches.

OTHER FORMS Fastigiate English oak or Cypress oak (*Quercus robur* 'Fastigiata'). Form with upright branches forming a narrow, columnar crown.

SIMILAR SPECIES May be confused with other members of the white oak group. (See illustrations.)

LOCATIONS
• Washington National Cathedral
• C Street, S.E., near House office buildings
• 16th Street, N.W. (Fastigiate form)
• Some public buildings and private homes in D.C.
• Audubon Naturalist Society, Woodend Sanctuary, Chevy Chase, Maryland (2007 Montgomery County Champion English Oak)

Downy Oak

Quercus pubescens Willd. • Beech Family *Fagaceae*

This is the famous Library of Congress Hungarian Oak, which may have come from Hungary but is not the species (*Quercus frainetto* Ten.) botanists once believed it to be. A very rare tree.

NATIVE RANGE Southern Europe, western Asia.

LEAVES Simple, alternate, deciduous. Lobes rounded or bluntly pointed, sinuses shallow. Pubescent along the veins below and on the petiole.

FRUIT Acorn, ½ to 1 inch (1.3–2.5 cm) long, with a pubescent cup. Short-stalked or sessile.

GROWTH HABIT Small tree.

LOCATION
• Library of Congress grounds

The Red and Black Oak Group

Leaves usually with pointed, bristle-tipped lobes or apices. Acorns usually maturing during the second year. (Compare to White Oak Group, page 224.)

Red and Black Oaks Native to North America

Southern Red Oak (Spanish Oak)

Quercus falcata Michx. • Beech Family *Fagaceae*

A graceful native oak with narrow, irregularly lobed leaves. Not as frequently grown in Washington as the following species, but often planted in southern towns, where it reaches impressive stature.

NATIVE HABITAT AND RANGE   Dry or sandy soils in the eastern part of its range, and often in richer and moister soils elsewhere; southeastern New York west to southern Illinois, southern Missouri, and eastern Texas, south to Louisiana and northern Florida.

LEAVES   Simple, alternate, deciduous. 3½ to 10 inches (9–25.3 cm) long, with three to seven narrow, often sickle-shaped, bristle-tipped lobes. Dark green above, paler and more or less woolly below. Petiole 1 to 2 inches (2.5–5 cm) long.

FRUIT   Acorn, maturing in two years. Short-stalked, about ½ inch (1–1.5 cm) long. Enclosed for one-third of its length or less by a cup covered with pubescent, appressed scales.

BARK AND TWIGS   Bark dark, thick, and furrowed. Twigs stout, reddish brown, usually pubescent. Winter buds ovoid, pubescent, dark red or chestnut.

GROWTH HABIT   Medium-sized to large tree with a full, rounded crown.

DISTINGUISHING CHARACTERISTICS No other oak planted in the area has leaves like this tree. (See illustration.)

LOCATIONS
- East Potomac Golf Course
- National Arboretum
- Soldiers' Home
- Some public building grounds and private yards
- Capital Crescent Trail
- Rock Creek Park, including Carter Barron Amphitheatre; Wheaton Regional Park, Northwest Branch Stream Valley Park; and other regional woodlands
- Potomac, Maryland (2007 Montgomery County Champion Southern Red Oak)

Red Oak (Northern Red Oak)

Quercus rubra L. (*Quercus borealis* F. Michx.) • Beech Family *Fagaceae*

STATE TREE OF NEW JERSEY

Widely planted throughout the city along streets, in parks, and around public buildings and private homes. Also common in regional woodlands.

NATIVE HABITAT AND RANGE Wide variety of soils and habitats; southeastern Canada, Michigan, and Minnesota, south to eastern Oklahoma, Alabama, and Georgia.

LEAVES Simple, alternate, deciduous. 4 to 10 inches (10–25.3 cm) long. Seven to eleven toothed, bristle-tipped lobes are cut about halfway to the midrib. Lobes pointed forward. Dull, medium green above, paler below and glabrous, except for occasional small tufts of brownish hairs in the vein axils. Petiole up to 2 inches (5 cm) long.

FRUIT   Acorn, maturing in two years. Oblong-ovoid, ⅔ to 1 inch (1.5–2.5 cm) long, sessile or nearly so. Enclosed for one-third or less of its length by a reddish brown, saucer-shaped cup with many small, closely appressed scales.

BARK AND TWIGS   Bark of mature trees has dark, narrow, vertical furrows between flat, often lighter-colored ridges. The furrows are sometimes described as "ski tracks." Twigs reddish brown, becoming glabrous, with scaly, reddish brown, ovoid winter buds. Buds have scales that are usually pubescent along their margins.

GROWTH HABIT   Medium to tall tree with large branches forming a rounded crown.

SIMILAR SPECIES   The black oak (*Quercus velutina*) is less commonly planted in Washington. Its leaves are similar in shape, but they are dark glossy green above, and usually have scurfy (dandruff-like) pubescence below, in addition to hair tufts in the vein axils. The scarlet oak (*Quercus coccinea*), the pin oak (*Q. palustris*), and the Shumard oak (*Q. shumardii*) have leaves that are cut more than halfway to the midrib.

LOCATIONS
• White House grounds
• U.S. Capitol grounds
• McPherson Square (Casey Trees' 2006 D.C. Champion Red Oak)
• Union Station (trees planted by the Daughters of the American Revolution in honor of U.S. presidents)
• Dumbarton Oaks
• Logan Circle
• 37th Street, N.W.
• Streets throughout the city, including South Dakota Avenue, N.E., and 34th Place, N.W.
• Cleveland Park
• Vice President's Residence
• Windy Run Park, Arlington County (two trees tied for second largest Virginia Champion Red [or Northern Red] Oak)
• Capital Crescent Trail
• Rock Creek Park and other regional parks

Black Oak

Quercus velutina Lam. • Beech
Family *Fagaceae*

NATIVE HABITAT AND RANGE
Usually in dry upland
soils, often on rocky or
sandy slopes; Maine to
Florida, west to Minne-
sota and Texas.

LEAVES   Simple, alternate,
deciduous. 4 to 10 inches
(10–25.4 cm) long. Five to nine
lobes with pointed, bristle-
tipped teeth. Dark glossy
green above, paler below, and
usually with hair tufts in some
vein axils and scurfy (dandruff-
like) pubescence on the lower blade.

FRUIT   Sessile or short-stalked acorn,
maturing in two years. Ovoid, ½ to ¾ inch
(1.3–2 cm) long, enclosed for one-third to
one-half of its length by a pubescent, bowl-shaped cup. Tips of
scales on the edge of the cup form a fringe-like edge.

BARK AND TWIGS   Bark nearly black, thick, furrowed. Twigs with
woolly winter buds.

SIMILAR SPECIES   The red oak (*Quercus rubra*) is far more commonly cultivated in Washington. Its leaves are dull medium
green above and glabrous below, except for small tufts of hairs
in the vein axils. Its acorn has a shallow, saucer-shaped cup, and
its winter buds are reddish brown, with scales usually pubescent
only along the margins. The bark of mature red oaks has flat,
vertical ridges separated by darker furrows ("ski tracks"). The
uncommon shumard oak (*Q. shumardii*) has leaves more deeply
lobed and acorns similar to the red oak.

LOCATIONS
• National Arboretum
• Dumbarton Oaks
• Anacostia Road, S.E. (Casey Trees' 2006 D.C. Champion Black
  Oak)
• Some parks, streets, public buildings, and homes citywide
• Outdoor Nursery School, Chevy Chase, Maryland

- Oakridge Avenue, Chevy Chase, Maryland
- Rock Creek Park, Northwest Branch Stream Valley Park, and other regional woodlands

Scarlet Oak

Quercus coccinea Muenchh. • Beech Family *Fagaceae*

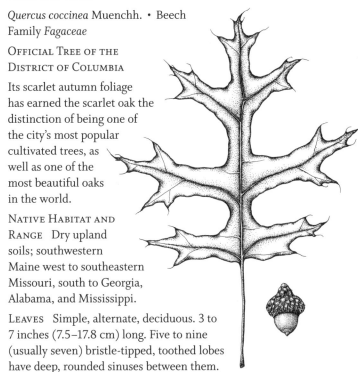

OFFICIAL TREE OF THE DISTRICT OF COLUMBIA

Its scarlet autumn foliage has earned the scarlet oak the distinction of being one of the city's most popular cultivated trees, as well as one of the most beautiful oaks in the world.

NATIVE HABITAT AND RANGE   Dry upland soils; southwestern Maine west to southeastern Missouri, south to Georgia, Alabama, and Mississippi.

LEAVES   Simple, alternate, deciduous. 3 to 7 inches (7.5–17.8 cm) long. Five to nine (usually seven) bristle-tipped, toothed lobes have deep, rounded sinuses between them. Side lobes point straight outward or slightly forward. Bright shiny green above, paler below and glabrous, except for tufts of hairs in the vein axils. Petiole 1¼ to 3 inches (3–7.5 cm) long. Autumn color: scarlet, lasting late into the season.

FRUIT   Acorn, maturing in two years. Short-stalked or sessile. ½ to 1 inch (1.3–2.5 cm) long, usually with several concentric rings near the apex. Reddish brown, enclosed for one-half of its length, more or less, by a scaly, bowl-shaped cup.

BARK AND TWIGS   Bark shallowly fissured on mature trees. Twigs slender, soon glabrous or nearly so, reddish brown. Red-brown winter buds have silky pubescence on the upper half of their scales.

GROWTH HABIT   Medium-sized to tall tree with ascending branches forming an open, rounded or irregular crown.

Sɪᴍɪʟᴀʀ Sᴘᴇᴄɪᴇs   In the absence of fruit, it is very difficult to distinguish this tree from the pin oak (*Quercus palustris*). Pin oak acorns are smaller, with shallow, saucer-shaped cups. During spring and summer, the best way to tell the two trees apart is by their growth habits. The pin oak has an egg-shaped crown and many horizontal branches with drooping lower ones. However, some pin oaks have had their lower branches pruned. The uncommon Shumard oak (*Q. shumardii*) has acorns with shallow, saucer-shaped caps.

Lᴏᴄᴀᴛɪᴏɴs
- 3374 Minnesota Avenue, S.E. (Casey Trees' 2006 D.C. Champion Scarlet Oak)
- New Hampshire Avenue, N.W.
- Eastern Avenue, N.E.
- Tudor Place, Georgetown
- White House grounds
- Hillwood Estate
- Constitution Gardens
- U.S. Supreme Court and Capitol grounds
- Rock Creek Park and regional woodlands
- Bethesda, Maryland (2007 Montgomery County Champion Scarlet Oak)
- Chestnut Hills Park and Lee Arts Center (2007–2008 Arlington County Co-champion Scarlet Oaks)

Pin Oak

Quercus palustris Muenchh. • Beech Family
Fagaceae

Pin oak leaves are similar to the scarlet oak, but the tree's acorns are smaller and its growth habit is distinctive. The pin oak has an egg-shaped or pyramidal crown with many small branches radiating outward and the lower ones drooping.

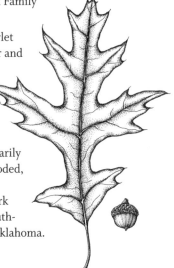

Nᴀᴛɪᴠᴇ Hᴀʙɪᴛᴀᴛ ᴀɴᴅ Rᴀɴɢᴇ   Primarily in lowlands that are periodically flooded, but thrives in a number of habitats; southern New England and New York south to North Carolina, west to southeastern Iowa, eastern Kansas, and Oklahoma.

Leaves   Simple, alternate, deciduous. 3 to 7 inches (7.5–17.8 cm) long. Five to seven bristle-tipped, toothed lobes have deep sinuses between them. Side lobes point slightly forward or straight outward. Bright green above, paler below and glabrous, but for tufts of hairs in the vein axils. Petiole ¾ to 2 inches (2–5 cm) long.

Fruit   Small acorn, about ½ inch (1.3 cm) long, maturing in two years. Short-stalked or sessile. Light brown, often with thin, vague, vertical stripes. Shallow, saucer-shaped cup is covered with small, reddish brown scales.

Bark and Twigs   Bark grayish brown, smooth on young trees, becoming furrowed and scaly with age. Twigs olive-gray or reddish brown; winter buds brown or reddish brown, scaly.

Growth Habit   Egg-shaped or pyramidal crown. Many branches usually radiate outward from a tall, central trunk; lower branches droop (but often are pruned in the city).

Similar Species   Very similar to the scarlet oak (*Quercus coccinea*), which has a larger acorn that may be enclosed for up to one-half of its length by a bowl-shaped cup. (See illustrations.) In the absence of fruit, the best way to distinguish the two trees is by growth habit. The pin oak's central trunk often continues almost to the top of its egg-shaped crown, with many small branches radiating outward and downward. The scarlet oak trunk splits into several large ascending and spreading limbs. The uncommon Shumard oak (*Q. shumardii*) also lacks drooping lower branches.

Locations
- White House grounds
- U.S. Capitol grounds
- Hains Point, East Potomac Park
- 2901 Legation Street, N.W. (Casey Trees' 2006 D.C. Champion Pin Oak)
- Smithsonian National Museum of American History
- Streets, parks, and private yards throughout the city and suburbs
- Northwest Branch Stream Valley Park
- Arlington National Cemetery (2007–2008 Arlington County Champion Pin Oak)
- George Washington Memorial Parkway, Fort Hunt Park (Witness Tree Protection Program specimen)

Shumard Oak

Quercus shumardii Buckley • Beech Family *Fagaceae*

The Shumard oak, a state rare (S2) species in Maryland, usually grows in moist, lowland soils and ranges from Pennsylvania, Maryland, and Virginia to Indiana, Michigan, and Kansas, and south to Texas and Florida. Uncommon to rare in the Washington area, both in cultivation and in the wild, the Shumard oak has leaves that are deeply cut, similar to the scarlet oak (*Q. coccinea*) and pin oak (*Q. palustris*). Shumard oak acorns have shallow, saucer-shaped cups, similar to the pin oak, but the acorns are slightly larger and more oblong. The tree doesn't have the drooping lower branches typical of the pin oak.

Locations
• C&O Canal (several large specimens near Lock 7)
• Theodore Roosevelt Island
• Algonkian Regional Park, Loudoun County, Virginia

Willow Oak

Quercus phellos L. • Beech Family *Fagaceae*

A beautiful oak with strong, clean lines and delicate willow-like foliage. The willow oak was Thomas Jefferson's favorite tree. It has been planted along streets and in parks throughout the city.

Native Habitat and Range   Moist lowlands, including swamps and stream banks, and rich, shady, upland soils; southeastern New York to parts of northern Florida, west to eastern Oklahoma and Texas.

Leaves   Simple, alternate, deciduous. 2 to 5 inches (5–12.6 cm) long, about ½ inch (1–1.5 cm) wide. Linear-oblong to lanceolate. Unlobed. Margin smooth or slightly wavy. Apex bristle-tipped, base wedge-shaped or rounded. Lustrous green and glabrous above, paler below and pubescent or glabrous. Petiole very short.

Fruit   Small acorn, sessile or short-stalked, maturing in two years. Enclosed only at the base by a scaly, saucer-shaped cup.

Bark and Twigs   Bark dark, thick, shallowly furrowed. Twigs slender, reddish brown. Winter buds small, narrow, sharply pointed, reddish brown.

GROWTH HABIT   Tall tree with a large, straight trunk and full, rounded crown.

SIMILAR SPECIES   The rarely planted laurel (or darlington) oak (*Quercus laurifolia*) of the southeastern U.S. has similar leaves, but they are thickly textured, leathery, and nearly evergreen.

LOCATIONS
- Franklin Delano Roosevelt Memorial
- Rhode Island Avenue
- Chevy Chase Parkway, N.W.
- Military Road
- Loughboro Road
- Tilden Street, N.W. (Casey Trees' 2006 D.C. Champion Willow Oak)
- Reno Road
- Harvard Street, N.W.
- Skyland Place, S.E.
- 31st Place, S.E.
- 19th Street, N.E.
- Logan Circle
- U.S. Capitol grounds
- George Washington Memorial Parkway (Belle Haven parking lot, Witness Tree Protection Program specimen)
- Arlington National Cemetery (2007–2008 Arlington County Champion Willow Oak)

Bartram's Oak

Quercus × *heterophylla* F. Michx. (*Quercus phellos* × *Quercus rubra*) • Beech Family *Fagaceae*

This handsome hybrid oak is a cross between two native species, the willow oak (*Quercus phellos*) and the red oak (*Q. rubra*).

LEAVES   Simple, alternate, deciduous. 3 to 7 inches (7.5–17.8 cm) long, 1 to 3 inches (2.5–7.5 cm) wide. Oblong-lanceolate. Various leaf shapes may be found on a single tree. Variable number of pointed, bristle-tipped lobes or large teeth, or with a smooth margin. Base rounded or wedge-shaped. Medium green and glabrous above, paler below and glabrous, except for small tufts of light brown hairs in the vein axils.

FRUIT Acorn, similar to red oak, but slightly smaller and rounder.

SIMILAR SPECIES See water oak (*Quercus nigra*).

LOCATIONS
• National Zoo
• U.S. Capitol grounds
• Some parks, public buildings, and private homes

Shingle Oak

Quercus imbricaria Michx. • Beech Family *Fagaceae*

NATIVE HABITAT AND RANGE A number of habitats from dry uplands to moist riverbanks; Pennsylvania south to Alabama, west to Kansas and Iowa. Uncommon in the East, common in the lower Ohio River Valley.

LEAVES Simple, alternate, deciduous. 3 to 7 inches (7.5–17.8 cm) long, 1 to 2 inches (2.5–5 cm) wide. Oblong or oblong-lanceolate. Un-lobed. Smooth or barely wavy margin. Rounded or pointed apex is usually bristle-tipped; base rounded or wedge-shaped. Shiny dark green and glabrous above, paler and pubescent below. Petiole ¼ to ¾ inch (0.5–2 cm) long.

FRUIT Short-stalked acorn, maturing in two years. Ovoid, chestnut-brown, ½ to ¾ inch (1.3–2 cm) long, enclosed for one-third to one-half of its length by a bowl-shaped, pubescent, reddish brown cup.

BARK Grayish brown, shallowly furrowed.

SIMILAR SPECIES The far more common willow oak (*Quercus phellos*) has narrower leaves.

LOCATIONS
• Soldiers' Home
• The Mall, near the U.S. Capitol Reflecting Pool
• Constitution Avenue and 21st Street, N.W.
• Some parks, public buildings, and private homes throughout the city and suburbs
• Rock Creek and its tributaries
• Sandy Spring, Maryland (2007 Montgomery County Champion Shingle Oak)

Water Oak

Quercus nigra L. • Beech Family *Fagaceae*

NATIVE HABITAT AND RANGE   Damp and
moist soils of floodplains, streamsides, and
riverbanks; southern New Jersey to central
Florida, west to eastern Texas, Oklahoma,
and southeastern Missouri.

LEAVES   Simple, alternate, deciduous. 2 to
6 inches (5–15 cm) long. Size and shape variable. Widest at the apex, which may be shallowly three-lobed, rounded, or with as many
as seven lobes. Lobes are usually rounded, but
may come to a sharp, abrupt point that is barely
bristle-tipped. Leaf narrows to a wedge-shaped
base. Bluish green and glabrous, except for small
tufts of brownish hairs in the vein axils below. Petiole
short, less than ½ inch (1 cm) long.

FRUIT   Short-stalked or sessile acorn, maturing in two years.
Dark, nearly round, ⅓ to ¾ inch (1–2 cm) long. Enclosed at base
only or for up to one-third of its length by a shallow cup covered
with thin scales.

BARK   Dark gray-black, smooth or shallowly furrowed and scaly.

SIMILAR SPECIES   Leaf shape is unique. Blackjack oak (*Quercus
marilandica*) has leaves with wider apices and usually rounded
or subcordate bases. Bartram's oak (*Quercus* × *heterophylla*) has
leaves with narrow, pointed, bristle-tipped lobes, teeth, and/or
apices. (See illustrations.)

LOCATIONS
• East Potomac Golf Course
• Chevy Chase, Maryland (2007 Montgomery County Champion
  Water Oak)
• Arlington National Cemetery (Virginia State Champion Water
  Oak, and water oak tied for third largest in Virginia)
• Some parks, public buildings, and private homes
• Regional native occurrence—Eastern Shore

Blackjack Oak

Quercus marilandica
Muenchh. • Beech Family
Fagaceae

NATIVE HABITAT AND
RANGE   Dry, often sandy
soils; southern New York
to northern Florida, west
to Kansas and Texas.

LEAVES   Simple, alternate, deciduous. 3 to 7 in. (7.5–17.8 cm) long.
Shape variable, but always wide at apex
and usually rounded or subcordate at base.
Apex may be rounded, shallowly three-lobed,
or with a few shallow, rounded, barely pointed
or bristle-tipped teeth. Thick and somewhat
leathery. Dark green and glabrous above, pubescent
below. Petiole pubescent, ⅓ to 1 inch (1–2.5 cm) long.

FRUIT   Sessile or short-stalked acorn, maturing in two years.
About ¾ inch (2 cm) long, enclosed for one-third to two-thirds
of its length by a bowl-shaped, pubescent, reddish brown cup.

BARK AND TWIGS   Bark dark gray or black, sometimes separated
into squarish segments. Twigs with rusty-pubescent buds.

GROWTH HABIT   Small to medium-sized tree with a rounded or
irregular crown.

SIMILAR SPECIES   Water oak (*Quercus nigra*) has leaves with narrower apices and wedge-shaped bases.

LOCATIONS
• Soldiers' Home
• Washington National Cathedral
• National Arboretum
• Some parks, private homes, and public buildings citywide
• Wheaton Veterans Park, Maryland (2007 Montgomery County
  Champion Blackjack Oak)
• Pimmit Run Park (2007–2008 Arlington County Champion
  Blackjack Oak)
• Regional native occurrence—Coastal Plain and Piedmont,
  including the summit of Sugarloaf Mountain, Maryland

Red and Black Oaks Not Native to North America

Saw-Toothed Oak

Quercus acutissima Carruth. • Beech Family *Fagaceae*

Named for its sharply bristle-tipped teeth resembling those of a saw. This unique Asian tree has been a successful urban tree, widely planted in Washington and its suburbs. However, botanists are concerned about its escape from cultivation and its invasiveness in regional fields and woodlands.

NATIVE RANGE   China, Korea, Japan.

LEAVES   Simple, alternate, deciduous. 3 to 9 inches (7.5–22.8 cm) long, 1 to 2½ inches (2.5–6.3 cm) wide. Oblong to lanceolate. Wedge-shaped or rounded base; sharply pointed apex. Pointed teeth end in long, thin bristle-tips. Dark glossy green above, paler below and glabrous, except for occasional tufts of hairs in the vein axils. Petiole ½ to 1¾ inches (1.3–4.5 cm) long.

FRUIT   Chestnut-brown round acorn, ½ to 1 inch (1–2.5 cm) long, sessile. Almost entirely enclosed by a thick cup covered with long, light brown scales. The cup looks like a shaggy wig. (See illustration.)

BARK AND TWIGS   Bark gray or grayish brown, with rough ridges and fissures. Twigs pale orange-brown or gray brown, with small, pointed winter buds. Dry leaves often persist into winter.

GROWTH HABIT   Handsome tree with a rounded, open crown.

SIMILAR SPECIES   Not likely to be confused with any other oak commonly planted in the District of Columbia. Somewhat similar to the extremely rare Chinese cork oak (*Quercus variabilis* Bl.), which is planted in Chevy Chase, Maryland. However, the saw-toothed oak bears a close resemblance to the Chinese chestnut (*Castanea mollissima*), which is widely planted around the Washington area. The Chinese chestnut has leaves that are whitish or very pale green and usually woolly below. It produces showy yellowish or cream-colored catkins in late spring or early summer, and its fruit is an edible chestnut enclosed by a sharply spiny husk.

LOCATIONS
- National Zoo
- Kenilworth Aquatic Gardens
- City streets, including 7th Street, N.W., between Geranium and Juniper Streets
- Suburban streets, including those in Chevy Chase, Maryland
- Lafayette Park and some other parks in D.C.
- Some public buildings and private grounds

Rare Oaks Occasionally Planted in Washington

Laurel Oak (*Quercus laurifolia* Michx.) of the southeastern U.S.

Darlington Oak (*Quercus hemisphaerica* Bartram) of the southeastern U.S. (Trees planted in Enid A. Haupt Garden of the Smithsonian Castle.)

Turkey Oak (*Quercus cerris* L.) of southern Europe, western Asia

Chinese Cork Oak (Oriental Cork Oak) (*Quercus variabilis* Bl.) of northern China, Korea, and Japan. Located at the Outdoor Nursery School, Chevy Chase, Maryland (2007 Maryland State Champion Chinese or Oriental Cork Oak)

Chinese Evergreen Oak (*Quercus myrsinifolia* Bl.) of Asia

Black Alder (European Alder)

Alnus glutinosa (L.) Gaertn. • Birch Family
Betulaceae

The woody fruit of this tree looks as if it belongs on a conifer.

NATIVE RANGE   Europe to Siberia, northern Africa.

LEAVES   Simple, alternate, deciduous. 1½ to 4 inches (3.8–10 cm) long. Obovate, ovate, or nearly round, with irregularly toothed margins.

FLOWERS AND FRUIT   Male catkins shed pollen in early spring. Tiny female flowers are reddish; young fruit is green, ½ to ¾ inch (1–2 cm) long, becoming cone-like, woody, and brown, and remaining on the tree through winter.

BARK   Dark grayish or purplish brown, cracked and fissured.

SIMILAR SPECIES   The rare Italian alder (*Alnus cordata*) has heart-shaped leaves. The native common, smooth, or hazel alder

[*Alnus serrulata* (Aiton) Willd.] is a shrub or small tree that is common in swamps and along regional streams, springs, and pond edges, but it is rarely cultivated.

LOCATIONS
• Some private yards and public buildings
• Rock Creek Park

Italian Alder

Alnus cordata Desf. • Birch Family *Betulaceae*

NATIVE RANGE   Southern Italy, Corsica.

LEAVES   Simple, alternate, deciduous. 2 to 3½ inches (5–9 cm) long. Ovate, with a cordate base. Margin toothed, but smooth near the petiole.

FRUIT   Similar to black alder (*Alnus glutinosa*) but larger (about an inch [2.5 cm] long).

SIMILAR SPECIES   Heart-shaped leaves separate this alder from the more commonly planted black alder.

LOCATIONS
• Rare in Washington

The Birches

European White Birch
(European Weeping Birch)

Betula pendula Roth • Birch Family *Betulaceae*

The European white birch was once widely planted as a stand-in for the white birch (*Betula papyrifera*), a northern American tree that struggles in D.C.'s summer heat. However, the European tree is planted less often today due to its susceptibility to the birch borer, a devastating pest.

NATIVE RANGE   Europe, northern Asia.

LEAVES   Simple, alternate, deciduous. 1¼ to 3 inches (3–7.5 cm) long. Triangular-ovate. Margin sharply and irregularly toothed.

Base straight across or wedge-shaped, apex long-pointed. Glabrous above and below, on a slender petiole.

FLOWERS AND FRUIT   Male catkins, ¾ to 1¼ inches (2–3 cm) long, are on the tree through winter; in spring they shed yellow pollen. Smaller female flowering catkins become cone-like structures, 1 to 1¼ inches (2.5–3 cm) long, that are green at first and then turn brown, releasing their small, winged seeds and breaking up.

BARK AND TWIGS   Bark shiny reddish brown on very young trees, becoming white or pinkish white with large, black, horizontal diamonds. The bark peels, but not as readily as that of the native North American white birch. Twigs are glabrous and resinous-glandular. Winter buds ovoid, purplish brown or greenish.

GROWTH HABIT   Graceful, small to medium-sized tree that is upright when young but usually assumes a pendulous form with age.

OTHER FORMS   The cultivar 'Dalecarlica' has deeply cut, very sharply toothed leaves.

SIMILAR SPECIES   The gray birch (*Betula populifolia* Marshall), not included in this guide, is native to the northeastern states and southeastern Canada (extending in the mountains to North Carolina). Its leaves are similar to the European white birch, but it is rare in cultivation. Gray birch bark is chalky white, rather than creamy. The white or paper birch (*Betula papyrifera*) has ovate or oblong-ovate (rather than triangular-ovate) leaves and twigs that are often pubescent, at least when young.

LOCATION
• National Arboretum

White Birch (Paper or Canoe Birch)

Betula papyrifera Marshall • Birch Family
Betulaceae

STATE TREE OF NEW HAMPSHIRE

Despite repeated attempts to coax the white birch into cultivation, it just doesn't seem to like Washington's summer heat. However, a few specimens do manage to survive. The white birch is one of North America's most striking trees, its creamy bark a hallmark of northern forests across the continent. The tree supplies important browse for wildlife, and it has tradition-ally been used to make birchbark canoes.

NATIVE HABITAT AND RANGE   A variety of habitats, both wet and dry soils; one of the first trees to establish itself after fires. Much of Canada and south in the U.S. to Pennsylvania, West Virginia, Iowa, South Dakota, and parts of Nebraska, Idaho, and northern Oregon. Ranges farther south in isolated parts of the Appala-chians and Rockies.

LEAVES   Simple, alternate, deciduous. 2 to 5 inches (5–12.5 cm) long. Ovate or oblong-ovate. Coarsely and irregularly toothed.

BARK AND TWIGS   Bark creamy white, marked with horizontal lenticels, peeling off in thin, papery layers to reveal pale orange inner bark. Twigs often pubescent, at least when young.

SIMILAR SPECIES   The European white birch (*Betula pendula*), already described, is more commonly cultivated here. Several other Eurasian and Asian species of white birch, which are similar to the American species, are in cultivation at the National Arboretum.

LOCATIONS
• A few private yards and public buildings

River Birch

Betula nigra L. • Birch Family *Betulaceae*

The river birch grows along streams and rivers throughout the Washington area and has gained popularity in recent years as a culti-vated tree. The cultivar 'Heritage' is frequently planted.

NATIVE HABITAT AND RANGE   Riversides, stream-sides, swamps, and pond sides; southern New En-gland to northern Florida, west to eastern Texas and Oklahoma, much of Missouri, eastern Iowa, and southeastern Minnesota.

LEAVES   Simple, alternate, deciduous. 1 to 5 inches (2.5–12.5 cm) long. Triangular-ovate. Irregularly toothed and sometimes slightly lobed. Usually pubescent below.

BARK   Pinkish, reddish, or orange-brown; separated into large, curly strips.

GROWTH HABIT   Small to medium-sized tree.

Locations
- Rock Creek Park
- Potomac and Anacostia Rivers
- Hains Point, East Potomac Park
- U.S. Botanic Garden: Bartholdi Park
- Smithsonian National Museum of the American Indian
- Smithsonian National Museum of American History
- Parks, public buildings, and private homes throughout the city and suburbs

Other Native Birches

The black, sweet, or cherry birch (*Betula lenta* L.) is native to the Piedmont and mountains of nearby Maryland (including Sugarloaf Mountain) and western Virginia. The yellow birch (*Betula alleghaniensis* Britton) is native to the Maryland and Virginia mountains. Both species are planted at the National Arboretum. For the story of another native Virginia birch, one that was believed extinct for many years, see page 68–70.

European Hornbeam

Carpinus betulus L. • Birch Family *Betulaceae*

The European hornbeam is very similar to the native American hornbeam, ironwood, musclewood, or blue-beech (*Carpinus caroliniana*). It is slightly more frequently cultivated than the native species.

Native Range   Europe, Asia Minor.

Leaves   Simple, alternate, deciduous. 2 to 5 inches (5–12.5 cm) long. Oblong-ovate. Rounded or cordate base, pointed apex, and sharply, finely, double-toothed margin. Glabrous except for some pubescence along the veins below and in the vein axils.

Fruit   Nutlet attached to a leafy bract, borne in clustered pairs. Bract with ovate-lanceolate central lobe and ovate side lobes; margin smooth or with remote teeth.

Bark   Gray, sometimes with vertical brown stripes; trunk often fluted. Muscular-looking.

Growth Habit   Small tree, frequently with a fluted trunk.

SIMILAR SPECIES   Very similar to American hornbeam.

LOCATIONS
- U.S. Capitol grounds
- U.S. Botanic Garden: Bartholdi Park
- National Park Service National Capital Region Headquarters, East Potomac Park

American Hornbeam (Ironwood, Musclewood, or Blue-Beech)

Carpinus caroliniana Walter • Birch Family *Betulaceae*

Very difficult to distinguish from the European species, previously described. The American hornbeam's hard and heavy wood traditionally was used to make bowls and hammer handles. It's easy to identify this small to medium-sized tree in its native habitat by its smooth, muscular-looking bark and fluted trunk.

NATIVE HABITAT AND RANGE   Moist woodlands, often along rivers and streams; southeastern Canada to northern Florida, west to eastern Texas and eastern Minnesota.

LEAVES   Very similar to the preceding species, slightly thinner textured, with less deeply impressed veins.

FRUIT   Similar to European hornbeam, but with leafy bracts with usually one to several pointed teeth.

BARK   Very muscular-looking; trunk usually fluted.

LOCATIONS
- Rock Creek Park
- Potomac River, Seneca Creek, and other regional rivers and streams
- National Garden of the U.S. Botanic Garden
- Dumbarton Oaks
- National Arboretum
- Some parks, public buildings, and private yards

Eastern Hop-Hornbeam

Ostrya virginiana (Mill.) K. Koch • Birch Family *Betulaceae*

Very similar to the hornbeams (*Carpinus* spp.), already described. The distinctive characteristics of the hop-hornbeam are its bark, which

often peels into long, thin strips, and its hop-like autumn fruit. (See illustration.)

NATIVE HABITAT AND RANGE   Moist or dry woods, slopes, and ridges; southeastern Canada, eastern U.S., Mexico.

LOCATIONS
• U.S. Capitol grounds
• National Garden of the U.S. Botanic Garden
• Georgetown
• National Arboretum
• Private yards
• Naturally occurring in Rock Creek Park and other regional woodlands (not common)

European Filbert (European Hazelnut, Hazel, or Cobnut)

Corylus avellana L., Corylus avellana 'Purpurea' • Birch Family *Betulaceae*

Although the European filbert is usually a shrub, we include it here because it can attain a height of twenty feet. With its large leaves and interesting fruit, it is very conspic-uous. The European filbert is widely cultivated in this country and abroad for its edible nuts. The European filbert most often planted in Washington is a purple-leaved form (*Corylus avellana* 'Pur-purea').

NATIVE RANGE   Europe, Asia Minor.

LEAVES   Simple, alternate, deciduous. 2 to 6 inches (5–15.2 cm) long, 1¼ to 5 inches (3–12.6 cm) wide. Broadly obovate, ovate, or elliptic. Margin doubly toothed, often with small, jagged lobes. Apex abruptly pointed or rounded, base usually cordate. Green, purplish, or reddish. Downy below and sometimes above.

FLOWERS   Males in catkins 1¼ to 2½ inches (3–6.3 cm) long. Early spring, before the leaves.

FRUIT   Edible nut, ⅔ to ¾ inch (1.5–2 cm) long, enclosed by two lobed, often toothed leafy bracts that are a little shorter or (rarely) longer than the nut.

GROWTH HABIT   Usually a tall, broad shrub with many ascending branches.

SIMILAR SPECIES   The rare Turkish hazel (*Corylus colurna*). The native American hazelnut (*Corylus americana* Walter), not included in this guide, is a shrub of regional moist woodlands and thickets. It grows in Rock Creek Park.

LOCATIONS
• Library of Congress grounds
• Dumbarton Oaks
• Tidal Basin

Turkish Hazel (Turkish Hazelnut or Filbert)

Corylus colurna L. • Birch Family *Betulaceae*

The following characteristics separate the rare Turkish hazel from the common European filbert.

NATIVE RANGE   Southeastern Europe, western Asia.

LEAVES   Slightly larger than the European filbert, often with distinct small lobes.

FRUIT   The leafy bracts surrounding the nut are deeply divided into lobes that are somewhat curled back.

GROWTH HABIT   Single-trunked tree with a pyramidal crown.

LOCATIONS
• Walter Reed Army Medical Center
• Glenn Dale, Maryland
• Rare in Washington

Mockernut Hickory

Carya tomentosa (Poiret) Nutt. • Walnut Family *Juglandaceae*

A native tree, common in area woodlands. The nuts of the mockernut and other hickories are prized by black bears, foxes, raccoons, squirrels, white-tailed deer, and large birds.

NATIVE HABITAT AND RANGE   Woodlands; southern New Hampshire, New York, and Ontario, southeastern Iowa to eastern Texas and northern Florida.

LEAVES   Compound, alternate, deciduous. 8 to 12 inches (20–30.5 cm) long, with seven to nine leaflets. Terminal leaflet slightly longer than side leaflets. Margins finely or coarsely toothed. Leaflets fragrant and pubescent below.

Fruit   Nut enclosed by a rounded or obovoid husk, 1½ to 2 inches (3.8–5 cm) long. Husk ⅛ to ¼ inch (3–6 mm) thick, splitting nearly to base.

Bark and Twigs   Bark gray, shallowly furrowed. Twigs stout, pubescent when young. Large terminal winter buds.

Growth Habit   Medium-sized to tall tree with a large, open crown.

Similar Species   Pignut hickory (*Carya glabra*).

Locations
- Some public buildings, private yards, and parks
- Naturally occurring in regional woodlands, including Rock Creek Park
- Sugarloaf Mountain, Maryland
- Arlington House (Virginia State Co-champion Mockernut Hickory)

Pignut Hickory

Carya glabra (Mill.) Sweet • Walnut Family *Juglandaceae*

The pignut hickory, like the mockernut, is native to Rock Creek Park and surrounding woodlands. Its distribution in the eastern U.S. and southeastern Canada corresponds closely to the mockernut's native range. The pignut differs from the mockernut in having leaves with usually five (rarely seven) leaflets, which are mostly glabrous. The fruit of the pignut is slightly smaller, with a thinner husk that splits only partway to the base.

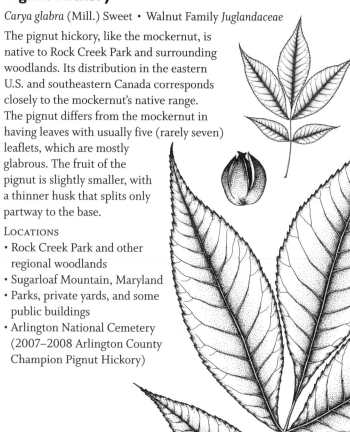

Locations
- Rock Creek Park and other regional woodlands
- Sugarloaf Mountain, Maryland
- Parks, private yards, and some public buildings
- Arlington National Cemetery (2007–2008 Arlington County Champion Pignut Hickory)

*Other hickories that are indigenous to the Washington area
or nearby Maryland and Virginia include the following:*

Bitternut Hickory

Carya cordiformis (Wangenh.) K. Koch

Bitternut hickory favors moist woods and bottomlands. Its leaves
have seven to eleven (usually nine) leaflets, and its nuts are
smaller than the mockernut, with a thin-walled husk that splits
partway to the base and has slight wings or ridges along the lines
of separation. The kernel is bitter. Winter buds are bright sulfur-
yellow.

LOCATIONS
• Rock Creek Park and other woodland parks
• Northwest Branch Stream Valley Park
• Sugarloaf Mountain, Maryland
• Roaches Run Waterfowl Sanctuary (second largest Virginia
  Champion Bitternut Hickory)

Shagbark Hickory

Carya ovata (Mill.) K. Koch

This hickory grows most commonly in the mountains. It has
shaggy bark that breaks into long strips or plates that often curl
at the ends. The five (sometimes seven) leaflets are softly pubescent below when young, becoming mostly glabrous, except for
tufts of hairs at the tips of fine teeth. Fruit is nearly round, with a
thick husk that eventually splits to the base. Kernel is edible and
sweet.

LOCATIONS
• Rock Creek Park
• Blockhouse Point Conservation Park

Shellbark Hickory

Carya laciniosa (F. Michx.) Loudon

Shellbark hickory has shaggy bark and mostly seven to nine
leaflets that are pubescent below. It is not common in our region,
either as a cultivated or a native tree, but grows naturally mainly
on floodplains and bottomlands.

LOCATION
• Rock Creek Park

Pecan

Carya illinoensis (Wangenh.) K. Koch • Walnut Family
Juglandaceae

State Tree of Texas

The pecan is cultivated throughout the southern states for its edible fruit. Prized for centuries by American Indians and early European explorers and settlers, it has become the most important native nut-producing tree in North America. Not surprisingly, the pecan is also a significant food source for wildlife. Several magnificent specimens of the pecan tree are growing on the Capitol grounds, at Tudor Place in Georgetown, and in front of George Washington's home at Mount Vernon.

Native Habitat and Range   Rich, moist bottomland soils, primarily of the Mississippi River Valley; Indiana and Alabama west to Iowa, eastern Kansas, Texas, and parts of Mexico.

Leaves   Compound, alternate, deciduous. 12 to 20 inches (30.5–50.5 cm) long. Eleven to seventeen toothed, lanceolate leaflets are usually slightly sickle-shaped.

Fruit   Oblong husk, 1 to 2 inches (2.5–5 cm) long, contains the nut.

Bark   Deeply furrowed.

Locations
- Mount Vernon (one of two historic trees was lost after Hurricane Isabel in 2003)
- Tudor Place, Georgetown (Casey Trees' 2006 D.C. Champion Pecan)
- U.S. Capitol grounds

Black Walnut

Juglans nigra L. • Walnut Family *Juglandaceae*

The black walnut has long been valued for its delicious nuts—used to flavor ice cream and candy—and its beautifully grained dark wood, for which naturally occurring large specimens of this slow-growing tree have been heavily harvested. There is a large black walnut next to the driveway at Woodend Sanctuary, the Audubon Naturalist Society headquarters in Chevy Chase, Maryland; and there are two large trees at the American Horticultural Society's River Farm near Mount Vernon that may date to George Washington's time.

NATIVE HABITAT AND RANGE   Rich, moist soils; eastern U.S. from southern New England to the Florida panhandle, west to Texas and South Dakota.

LEAVES   Pinnately compound, alternate, deciduous. 8 inches to 2 feet (20–60 cm) long, with eleven to twenty-three leaflets. Leaflets lance-shaped, often unequal at the base, sharply toothed. The end leaflet is smaller than the side ones or absent. Yellow-green (turning a clear yellow in fall), usually pubescent below.

FRUIT   Round nut 1 to 2 inches (2.5–5 cm) in diameter, with a furrowed shell, borne singly or in pairs. Contained within a thick, round, green lime-like husk.

BARK AND TWIGS   Mature trees have dark, deeply furrowed, ridged bark. Twigs have pubescent winter buds.

GROWTH HABIT
Tall tree with a long, straight trunk and rounded crown.

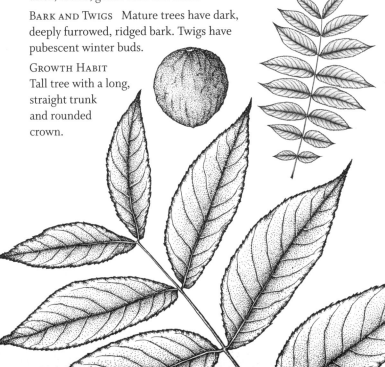

SIMILAR SPECIES   The butternut or white walnut (*Juglans cinerea* L.) is native to the eastern U.S., including the Washington area, but is rarely grown in the city. It can be distinguished from the black walnut by its oblong-ovoid (rather than round) fruit, which is borne singly or in clusters of up to five. The English or Persian walnut (*Juglans regia*) has smooth-margined leaves with fewer leaflets.

LOCATIONS
- Audubon Naturalist Society, Woodend Sanctuary, Chevy Chase, Maryland
- Rock Creek Park and other regional woodlands and fields
- Mouth of Tidal Basin near Ohio Drive (Casey Trees' 2006 D.C. Champion Black Walnut)
- Theodore Roosevelt Island
- National Arboretum
- River Farm
- Private homes and public buildings in the city and suburbs

Butternut (White Walnut)

Juglans cinerea L. • Walnut Family *Juglandaceae*

Although not nearly as common as the black walnut (*Juglans nigra*), the butternut is occasionally encountered in cultivation and in the wild in the Washington area. Butternut has oblong-ovoid fruit, compound leaves that usually have an end leaflet present (those of the black walnut often are absent or smaller than side leaflets), and leaf scars with a hairy fringe along the upper edge (like an eyebrow).

LOCATIONS
- Rock Creek Park
- Turkey Run Park

English Walnut (Persian or Common Walnut)

Juglans regia L. • Walnut Family *Juglandaceae*

This tree has been in cultivation in Europe and North America for many years for its fruit and timber.

NATIVE RANGE   Southeastern Europe, Asia.

LEAVES   Pinnately compound, alternate, deciduous. Five to nine leaflets (rarely more), mostly glabrous (may have small axillary tufts of hairs below), with smooth margins. Young trees may have obscurely toothed leaflets.

FRUIT   Smooth or slightly wrinkled, 1½ to 2 inches (4–5 cm) in diameter, thick-shelled, roundish.

SIMILAR SPECIES   The black walnut (*Juglans nigra*) has toothed leaflets. Another exotic species (extremely rare here) is the Japanese walnut (*Juglans ailanthifolia* Carr.). It has toothed leaflets and nuts borne in long, pendulous clusters. The Japanese walnut is planted at the National Arboretum.

LOCATIONS
• U.S. Capitol grounds
• Private homes and public buildings (not common)

Franklin Tree (Franklinia)

Franklinia alatamaha Bartr. ex Marshall • Tea Family *Theaceae*

Native to Georgia, the mysterious Franklin tree has not been documented as growing in its natural habitat since 1790 and is believed by many to be extinct in the wild. In 1973, Congress authorized the Smithsonian Institution to prepare a list of the country's extinct and endangered plants. The Smithsonian listed two trees as extinct: the Franklin tree and the Virginia round-leafed birch (*Betula uber*). After the list was compiled, *Betula uber* was rediscovered in the wild (see story on page 68). The Franklin tree is named for Benjamin Franklin.

LEAVES   Simple, alternate, deciduous. 4¾ to 9 inches (12–23 cm) long. Obovate-oblong. Remotely toothed. Bright lustrous green above, pubescent below. Petiole short.

FLOWERS   Five creamy-white petals and a bright yellow center. Large and showy, cup-shaped. Fragrant. Mid to late summer and early fall. (See color close-up.)

GROWTH HABIT   Small tree or shrub.

LOCATIONS
• Audubon Naturalist Society, Woodend Sanctuary, Chevy Chase, Maryland
• Fern Valley, National Arboretum
• River Farm

Japanese Stewartia (Deciduous Camellia)

Stewartia pseudocamellia Maxim. • Tea Family *Theaceae*

This small Japanese tree has ornamental bark and striking midsummer flowers.

NATIVE RANGE   Japan.

LEAVES   Simple, alternate, deciduous. 1¼ to 3¼ inches (3–8 cm) long. Ovate-lanceolate to obovate-elliptic. Margin wavy or with a few remote, shallow teeth. Long-pointed apex, wedge-shaped base.

FLOWERS   White, cup-shaped, with showy orange anthers in the center. 1¾ to 2½ inches (4.5–6.3 cm) wide.

BARK   Orange-brown, peeling away in plane tree fashion to reveal paler orange-brown inner bark.

LOCATIONS
• U.S. Capitol grounds
• City gardens

Since earlier editions of City of Trees *were published, several other members of the* Stewartia *genus have been planted in area gardens and cultivated landscapes. They include the following trees and shrubs:*

Korean Stewartia

Stewartia koreana Rehd.

Similar in appearance to the Japanese stewartia, this small tree has flaky, richly hued, ornamental bark and showy flowers that are more flattened than cup-shaped.

Tall Stewartia

Stewartia monadelpha Sieb. & Zucc.

Native to Japan, this small tree may grow tall, especially in the wild. The brown, scaly bark on young trees becomes smooth with age. The flowers are slightly smaller than the Japanese stewartia and other species mentioned here.

Upright Stewartia

Stewartia rostrata Spongb.

This large, upright shrub is native to eastern China. Its flower buds are surrounded by reddish bracts, and it blooms earlier than previously mentioned species, which are summer bloomers. Bark is gray-brown and may be ridged and furrowed.

Silky Stewartia (Silky Camellia)

Stewartia malacodendron L.

This shrub or small tree is a native North American species principally indigenous to the southeastern Coastal Plain. Its summer flowers are large and white-petaled. The showy flowers have stamens with blue anthers and purple filaments. The gray-brown bark is not as ornamentally striking as the *Stewartia* species already mentioned. A state endangered plant of Arkansas and Florida and state rare plant in Georgia, according to the U.S. Department of Agriculture's plants database. Silky stewartia grows in the National Arboretum's Fern Valley.

Idesia (Igiri Tree)

Idesia polycarpa Maxim. • Flacourtia Family *Flacourtiaceae*

This Asian tree is extremely rare in Washington.

NATIVE RANGE   Japan, China.

LEAVES   Simple, alternate, deciduous. 4 to 10 inches (10–25.5 cm) long. Heart-shaped, with large, coarse teeth. Petiole very long.

FLOWERS   Greenish yellow, fragrant, in long clusters. Early summer.

FRUIT   Very showy hanging clusters of round, reddish brown berries.

SIMILAR SPECIES   Two other rare exotic trees, the Japanese raisin-tree (*Hovenia dulcis*) and the dove or handkerchief tree (*Davidia involucrata*), have similar foliage, but the fruit of each is distinctive.

LOCATIONS
• National Arboretum
• A few private yards

The Tamarisks

Tamarix spp. • Tamarisk Family *Tamaricaceae*

Botanists are still puzzling over this confusing genus, so we will not attempt to describe species characteristics in detail. Probably most of the tamarisks planted in Washington are the species *Tamarix ramosissima* Ledeb., which is also known as *T. pentandra* Pall. and may also go by the name *T. chinensis* Lour. If you're like us, you'll be happy to enjoy these gorgeous shrubs or small trees on an aesthetic level and let the taxonomists worry about how to classify them.

NATIVE RANGE   Several dozen tamarisk species are found in the Mediterranean area and Asia.

LEAVES   Delicate, fern-like leaves are grayish green and, upon close examination, scale-like.

FLOWERS   Pink, wispy, as delicate as the foliage. (See color close-up.)

GROWTH HABIT   Extremely delicate branches, often spreading or weeping.

LOCATIONS
• National Arboretum
• Logan Circle, Rhode Island Avenue, N.W.
• Private yards and gardens on Capitol Hill, in Georgetown, and elsewhere

Weeping Willow

Salix babylonica L. • Willow Family *Salicaceae*

The weeping willow is such a familiar part of the landscape that most people probably don't realize that it's an exotic tree. Graceful weeping willows line Washington's Potomac shoreline.

NATIVE RANGE   China.

LEAVES   Simple, alternate, deciduous. 3 to 7 inches (7.5–17.8 cm) long. Linear-lanceolate. Long-pointed apex, wedge-shaped base. Margin with rounded or pointed teeth. Dark green above, paler grayish green below, usually glabrous.

GROWTH HABIT   One of the world's most beautiful trees, with gracefully pendulous branches and foliage that streams in the wind.

OTHER FORMS   *Salix babylonica* 'Crispa' has leaves that are spirally curled.

SIMILAR SPECIES   Golden weeping willow (*Salix* × *chrysocoma*).

LOCATIONS
- East and West Potomac Parks
- National Arboretum
- Common throughout the city, especially along the water

Golden Weeping Willow

Salix × *chrysocoma* Dode • Willow Family *Salicaceae*

The golden weeping willow is very similar to the weeping willow (*Salix babylonica*), but it has golden twigs and branches. The leaves of the golden weeping willow are usually pubescent.

LOCATIONS
- National Arboretum
- Common in Washington

Other Willows of the Washington Area

Several other species of willow—some trees, some shrubs—grow in Washington, including the pussy willow (*Salix discolor* Muhl.), the exotic goat willow (*Salix caprea* L.), and the black willow (*Salix nigra* Marshall). The black willow occurs naturally along area streams and in bottomlands. The willows are an extremely difficult genus, even for botanists, so we have described and illustrated only the ones that are important ornamental trees in Washington. For a list of native and exotic willows growing in D.C., consult Shetler and Orli's *Annotated Checklist of the Vascular Plants of the Washington-Baltimore Area.* For illustrated descriptions of willows native to Maryland, consult Brown and Brown's *Woody Plants of Maryland.*

Eastern Cottonwood

Populus deltoides Bartram ex Marshall • Willow Family *Salicaceae*

STATE TREE OF KANSAS AND NEBRASKA

Several magnificent old cottonwood trees grow on both sides of the Potomac in the Washington area.

NATIVE HABITAT AND RANGE   Riverbanks, lowlands, moist prairies; eastern U.S. (excluding northern New England), much of Florida and the high Appalachians.

LEAVES   Simple, alternate, deciduous. 3 to 7 inches (7.5–17.8 cm) long, deltoid, with large, coarse, rounded or pointed teeth. Glabrous. Petiole thick, flattened, with two conspicuous glands at the point where it attaches to the base of the leaf.

FRUIT   Fruiting catkins, 8 to 12 inches (20–30.5 cm) long, bear small ovoid capsules that release cottony-haired seeds that are spread by wind and water.

BARK   Greenish and smooth on young trees, becoming gray, thick, and deeply furrowed with age.

LOCATIONS
- Hains Point, East Potomac Park (including Casey Trees' 2006 D.C. Champion Cottonwood)
- Rock Creek Park
- Lady Bird Johnson Park
- Shirlington Park (2007–2008 Arlington County Champion Eastern Cottonwood)
- Regional rivers and bottomlands

The Poplars

Populus L. • Willow Family *Salicaceae*

Once popular (no pun intended) throughout the city, the *Populus* genus is now significantly represented in Washington only by the Eastern cottonwood (*Populus deltoides*). During the nineteenth century, poplars were widely planted for their fast growth and attractive foliage. But they proved to be bad city trees. Their shallow roots tore into roads and sidewalks, so over the years these surface rooters, as they came to be called, were replaced by more suitable species. Brief descriptions of three poplars that are still found in the area follow. In addition to these trees, Shetler and Orli list additional exotic poplars growing in Washington in their *Annotated Checklist of the Vascular Plants of the Washington-Baltimore Area*: balsam poplar (*Populus balsamifera* L.) and gray poplar [*P. × canescens* (Aiton.) Sm.]. Consult Brown and Brown's *Woody Plants of Maryland* for poplars found in other parts of the state.

Lombardy Poplar

Populus nigra L. 'Italica'

Thomas Jefferson personally se-lected this Italian clone for planting along Pennsylvania Avenue during his administration. The tree has tri-angular leaves and a distinctive narrow, columnar growth habit with many small, steeply ascending branches.

White Poplar (Silver Poplar)

Populus alba L.

Native to Europe and Asia, the white poplar has naturalized in many parts of North America, becoming invasive in places. Easily recognized by its distinctive palmately lobed leaves, which are white or silver and densely pubescent below.

Big-Toothed Aspen (Large-Toothed Aspen)

Populus grandidentata Michx.

The big-toothed aspen is native to the northeastern U.S. (including the Washington area) and southeastern Canada. Its leaves are similar to the Eastern cottonwood, but they are smaller (2 to 3 inches [5–7.5 cm] long) and ovate rather than deltoid.

Sourwood (Sorrel-Tree)

Oxydendrum arboreum (L.) DC. • Heath Family *Ericaceae*

This small tree is inconspicuous most of the year, but in fall it steals the show. Decorative hanging clusters of small, bell-shaped, ivory flowers appear in midsummer and are followed by showy fruit that is set off by gorgeous, long-lasting autumn color, varying from scarlet to dark wine. This tree is the source of sourwood honey.

NATIVE HABITAT AND RANGE   Woodlands; New Jersey and Pennsylvania, west to southern Illinois, south to Florida and Louisiana.

LEAVES   Simple, alternate, deciduous. 4 to 7 inches (10–17.7 cm) long. Oblong-elliptic to oblong-lanceolate. Finely and irregularly toothed. Broadly wedge-shaped at base, somewhat abruptly pointed at apex. Glossy and glabrous above, paler below and slightly pubescent along the veins.

FLOWERS   Ivory, bell-shaped flowers in thin, pendulous, delicately curved clusters. Clusters are 4 to 10 inches (10–25.3 cm) long and hang from the ends of the branches. Midsummer.

FRUIT   Small, five-angled, grayish brown capsules in long clusters. Late summer and autumn into winter.

BARK AND TWIGS   Bark gray, sometimes tinged with red; thick, furrowed, ridged, and scaly. Twigs reddish to yellow-green, glabrous, with small winter buds and false end bud.

Growth Habit   Small to medium-sized tree. Ascending branches form a narrow, rather top-heavy, rounded crown.

Similar Species   Distinctive. The tupelo or sour-gum (*Nyssa sylvatica*) has somewhat similar leaves, but they are smaller, with smooth or slightly wavy margins. See also common persimmon (*Diospyros virginiana*) "Similar Species."

Locations
• Glenwood Cemetery
• Arlington National Cemetery
• National Garden of the U.S. Botanic Garden
• George Washington Memorial Parkway
• Private yards and gardens throughout the city and suburbs

Japanese Snowbell

Styrax japonicus Siebold & Zucc. • Storax Family *Styracaceae*

A small tree with slender, widely ascending branches and attractive clustered white flowers in early summer.

Native Range   China, Japan, Korea.

Leaves   Simple, alternate, deciduous. 1½ to 3½ inches (3.8–9 cm) long. Ovate or elliptic, with abruptly or gradually pointed apex and wedge-shaped base. Margin wavy, often with a few irregular, shallow teeth. Soon glabrous, except for tufts of hairs in the vein axils below. Petiole ¼ to ⅓ inch (less than 1 cm) long.

Flowers   White, stamens orange or yellow. Slightly fragrant. Usually five-lobed. Each flower an inch or less (1.5–2.5 cm) across. Many clusters, each containing three to six flowers, hang close to the undersides of the branches. Late spring or early summer. (See color close-up.)

Fruit   Smooth, greenish gray, ovoid or rounded, ½ to ⅔ inch (1.2–1.6 cm) long on a long stalk.

Similar Species   The fragrant snowbell (*Styrax obassia*) has very fragrant flowers and larger, rounder leaves. American snowbell (*Styrax americanus* Lam.) is occasionally cultivated. Its white, bell-shaped flowers have very reflexed (swept back) lobes. Because it is a shrub, it is not treated individually in this guide. It grows in Fern Valley at the National Arboretum and is native to the southeastern U.S. from Virginia to Florida west to Missouri, Arkansas, and Louisiana, and in scattered spots in the Midwest.

LOCATIONS
- Soldiers' Home
- National Arboretum
- Smithsonian Castle: Enid A. Haupt Garden
- Private yards and gardens throughout the city
- Some parks and public buildings

Fragrant Snowbell (Big-Leaf Storax)

Styrax obassia Siebold & Zucc. • Storax Family *Styracaceae*

An attractive ornamental tree with large, nearly round leaves and fragrant flowers.

NATIVE RANGE Japan, Korea, Manchuria.

LEAVES Simple, alternate, deciduous. 3 to 8 inches (7.5–20.3 cm) long and usually about as wide or slightly wider. (Some leaves are narrower.) Very rounded, with an abruptly pointed apex and a wedge-shaped or rounded base. Margin slightly wavy, often with a few small teeth toward the apex. Densely and softly pubescent below.

FLOWERS Similar to the Japanese snowbell (*Styrax japonicus*), but earlier, much more fragrant, and with more flowers per cluster. Hanging clusters are 4 to 8 inches (10–20 cm) long and often are partly hidden behind the leaves. May.

FRUIT Gray-green, ovoid or nearly round, about ¾ inch (2 cm) long. Pubescent, at least on the persistent calyx. This and the fruit of the Japanese snowbell are shaped like tiny eggplants.

SIMILAR SPECIES Although the flowers and fruit are similar to the Japanese snowbell, the large, rounded leaves of this species easily identify it.

LOCATIONS
- Dumbarton Oaks

- National Arboretum (near Magnolia Collection and Mount Hamilton azaleas)
- Sparsely planted in Washington, mostly in private and public gardens and private yards

Carolina Silverbell

Halesia carolina L. (*Halesia tetraptera* Ellis) • Storax Family *Styracaceae*

A small tree or large shrub with bell-shaped spring flowers.

Native Habitat and Range Moist, rich woods; southeastern U.S., mainly in the mountains and/or along streambanks, Virginia to the Florida panhandle, west to Oklahoma.

Leaves Simple, alternate, deciduous. 3 to 7 inches (7.5–18 cm) long. Finely toothed.

Flowers White, in drooping clusters of two to five. Each flower bell-shaped with four fused petals. (See color close-up.)

Fruit Dry, four-winged, oblong fruit, up to 1½ inches (4 cm) long.

Similar Species Compare leaves of the two preceding species, which both have smooth (not winged) fruit. See two-winged silverbell.

Locations
- National Arboretum
- Lowell Street, N.W.
- Some parks, private yards, and public and private gardens throughout the Washington area

Two-Winged Silverbell

Halesia diptera Ellis • Storax Family *Styraceae*

This small tree or shrub is native to the southeastern U.S. from South Carolina and Florida to Texas. It blooms slightly later than the Carolina silverbell, and its fruit is two-winged rather than four-winged.

Location
- U.S. Botanic Garden: Bartholdi Park

Common Persimmon

Diospyros virginiana L. • Ebony Family *Ebenaceae*

The common persimmon produces autumn fruit that is an important food source for white-tailed deer, raccoons, foxes, other mammals, and birds. It also makes a succulent snack for humans once cold autumn weather has sweetened the flavor and improved the texture. The common persimmon is not widely cultivated in Washington.

NATIVE HABITAT AND RANGE
A variety of habitats, including dry, rocky woods, rich bottomlands, hedgerows, and roadsides; southeastern Connecticut and southern New York through all of Florida, west to eastern Texas, eastern Kansas, and southeastern Iowa.

LEAVES   Simple, alternate, deciduous. 3 to 6 inches (7.5–15 cm) long. Oblong-ovate to ovate-elliptic. Margin smooth. Lustrous green and glabrous above, sometimes slightly pubescent below.

FRUIT   Large, round, orange, purple-tinged berry, 1 to 1½ inches (2.5–3.8 cm) across. The smooth skin becomes wrinkled when the fruit is ripe and edible. The persistent calyx is thick and leathery. Large, smooth, shiny reddish brown seeds.

BARK   Very distinctive: bark is dark gray and separated into small, thick squares.

SIMILAR SPECIES   The tupelo or black gum (*Nyssa sylvatica*) has fruit that is a small blue-black drupe.

LOCATIONS
• Some parks (including Rock Creek Park) and private homes in the District
• Woods, hedgerows, and roadsides in the surrounding countryside

Chinese Kaki Persimmon (Japanese Persimmon)

Diospyros kaki L. • Ebony Family *Ebenaceae*

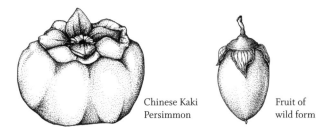

Chinese Kaki
Persimmon

Fruit of
wild form

This tree is cultivated in Asia, Europe, and North America for its edible fruit.

NATIVE RANGE   Asia.

LEAVES   Similar in shape to the native species, but longer and broader.

FRUIT   1½ to 3½ inches (3.8–8.8 cm) across, rounded to ovoid (often squat like a tomato), bright yellow to orange. (The fruit of the wild form of the tree, *D. kaki* var. *sylvestris* Mak., is considerably smaller.)

LOCATIONS
• National Arboretum
• Hillwood Estate (wild form)

The Lindens (Basswoods, Limes)

Tilia L. • Linden Family *Tiliaceae*

Bees are fonder of lindens than botanists are. Linden nectar makes great honey, but the trees themselves are a nightmare to identify and classify. The European species pose particular problems because they have been so heavily hybridized.

Washington's streets, avenues, and parks are well endowed with linden trees, whose fragrant flowers perfume the air for much of the month of June.

LEAVES   Simple, alternate, deciduous. Usually heart-shaped, with unequal bases and toothed margins.

FLOWERS AND FRUIT   Flowers yellow or whitish, fragrant, in clusters attached to a leafy bract. Fruit small, round or ovoid, sometimes conspicuously ribbed, attached to the leafy bract. [See American linden (*Tilia americana*) illustration.]

TWIGS Winter buds quite large, obtuse; terminal bud absent.

American Linden (American Basswood or Lime)

Tilia americana L. • Linden Family *Tiliaceae*

During the nineteenth and early twentieth centuries, Massachusetts Avenue was lined with double rows of American linden (or basswood) trees that framed the walkways on both sides of the street. Some lindens remain from the original plantings.

The city's Urban Forestry Administration still maintains the tradition of planting lindens on Massachusetts Avenue. Restore Mass Ave, a nonprofit citizens group, is working with the city to help protect and restore the historic lindens along the Embassy Row section of Massachusetts Avenue. In June, the linden blossoms on the avenue and throughout the city fill the air with a summery perfume.

A 1923 visitor to the capital had this to say about the lindens: "Its praises have been less sung than the praises of the oak, the elm, the maple, or the chestnut, but let one drive under the lindens of Massachusetts Avenue on a damp night in June, when the trees are in full bloom, and the haunting fragrance of that drive will long remain. Some day American poets may sing its praises."[85]

NATIVE HABITAT AND RANGE A variety of habitats from low, moist, well-drained woodlands to rich upland woods and rocky ridges; New Brunswick and Maine, south to western North

Carolina, west to southeastern Manitoba, the eastern Dakotas, eastern Kansas, and eastern Oklahoma.

Leaves   Simple, alternate, deciduous. 4 to 10 inches (10–25.3 cm) long. Heart-shaped, with an unequal base. Coarsely toothed. Dull dark green above, paler below and usually glabrous, except for a few small tufts of hairs in the vein axils. Petioles slender, 1 to 2 inches (2.5–5 cm) long.

Flowers   Yellow, fragrant, in pendulous clusters of six to fifteen on a long, slender stalk attached to a leafy bract. 3 to 5½ inches (7.5–14 cm) long.

Fruit   Round or ellipsoid, nut-like, without ribs. ¼ to ½ inch (5–12 mm) long, attached in small clusters to a leafy bract.

Bark and Twigs   Bark gray, becoming narrowly, vertically ridged and furrowed. Twigs with rather large, reddish winter buds; terminal bud absent.

Growth Habit   Tall trunk and a dense, rounded crown.

Similar Species   The white basswood (*Tilia heterophylla* Vent.) is considered a separate species by some botanists and a variety of the American linden or basswood [*Tilia americana* var. *heterophylla* (Vent.) Loudon] by others. It ranges farther south and is characterized by leaves that are whitish woolly or brownish woolly below. The tree is planted in Washington, though not nearly as commonly as the American linden. The European lindens have smaller leaves than the American species. The leaves of the European big-leafed linden (*Tilia platyphyllos*), which are almost as large as the American species, are pubescent below, with conspicuous tufts of hairs in the vein axils.

Locations
• Massachusetts Avenue
• U.S. Capitol grounds
• Streets, parks, and public buildings throughout the city
• Audubon Naturalist Society, Woodend Sanctuary, Chevy Chase, Maryland (2007 Montgomery County Champion American Linden or Basswood)
• Arlington National Cemetery (2007–2008 Arlington County Champion American Linden or Basswood)

Big-Leafed Linden (Large-Leafed Lime)

Tilia platyphyllos Scop. • Linden Family *Tiliaceae*

NATIVE RANGE   Europe, the Caucasus, Asia Minor.

LEAVES   Simple, alternate, deciduous. Variable in size, 2½ to 6½ inches (6.3–16.5 cm) long. More or less heart-shaped, with unequal base and sharply toothed margin. Pubescent below, especially along the veins, with conspicuous tufts of hairs in the vein axils. Petiole pubescent.

FLOWERS AND FRUIT   Flowers yellow-white, fragrant, attached to a leafy bract. The first linden to bloom in Washington (late May or early June). Fruit small, round, and nut-like, conspicuously five-ribbed, pubescent, attached to a leafy bract.

OTHER FORMS   A beautiful specimen of the cultivar 'Vitifolia' used to stand behind the Smithsonian Castle (Independence Avenue side). Many of its leaves were slightly three-lobed.

SIMILAR SPECIES   The common American linden (*Tilia americana*) has larger leaves that are glabrous except for small tufts of hairs in the vein axils. The white basswood (see American linden "Similar Species") has leaves that are usually whitened below.

LOCATIONS
• U.S. Capitol grounds
• Moderately common in the city

Little-Leafed Linden (Small-Leafed Lime)

Tilia cordata Mill. • Linden Family *Tiliaceae*

This European tree is widely planted in Washington, but is very difficult to distinguish from the hybrid European linden (*Tilia × europaea*), which is a cross between this species and the big-leafed linden (*Tilia platyphyllos*). Franklin Delano Roosevelt planted two little-leafed lindens on the south lawn of the White House.

NATIVE RANGE   Europe.

LEAVES   Simple, alternate, deciduous. 1 to 3 inches (2.5–7.5 cm) long. Deeply heart-shaped. Apex abruptly pointed, margin sharply and finely toothed. Pale bluish green below, with orange tufts of hairs in the vein axils.

FLOWERS AND FRUIT   Pale yellow, fragrant, in erect or spreading clusters attached to a leafy bract. June. Fruit small, round, glabrous, and nut-like, not ribbed or only scarcely so, attached to a leafy bract.

OTHER FORMS   'Greenspire' is one of many cultivars of *Tilia cordata*.

SIMILAR SPECIES   The European linden (*Tilia* × *europaea*) has slightly larger leaves that tend to be more pubescent than the little-leafed linden. A few small hairs scattered along the leaf margin of the European linden often are visible with a hand lens. Little-leafed linden leaves usually have no hairs along their margins.

LOCATIONS
• White House grounds
• National Park Service National Capital Region Headquarters, East Potomac Park
• U.S. Capitol grounds
• Smithsonian Castle: Enid A. Haupt Garden
• Streets, parks, and public buildings throughout the city

European Linden (Common Lime)

Tilia × *europaea* L. (*T. platyphyllos* × *T. cordata*) • Linden Family *Tiliaceae*

This hybrid of the big-leafed and little-leafed lindens is widely planted in Washington. It is difficult to distinguish from the little-leafed linden, even for botanists.

LEAVES   Simple, alternate, deciduous. 2¼ to 4¼ inches (5.5–10.5 cm) long. Very similar to the little-leafed linden (*Tilia cordata*), but slightly larger, sometimes more pubescent below, and sometimes less deeply cordate at the base. A very few hairs often are visible along the margin with a hand lens.

FLOWERS AND FRUIT   Flower clusters slightly more pendulous than the little-leafed linden. Nut-like fruit woolly pubescent and faintly ribbed.

SIMILAR SPECIES   Little-leafed linden. There are two reasons why the distinguishing characteristics of the European linden are so hard to pin down. Lindens in general are a difficult genus; and the European linden is the name for a large group of hybrids with widely varying characteristics.

LOCATIONS
- U.S. Capitol grounds
- National Park Service National Capital Region Headquarters, East Potomac Park (most trees in this planting are little-leafed lindens)
- Streets and parks throughout the District

Weeping Silver Linden (Weeping Silver Lime)

Tilia petiolaris DC. • Linden Family *Tiliaceae*

A beautiful weeping tree with leaves that look silvery below when blown by the wind. Quite rare in Washington.

NATIVE RANGE   Origin uncertain. Some botanists believe the tree is a form of the silver linden (*Tilia tomentosa* Moench.), native to southeastern Europe and western Asia.

LEAVES   Simple, alternate, deciduous. 2½ to 5 inches (6.3–12.5 cm) long. Heart-shaped. Sharply toothed. Lower leaf surface and petiole covered with short, soft, white pubescence, giving it a silvery look.

FLOWERS   Yellow, very fragrant. Their nectar has a narcotic effect on bees. Mid to late June.

DISTINGUISHING CHARACTERISTICS   The weeping growth habit and the soft, white undersides of the leaves distinguish this tree from other locally planted lindens.

LOCATIONS
- Rarely planted in Washington

Other Lindens of the Washington Area

At least two other species of linden (*Tilia*) are cultivated in Washington, although rarely.

The Caucasian linden or lime (*Tilia × euchlora* K. Koch) is planted along a few streets in Washington. Its leaves are 2 to 4 inches (5–10 cm) long and a deep glossy green, with large tufts of brownish hairs in the vein axils below.

Tilia dasystyla Stev. is an even rarer linden, believed to be one of the parents of the hybrid Caucasian linden. This tree has leaves that are 3 to 5½ inches (7.5–14 cm) long, with tufts of whitish yellow hairs in the vein axils below.

Rose-of-Sharon (Shrubby Althea)

Hibiscus syriacus L. • Mallow Family *Malvaceae*

The rose-of-sharon is very conspicuous in Washington during its long blooming time, midsummer to mid-autumn. Although usually a shrub, it is sometimes trained as a small tree.

NATIVE RANGE   China, India.

LEAVES   Simple, alternate, deciduous. 1¾ to 4 inches (4.5–10 cm) long. Usually three-lobed, with coarse rounded or pointed teeth.

FLOWERS AND FRUIT   Showy flowers may be pink, red, white, purple, blue, or a combination. Five-petaled, 2 to 4 inches (5–10 cm) across, vaguely rose-like. Fruit an upright capsule, persistent and brown into winter.

SIMILAR SPECIES   Viburnums (*Viburnum* spp.) have opposite leaves.

LOCATIONS
• Very common in public and private gardens and grounds throughout the city
• National Arboretum
• Sometimes escapes from cultivation

Chinese Parasol Tree (Phoenix-Tree)

Firmiana simplex (L.) W. F. Wight • Sterculia Family *Sterculiaceae*

NATIVE RANGE   China, Japan. The tree escapes from cultivation and is potentially invasive.

LEAVES   Simple, alternate, deciduous. Size varies: most leaves 6 to 10 inches (15–25.5 cm) long, but some are much larger.

Palmately three- to five-lobed. Petiole as long or almost as long as leaf blade.

BARK   Gray-green, very smooth.

GROWTH HABIT   Trunk very straight. Branches form a compact, rounded crown. Overall appearance vaguely suggests a parasol. According to Joan Feely, curator of Fern Valley at the National Arboretum, the tree tends to develop suckers.

LOCATIONS
• National Arboretum
• Rare in Washington

Common Box

Buxus sempervirens L. •
Box Family *Buxaceae*

Dozens of varieties of the common box are planted in Washington. Although most are shrubs, the box can become a small tree. Several attractive tree-like specimens are growing on the Capitol grounds.

NATIVE RANGE   Europe, northern Africa, western Asia.

LEAVES   Simple, opposite, evergreen. Tiny: ½ to 1¼ inches (1.3–3.2 cm) long. Elliptic or ovate. Dark glossy green.

LOCATIONS
• U.S. Capitol grounds
• White House grounds (form known as "American box" planted by Harry S. Truman)
• Dumbarton Oaks
• Common throughout the city

The Cherries, Peaches, and Plums

Prunus L. • Rose Family *Rosaceae*

The crème de la crème of Washington's flowering trees are among the most botanically elusive. Centuries of hybridization (mostly in Japan) have rendered many specimens of the genus virtually inscrutable, even to botanists and horticulturists specializing in the field. Thanks to one individual, Roland Jefferson of the National Arboretum, the history and taxonomy of Washington's famous flowering cherry trees were untangled and preserved during the latter part of the twentieth century. See Part I of *City of Trees* for the story of these living symbols of international friendship.

LEAVES   Simple, alternate, deciduous. Usually toothed.

FLOWERS   White, pink, or red (rarely green). Five petals.

FRUIT   Usually a one-seeded drupe.

Japanese Flowering Cherry Trees

Yoshino Cherry (Somei-Yoshino)

Prunus × *yedoensis* Matsum. (Hybrid of unknown origin) • Rose Family *Rosaceae*

This is the enchanting Japanese flowering cherry of Tidal Basin fame. Some of the original trees given to the United States by Japan in 1912 are still alive today.

LEAVES   Simple, alternate, deciduous. About 6 inches (15 cm) long. Elliptic-obovate. Coarsely toothed. Pubescent along the veins below.

FLOWERS   Pale pink at first, later turning white or nearly white, then often blushing pink near the base before falling. In clusters of two to five. Late March or early April, before the leaves. (See color close-up.)

FRUIT   Black when ripe (red and yellow when ripening), obovoid-ellipsoid, less than ½ inch (1 cm) long. Early summer.

OTHER FORMS   In the 1920s, the slightly pinker 'Akebono' was selected and propagated in a California nursery. This American form of the Japanese tree is widely planted in Washington today. Many of the old Yoshino cherries have been replaced by specimens of Akebono.

YOSHINO LOCATIONS
• Tidal Basin (West Potomac Park)
• East Potomac Park
• U.S. Capitol grounds
• Library of Congress grounds
• Fort McNair
• Kenwood neighborhood, Bethesda, Maryland

AKEBONO LOCATIONS
• Tidal Basin (West Potomac Park)
• East Potomac Park
• U.S. Capitol grounds
• Washington Monument
• Dumbarton Oaks

Weeping Cherry (Weeping Higan Cherry)

Prunus subhirtella pendula Maxim., *Prunus subhirtella pendula*
'Flora Plena' • Rose Family *Rosaceae*

The weeping cherry is one of Washington's most spectacular
flowering trees. In early spring its pendulous branchlets put forth
clouds of pink or white blossoms.

NATIVE RANGE Japan.

LEAVES Simple, alternate, deciduous. 2½ to 5 inches (6.3–12.5
cm) long. Oblong-elliptic. Sharply, sometimes doubly toothed.
Pubescent along the veins below.

FLOWERS Pink (rarely white), double or single. The single
flowers are star-shaped, the double flowers bell-shaped. March
or early April, before the leaves. (See color close-up of single-
blossomed form.)

FRUIT Less than ½ inch (8 mm) long, black.

GROWTH HABIT Gracefully weeping tree with delicate, very
pendulous branchlets.

SINGLE-BLOSSOMED PINK FORM LOCATIONS
• East Potomac Park
• U.S. Capitol grounds
• Dumbarton Oaks
• Smithsonian Castle: Enid A. Haupt Garden
• Parks and gardens throughout the city and suburbs

DOUBLE-BLOSSOMED PINK FORM LOCATIONS
• National Arboretum
• Parks and gardens throughout the city (not as common as the
  single-blossomed form)

SINGLE-BLOSSOMED WHITE FORM LOCATIONS
• East Potomac Park
• Parks and gardens throughout the city (uncommon)

Fall-Blooming Cherry

Prunus subhirtella Miq. 'Autumnalis' • Rose Family *Rosaceae*

The fall-blooming cherry belongs to the same species as the
weeping cherry. In late autumn and early winter, this unique tree
puts forth pale pink, gently nodding flowers. In spring, the tree

becomes covered with blossoms before the leaves appear and continues to bloom for a time after they have unfurled.

Locations
• Dumbarton Oaks
• Parks, gardens, and grounds throughout the city and suburbs

Kwanzan Cherry

Prunus serrulata Lindl. 'Kwanzan' [*Prunus* (Sato-Zakura group) 'Sekiyama'] • Rose Family *Rosaceae*

A deep pink, double-blossomed Japanese cherry that blooms approximately two weeks later than the Yoshino and Akebono. Kwanzan cherries are planted extensively in East Potomac Park.

Native Range   Origin unknown. Possibly a Chinese tree introduced into Japan early on as a single-flowered form.

Leaves   Simple, alternate, deciduous. 3 to 7½ inches (7.5–18.8 cm) long. Ovate, ovate-lanceolate, or obovate. Doubly toothed. Coppery or purplish at first, becoming green.

Flowers   Medium to deep pink. Large, double-flowered, in dense clusters of three to five. Mid to late April. (See color close-up.)

Growth Habit   Distinctive upright habit, with branches forming an inverse pyramid.

Similar Species   Several other double-blossomed cherries were part of the original 1912 gift from Japan to the United States. The Kwanzan is the only one that is still around in any numbers. One of the trees sent to the U.S. by Japan, the Gyoiko, is very rare today. The Gyoiko has unique, pale green blossoms shaped much like the Kwanzan. The specimens planted on the White House grounds have since died, but a large Gyoiko is thriving at Glenn Dale, Maryland.

Locations
• East Potomac Park
• U.S. Capitol grounds
• Library of Congress grounds
• Organization of American States headquarters
• Public and private gardens and grounds throughout the city and suburbs

Sargent Cherry

Prunus sargentii Rehd. • Rose Family *Rosaceae*

Sargent cherry has early, pink, single flowers and bronze and red fall foliage. This Japanese flowering cherry has gained popularity in Washington in recent years.

LOCATIONS
• East and West Potomac Parks
• Public and private gardens and grounds throughout the city and suburbs

Other Japanese Flowering Cherries

The Usuzumi cherry (*Prunus spachiana ascendens*)—with white-gray flowers—and the Takesimensis cherry (*Prunus takesimensis*) are also grown in Washington. The Usuzumi is found in West Potomac Park, and the Takesimensis grows in East Potomac Park.

The dream catcher cherry (*Prunus* 'Dream Catcher') and the first lady cherry (*Prunus* 'First Lady') are growing at the National Arboretum, where they were developed. The dream catcher cherry has medium pink, early-spring flowers, and the first lady cherry has nodding, dark rose-pink early blooms.

The Fuji cherry (*Prunus incisa* Thunb.) grows wild in the vicinity of Mount Fuji. It was selected for a ceremonial planting at the Freer Gallery by S. Dillon Ripley, secretary of the Smithsonian Institution, during a 1981 visit by the prime minister of Japan.

Other forms of *Prunus subhirtella* (Higan cherry) planted in Washington include *Prunus subhirtella* var. *ascendens* (Mak.) Wils.

Other Exotic *Prunus* Species Planted in Washington

Peach

Prunus persica (L.) Batsch • Rose Family (*Rosaceae*)

STATE FLOWER OF DELAWARE

The peach has long been cultivated throughout Asia, Europe, and North America for its delicious fruit and lovely flowers. Several forms of the peach, with blossoms ranging from white to deep red, are planted in Washington. Some have large double blossoms.

Native Range   Believed to be China.

Flowers   Red, pink, rose, or white. Late March to April.

Locations
• Public and private gardens and grounds throughout the city
• Peach orchards in surrounding farmlands, including Montgomery County's Agricultural Reserve

Purple-Leaved Plum (Pissard Plum)

Prunus cerasifera Ehrh. 'Atropurpurea' • Rose Family *Rosaceae*

The purple-leaved plum is one of Washington's loveliest ornamentals. Its small, pale pink blossoms open in very early spring and are soon offset by attractive, reddish purple leaves. The species is native to the Balkan Peninsula and Asia.

Locations
• Public and private gardens and grounds throughout the city

Double Cherry-Plum

Prunus × *blireana* André (*P. cerasifera* 'Atropurpurea' × *P. mume*) • Rose Family *Rosaceae*

The double cherry-plum is extremely rare in Washington. It has large, pink, double blossoms that open with the reddish purple leaves in spring.

Location
• Dumbarton Oaks

Additional Exotic *Prunus* Species Planted Here

Sweet cherry or Mazzard cherry (*Prunus avium* L.), an early-blooming Eurasian native with edible fruit, has become established as a naturalized tree in Washington-area woodlands. Sour cherry (*Prunus cerasus* L.), also of Eurasian origin, has been planted here. It has tarter fruit and is less common as an escaped species. Flowering almond (*Prunus triloba* Lindl.) is occasionally grown in Washington gardens.

Native North American *Prunus* Species

Black Cherry (Wild Cherry, Wild Black Cherry)

Prunus serotina Ehrh. • Rose Family *Rosaceae*

The black cherry, native to most of the eastern United States, southeastern Canada, and parts of Central America, blooms in Washington in April and May. Many songbirds favor the slightly bitter fruit.

LEAVES Simple, alternate, deciduous. 2 to 6 inches (5–15 cm) long. Elliptic to oblong-lanceolate. Small, incurved teeth. The lower leaf surface has a little orange pubescence near the base, and there usually are two small, glandular projections on the leaf blade near the petiole. Leaves, especially if wilted, are toxic to farm animals.

FLOWERS Small, white, five-petaled flowers in elongated, pendulous, or partially pendulous clusters, 4 to 5 inches (10–12.5 cm) long.

FRUIT Small, black or very dark red or dark purple cherries, ¼ to ½ inch (6–12 mm) long.

SIMILAR SPECIES The usually shrubby choke cherry (*Prunus virginiana* L.), a far less locally common native cherry that is indigenous to much of the U.S., has red fruit and leaves with spreading, rather than incurved, teeth. I have never seen it growing in the city; and in their *Annotated Checklist of the Vascular Plants of the Washington-Baltimore Area,* Shetler and Orli place a question mark after its D.C. listing. In their *Woody Plants of Maryland*, Brown and Brown describe its range as "[m]ostly in the mountain counties."

LOCATIONS
• National Arboretum
• Montrose Park
• Rock Creek Park
• Parks, woodlands, and roadsides throughout the city and surrounding suburbs and countryside

Carolina Laurelcherry

Prunus caroliniana (Mill.) Ait. • Rose Family *Rosaceae*

The Carolina laurelcherry, which grows from North Carolina to Texas, is just barely hardy here if planted in a sheltered place. Its leaves are evergreen, and its tiny white flowers are borne in elongated clusters in early spring.

LOCATIONS
• White House grounds
• National Garden of the U.S. Botanic Garden
• Kenilworth Aquatic Gardens

The Flowering Crabapples

Malus Mill. • Rose Family *Rosaceae*

Like the Japanese flowering cherry trees, Washington's flowering crabapples are an important part of the landscape. A steady procession of crabapple blossoms adorns the city during April and May. For many years, a crabapple festival was held in the nation's capital each spring, with nearly as much fanfare as the Cherry Blossom Festival. A crabapple parade was held, and a young lady was crowned crabapple queen. The festival was discontinued in the 1950s, but some of the old trees still bloom each year along the banks of the Anacostia in Southeast Washington.

The genus *Malus*, to which the flowering crabapples belong, is an extremely confusing one. So much hybridization has taken place among the crabapples that even botanists specializing in the genus have trouble distinguishing among them. Therefore, we've chosen one of the most commonly planted crabapples as an exemplary species. A list of some of the other crabapples traditionally cultivated in Washington follows. (Some botanists now use the genus name *Pyrus* for *Malus* species.)

Japanese Flowering Crab

Malus floribunda Siebold ex Van Houtte • Rose Family *Rosaceae*

NATIVE RANGE   Japan.

LEAVES   Simple, alternate, deciduous. 2 to 3 inches (5–7.5 cm) long. Elliptic-ovate or oblong-ovate. Long-pointed apex, usually wedge-shaped base, sharply toothed margin. Dark green. Pubescent along the veins below or nearly glabrous.

FLOWERS Deep rose-pink buds, opening up paler pink to nearly white. 1 to 1¼ inches (2.5–3 cm) across. The deep pink buds against the paler pink open flowers and dark green leaves present a striking picture. (See color close-up.)

FRUIT Small pome, yellowish or sometimes blushed red, ¼ to ½ inch (6–12 mm) across.

GROWTH HABIT Small tree with widely spreading branches.

LOCATIONS
• Common throughout the city

The following list includes crabapples traditionally planted in Washington. Some of them are now hard to find, but we have retained most of the cultivated varieties listed in earlier editions of *City of Trees*.

CRABAPPLES WITH WHITE OR PALE PINK FLOWERS

Adirondack Crabapple (*Malus* 'Adirondack')
Fuji Crab [*Malus sieboldii* (Reg.) Rehd.] 'Fuji' (This cultivar produces a profusion of white double blossoms.)
Katherine Crab (*Malus* × 'Katherine')
Arnold Crab [*Malus* × *arnoldiana* (Rehd.) Sarg.] (*M. floribunda* × *M. baccata*)
Siberian Crab [*Malus baccata* (L.) Borkh.]
Tea Crab [*Malus hupehensis* (Pampan.) Rehd.]
Iowa or Prairie Crab [*Malus ioensis* (Wood) Britt.]
Bechtel Crab (*Malus ioensis* 'Plena')
Pear or Plum-Leaved Crab [*Malus prunifolia* (Willd.) Borkh.]
Cherry Crab [*Malus* × *robusta* (Carr.) Rehd.] (*M. baccata* × *M. prunifolia*)
Sargent Crab (*Malus sargentii* Rehd.)
Zumi Crab [*Malus* × *zumi* (Matsum.) Rehd.]

CRABAPPLES WITH MEDIUM PINK, DARK PINK, REDDISH, OR PURPLISH FLOWERS

Dorothea Crab (*Malus* × 'Dorothea')

Hopa Crab (*Malus* × 'Hopa')
Radiant Crab (*Malus* × 'Radiant')
Carmine Crab [*Malus* × *atrosanguinea* (Spaeth) Schneid.]
Wild Sweet Crab [*Malus coronaria* (L.) Mill.]
Purple Crab [*Malus* × *purpurea* (Barbier) Rehd.] (*M. atrosan-guinea* × *M. pumila* var. *niedzwetzkyana*)
Scheidecker Crab [*Malus* × *scheideckeri* (Spaeth) Zab.] (*M. floribunda* × *M. prunifolia*)
Chinese Flowering Crab [*Malus spectabilis* (Ait.) Borkh.]

The Pears

Pyrus L. • Rose Family *Rosaceae*

The pears have long been cultivated for their delicious fruit and showy early-spring flowers.

Bradford Pear

Pyrus calleryana Decne. 'Bradford' • Rose Family *Rosaceae*

In the previous editions of *City of Trees* I wrote: "The Bradford pear is an increasingly popular cultivar. Its snowy white, early-spring flowers are borne on a beautiful egg-shaped crown. In the fall, Bradford pear leaves turn wine-red. With so much to recommend this tree it's no wonder we've heard it criticized . . . for being too perfect!"

What a difference a quarter century can make. The Bradford pear is now considered an undesirable tree, both for the hazards of its weak limbs, which are prone to splitting during storms, and its invasiveness. This once-heralded ornamental's star has definitely fallen. And yet, as I sit here on a clear March morning, I can't help admiring the creamy flowers on the neighbors' tree outside my window.

NATIVE RANGE   A cultivar of the Callery pear (*Pyrus calleryana*), which is native to China and Korea.

LEAVES   Simple, alternate, deciduous. 1½ to 4 inches (4–10 cm) long. Egg- or heart-shaped, with small, rounded teeth. Bright yellow-green when they unfold in spring, becoming gray-green. Smooth, some pubescence when young, then becoming glabrous.

FLOWERS   White, five-petaled, with long stamens with purple or red anthers. Early spring, before or with the leaves. (See color close-up.)

FRUIT   Small, rounded, slender-stalked pome, less than ½ inch (1 cm) in diameter.

GROWTH HABIT   Small tree with a distinctive egg-shaped crown and narrow, ascending branches. Tree prone to limb-splitting during ice storms and thunderstorms. Many older trees lose the clean lines of their crowns due to storm damage.

DISTINGUISHING CHARACTERISTICS   The Bradford pear is best distinguished from other pears, cherries, and apples by its egg-shaped crown.

LOCATIONS
• National Capital YMCA (Rhode Island Avenue)
• U.S. Department of Agriculture, the Mall (tree planted by Lady Bird Johnson in 1966 replaced on May 2, 1987)
• Common throughout the city and suburbs and in surrounding woodlands, where it has escaped from cultivation and become invasive

Callery Pear

Pyrus calleryana Decne. • Rose Family *Rosaceae*

This pear is less frequently planted than its popular cultivar. The Callery pear closely resembles the Bradford, but lacks the egg-shaped crown.

LOCATIONS
• National Arboretum
• Washington Avenue, S.W., U.S. Botanic Garden: Bartholdi Park

Common Pear

Pyrus communis L. • Rose Family *Rosaceae*

Another flowering pear with beautiful white spring blossoms. This tree is planted in Lady Bird Johnson Park along the Potomac.

NATIVE RANGE   Europe, Asia.

LEAVES   Simple, alternate, deciduous. 1 to 3 inches (2.5–7.5 cm) long. Ovate, almost rounded or elliptic, with wavy-toothed and/or sharply toothed margin.

FLOWERS   White, about 1 inch (2.5 cm) across, with five petals. Early spring.

GROWTH HABIT   Small to medium-sized tree with a rounded or pyramidal crown.

SIMILAR SPECIES   Ussurian Pear (*Pyrus ussuriensis* Maxim.) is a rare species also planted in Lady Bird Johnson Park. This Asian native has sharp, bristly teeth on its leaf margins. The Callery and Bradford pears (*Pyrus calleryana* and *P. calleryana* 'Bradford') have very small fruit.

LOCATIONS
• Lady Bird Johnson Park
• Some parks, public buildings, and private homes

Medlar

Mespilus germanica L. • Rose Family *Rosaceae*

This rare tree or shrub grows on the grounds of the National Library of Medicine in Bethesda.

NATIVE RANGE   Southeastern Europe, western Asia.

LEAVES   Simple, alternate, deciduous. Margins with rounded teeth, sometimes nearly smooth.

FLOWERS   White, with five petals, borne singly.

FRUIT   Pome-like drupe that is open at the top and reddish brown or dark orange when mature. Edible only when over-ripe (usually after a frost). Eaten raw or used to make jelly and wine.

Chinese Photinia

Photinia serrulata Lindl. • Rose Family *Rosaceae*

A small tree or large shrub with shiny evergreen leaves, attractive white blossoms, and bright red fruit.

NATIVE RANGE   China.

LEAVES   Simple, alternate, evergreen. 3 to 7 inches (7.5–17.8 cm) long, 1 to 1¾ inches (2.5–4.5 cm) wide. Oblong, abruptly pointed, with a rounded or wedge-shaped base. Margin with small rounded or pointed teeth. Reddish when young. Leathery and glabrous. Lustrous dark green above, paler below.

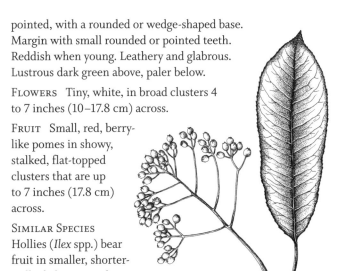

Flowers   Tiny, white, in broad clusters 4 to 7 inches (10–17.8 cm) across.

Fruit   Small, red, berry-like pomes in showy, stalked, flat-topped clusters that are up to 7 inches (17.8 cm) across.

Similar Species   Hollies (*Ilex* spp.) bear fruit in smaller, shorter-stalked clusters. Other photinia species and hybrids are in cultivation, including Fraser photinia (*Photinia* × *fraseri* Dress), a tall shrub with toothed evergreen leaves that are copper-red when they first emerge.

Locations
• U.S. Capitol grounds
• Some public and private gardens and grounds

Chinese Quince

Pseudocydonia sinensis (Thouin) Schneid. [*Chaenomeles sinensis* (Thouin) Koehne] • Rose Family *Rosaceae*

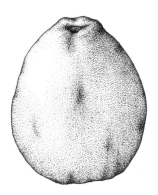

A beautiful little tree with a fluted trunk, mottled bark, and large, fragrant fruit. Gail Griffin, the director of gardens at Dumbarton Oaks, enjoys making Chinese quince pie.

Native Range   China.

Leaves   Simple, alternate, deciduous. 2 to 4 inches (5–10 cm) long. Elliptic-ovate or oblong-elliptic. Sharply and finely toothed.

Flowers   Pale pink, 1 to 1½ inches (2.5–3.8 cm) across. Spring, after the leaves.

FRUIT   Dark yellow, oblong, 4 to 6 inches (10–15 cm) long.

SIMILAR SPECIES   Quince (*Cydonia oblonga* Mill.), not included in this guide, is planted at the National Arboretum. It has leaves that are downy below, with smooth margins.

LOCATIONS
• Dumbarton Oaks
• Gardens in the Washington area

Common or Downy Serviceberry
(Shadbush, Shadblow, or Juneberry)

Amelanchier arborea (F. Michx.) Fernald and other *Amelanchier* species • Rose Family *Rosaceae*

The common serviceberry or shadbush is one of the first trees to bloom in woodlands throughout the eastern United States and southeastern Canada. The tree was named serviceberry because it blooms soon after the ground has thawed, when burial services traditionally were held for people who had died during winter. Its blooming time often coincides with the running of shad in the northeast, thus the names shadbush and shadblow. George Washington was fond of the serviceberry and planted it on the grounds of his Mount Vernon estate.

NATIVE HABITAT AND RANGE   Woodlands; New Brunswick to Florida, west to eastern Minnesota and eastern Texas.

LEAVES   Simple, alternate, deciduous. 1 to 4 inches (2.5–10 cm) long. Ovate, oblong, or obovate. Small, sharply pointed teeth. Gradually or abruptly pointed apex, cordate or rounded base. Often copper-colored and folded when young during flowering time. Densely pubescent on lower surface when young, but may become glabrous.

FLOWERS   Creamy white or pale pink, ¾ to 1½ inches (2–3.8 cm) across, with five thin petals. Slightly asymmetrically star-shaped. Flowers borne in loose clusters toward the ends of the branches with the emerging leaves. March to April. (See color close-up.)

FRUIT   Small, round, red, purple, or blackish pome, ¼ to ½ inch (1 cm or less) in diameter. The fruit is eaten by songbirds and mammals, including black bears. June to August.

GROWTH HABIT   Shrub or small to medium-sized tree.

Similar Species Several other species of *Amelanchier* grow in the Washington area, including smooth serviceberry or shadbush (*Amelanchier laevis* Wiegand), which is a commonly cultivated woody plant. Its leaves are glabrous or only slightly pubescent beneath, and its fruit is sweeter and juicier. A third native species growing here is the shrubby *Amelanchier canadensis* (L.) Medik. Another serviceberry that sometimes goes by the name snowy mespilus (*Amelanchier lamarckii*), and is of uncertain origin, has gained popularity as a cultivated tree in Washington for its abundant white flowers and brilliant orange and red autumn foliage. It has been planted in the National Gallery of Art Sculpture Garden and in Bartholdi Park of the U.S. Botanic Garden. As serviceberries grow in popularity, more cultivated varieties and hybrids are becoming available. Distinguish locally grown serviceberries from other members of the rose family by their thin petals and star-shaped flowers.

Locations of serviceberry species
- Fern Valley, National Arboretum
- Mount Vernon
- Woodlands throughout the region
- Gulf Branch Park (2007–2008 Arlington County Champion Serviceberry or Shadbush *Amelanchier arborea*)
- Parks and public and private gardens and grounds

The Hawthorns

Crataegus L. • Rose Family *Rosaceae*

English May

Hybrid
Cockspur
Thorn

Because the hawthorns are extremely difficult even for botanists to identify, we simply describe the characteristics of the genus here, with a list of some of the species planted in Washington. The hawthorns are a large and complex genus, containing more than a hundred species (and many more, according to some botanists). They typically are small trees or shrubs and usually bear sharp thorns. The single most interesting hawthorn in

Washington is undoubtedly the rare Glastonbury thorn (*Crataegus monogyna* Jacq. 'Biflora'), which is planted in a circle near the Washington National Cathedral. This rather scrappy-looking old tree is reputed to have been raised from a cutting brought to the country from Glastonbury Abbey in England around the turn of the twentieth century. According to legend, the Glastonbury thorn blooms when royalty is present. But royalty or no, this particular tree has been known to bloom at nearly every time of year. The original Glastonbury thorn is said to have sprung to life from the wooden staff of Joseph of Arimathea after the death of Christ. The descendants of the legendary tree bloom in England at Christmas, as well as during spring. Traditionally, flowering branchlets are sent from Glastonbury to the Queen of England at Christmastime.

LEAVES Simple, alternate, almost always deciduous. Lobed or unlobed, usually toothed.

FLOWERS White or pink, with five petals (except in double-blossomed forms such as 'Paul's Scarlet') and five sepals.

FRUIT Small, often brightly colored pome that resembles a tiny apple. Fruit on some species remains on the tree into winter.

BARK AND TWIGS Bark scaly and/or shallowly furrowed. Twigs usually armed with sharp, stiff thorns. Winter buds small, round, brown, and scaly.

HAWTHORNS COMMONLY PLANTED LOCALLY
Cockspur Thorn *Crataegus crus-galli* L.
English May or Hawthorn *Crataegus laevigata* (Poir.) DC. (*C. oxyacantha* L.)
Paul's Scarlet Hawthorn *Crataegus laevigata* 'Paul's Scarlet' (*C. oxyacantha* 'Paul's Scarlet')
Downy Hawthorn *Crataegus mollis* (Torr. & A. Gray) Scheele
Common Hawthorn (One-Seeded Hawthorn) *Crataegus monogyna* Jacq.
Glastonbury Thorn *Crataegus monogyna* Jacq. 'Biflora'
Hybrid Cockspur Thorn (Lavalle Hawthorn) *Crataegus × lavallei* Henriq. ex Lav.
Frosted Hawthorn (Waxy-Fruited Hawthorn) *Crataegus pruinosa* (J. C. Wendl.) K. Koch
Washington Thorn *Crataegus phaenopyrum* (L.f.) Medik
Dotted Hawthorn *Crataegus punctata* Jacq.
Fireberry Hawthorn *Crataegus dodgei* Ashe
Biltmore Hawthorn *Crataegus intricata* Lange

One-Flowered Hawthorn (Dwarf Hawthorn) *Crataegus uniflora* Muenchh.

LOCATIONS
• Parks and public and private gardens and grounds

Rowan Tree (European Mountain-Ash)

Sorbus aucuparia L. • Rose Family *Rosaceae*

The Rowan tree or European mountain-ash is similar to the native American mountain-ash (*Sorbus americana* Marshall), which grows in the northeastern states and in the mountains to northern Georgia. The Rowan tree is widely cultivated and has become naturalized in parts of the northern U.S. and Canada.

NATIVE RANGE   Europe to western Asia and Siberia.

LEAVES   Pinnately compound, alternate, deciduous. 6½ to 10 inches (16.5–25 cm) long. Nine to fifteen sessile leaflets, each 1¼ to 3 inches (3–7.5 cm) long. Margins evenly toothed, but smooth near their bases, which are slightly unequal. Apices pointed. Pubescent below at first, but may become glabrous.

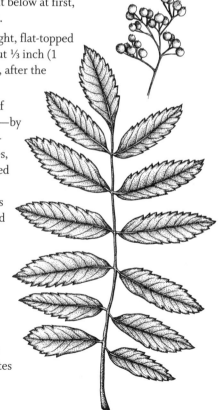

FLOWERS   White, in upright, flat-topped clusters. Each flower about ⅓ inch (1 cm or less) across. Spring, after the leaves.

FRUIT   Upright clusters of yellow, then orange, then—by midsummer—brilliant orange-red, berry-like pomes, which are quickly devoured by birds. The fruit of this tree and the native species has traditionally been used to make medicines and beverages.

SIMILAR SPECIES   The American mountain-ash (*Sorbus americana*) and the showy mountain-ash [*S. decora* (Sarg.) C. K. Schneid.], which are both native to the northern states (with the first species ranging into the southern Appalachian Mountains), are unlikely to be encountered in cultivation here. Korean mountain-ash [*Sorbus alnifolia* (Sieb. & Zucc.) K. Koch] has simple, alternate leaves resembling the alder (*Alnus*), as the scientific name implies. It has showy, pinkish red to scarlet fruit. Korean mountain-ash grows at the National Arboretum.

LOCATIONS
• Some gardens and grounds throughout the city and suburbs

Mimosa (Silk-Tree or Persian Acacia)

Albizia julibrissin Durrazz. • Pea Family *Fabaceae* (Some taxonomists place this tree in the Mimosa Family *Mimosaceae*.)

A small, delicate tree, conspicuous in summer with its wispy pink flowers and feathery leaves. Once, on a bicycle ride in the Montgomery County countryside, my husband and I came upon a pair of mimosa trees in a small yard that were surrounded by dozens of ruby-throated hummingbirds.

NATIVE RANGE   Central China to Iran. Escaped from cultivation and widely naturalized in the southeastern U.S., where it has become a problematic invasive in places.

LEAVES   Bipinnately compound, alternate, deciduous. 6 to 13 inches (15–33 cm) long. Each tiny leaflet ¼ to ½ inch (1–1.5 cm) long. Fern-like.

FLOWERS   Pink, fragrant, "powder puff" clusters. June to August. (See color close-up.)

FRUIT   Many-seeded green legume, 3½ to 6 inches (9–15 cm) long, about ¾ inch (2 cm) wide, very thin. Seeds visible inside legume, horizontally oval, seven to fifteen per pod.

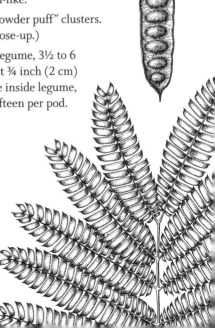

BARK AND TWIGS Bark light brown, smooth. Twigs slender, glabrous, with small winter buds and leaf scars.

GROWTH HABIT Small tree with a broad crown, graceful branching pattern, and overall airy appearance.

SIMILAR SPECIES The only other commonly grown trees in Washington with bipinnately compound leaves are the Kentucky coffee-tree (*Gymnocladus dioicus*), honey-locust (*Gleditsia triacanthos*), and devil's walkingstick (*Aralia spinosa*). All have larger leaflets.

LOCATIONS
• Rock Creek Park
• A popular garden tree that has escaped from cultivation in the city and suburbs

Redbud (Judas-Tree)

Cercis canadensis L. •
Pea Family *Fabaceae* (Some taxonomists place the redbud species in the Caesalpinia Family *Caesalpiniaceae*.)

STATE TREE OF OKLAHOMA

The redbud graces parks, gardens, and native woodlands with purplish pink early-spring flowers that are clustered along the tree's branchlets. It is a host plant for the Henry's elfin butterfly.

NATIVE HABITAT AND RANGE Moist woods; Connecticut and southern New York to northern Florida, west to southern Michigan, Iowa, eastern Nebraska, Texas, and northern Mexico.

LEAVES Simple, alternate, deciduous. 2 to 5 inches (5–12.5 cm) long, 3 to 5 inches (7.5–12.5 cm) wide. Heart-shaped, margin smooth. Five to seven palmately arranged veins arise from the base. Petiole slender; small

stipules soon fall. The first leaves unfold at the tips of the branchlets when the tree is in full bloom in spring.

FLOWERS   Deep purplish pink, rarely white. Tiny pea-like
flowers cluster along the branchlets and limbs and down the
trunk. Late March to April. (See color close-up.)

FRUIT   Legume, 2 to 3½ inches (5–9 cm) long. Pointed at both
ends, on a thin stalk about ½ inch (1.2 cm) long.

BARK AND TWIGS   Bark gray, may be smooth or scaly. Twigs
reddish brown or reddish gray, somewhat zigzagged, with small
lateral buds and no terminal bud.

GROWTH HABIT   Small tree with a rounded crown or upright
shrub with few ascending branches.

SIMILAR SPECIES   Very similar to Chinese redbud (*Cercis
chinensis*). The white-flowered Texas redbud (*Cercis reniformis*
'Alba') grows in the National Gallery of Art Sculpture Garden on
the Mall and in a few other locations in Washington. Redbuds
may be confused with catalpas (*Catalpa* spp.), but catalpas have
whorled or opposite leaves. See Katsura-tree (*Cercidiphyllum
japonicum*) "Similar Species."

LOCATIONS
• Mount Vernon
• George Washington Memorial Parkway
• National Zoo
• National Arboretum
• Smithsonian National Museum of Natural History
• Rock Creek Park
• Thrifton Park (2007–2008 Arlington County Champion
  Redbud)
• North Chevy Chase, Maryland (New National Co-Champion
  Redbud)
• Common throughout the area as a cultivated and naturally oc-
  curring tree

Chinese Redbud (Chinese Judas-Tree)

Cercis chinensis Bunge • Pea Family *Fabaceae* (Caesalpinia Family
Caesalpiniaceae)

Very similar to the native redbud, with obscure differences in
leaves and fruit. Chinese redbud flowers tend to be deeper purplish pink and slightly larger than the native species. However,
the best way to distinguish the two is by growth habit. The Chi-

nese redbud is usually shrubby in cultivation. While the native redbud is also shrub-like when young, it has fewer branches and is not as full as the Chinese species.

Locations
• Common throughout the city

Yellowwood

Cladrastis kentukea (Dum.-Cours.) Rudd [*Cladrastis lutea* (Michx.) K. Koch] • Pea Family *Fabaceae*

An attractive tree with smooth gray bark, fragrant white flowers, and yellow autumn leaves.

Native Habitat and Range   Rich soils of slopes, ridges, streamsides, and river valleys. Southern Illinois and Indiana to northern Georgia and Alabama; also southwestern Missouri, Arkansas, and eastern Oklahoma.

Leaves   Pinnately compound, alternate, deciduous. 6 to 12 inches (15–30 cm) long. Five to eleven leaflets, each 2 to 4 inches (5–10 cm) long, broadly ovate or occasionally obovate. More or less abruptly, and rather bluntly, pointed. Leaflet bases rounded, wedge-shaped, or subcordate. Margins smooth. Leaflets glabrous above, sometimes silky below, each with a very short petiolule. Alternately arranged along rachis with a terminal leaflet.

Flowers   White, fragrant, in pendulous clusters. Each flower ¾ to 1¼ inches (2–3 cm) long. May. (See color close-up.)

FRUIT   Flat, pale green legume (turning brown), 2 to 4 inches (5–10 cm) long, containing several seeds.

BARK AND TWIGS   Bark clear gray, smooth. (Wood underneath is yellow, and the roots yield a yellow dye.) Twigs slender, glabrous, with naked winter buds hidden by hollow petioles before leaves fall in autumn.

GROWTH HABIT   Small to medium-sized tree with graceful branching and a rounded crown.

SIMILAR SPECIES   There is no other tree planted in our area—or occurring naturally—with the combination of smooth gray bark and alternate, odd-pinnately compound leaves. Naked winter buds distinguish it from the beeches (*Fagus* spp.) in winter. [Flowers and fruit are somewhat similar to black locust (*Robinia pseudoacacia*).]

LOCATIONS
• National Zoo
• Folger Park
• Lafayette Park
• Vietnam Women's Memorial and World War II Memorial
• Smithsonian Air and Space Museum
• National Gallery of Art Sculpture Garden
• Montrose Park
• Town of Chevy Chase, Maryland
• Arlington National Cemetery (second largest Virginia State Champion Yellowwood)
• Growing in popularity as a desirable tree for city and suburban gardens and yards

Honey-Locust

Gleditsia triacanthos L. • Pea Family *Fabaceae* (Some taxonomists place honey-locust in the Caesalpinia Family *Caesalpiniaceae*.)

Although the honey-locust is usually identified by its fierce-looking thorns, nurseries are now propagating many thornless cultivars. Most trees planted for ornament in recent years are thornless.

NATIVE HABITAT AND RANGE   Rich, moist woods; western Pennsylvania to South Dakota, south to Florida and Texas. Escaped from cultivation and widely naturalized in many other parts of the eastern U.S. and southeastern Canada.

LEAVES Pinnate or bipinnately compound, alternate, deciduous. Individual leaflets ½ to 1 inch (1.2–2.5 cm) long, elliptic-lanceolate, with blunt apices and rounded or wedge-shaped bases. Margins smooth or with very shallow, rounded teeth. Delicate and somewhat feathery looking. Petiolules extremely short. Rachis grooved, pubescent.

FLOWERS Greenish yellow, hanging in clusters of small, closely arranged flowers. May.

FRUIT Very long, twisted, rust-brown legume, 8 to 18 inches (20–45.5 cm). Contains many flattened oval seeds with sweet pulp between them. White-tailed deer, squirrels, quail, and other wildlife eat the seeds and sometimes the pods.

BARK AND TWIGS Bark dark, fissured and scaly, with or without stout, often branched thorns. Twigs with very small winter buds and false end buds.

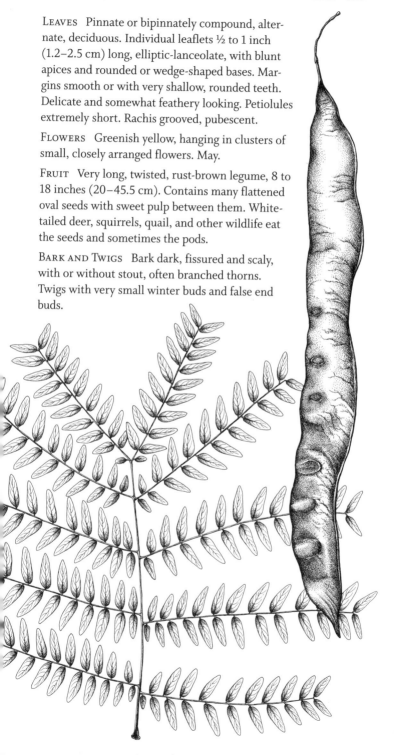

Growth Habit   Medium to tall tree with wide-spreading, rounded or slightly flat-topped crown.

Other Forms   Thornless honey-locust [*Gleditsia triacanthos* f. *inermis* (L.) Zab.]. The thornless forms are now propagated almost exclusively for ornament. Many thornless cultivars have been developed, including 'Sunburst,' 'Majestic,' 'Imperial,' and 'Shademaster.'

Distinguishing Characteristics   In the absence of flowers or mature fruit, leaflet size, shape, and margin are the characteristics that set the honey-locust apart from other members of the pea family. (See illustrations.)

Locations
• First Street, S.E., near Independence Avenue
• U.S. Capitol grounds
• Franklin Delano Roosevelt Memorial
• Common throughout the city and suburbs

Kentucky Coffee-Tree

Gymnocladus dioicus (L.) K. Koch • Pea Family *Fabaceae* (Some taxonomists place Kentucky coffee-tree in the Caesalpinia Family *Caesalpiniaceae*.)

State Tree of Kentucky

Conspicuous from afar in winter with its large, sickle-shaped legumes. During the Civil War, Kentucky coffee-tree seeds were roasted and used as a coffee substitute.

Native Habitat and Range   Rich, moist woods; western New York and Pennsylvania, west to southern Minnesota and southeastern South Dakota, south to Tennessee and Oklahoma.

Leaves   Bipinnately compound, alternate, deciduous. 12 to 36 inches (30–90 cm) long. Numerous leaflets, each 1 to 2½ inches (2.5–6.3 cm) long. Ovate, smooth-margined, usually with a sharply pointed apex. Leaflet bases most often rounded, but may be wedge-shaped. Glabrous or slightly pubescent below when young, on a short petiolule. Late to leaf out in spring.

Flowers   Pale greenish white, fragrant. Males and females on separate trees. Flowers not typical of pea family. Early to mid-May.

Fruit   Thick, reddish brown, somewhat sickle-shaped legume. 3 to 9 inches (7.5–23 cm) long. Contains several rounded seeds with a sweet pulp between them. Formed by early fall (on female trees only) and remaining on the tree after the leaves have fallen.

BARK AND TWIGS   Bark gray or gray-brown, roughly fissured and scaly. Twigs stout, somewhat whitened, with small, silky, partially depressed winter buds and false end buds.

GROWTH HABIT   Tall tree with an open crown.

SIMILAR SPECIES   The Kentucky coffee-tree is the only tree in our area besides the prickly devil's walkingstick (*Aralia spinosa*) with bipinnately compound leaves on which the leaflets are more than an inch (2.5 cm) long. Japanese pagoda tree (*Sophora japonica*) and black locust (*Robinia pseudoacacia*) are the most similar species.

LOCATIONS
• U.S. Capitol grounds
• Corregidor Street, N.W., near Massachusetts Avenue
• Washington National Cathedral
• National Gallery of Art Sculpture Garden
• Lafayette Park
• Chestnut Hills Park (2007–2008 Arlington County Champion Kentucky Coffee-Tree)

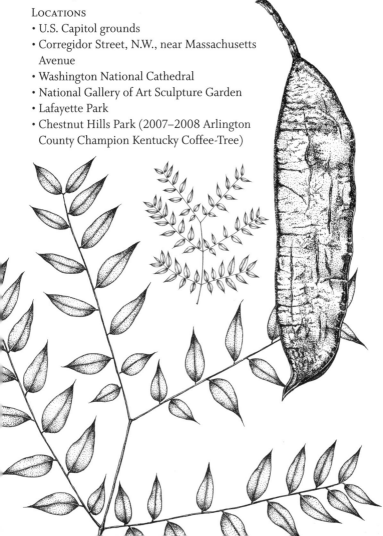

Black Locust (False Acacia)

Robinia pseudoacacia L. • Pea Family *Fabaceae*

The black locust, native to the eastern U.S., has been widely planted throughout the world. Since it was first introduced in Europe in the seventeenth century, the black locust has been planted for timber and ornament in nearly every European country. The tree is a favorite ornamental in China, and is also widely grown in parts of Africa, Australia, New Zealand, and South America. The black locust is so well loved in other parts of the world for its fragrant white blossoms and sturdy wood that many foreign visitors to Washington may be more familiar with it than D.C. residents are. As Michael A. Dirr writes in his comprehensive *Manual of Woody Landscape Plants*: "Europeans have grown, appreciated and selected superior forms of this tree while Americans treat it as some pedestrian weed."[86]

Since writing the first two editions of *City of Trees,* I have come to appreciate the black locust for its fragrant spring floral display in the rolling countryside surrounding Sugarloaf Mountain. The tree is a larval host plant for the silver-spotted skipper butterfly.

NATIVE HABITAT AND RANGE Woods, fields, hedgerows, roadsides. Pennsylvania south to northern Georgia and Alabama, west to central Kentucky, Tennessee, and parts of southern Indiana and Illinois; also, southern Missouri, central and western Arkansas, and eastern Oklahoma. Naturalized in many other parts of the U.S. and Europe.

LEAVES Pinnately compound, alternate, deciduous. 6 to 11 inches (15–28 cm) long. Seven to twenty-one leaflets, including a terminal one. Each leaflet ¾ to 2¼ inches (2–5.7 cm) long. Elliptic-ovate, with a smooth or very slightly wavy margin. Apex rounded or indented, often with a tiny spine barely visible. Base rounded, wedge-shaped, or almost straight across. Blue-green or gray-green. Glabrous at maturity; may be finely pubescent below when young and along the short petiolule.

Flowers White, fragrant, in pendulous clusters of typically pea-like flowers. Individual flowers an inch (2.5 cm) or less long. April to May. (See color close-up.)

Fruit Flat, reddish brown legume, tapered to a point at both ends. 2 to 4 inches (5–10 cm) long, containing several flat brown seeds.

Bark and Twigs Bark brown, reddish brown, or gray; thick, deeply furrowed and ridged. Twigs usually have stipular spines about ½ inch (1.2 cm) long. Winter buds small, end buds false.

Growth Habit Medium-sized tree with an open, scraggly crown.

Similar Species Honey-locust (*Gleditsia triacanthos*) has smaller leaflets. Kentucky coffee-tree (*Gymnocladus dioicus*) has bipinnately compound leaves. The Japanese pagoda tree (*Sophora japonica*) is the most similar, but its leaflets are pointed at apices and whitened below. Clammy locust (*Robinia viscosa*) is discussed below.

Locations
• Cedar Hill, Frederick Douglass National Historic Site
• Mount Vernon and George Washington Memorial Parkway
• C&O Canal
• Rock Creek Park
• Common throughout the city, suburbs, and surrounding countryside

Clammy Locust

Robinia viscosa Vent. • Pea Family *Fabaceae*

Grows mostly in the mountains from Pennsylvania to Georgia and Alabama, but widely escaped from cultivation and growing along roadsides in the eastern U.S. Usually shrubby in our area, the clammy locust has clustered pink flowers, and its branchlets have glands that exude a sticky, "clammy" substance.

Locations
• Not common here

Japanese Pagoda Tree (Chinese Scholar Tree)

Sophora japonica L. • Pea Family *Fabaceae*

During the Chou Dynasty (ca. 1122–240 B.C.) in China, this tree was planted near the tombs of high officials. Long cultivated on temple grounds in Japan, the Japanese pagoda tree has gained great popularity in the West. Its profuse, fragrant blossoms provide refreshment for those who spend the steamy months of July and August in Washington.

NATIVE RANGE   China, Korea. (Not native to Japan.)

LEAVES   Pinnately compound, alternate, deciduous. 6 to 10 inches (15–25 cm) long. Seven to seventeen leaflets, 1 to 2 inches (2.5–5 cm) long. Ovate, with smooth margins, rounded or wedge-shaped bases, and pointed apices. Leaflets lustrous dark green above, glaucous and very finely pubescent below. Short, pubescent petiolules.

FLOWERS   Pale yellow-green or creamy flowers in spreading, loosely pyramidal clusters. Fragrant. Individual flowers typically pea-like, 1/3 to 2/3 inch (0.7–1.5 cm) long. Early to mid-July through much of August; some trees bloom into September. (See color close-up.)

FRUIT   Numerous clusters of sausage-like legumes. Bright yellow-green, divided into several round segments, each containing a seed. Length varies according to the number of segments. Late summer to fall.

BARK AND TWIGS   Bark gray-brown or brown, often with wavy ridges. Young branchlets green, glabrous or nearly so. Winter buds small, hidden by petioles before leaves fall.

GROWTH HABIT   Crown usually full and rounded. Branches spreading.

SIMILAR SPECIES   Black locust (*Robinia pseudoacacia*) has leaflets that are rounded or slightly indented at the apex and not whitened below. Kentucky coffee-tree (*Gymnocladus dioicus*) has bipinnately compound leaves. No similar species blooms in midsummer, but from a distance the greenish ripening capsules of golden-rain-tree (*Koelreuteria paniculata*) may be mistaken for Japanese pagoda tree flowers.

LOCATIONS
- U.S. Capitol grounds
- President's Park near E Street and 15th Streets, N.W. (Casey Trees' 2006 D.C. Champion Pagoda Tree)
- New Hampshire Avenue and 21st Street, N.W.
- Dupont Circle
- Washington National Cathedral
- U.S. Department of Agriculture, the Mall
- Farragut Square
- Lincoln Park

Maackia (Amur Maackia)

Maackia amurensis Rupr. & Maxim. • Pea Family *Fabaceae*

Rare tree, native to Manchuria. Somewhat similar to yellowwood (*Cladrastis kentukea*), but with leaflets arranged oppositely (or nearly so) along the rachis, and white flowers in upright clusters.

LOCATION
- National Arboretum

Golden Chain Tree (Common Laburnum)

Laburnum anagyroides Medik. • Pea Family *Fabaceae*

Small tree with alternate clover-like leaves and hanging clusters of bright yellow flowers in late April or early May.

NATIVE RANGE   Central and southern Europe.

LEAVES   Trifoliate, alternate, deciduous. Three leaflets, 1¼ to 3¼ inches (3–8 cm) long. Usually elliptic. Smooth-margined. Silky-pubescent below when young.

FLOWERS   Yellow, typically pea-like, in long, narrow, pendulous clusters.

FRUIT   Twisted legume containing poisonous black seeds.

LOCATIONS
- Private and public gardens and grounds

Voss's Laburnum (Golden Chain Tree)

Laburnum × watereri (Kirchn.) Dipp. (*L. anagy-roides × L. alpinum*) • Pea Family *Fabaceae*

A hybrid, very similar to the preceding species, but with fuller flower clusters and foliage.

LOCATIONS
• Washington National Cathedral
• Private and public gardens and
  grounds

Crape-Myrtle

Lagerstroemia indica L. (*L. indica × L. fauriei* cultivars) • Loose-strife Family *Lythraceae*

From late July through September, crape-myrtles ornament the Washington landscape with their boldly hued flowers. Deep dark pink is the most common color of the clusters of frilly blossoms adorning these small trees or large shrubs, but lavender, white, pale pink, and cherry-red forms are also planted in the city and suburbs. The National Arboretum has developed many crape-myrtle cultivars arising from hybrids of *Lagerstroemia indica* and *L. fauriei*. In his classic *Manual of Woody Landscape Plants,* Michael A. Dirr sings the praises of the National Arboretum horticulturist responsible for many of these cultivars: "Dr. Don Egolf was one of the greatest woody plant breeders that history will ever recognize. He was a scientist, breeder, horticulturist, plantsman, and gardener. . . . His plants will withstand the test of time. Like the masterpieces of great artists, writers, and musicians, Dr. Egolf's plants stand out from those of mere mortals."[87]

NATIVE RANGE   China, Korea. Widely cultivated throughout the southern United States.

LEAVES   Simple; opposite, sub-opposite, whorled, or alternate; deciduous. 1¼ to 2¾ inches (3–7 cm) long. Elliptic or obovate, on an extremely short petiole. Autumn color: orange, yellow, and red.

FLOWERS   Pink, red, lavender, purple, or white flowers in large, lilac-like clusters. Each crinkly flower about 1½ inches (3–4 cm) across. (See color close-up.)

FRUIT   Small, round, woody capsule that resembles a flower bud when closed, then opens to release seeds. Often remains on the plant into winter.

BARK   Gray-brown and pink, very smooth and ornamental, with thin shreds peeling away.

GROWTH HABIT   Small tree or large shrub with variable growth habit.

LOCATIONS
• National Arboretum
• North Carolina Avenue and 7th Street, S.E.
• Common throughout the city in parks and public and private gardens and grounds

European Smoke-Tree

Cotinus coggygria Scop. • Cashew Family
Anacardiaceae

A unique and striking ornamental. Translucent, feathery, fruiting panicles that look like puffs of smoke appear in early summer and last well into the season. They are especially beautiful in the early-morning and evening light.

NATIVE RANGE   Southern Europe to central China and Himalayas.

LEAVES   Simple, alternate, deciduous. 1¼ to 3½ inches (3–9 cm) long. Ovate, elliptic, or obovate. Rounded, broadly pointed, or slightly indented apex; broadly wedge-shaped or rounded base. Young leaves are purple in some cultivated forms. Becoming glabrous, but petiole and midrib below may be pubescent when young.

FLOWERS AND FRUIT   Flowers and kidney-shaped fruit are small and inconspicuous. The showy, "smoky," erect or gently drooping fruiting panicles are 6 to 9 inches (15–22.8 cm) long. The purplish, greenish, or gray-pink smoky effect is created by many small feathery hairs. (See color close-up.)

GROWTH HABIT   Full shrub or small tree.

OTHER FORMS   There are many cultivars of the European smoke-tree, including forms with purplish panicles and deep purple young leaves. 'Grace' is a popular hybrid arising from *Cotinus coggygria* 'Velvet Cloak' and the American smoke-tree (*C. obovatus*). It has large, showy, pink panicles.

LOCATIONS
• National Arboretum
• U.S. Botanic Garden: Bartholdi Park
• Fairly common in private yards and gardens

American Smoke-Tree (Chittamwood)

Cotinus obovatus Raf. (*Cotinus americanus* Nutt.) • Cashew Family *Anacardiaceae*

The American smoke-tree is infrequently planted for ornament and is, therefore, rare in the D.C. area.

NATIVE HABITAT AND RANGE   Mountains, plateaus, canyons, rocky slopes, often in limestone soils. Spotty distribution in south-central states from Kentucky and Tennessee to southern Missouri, eastern Oklahoma, and Texas.

LEAVES   Simple, alternate, deciduous. 2⅓ to 4¾ inches (6–12 cm) long. The leaves are slightly longer than those of the European species and are covered with silky pubescence when young. Autumn color: brilliant orange and scarlet.

FLOWERS AND FRUIT   The fruiting panicles are less spectacular than the European tree, with rather inconspicuous brownish or purplish feathery hairs.

LOCATIONS
• A few private gardens and yards
• U.S. Botanic Garden: Bartholdi Park
• National Arboretum

Ailanthus (Tree of Heaven)

Ailanthus altissima (Mill.) Swingle • Quassia Family *Simaroubaceae*

While the poetic Chinese name Tree of Heaven refers to the short time it takes this tree to reach the sky, many District residents have less ethereal feelings about the prolific, fast-growing ailanthus. Some Washingtonians consider it an attractive shade tree, but many others have been at war with ailanthus seedlings and suckers for years. In 1875, the District passed an ordinance declaring ailanthus ownership a crime: "That ailanthus trees, the flowers of which produce offensive and noxious odors, in bloom, in the cities of Washington or Georgetown, or the more densely populated suburbs of said cities, are hereby declared nuisances injurious to health; and any person maintaining such nuisance, who shall fail, after due notice from this board, to abate the same, shall, upon conviction, be fined not less than five nor more than ten dollars for every such offence."[88]

Once considered an ideal urban tree, and able to survive in the most impoverished city soils, this is the species that inspires a young girl in the novel *A Tree Grows in Brooklyn*. Over time, the tenacious ailanthus has become one of the most troublesome invasive trees in the mid-Atlantic region and elsewhere.

NATIVE RANGE China. Brought into the United States in the late eighteenth century and now naturalized over much of the East.

LEAVES Odd-pinnately compound, alternate, deciduous. Large: 7 to 27 inches (17.5–61 cm) long. Thirteen to twenty-five leaflets, each 2 to 6 inches (5–15 cm) long. Ovate-lanceolate, usually with one to four blunt or pointed glandular teeth near the base. Base straight across or unequal. Glabrous or slightly pubescent below.

FLOWERS Large, greenish clusters. Male and female flowers usually on separate trees (dioecious), but may be unisexual on the same tree or occasionally perfect. Early to midsummer.

FRUIT Large clusters of samaras remaining after the leaves have fallen.

Each samara about 1½ inches (3.8 cm) long, twisted, and with a single seed in the middle.

BARK AND TWIGS   Bark usually light brown or gray, smooth, sometimes with lighter vertical stripes or shallow ridges. Winter twigs distinctive: stout, yellowish or orange-brown, and soft to the touch. No terminal bud. Leaf scars large, heart-shaped; lateral buds roundish, dark brown.

GROWTH HABIT   Fast-growing, small to medium-sized tree with a slender trunk. Tropical-looking, with few branches, a rounded crown, and large, compound leaves.

SIMILAR SPECIES   Somewhat similar to the Cedrela or Chinese cedar (*Toona sinensis*), but far more commonly grown. Could be confused with native sumacs (*Rhus* spp.), shrubs that are not included in this guide.

LOCATIONS
- Rock Creek Park
- Common in unused lots and at fringes of parking lots and highways
- Yards, parks, and grounds throughout D.C.

Amur Cork-Tree

Phellodendron amurense Rupr. • Rue Family *Rutaceae*

The Amur cork-tree is one of Washington's most beautiful Asian ornamentals. The tree is particularly striking in winter, with its persistent fruit, grooved bark, and dramatic profile.

NATIVE RANGE   China, Manchuria, Japan.

LEAVES   Pinnately compound, opposite, deciduous. 10 to 15 inches

(25.3–38 cm) long. Seven to thirteen ovate leaflets come to a long, somewhat curved point. Dark green. Glabrous below, or with tufts of hairs in the vein axils. Petiolules and rachis yellow-green.

FRUIT   Small, berry-like drupes in upright clusters, becoming black and sometimes remaining on the tree into winter.

BARK   Pale or medium gray, thick and deeply fissured, with corky ridges.

GROWTH HABIT   Broadly spreading branches, a rounded crown, and a short trunk create a striking profile.

SIMILAR SPECIES   The rare Japanese Phellodendron (*Phelloden-dron japonicum* Maxim.) is very difficult to distinguish from the more commonly grown Amur cork-tree. The Japanese species tends to be more pubescent. While a consensus has not yet been reached in Washington's botanical community, some believe that the tree on the southeast side of the Library of Congress may be the rare Japanese species, while the tree standing just a few yards to the north is undoubtedly the more common Chinese tree.

LOCATIONS
• Library of Congress grounds
• Tidal Basin
• National Arboretum

Trifoliate Orange

Poncirus trifoliata (L.) Raf. • Rue Family
Rutaceae

Small tree or shrub with spiny green branchlets. Often used as grafting stock for orange trees. Planted in hedges in southern states, where it has escaped from cultivation and become invasive in many places.

NATIVE RANGE   China, Korea.

LEAVES   Compound, alternate, deciduous. Three clover-like leaflets with slightly wavy margins or a few shallow, rounded teeth. Petiole winged.

FLOWERS   White, five-petaled, 1¼ to 2 inches (3–5 cm) across. Spring, before the leaves.

FRUIT   Small, yellow "orange" with bitter juice, up to 2 inches (5 cm) in diameter. In his *Manual of Woody Landscape Plants*,

Michael A. Dirr writes: "Ripe fruits set aside for several weeks become juicy and develop a sprightly, slightly acid flavor. Serves as a substitute for lemon, pulp can be made into marmalade, and peel can be candied."[89]

TWIGS   Green, glabrous, with thorns up to an inch (2.5 cm) or more long.

LOCATIONS
• U.S. Capitol grounds
• U.S. Botanic Garden: Bartholdi Park
• Some gardens and grounds throughout the city and suburbs

Common Hop-Tree (Wafer-Ash)

Ptelea trifoliata L. • Rue Family *Rutaceae*

A small native tree or shrub. American Indians and early American physicians used the root, bark, shoots, and leaves medicinally. The bitter fruit has been used as a substitute for hops in brewing beer.

NATIVE HABITAT AND RANGE   Moist woods, woodland edges, and rich, rocky slopes; scattered throughout the eastern U.S., southeastern Canada, and Mexico and a few places in the western states.

LEAVES   Compound, alternate, deciduous. Trifoliate leaflets 2 to 6 inches (5–15 cm) long, the middle one usually longest.

FRUIT   Roundish, flattened, elm-like samara containing two seeds.

SIMILAR SPECIES   The laburnums (*Laburnum* spp.)—including the golden chain tree—and the trifoliate orange (*Poncirus trifoliata*) also have alternate trifoliate leaves, but their other features differ. The bladdernut (*Staphylea trifolia*) is a small native tree or shrub with opposite trifoliate leaves and fruit that is a thin-walled, papery capsule.

LOCATIONS
• National Arboretum
• Some parks and private yards

Cedrela (Chinese Cedar, Chinese Toon)

Toona sinensis (A. Juss.) M. Roem. (*Cedrela sinensis* A. Juss.) • Mahogany Family (*Meliaceae*)

Rare in Washington. See page 31 to read about Frederick Law Olmsted's nineteenth-century Capitol Hill plantings, which included this still-thriving tree. The leaves are prized as a boiled vegetable in China, and the tree is used in traditional Chinese medicine.

NATIVE RANGE   China.

LEAVES   Pinnately compound, alternate, deciduous. Very long: up to 24 inches (60 cm). Similar to the tree of heaven (*Ailanthus altissima*), but with no large glandular teeth at the leaflet bases. Ten to thirty leaflets (usually an even number), 3 to 6 inches (7.5–15.2 cm) long. Long-pointed, slightly unequal at base. Margins nearly smooth or with a few small, remote teeth. Pubescent along the veins below, or glabrous.

FLOWERS   Small, white flowers in fragrant clusters. Early summer.

FRUIT   Small, tulip-shaped, woody capsule.

BARK   Dark, pinkish gray, becoming shaggy with age.

SIMILAR SPECIES   Ailanthus or tree of heaven is far more common and usually has an odd number of leaflets with coarse teeth near their bases.

LOCATION
• U.S. Capitol grounds, near the Olmsted grotto

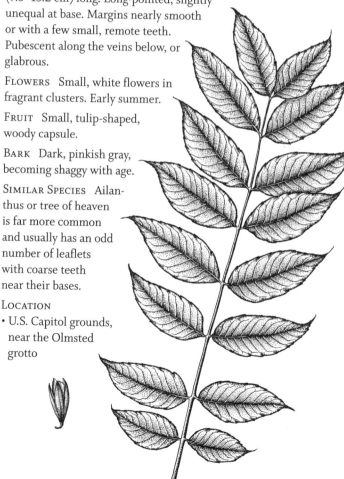

Bladdernut

Staphylea trifolia L. • Bladdernut Family *Staphylaceae*

The bladdernut, a small tree or shrub, grows along Rock Creek and in rich, moist woodlands in the Washington area.

Native Habitat and Range   Moist woods, streamsides, and thickets; southeastern Canada to Minnesota, south to Georgia, western Florida, and Oklahoma.

Leaves   Compound, opposite, deciduous. Trifoliate leaflets 2 to 4 inches (5–10 cm) long. Oblong, ovate, or elliptic; finely toothed.

Flowers   Greenish white, somewhat bell-shaped, in drooping clusters. April to May, with the leaves.

Fruit   Thin-walled, three-lobed, inflated, papery capsule.

Bark   Smooth, may be striped.

Growth Habit   Erect shrub or small tree.

Similar Species   The common hop-tree (*Ptelea trifoliata*) has alternate trifoliate leaves and fruit that is a two-seeded, roundish samara. Exotic shrubs of the *Staphylea* genus also are occasionally planted in the area. Colchis bladdernut (*S. colchica* Steven.), native to the Caucasus, has leaves with five (sometimes three) leaflets and fragrant flowers in upright clusters that bloom later in spring than the native species.

Locations
• Rock Creek Park and other moist area woodlands

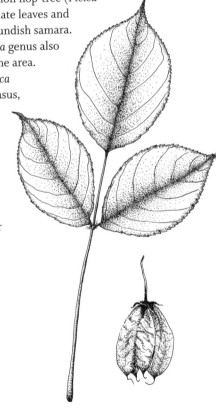

The Maples

Acer L. • Maple Family *Aceraceae*

Famous for their autumn foliage, and attractive throughout the year, maples abound in Washington. The city's most common maples hail from four continents: Asia, Europe, North America, and Africa. Maples are planted as street trees in parks, and in public and private gardens and grounds. They are second only to oaks in their popularity as shade trees. Several native maples grow in area woodlands, where their seeds are important in the diets of mammals and birds and their twigs are browsed by deer.

LEAVES   Simple or compound, opposite, deciduous. Simple leaves palmately veined.

FLOWERS   Small, clustered. Spring, before or after the leaves.

FRUIT   Pairs of distinctive winged samaras that are sometimes called "keys."

DISTRIBUTION   More than a hundred species in North America, Europe, Asia, and northern Africa.

SIMILAR SPECIES   The sweetgum (*Liquidambar styraciflua* L.) has alternate leaves and fruit that is pendulous, prickly, and round. Some hawthorns (*Crataegus* spp.) have small, maple-like leaves, but they are alternately arranged, and hawthorn branches are usually thorny. Viburnums (*Viburnum* spp.) are large shrubs or, rarely, small trees.

Maples Native to North America

Sugar Maple (Rock Maple)

Acer saccharum Marshall • Maple Family *Aceraceae*

STATE TREE OF NEW YORK, VERMONT, WEST VIRGINIA, AND WISCONSIN

The sugar maple is the most important part of the world-renowned New England autumn. Its fall colors, unrivaled even among maples, range from yellow to orange to deep red. Although sugar maples in Washington infrequently attain the glorious reds more common farther north, they are beautiful nonetheless, often coloring a deep orange. The tree is the major source of the sap that is boiled down to make maple syrup, an art taught to European settlers by American Indians. The beautiful wood is highly prized. The tree is favored by wildlife: birds and mammals eat the seeds, and deer and smaller mammals browse the twigs, buds, leaves, and bark.

NATIVE HABITAT AND RANGE   A woodland tree that is often planted in open fields. Thrives in a variety of soil conditions, but does best in rich soils. Southeastern Canada, northeastern United States to northern Georgia and Alabama, west to Missouri.

LEAVES   Simple, opposite, deciduous. 3 to 5 inches (7.5–12.5 cm) long, 3¼ to 6½ inches (8–16 cm) wide. Three to five coarsely and sparingly toothed lobes with fairly deep sinuses between them. Heart-shaped, rounded, or truncate base. Dark green above, paler and usually glabrous below (but may have some pubescence, especially along the veins). Long, slender, glabrous petiole.

FLOWERS   Yellowish, long-stemmed and drooping, with no petals. Spring, with the leaves.

FRUIT   Twin, winged, slightly divergent samaras, 1 to 1½ inches (2.5–4 cm) long.

BARK AND TWIGS   Bark gray, becoming deeply and irregularly furrowed with age, often breaking into plates. Twigs may be olive when young, turning reddish brown. Winter buds pointed, reddish brown, with four to eight pairs of scales.

GROWTH HABIT   Medium-sized to tall tree with a full, rounded, oval or oblong crown.

VARIETIES   Some botanists consider the black maple (*Acer nigrum*) to be a variety of the sugar maple (*Acer saccharum* var. *nigrum*).

SIMILAR SPECIES   The sugar maple is similar in appearance to the Norway maple (*Acer platanoides*). Although the Norway maple usually has wider, more shallowly sinused leaves, the best way to make a positive identification is to break the tip of a petiole. If the liquid exuded is milky in color, the tree is a Norway maple. (The sugar maple exudes clear sap.) Sugar maple foliage turns earlier in autumn than the Norway maple. Also note the differences in fruit, flowers, and bark.

LOCATIONS
- U.S. Capitol grounds
- World War II Memorial
- Cleveland Park
- Georgetown
- Rock Creek Park
- Turkey Run Park
- Scott's Run Nature Preserve
- Streets, parks, and private yards throughout the city and suburbs

Black Maple

Acer nigrum F. Michx. (*Acer saccharum* var. *nigrum*) • Maple Family *Aceraceae*

The black maple is considered a variety of the sugar maple by some botanists and a separate species by others. The black maple bears the same famous sap that goes into the making of maple syrup, and apart from the following characteristics, the two trees are very similar.

NATIVE HABITAT AND RANGE   Often in slightly moister sites than sugar maple, such as streamsides and riversides. Spotty distribution in northeastern states and southeastern Canada, more common in the Midwest, and ranging west to Minnesota and northern Arkansas.

LEAVES   Simple, opposite, deciduous. Similar to the sugar maple, but usually with fewer, more bluntly pointed teeth. Leaf margin gently drooping with age. Leaf blade thicker than the sugar maple, lighter green beneath, and slightly downy.

BARK AND TWIGS   Bark darker than the sugar maple, sometimes almost black, and deeply furrowed. Twigs orange-brown.

LOCATIONS
• Garfield Park
• Streets, yards, and parks citywide

Southern Sugar Maple

Acer barbatum Michx. • Acer Family *Aceraceae*

A few specimens of the southern sugar maple are planted along Independence Avenue next to the National Garden of the U.S. Botanic Garden. This species occurs on the Coastal Plain and in the Piedmont from southeastern Virginia to northern Florida, eastern Texas, and eastern Oklahoma. It differs from the two previous species by having leaves with rounded, rather than pointed, lobes and smooth bark that becomes shallowly grooved and scaly with age.

Red Maple

Acer rubrum L. • Maple Family *Aceraceae*

STATE TREE OF RHODE ISLAND

The first arboreal signs of spring in Washington are weeks ahead of the cherry blossoms. Early in March, the red maple—along with the silver maple and the American elm—blooms at a time when it seems winter will never end. With its abundant red flowers and pale gray bark, the red maple is the most striking of Washington's first-blooming trees, creating a crimson glow in the treetops. This maple continues its colorful show when its red samaras follow the flowers, and it dazzles onlookers again in autumn with multicolored foliage displays.

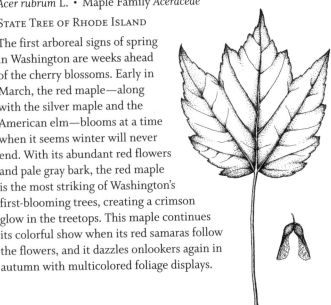

NATIVE HABITAT AND RANGE   A variety of habitats, from swamps to dry uplands; Newfoundland to southeastern Manitoba, south to Florida and Texas.

LEAVES   Simple, opposite, deciduous. 2 to 6 inches (5–15 cm) long and roughly as wide. Three to five broad lobes with shallow sinuses between them. Margin singly or doubly toothed. Dark green above, paler and usually glaucous beneath, sometimes pubescent along the veins. Petiole 2 to 4 inches (5–10 cm) long, often red. Autumn color: red, yellow, purple, and orange, sometimes all on a single leaf.

FLOWERS   Usually red, sometimes yellow-green, with small petals. Borne in dense clusters. May be unisexual or perfect. Early spring, before the leaves. (See color close-up.)

FRUIT   Twin, winged samaras, usually ⅔ to 1 inch (1.5–2.5 cm) long, on a long, thin stalk. Pale pink to bright red or yellow wings connected at a V-shaped angle. April or May.

BARK AND TWIGS   Bark smooth and pale gray on young trees, usually darkening and breaking into large plates with age. Twigs greenish, turning reddish or orange with age. Red, scaly winter buds. No unpleasant odor when twig is broken.

GROWTH HABIT   Medium to tall tree with a straight trunk and narrow or rounded crown.

SIMILAR SPECIES   The red maple is easily distinguished from other maples cultivated in the Washington area by its heavily toothed, shallowly and broadly lobed leaves. A similar species, the silver maple (*Acer saccharinum*), has very deeply and narrowly sinused leaves and more coarsely flaking, almost shaggy bark on mature trees. However, the two trees are easily confused when they are both in bloom before the leaves in spring. Silver maple flowers have no petals and are more often greenish yellow than red. Its twigs have a rank odor when broken, while red maple twigs do not.

LOCATIONS
• Smithsonian National Museum of the American Indian
• U.S. Capitol grounds
• White House grounds (tree planted by Jimmy Carter)
• Everett Street, N.W. (Casey Trees' 2006 D.C. Champion Red Maple)

- Vietnam Veterans Memorial
- Franklin Delano Roosevelt Memorial
- City and suburban streets, parks, and yards
- Rock Creek Park and parks throughout the region
- St. John the Baptist Catholic Church, Silver Spring, Maryland (2007 Montgomery County Champion Red Maple)
- Sugarloaf Mountain, Maryland
- Upton Hill Park (2007–2008 Arlington County Champion Red Maple)

Silver Maple (Soft Maple)

Acer saccharinum L. • Maple Family *Aceraceae*

In the 1870s and '80s, Washington arborists considered the fast-growing silver (or soft) maple to be the ideal street tree. More than eleven thousand silver maples were planted along the streets of the nation's capital in 1883. Over the years, the silver maple lost its status as Washington's favorite street tree because it proved to be difficult to maintain. However, it remains common throughout the District and neighboring Maryland and Virginia, as both a cultivated and a naturally occurring tree.

NATIVE HABITAT AND RANGE   Moist or wet soils, especially riverbanks and bottomlands; southeastern Canada and most of the eastern U.S. (excluding the southeastern Coastal Plain and much of Florida), west to Minnesota, Nebraska, Kansas, and Oklahoma.

LEAVES   Simple, opposite, deciduous. 4 to 8 inches (10–20 cm) long and wide. Five-lobed, very deeply cut, with the middle lobe itself sometimes three-lobed. Sharply, irregularly, and sometimes doubly toothed. Delicate, almost fern-like. Bright green or yellowish green above, pale silvery white below. Petiole slender, often pink or red above, from 2½ to 5 inches (6.5–12.5 cm) long. Autumn color: usually pale yellow, occasionally reddish.

FLOWERS   May be yellow-green or reddish. Similar to red maple (*Acer rubrum*), but with no petals. Very early spring, before the leaves.

FRUIT   Paired, winged samaras, connected at a broad V-shaped angle or with one samara aborted. Green and glabrous, 1½ to 2½ inches (3.8–6.3 cm) long. Maturing in spring, with the leaves, and soon falling.

BARK AND TWIGS Bark gray and smooth on young trees, furrowed and flaking into shaggy plates with age. Twigs slender, often reddish brown, usually with dark red or reddish brown winter buds. Twigs have a rank odor when broken.

GROWTH HABIT Fast-growing tree with a long, tall, irregularly shaped crown.

SIMILAR SPECIES The silver maple is distinctive in summer with its deeply lobed, sharply toothed leaves. See red maple (*Acer rubrum*) "Similar Species" for similarities in early spring.

LOCATIONS
- U.S. Capitol grounds
- Butterworth Place, N.W. (Casey Trees' 2006 D.C. Champion Silver Maple)
- Streets, parks, and yards throughout the city and suburbs
- Theodore Roosevelt Island
- Rock Creek Park
- Potomac River and C&O Canal, into Maryland (2007 Montgomery County Champion Silver Maple near Dickerson)
- Parkhurst Park (2007–2008 Arlington County Champion Silver Maple)

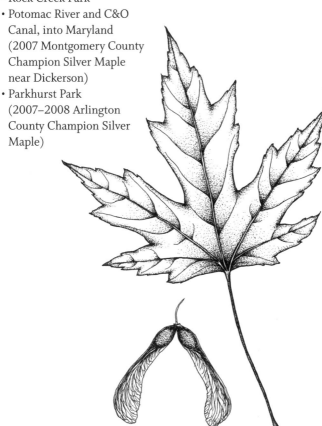

Boxelder (Ash-Leaved Maple)

Acer negundo L. • Maple Family *Aceraceae*

The boxelder or ash-leaved maple is the only naturally occurring maple in the Washington area with compound, rather than simple, leaves. [See also paperbark maple (*Acer griseum*)]. The boxelder's hanging clusters of greenish yellow flowers are one of the first signs of spring along Rock Creek. Its leaves resemble those of the ash tree, thus the second common name.

NATIVE HABITAT AND RANGE   Usually growing in moist soils of streambanks, riverbanks, pondsides, and floodplains. Much of U.S.: New England to Florida, west to California, with scattered distribution throughout the West; southern Canada and parts of Mexico and Guatemala.

LEAVES   Pinnately compound, opposite, deciduous. Three to five (rarely seven) leaflets, each 1½ to 4 inches (3.8–10 cm) long, ¾ to 1½ inches (2–3.8 cm) wide. Ovate to lanceolate. Coarsely and irregularly toothed, with the end leaflet sometimes three-lobed. Glabrous above, often slightly pubescent below. Petiolules short and slender; petiole 2 to 3¼ inches (5–8 cm) long, pale yellow or pinkish.

FLOWERS   Greenish yellow, small, with no petals, in hanging clusters. Spring, before and/or with the young leaves.

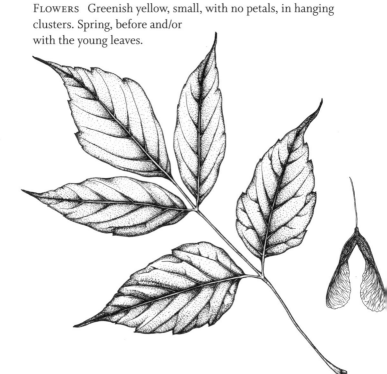

FRUIT   Paired, winged samaras in pendulous clusters. Each samara 1 to 1¾ inches (2.5–4.5 cm) long; pair joined at acute angle. Wings slightly incurved. Yellowish green, becoming brown and persisting into winter.

BARK AND TWIGS   Light brown or gray, ridged and furrowed. Twigs green, brown, or gray; glabrous. Winter buds with grayish or whitish pubescence.

SIMILAR SPECIES   Ashes (*Fraxinus* spp.) and cork trees (*Phellodendron* spp.) also have opposite, pinnately compound leaves.

LOCATIONS
• Common throughout D.C., suburbs, and surrounding country-
  side, both in cultivation and in the wild
• Rock Creek Park
• Potomac River and C&O Canal
• Seneca Creek State Park and other parks throughout the region

Striped Maple (Moosewood, Goosefoot Maple)

Acer pensylvanicum L. • Maple Family *Aceraceae*

A small, slender maple native to the mountains and cool woods of western Maryland and Virginia. Distinguished by its thin, green bark (sometimes becoming reddish with age), which is vertically striped white. The leaf is shallowly three-lobed, and the fruit is borne in slender, pendu-lous clusters.

NATIVE HABITAT AND RANGE
Moist, rich woods; northeastern
U.S. and southeastern Canada,
south in the mountains to
North Carolina,
Tennessee, and
northern Georgia.

LOCATIONS
• Mount Vernon
• Fern Valley, National
  Arboretum
• Mountains of western Mary-
  land and Shendandoah National
  Park

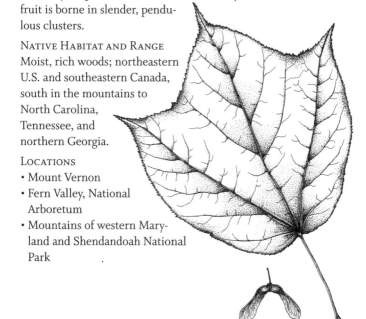

Maples Not Native to North America

Norway Maple

Acer platanoides L. • Maple Family *Aceraceae*

This popular tree has been widely planted throughout D.C. along streets, in parks, and around public buildings and private homes. The Norway maple retains its foliage until late autumn, when it turns a bright clear yellow or (less frequently) orange. This European import became one of the most commonly cultivated trees in North America because it is fast-growing and tolerates urban conditions. Unfortunately, it has escaped from cultivation and become invasive in our region and elsewhere.

NATIVE RANGE   Europe.

LEAVES   Simple, opposite, deciduous. Often slightly wider than long, 4 to 8 inches (10–20 cm) across. Five- to seven-lobed, with finely pointed teeth. Sinuses between lobes rather shallow. Bright or dark green and glabrous above, slightly paler below, with tufts of hairs in the vein axils. Petiole exudes a milky sap when broken.

FLOWERS   Bright yellow-green, in roundish erect clusters. Often quite fragrant. Early spring, just before the leaves, then remaining after they have unfolded.

FRUIT   Twin, winged samaras attached at a widely divergent angle. Each samara 1¼ to 2¼ inches (3–5.5 cm) long, yellow-green, then turning brown.

BARK AND TWIGS   Bark light brown or gray, broken into thin, shallow, vertical furrows and ridges on mature trees. Winter buds large, ovoid, green or reddish.

GROWTH HABIT   Well-formed tree with a full, rounded crown and dense foliage.

OTHER FORMS   Many cultivated forms of the Norway maple have been planted in our region. Several forms with more or less purple leaves are popular, including 'Goldsworth Purple,' 'Crimson King,' and 'Schwedleri.' The columnar Norway maple (*Acer platanoides* 'Columnare') has been planted along city streets where a narrow crown is desirable, including I Street, N.W., and W Street, N.W.

SIMILAR SPECIES   The very similar sugar maple (*Acer saccharum*) has leaves with petioles that do not exude a milky juice when broken. Sugar maple bark on older trees is usually broken into large scales or plates.

LOCATIONS
• U.S. Capitol grounds
• A popular street tree citywide
• Parks and private yards throughout the city and suburbs
• Escaped from cultivation in many places, including Rock Creek Park

Hedge Maple (Field Maple)

Acer campestre L. • Maple Family
Aceraceae

These trees are often pruned to
form hedges in Europe, thus the
name.

NATIVE RANGE   Europe, western Asia,
northern Africa.

LEAVES   Simple, opposite, deciduous.
1¾ to 4 inches (4.5–10 cm) long, 2¼
to 4 inches (5.5–10 cm) wide. Usually
five-lobed, the middle three lobes with large, rounded teeth.
Lobe apices rounded. Glabrous, except for buff-colored hairs
along the veins below. Petiole slender, 1¼ to 3½ inches (3–9 cm)
long. Autumn color: yellow.

FLOWERS   Yellow-green. Spring, with the leaves.

FRUIT   Paired, winged samaras with pubescent nutlets and finely
pubescent wings. Pair attached at a wide angle, resembling the
silhouette of a bird in flight. Each samara about 1 to 1¾ inches
(2.5–4.5 cm) long.

BARK AND TWIGS   Bark of mature trees usually dark gray (sometimes brown), with many thin vertical ridges and furrows. Twigs
sometimes develop corky wings. Winter buds often with grayish
pubescence at apices.

GROWTH HABIT   Short trunk, several long sinuous limbs, and
broad crown.

DISTINGUISHING CHARACTERISTICS   All other maples commonly cultivated or growing wild in the Washington area have
pointed lobes.

LOCATIONS
• U.S. Capitol and Library of Congress grounds
• Between 17th Street, N.W., and the Ellipse
• Soldiers' Home
• The Mall, near the Vietnam Veterans Memorial
• Some city and suburban parks
• Elm Street, Chevy Chase, Maryland

Sycamore Maple (Plane-Tree Maple)

Acer pseudoplatanus L. • Maple Family *Aceraceae*

A maple with large, pendulous clusters of flowers and fruit. Its leaves resemble those of the American sycamore and London plane tree.

NATIVE RANGE   Europe, western Asia.

LEAVES   Simple, opposite, deciduous. 3 to 7 inches (7.5–17.7 cm) long, often slightly wider than long. Usually five-lobed. Margin with coarse, irregular, bluntly or sharply pointed teeth. Thick, leathery, slightly wrinkly. Deep dark green above, pale green or whitish beneath, with prominent veins. Glabrous or with some pubescence along the veins below. Petiole slender, reddish or yellow-green, 3 to 7½ inches (7.5–19 cm) long.

FLOWERS   Greenish yellow, in conspicuous clusters, which may be upright at first, becoming pendulous. Late April and May, with the young leaves.

FRUIT   Twin, winged samaras in long, hanging clusters. Samaras attached at varying angles, from acute to nearly horizontal; each samara 1 to 1¾ inches (2.5–4.5 cm) long. Nutlet often pubescent. Late summer to fall.

BARK AND TWIGS
Bark gray or reddish brown, flaking into scales. Twigs glabrous, with green, ovoid winter buds.

GROWTH HABIT
Large tree with spreading branches and a full, rounded crown.

SIMILAR SPECIES
The leaf shape and coarse, irregular teeth set the sycamore maple apart from other maples planted in Washington. (See illustration.) True sycamores

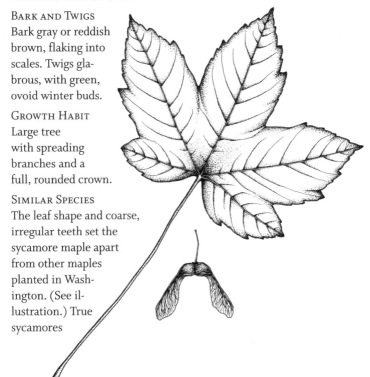

and London plane trees (*Platanus* spp.) have alternate leaves and whitish, peeling bark.

LOCATIONS
• U.S. Capitol grounds
• Smithsonian National Museum of Natural History
• Between 17th Street, N.W., and the Ellipse
• Some city and suburban parks, streets, public buildings, and private yards

Amur Maple

Acer tataricum L. spp. *ginnala* (Maxim.) Wesm. (*Acer ginnala* Maxim.) • Maple Family *Aceraceae*

A small, shrubby tree that has naturalized and become invasive in places.

NATIVE RANGE China, Manchuria, Japan.

LEAVES Simple, opposite, deciduous. 1½ to 3½ inches (3.8–9 cm) long, 1 to 2½ inches (2.5–6.5 cm) wide. Three-lobed, with the middle lobe the longest. Heavily toothed. Petiole thin, ¾ to 2 inches (2–5 cm) long. Autumn color: red, dropping early.

FLOWERS Yellowish white, conspicuous, clustered. Fragrant. Spring, with the leaves.

FRUIT Twin, winged samaras in hanging clusters. Wings attached at an acute angle; each samara about an inch (2.5 cm) long. Fruit persists into winter.

BARK AND TWIGS Bark dark gray or gray-brown, with darker striations or shallow fissures with age. Winter buds tiny, reddish brown.

GROWTH HABIT Shrub or small tree with many limbs.

SIMILAR SPECIES Trident maple (*Acer buergerianum*) leaves are untoothed or barely toothed.

LOCATIONS
• National Zoo
• Private yards throughout the city and suburbs
• Streets, Chevy Chase, Maryland

Cappadocian Maple (Coliseum Maple, Caucasian Maple)

Acer cappadocicum Gleditsch. • Maple Family *Aceraceae*

Rare in the Washington area. A tree that grew on the Capitol grounds, mislabeled years ago, was once believed to be the largest mountain maple (*Acer spicatum* Lam.) in the United States.

NATIVE RANGE   Caucasus Mountains, Himalayas, China.

LEAVES   Simple, opposite, deciduous. 3 to 6½ inches (7.5–16.5 cm) wide, 2 to 4 inches (5–10 cm) high. Usually five-lobed; each lobe broad, tapering to a fine point at apex. Sinuses shallow, base broadly cordate, margin untoothed. Glabrous but for tufts of hairs in the vein axils beneath. Petiole slender, yellow or pinkish, 1½ to 3½ inches (3.8–9 cm) long. Autumn color: yellow.

FLOWERS   Pale yellow. Spring, with the leaves.

FRUIT   Twin samaras, attached at a wide angle (nearly horizontal); each samara ¾ to 2¾ inches (2–7 cm) long.

BARK AND TWIGS Bark gray; winter buds small, ovoid.

GROWTH HABIT Trunk short, crown broad.

SIMILAR SPECIES May be confused with Norway maple (*Acer platanoides*).

LOCATION
• National Arboretum

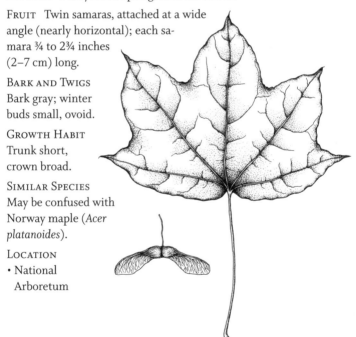

Trident Maple

Acer buergerianum Miq. • Maple Family
Aceraceae

A small tree that is infrequently planted in
Washington. This maple is com-
monly cultivated as a street tree in
Japan, and it is a good bonsai plant.

NATIVE RANGE   China.

LEAVES   Simple, opposite, deciduous.
1¾ to 3½ inches (4.5–9 cm) long,
1¼ to 2¾ inches (3–7 cm) wide. Three-
lobed, with three prominent veins radiating
from the base. Lobes triangular; base broadly
wedge-shaped, rounded, or subcordate. Margin
smooth or barely toothed. Somewhat leathery.
Dark green above, pale beneath. Petiole very
slender, 1¼ to 3¼ inches (3–8 cm) long. Autumn color: yellow, red, purple, or orange.

FLOWERS   Greenish yellow, small. Early
spring.

FRUIT   Small twin, winged samaras, about
¾ inch (2 cm) long.

BARK AND TWIGS   Bark pinkish and flaking, twigs glabrous.
Winter buds reddish brown, conic.

GROWTH HABIT   Small to medium tree with a full, rounded
crown and often with low branches. (Grows larger in its native
habitat in China.)

SIMILAR SPECIES   Amur maple (*Acer ginnala*) leaves are sharply
toothed.

LOCATIONS
• National Arboretum
• Streets, Chevy Chase, Maryland

Japanese Maple

Acer palmatum Thunb. • Maple Family *Aceraceae*

In Japan, the autumn colors of the Japanese maple are as highly revered as the
spring cherry blossoms. Although the
Japanese maples planted in Washington
are not nearly as well known as our Japanese cherry trees, their fall colors are the
most brilliant among locally planted maples.
Dozens of forms of this delicate tree are popular
here, with autumn color ranging from scarlet to
bright yellow. The Japanese maple can escape from cultivation,
and botanists are monitoring the species to determine its level of
invasiveness.

NATIVE RANGE   Japan, Korea, China.

LEAVES   Simple, opposite, deciduous. 1½ to 5 inches (3.8–12.5
cm) long and wide. Star-like, with five to seven (sometimes nine)
pointed lobes. Small, sharply pointed teeth; prominent palmate
venation. Base slightly cordate, straight across or broadly wedge-
shaped. Bright green in summer or, in some forms, purplish,
reddish, coppery, or yellow-green. Glabrous, or with tufts of hairs
in the vein axils below. Petiole slender, glabrous. Autumn color:
scarlet, red, purple, orange, or yellow, lasting late in the season.

FLOWERS   Purplish red, in small erect or spreading clusters.
Spring, with the leaves.

FRUIT   Delicate twin, winged samaras attached at a wide angle
(sometimes nearly horizontally), each ½ to 1¼ inches (1–3 cm)
long.

BARK AND TWIGS   Bark light brown or gray,
smooth, often marked with pale vertical
stripes. Twigs slender, glabrous, with
small, ovoid, usually red winter buds.

GROWTH HABIT   Small, graceful
tree with slender, sinuous branches
forming a rounded or flat-topped
crown. Some forms pendulous.

OTHER FORMS   Many cultivars of
the Japanese maple are planted in
Washington, with varying leaf colors and
shapes and fanciful growth habits. Two

Japanese fern-
leafed maple
('Dissectum')

commonly planted cultivated forms are 'Atropurpureum,' with deep purple leaves, and the Japanese fern-leafed maple ('Dissectum'), a weeping form with deeply cut, fern-like leaves.

SIMILAR SPECIES　The small, star-like leaves are distinctive among maples. May be confused with the sweetgum (*Liquidambar styraciflua*), which has larger, alternately arranged leaves and fruit that is spherical, pendulous, and prickly.

LOCATIONS
- Dumbarton Oaks
- U.S. Capitol and Library of Congress grounds
- White House grounds
- Franklin Delano Roosevelt Memorial
- Hillwood Estate
- Cleveland Park, including Newark Street, N.W.
- Audubon Naturalist Society, Woodend Sanctuary, Chevy Chase, Maryland (2007 Montgomery County Champion Japanese Maple)
- Common around public buildings and private homes

'DISSECTUM' LOCATIONS
- Rock Creek Cemetery
- Public and private gardens and grounds

Fullmoon Maple (Downy Japanese Maple)

Acer japonicum Thunb. • Maple Family *Aceraceae*

The rare fullmoon maple is somewhat similar in appearance to the commonly planted Japanese maple (*Acer palmatum*).

NATIVE RANGE　Japan.

LEAVES　Divided into seven to eleven lobes. Similar to Japanese maple, but often slightly larger and less deeply lobed. Very pubescent when young, pubescent later, at least along the lower veins.

OTHER FORMS　The cultivar 'Acontifolium' has leaves very similar to the smaller leaves of the Japanese fern-leafed maple (*Acer palmatum* 'Dissectum'), with deeply cut, delicate lobes. The 'Acontifolium' leaf is pubescent, at least along the veins below, while the Japanese fern-leafed maple leaf is glabrous or nearly so.

LOCATIONS
- Tudor Place, Georgetown
- Some private yards

Paperbark Maple

Acer griseum (Franch.) Pax • Maple Family *Aceraceae*

A small tree with striking cinnamon-colored, peeling, paper-like bark and trifoliate leaves. This is a new addition to *City of Trees*. I became acquainted with this species when friends gave our family a paperbark maple as a housewarming gift for our first country home near Sugarloaf Mountain.

NATIVE RANGE   Central China.

LEAVES   Compound, opposite, deciduous. Three leaflets, 2 to 5 inches (5–12.5 cm) long. Middle leaflet short-stalked and coarsely toothed; side leaflets almost sessile and less toothed. Blue-green above, paler below; petiole pubescent. Autumn color: green to reddish brown to a striking red. (Our tree colored red late in the season.)

BARK   Pinkish brown bark, peeling, very distinctive. In his *Manual of Woody Landscape Plants,* Michael A. Dirr writes: "Verbal descriptions cannot do justice to this ornamental asset and only after one has been privileged to view the bark first hand can he or she fully appreciate the character; snow acts as a perfect foil for the bark and accentuates its qualities."[90]

LOCATIONS
• National Arboretum
• Smithsonian Arts and Industries Building: Mary Livingston Ripley Garden
• U.S. Botanic Garden: Bartholdi Park
• 32nd Street, N.W., Georgetown
• Streets, Chevy Chase, Maryland

Golden-Rain-Tree (Pride-of-India, China-Tree, Varnish Tree)

Koelreuteria paniculata Laxm. • Soapberry Family *Sapindaceae*

The golden-rain-tree is one of Washington's most beautiful non-native ornamentals. Its fern-like leaves unfold in early spring and are followed by large clusters of yellow flowers in early summer and copper-colored, lantern-shaped fruit in autumn. During the Chou dynasty of ancient China, the golden-rain-tree, one of five official memorial trees, was planted on the tombs of scholars. This Asian tree has escaped from cultivation in this country and is being monitored for invasiveness.

NATIVE RANGE   China, Japan, Korea.

LEAVES   Pinnately (sometimes bipinnately) compound, alternate, deciduous. 6 to 14 inches (15–35.5 cm) long. Ovate. Seven to fifteen leaflets, each 1 to 3½ inches (2.5–9 cm) long. Feathery-looking, with large teeth and often with one, two, or more small lobes. Glabrous above, glabrous or slightly pubescent below.

FLOWERS   Small, bright yellow flowers tinged with red in branched horizontal or erect clusters up to 13 inches (33 cm) long. June to July. (See color close-up.)

FRUIT   Papery, lantern-like hanging capsule, 1½ to 2 inches (3.8–5 cm) long. Widest at the top, tapered to a point and open at the bottom. Pale green when it first appears in summer, becoming coppery pink and remaining on the tree into winter. Contains three black, berry-like seeds.

BARK AND TWIGS   Bark brown, gray-brown, or purplish brown, fissured and often marked with orange. Twigs light brown with darker brown, beaked winter buds.

GROWTH HABIT   Small to medium-sized tree, with a rounded crown and sinuous, ascending limbs.

SIMILAR SPECIES   When the pale green, lantern-like fruit capsules appear in summer, they may be confused from afar with Japanese pagoda (*Sophora japonica*) blossoms. A second *Koelreuteria* species is rarely planted in Washington and is just barely able to survive the winters here. Chinese flame-tree or bougainvillea golden-rain-tree (*Koelreuteria bipinnata* Franch.) has large, twice-pinnately compound leaves with untoothed or barely toothed leaflets. The yellow flowers bloom during summer, and the fruit is similar to the golden-rain-tree, but it is ellipsoid or oval-shaped and not tapered to a point at the bottom. I have seen a single specimen of this tree in Washington, in Garfield Park near Capitol Hill. It also grows at the National Arboretum.

LOCATIONS
• National Zoo
• U.S. Capitol grounds
• Rhode Island Avenue at Logan Circle
• National Arboretum
• Common in parks and public and private gardens and grounds throughout the city and suburbs

The Horse-Chestnuts and Buckeyes

Aesculus L. • Horse-Chestnut Family *Hippocastanaceae*

Horse-chestnuts and buckeyes are widely planted in Washington for their showy, upright flower clusters and large, compound, fan-shaped leaves. The most popular member of the genus is the common horse-chestnut (*Aesculus hippocastanum*) of southeastern Europe. In April and May, it puts forth large, pyramidal clusters of white flowers. The sweet and Ohio buckeyes (*A. flava* and *A. glabra*), which are native to the midwestern and southern U.S., are also popular ornamental trees in the District. Both have yellow flowers that can be told apart by the length of their stamens (see "Similar Species"). Ohio is known as the Buckeye State in honor of the Ohio buckeye. Other members of the genus in cultivation in our region are the red buckeye (*Aesculus pavia*) of the southeastern states and at least two hybrids, the red horse-chestnut (*A. × carnea*) and the hybrid buckeye (*A. × hybrida*).

Buckeyes are named for their large, shiny, round seeds, each of which is marked with a single pale, circular scar, or "buck eye." Although they look good enough to eat, most buckeye and horse-chestnut seeds are poisonous.

LEAVES   Palmately compound, opposite, deciduous. Five to nine toothed leaflets on a long petiole.

FLOWERS   White, yellow, pink, red, or a combination, in showy, upright clusters. April to May.

FRUIT   Smooth or spiny nut-like capsule that splits open to release one to three shiny seeds marked with characteristic "buck eye." Autumn.

DISTRIBUTION   About twenty species in North America, Asia, and Europe.

KEY TO HORSE-CHESTNUTS AND BUCKEYES COMMONLY CULTIVATED IN WASHINGTON, D.C.

1a) Flower clusters white. Leaflets stalkless. Autumn fruit capsule green or dark brown, prickly..
.... Common Horse-Chestnut (*A. hippocastanum*)

1b) Flower clusters pink, red, yellow, or yellow and pink.

2a) Flowers usually yellow.

3a) Flowers pale yellow, with stamens longer than petals. Autumn fruit capsule tan, spiny................................
.... Ohio Buckeye (*A. glabra*)

3b) Flowers yellow or yellow and pink, with stamens not longer than petals. Autumn fruit capsule smooth ......
....Sweet Buckeye (*A. flava*)

2b) Flowers red, pink, or yellow and pink.

4a) Flowers dark red or dark pink, long, thin, with tubular calyx and petals not spreading widely apart. Leaflets pale to medium green, finely toothed. Autumn fruit capsule smooth ....
....Red Buckeye (*A. pavia*)

4b) Flowers red, pink, or pink and yellow, with petals spreading apart.

5a) Leaflets deep dark green, with coarse, jagged teeth. Autumn fruit capsule with a few small spines .... Red Horse-Chestnut (*A.* × *carnea*)

5b) Leaflets pale to medium green, with small, fine teeth. Autumn fruit capsule smooth ....
.... Hybrid Buckeye (*A.* × *hybrida*)

Common Horse-Chestnut (European Horse-Chestnut)

Aesculus hippocastanum L. • Horse-Chestnut Family
Hippocastanaceae

One of the most spectacular flowering trees growing in Washington. The common horse-chestnut is widely planted in legendary gardens and parks of Europe.

NATIVE RANGE Greece, Albania, Bulgaria.

LEAVES Palmately compound, opposite, deciduous. Five to seven stalkless leaflets, 3 to 10 inches (7.5–25.5 cm) long. Very narrow at the base, widening toward the apex and ending in an abrupt point. Side leaflets smallest, middle ones largest. Margin irregularly toothed. Petiole up to 10 inches (25.5 cm) long.

FLOWERS Large, showy, upright clusters. Overall color of cluster white, but individual flowers are often tinged with red and yellow. April to early May.

FRUIT Dark brown, sharply and heavily spined capsule, splitting open to release one or two shiny, dark reddish brown seeds. Each seed with whitish or pinkish circle (visible when free of capsule), approximately 1¼ to 2½ inches (3–5.5 cm) long.

BARK AND TWIGS   Bark often breaks into irregular scales that peel away slightly from trunk. Twigs usually glabrous. Winter buds conspicuous: large, sticky, mahogany-colored.

GROWTH HABIT   May grow to be a large tree. Crown tall and rounded.

DISTINGUISHING CHARACTERISTICS   White flowers, stalkless leaflets, and (from late summer through early spring) sticky buds distinguish the common horse-chestnut from other horse-chestnuts and buckeyes planted in the Washington area.

LOCATIONS

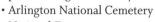

- U.S. Capitol grounds
- U.S. Capitol Reflecting Pool (Casey Trees' 2006 D.C. Champion Horse-Chestnut)
- Stanton Park, Lafayette Park, and other parks throughout the city
- Arlington National Cemetery
- National Zoo
- U.S. Botanic Garden: Bartholdi Park
- The Mall
- Common in public places throughout the region

Red Horse-Chestnut

Aesculus × carnea Hayne. (*A. hippocastanum × A. pavia*) • Horse-Chestnut Family *Hippocastanaceae*

A cross between the common horse-chestnut of Europe and the red buckeye of the southeastern United States.

LEAVES Palmately compound, opposite, deciduous. Five (sometimes seven) crinkly textured leaflets on extremely short stalks. Similar to common horse-chestnut (*Aesculus hippocastanum*), but darker, more coarsely toothed, and usually smaller.

FLOWERS Deep pink or red clusters (with yellow markings in some cultivated forms). April to early May. (See color close-up.)

FRUIT Smaller than common horse-chestnut, with fewer or no spines.

OTHER FORMS The cultivar 'Briotii' is the most frequently planted form. It has bright red flowers and dark green leaves. Another popular cultivar is 'Fort McNair,' named for Fort McNair in D.C. It has pink flowers with yellow markings.

SIMILAR SPECIES Red buckeye (*Aesculus pavia*) has deeper red but less spectacular flowers with tubular calyxes, thinner leaflets on longer stalks, and fruit that is always smooth. [See also common horse-chestnut (*A. hippocastanum*) and buckeyes.]

LOCATIONS
• National Zoo
• Georgetown
• Parks and private yards

Red Buckeye

Aesculus pavia L. • Horse-Chestnut Family *Hippocastanaceae*

An infrequently cultivated small tree or shrub.

NATIVE HABITAT AND RANGE Rich, moist woods and streambanks; southeastern U.S. from Virginia to Florida, west to Texas, Missouri, and southern Illinois.

LEAVES Palmately compound, opposite, deciduous. Similar to sweet or yellow buckeye (*Aesculus flava*), but with leaflets smaller and more irregularly toothed; overall leaf shape is less symmetrical. Leaflet stalk may be ½ inch (1.2 cm) long or longer.

FLOWERS Dark red, in tall clusters. Each flower has a red tubular calyx. April to May.

FRUIT Similar to sweet buckeye, but smaller. Capsule contains one or two seeds.

SIMILAR SPECIES See red horse-chestnut (*Aesculus* × *carnea*) and other buckeyes.

LOCATIONS
- National Garden of the U.S. Botanic Garden
- National Institutes of Health, Bethesda (2007 Montgomery County Champion Red Buckeye)
- Private gardens

Sweet Buckeye (Yellow Buckeye)

Aesculus flava Aiton (*A. octandra* Marshall) • Horse-Chestnut Family *Hippocastanaceae*

NATIVE HABITAT AND RANGE Rich, moist woods, streambanks, and river bottoms; mountains of southwestern Pennsylvania, west to southern Illinois, south to northern Georgia and Alabama.

LEAVES Palmately compound, opposite, deciduous. Usually with five (rarely up to seven) leaflets, 4 to 10 inches (10–25.5 cm) long. Widest in the middle, tapering smoothly and gradually to apex and base. Finely toothed. Yellow-green above, considerably paler

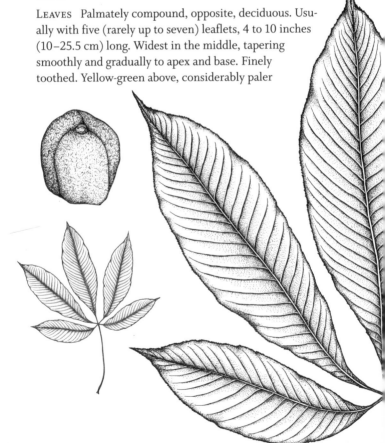

below. May be glabrous, pubescent, or partially pubescent below. Each leaflet usually stalked. Petiole 3 to 8 inches (7.5–20 cm) long. Autumn color: bright orange-yellow or yellow.

FLOWERS Yellow, pink, or yellow and pink clusters. Stamens not longer than petals. April to early May.

FRUIT Smooth, tan, shallowly etched capsule, about the size and shape of a small plum. Splits open to release (usually two) shiny, poisonous seeds, each with characteristic "buck eye."

BARK AND TWIGS Bark gray and grayish pink, smooth underneath, with shedding scales. Winter end buds large, but lighter colored than common horse-chestnut (*A. hippocastanum*) and not sticky.

GROWTH HABIT Medium to tall tree. Crown broad and somewhat rounded.

SIMILAR SPECIES Ohio buckeye (*A. glabra*) has thick, furrowed bark, flowers with stamens extending beyond the petals, and a spiny fruit capsule. See other buckeyes and horse-chestnuts (*Aesculus* spp.).

LOCATIONS
• U.S. Capitol grounds
• Sligo Creek Stream Valley Park (2007 Montgomery County Champion Sweet or Yellow Buckeye)

Ohio Buckeye

Aesculus glabra Willd. • Horse-Chestnut Family *Hippocastanaceae*
STATE TREE OF OHIO
The tree that named the Buckeye State.

NATIVE HABITAT AND RANGE Moist woods, streambanks, and river bottoms; western Pennsylvania to eastern Nebraska, Kansas, Oklahoma, and Texas, south to Tennessee and Alabama.

LEAVES Palmately compound, opposite, deciduous. Smallish for the genus, variable in size. Usually with five (sometimes seven) leaflets, 2 to 6 inches (5–15 cm) long. Widest at the middle, or just above it, and tapering to a point at either end. Finely toothed margins. Glabrous to pubescent below. Petiole thin, 2 to 6 inches (5–15 cm) long. Leaflet stalks very short, almost nonexistent on some leaves.

FLOWERS Pale yellow or yellow-green, bell-shaped, clustered. Stamens longer than petals. April to May.

Fʀᴜɪᴛ   Capsule the color of coffee with cream. An inch or more in diameter, covered with small, weak spines. Splits open to release one (usually) or more reddish brown seeds, marked with characteristic "buck eye."

Bᴀʀᴋ ᴀɴᴅ Tᴡɪɢs   Bark gray or brown, thick, furrowed and scaly. Twigs emit a foul odor when broken. (The tree is sometimes known as "fetid buckeye.") Winter end buds reddish brown, not sticky, with ridged scales.

Gʀᴏᴡᴛʜ Hᴀʙɪᴛ   Small to medium-sized tree with a broad, rounded crown.

Sɪᴍɪʟᴀʀ Sᴘᴇᴄɪᴇs   See sweet or yellow buckeye (*A. flava*). Fruit similar to common horse-chestnut (*A. hippocastanum*), but smaller, lighter colored, and with shorter, weaker spines.

Lᴏᴄᴀᴛɪᴏɴs
• Hains Point, East Potomac Park
• National Arboretum

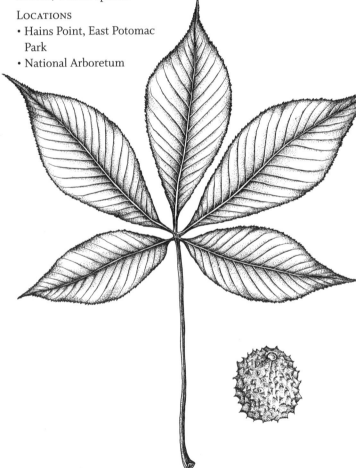

Hybrid Buckeye

Aesculus × *hybrida* DC. (*Aesculus flava* × *Aesculus pavia*) • Horse-Chestnut Family *Hippocastanaceae*

A cross between the sweet or yellow buckeye (*A. flava*) and the red buckeye (*A. pavia*).

LEAVES   Five long-pointed leaflets. Margins with small, pointed or rounded teeth. Pubescent along the veins below.

FLOWERS   Reddish and yellow, in upright clusters. Late April and early May.

FRUIT   Smooth, slightly etched, pale brown capsule. Splits open to release shiny seed with characteristic "buck eye."

LOCATIONS
• Uncommonly planted in Washington

Flowering Dogwood

Cornus florida L. • Dogwood Family *Cornaceae*

STATE TREE AND FLOWER OF VIRGINIA, STATE TREE OF MISSOURI, STATE FLOWER OF NORTH CAROLINA

Unsurpassed in beauty among our native flowering trees, the flowering dogwood dazzles the eye in city and suburban gardens and native woodlands during its April blooming time. Its autumn fruit is an important food source for songbirds and mammals. The tree has also enjoyed a rich herbal history. Its twigs were used as chewing sticks (primitive toothbrushes) by American Indians, colonial settlers, and slaves; and a tincture or tea made from dogwood root bark was used to treat malaria during the Civil War.

This cherished native tree is seriously threatened by a fungus called *Discula destructiva*, which causes a disease known as Discula anthracnose. The most obvious early symptom of the disease is lower branch die-back. Discula anthracnose has killed many dogwoods in the mid-Atlantic states and New England. I have watched it kill many on Sugarloaf Mountain, thirty-five miles northwest of Washington, and then move into the city, where it has affected cultivated trees, too. It has been heartbreaking to see our most beautiful native tree sicken and in many cases die. But as I write this, I can see dogwoods coming into bloom outside my window, and I hope the species will survive and return to its former glory throughout the mid-Atlantic. Thankfully, trees in many parts of the southern states remain unaffected so far.

NATIVE HABITAT AND RANGE   Woods; southern New England to Florida, west to Ontario, Michigan, eastern Texas, and northeastern Mexico.

LEAVES   Simple, opposite, deciduous. 2 to 6 inches (5–15 cm) long. Elliptic or ovate. Abruptly pointed, with broadly wedge-shaped or rounded base. Veins, characteristic of dogwoods, curve along the smooth or nearly smooth leaf margin. (See illustration.) Mostly glabrous above, paler below and usually glabrous, but may be somewhat pubescent, especially along the veins. Autumn color: brilliant scarlet, crimson, and wine.

FLOWERS   Usually white, but may be pink or red. (See "Other Forms.") 2 to 4 inches (5–10 cm) across. The four notched white "petals" are actually large bracts that surround the tiny yellowish or greenish true flowers clustered at the center. Mid-April to early May, just before or with the leaves. (See color close-up.)

FRUIT   Scarlet, berry-like drupes, each ½ inch (1 cm) or less long, in small clusters.

BARK AND TWIGS   Bark is broken into many small, squarish plates. Twigs greenish or purplish, with separate leaf and flower buds. The buds are distinctive—gray and onion-shaped, borne at the ends of the twigs—and especially showy in winter. They have always reminded me of Eastern Orthodox church spires.

GROWTH HABIT   Small tree with a flat, bushy crown.

OTHER FORMS   There are many cultivated forms of the flowering dogwood planted in the Washington area, including *Cornus florida* 'Pluribracteata,' which blooms slightly later and has six or more petal-like bracts; *C. florida* var. *rubra*, with bracts ranging from pale pink to red; and *C. florida* 'Cherokee Chief,' a popular cultivar with red, petal-like bracts. In recent years, an anthracnose-resistant form called 'Appalachian Spring' was developed at the Tennessee Agricultural Experiment Station from a tree growing in the Catoctin Mountains in Maryland. As time goes on, more disease-resistant forms of flowering dogwood are apt to be offered in the nursery trade.

Similar Species   The kousa dogwood (*Cornus kousa*) blooms after the leaves are out. It has pointed, rather than notched, petal-like bracts. In recent years, hybrid trees that are a cross between *Cornus florida* and *Cornus kousa*, known as stellar dogwoods, were developed at Rutgers University. Many have been planted in the region. Stellar dogwoods (*Cornus × rutgersensis*) bloom between the two species' blooming times and exhibit traits of both parents. (See color close-up.) Some trees tend to have pointed bracts, like the kousa, and some have more rounded and notched ones, like the flowering dogwoods. Most are white-bracted, and some are pink. Names include 'Celestial,' 'Aurora,' 'Constellation,' 'Stellar Pink,' 'Stardust,' and 'Ruth Ellen.' Each selection has moderate to good resistance to anthracnose. The town of Chevy Chase, Maryland, has planted stellar dogwoods along some of its streets.

Locations
- U.S. Capitol grounds
- National Arboretum, Dogwood Collection, and among the azaleas on Mount Hamilton
- Mount Vernon
- White House grounds
- Lady Bird Johnson Park and along the George Washington Parkway to Mount Vernon
- Franciscan Monastery
- Streets, Chevy Chase, Maryland
- Common throughout the city, suburbs, and surrounding woodlands (although less so since the blight)

Kousa Dogwood

Cornus kousa (Buerger ex Miq.) Hance   •   Dogwood Family
Cornaceae

A beautiful Asian tree or shrub. Similar to our native flowering dogwood, but with pointed, rather than notched, petal-like bracts and a later and longer blooming time. Some botanists are concerned that the kousa dogwood may be becoming invasive.

Native Range   Japan, Korea, China.

Leaves   Simple, opposite, deciduous. 2 to 5 inches (5–12.5 cm) long. Elliptic-ovate. Thinner and slightly less abruptly pointed than flowering dogwood (*Cornus florida*), with a smooth or barely wavy-toothed margin. Base broadly wedge-shaped or (rarely) rounded. Characteristic dogwood venation pattern. Glaucous below, with pale, minute, flattened hairs along lower surface and longer, rust-colored hairs in vein axils.

FLOWERS   Four pale green, white, or yellowish (rarely pink) petal-like bracts are gracefully pointed at apices. True flowers (and flower buds) tiny, in a prominent round, greenish head in the center. Mid or late May to late June, after the leaves. (See color close-up.)

FRUIT   Red, compound drupe that looks like a raspberry or strawberry.

BARK   Brown, mottled.

GROWTH HABIT   Either shrub-like, with spreading branches and a rounded crown, or with a tallish, narrow crown.

OTHER FORMS   *Cornus kousa* var. *chinensis*, native to China, has slightly larger petal-like bracts and leaves with very little or no rusty pubescence in the vein axils below. Many cultivated varieties of kousa dogwood are available.

SIMILAR SPECIES   Flowering dogwood (*Cornus florida*) blooms in April and early May and has notched, rather than pointed, petal-like bracts. See flowering dogwood "Similar Species" for information about stellar dogwoods, a hybrid group representing a cross between the flowering dogwood and kousa dogwood.

LOCATIONS
- U.S. Capitol northeast grounds (planted in honor of Lady Bird Johnson by Senate wives, 1968)
- Rock Creek Cemetery
- Smithsonian National Museum of Natural History
- Common throughout the city and suburbs in public and private gardens and grounds

Cornelian Cherry (Cornelian Cherry Dogwood)

Cornus mas L. • Dogwood Family *Cornaceae*

This small tree or shrub is really a dogwood, but its fruit is cherry-like. It is one of the first trees to bloom in Washington in the early spring. Its edible fruit is used to make preserves and syrups.

NATIVE RANGE   Central and southern Europe, western Asia.

LEAVES   Simple, opposite, deciduous. 1½ to 4 inches (4–10 cm) long. Similar to flowering dogwood (*Cornus florida*), but smaller and usually with tiny, pale, flattened hairs (visible with a hand lens) on both the upper and lower surfaces.

FLOWERS Tiny yellow flowers, in round clusters. March or very early April, before the leaves. (See color close-up.)

FRUIT Red drupe, up to ¾ inch (2 cm) long, resembling a cherry.

BARK Brown, flaky.

GROWTH HABIT Usually a tall, full shrub in our area.

SIMILAR SPECIES Rare Japanese Cornelian cherry (*Cornus officinalis*) is described below.

LOCATIONS
• Library of Congress grounds
• Tidal Basin
• National Arboretum
• National Zoo
• Public and private gardens and grounds throughout the city and suburbs.

Japanese Cornelian Cherry

Cornus officinalis Sieb. & Zucc. • Dogwood Family *Cornaceae*

This rare tree or shrub, native to Japan and Korea, is very similar to the Cornelian cherry. It differs in having leaves with conspicuous tufts of brownish hairs in the vein axils below, and minor differences in the flowers, fruit, and bark.

LOCATION
• National Arboretum

Alternate-Leaved Dogwood (Pagoda Dogwood, Green Osier)

Cornus alternifolia L.f. • Dogwood Family *Cornaceae*

Most dogwoods have oppositely arranged leaves. However, this tree and the table dogwood (*Cornus controversa*) have leaves arranged alternately.

NATIVE HABITAT AND RANGE Rich woods, thickets; New Brunswick west to Minnesota, south to Georgia and Alabama.

LEAVES Simple, alternate (although crowded near the branchlet tip and may appear opposite or whorled), deciduous. 2 to 5 inches (5–12.5 cm) long. Elliptic-ovate, with wedge-shaped base. Typical dogwood venation pattern. Flattened pubescence below (visible with a hand lens).

FLOWERS   Small, white, in flat-topped clusters that are 1½ to 2½ inches (4–6.3 cm) across. Late spring, after the leaves.

FRUIT   Small, bluish black, berry-like drupe on a reddish stalk.

SIMILAR SPECIES   See table dogwood, below.

LOCATIONS
• National Arboretum
• Town of Chevy Chase, Maryland

Table Dogwood (Giant Dogwood)

Cornus controversa Hemsl. • Dogwood Family *Cornaceae*

Native to Japan and China. Similar to the alternate-leaved dogwood, but with leaves usually rounded at the base and larger flower clusters.

Tupelo (Black Tupelo, Black-Gum, Sour-Gum)

Nyssa sylvatica Marshall • Tupelo or Black-Gum Family *Nyssaceae*

A handsome native tree. Leaves turn scarlet, peach, and wine-red in early autumn.

NATIVE HABITAT AND RANGE   Upland woods and wet low-lands, including swamps. [Botanists recognize a distinct variety growing in Coastal Plain wetland areas (*N. sylvatica* var. *biflora*)]. Southern Maine and southern Ontario and Michigan, south to Florida and Texas.

LEAVES   Simple, alternate, deciduous. 2 to 6 inches (5–15 cm) long. (Leaves crowded near the tips of branchlets may appear nearly opposite.) Obovate, with bluntly pointed apex and wedge-shaped or (rarely) rounded base. Margin smooth or slightly wavy. Often pubescent along the veins below. Petiole about ¾ inch (2 cm) long. Spectacular early autumn foliage.

FLOWERS   Small, greenish white. Males in many-flowered round heads; females, few per cluster. Spring, with the leaves.

FRUIT   Egg-shaped, dark blue, berry-like drupe, ⅓ to ⅔ inch (1–1.5 cm) long, on a slender stalk up to 1¾ inches (4.5 cm) long. Contains a stony, shallowly grooved pit.

BARK AND TWIGS   Bark dark, furrowed, often broken into squares. Twigs slender, with diaphragmed pith. Winter buds scaly, pointed, ovoid. Terminal bud present.

GROWTH HABIT   Medium-sized tree with rounded or cylindric and flat-topped crown. Branches and twigs horizontal or slightly drooping.

SIMILAR SPECIES   Common persimmon (*Diospyros virginiana*) has somewhat similar leaves and bark. See persimmon "Similar Species," and compare leaf and fruit illustrations. Water-tupelo (*Nyssa aquatica* L.) grows in freshwater swamps of the southeastern Coastal Plain from Virginia south. Ogeechee-tupelo or Ogeechee-lime (*Nyssa ogeche* Marsh.), native to the Coastal Plain from South Carolina to Florida, is planted along a stream in Fern Valley and elsewhere at the National Arboretum.

LOCATIONS
- Kenilworth Aquatic Gardens
- White House south lawn, just outside the Oval Office
- National Arboretum
- Rock Creek Park and other parks throughout the region
- Sugarloaf Mountain, Maryland

Dove Tree (Handkerchief Tree, Ghost Tree)

Davidia involucrata Baill. • Tupelo Family *Nyssaceae*

A very rare and beautiful tree.

NATIVE RANGE   China.

LEAVES   Simple, alternate, deciduous. 3 to 9 inches (7.5–23 cm) long. Heart-shaped, with large, coarse teeth.

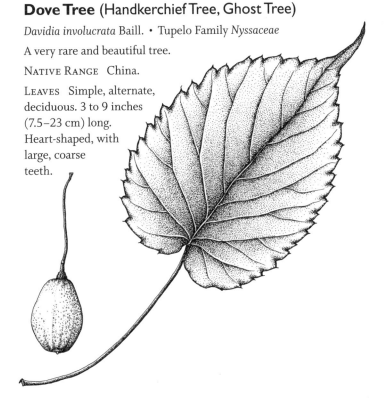

FLOWERS   Large, creamy white bracts are showy; true flowers small, in a round cluster. (See color close-up.)

FRUIT   Hanging drupe, about 1½ inches (3.5–4 cm) long.

SIMILAR SPECIES   Leaves of two other rare trees, Japanese raisin-tree (*Hovenia dulcis*) and Idesia (*Idesia polycarpa*), are similar, but the fruit of each is very distinctive.

LOCATIONS
• National Arboretum
• 34th Street, N.W., Cleveland Park
• Outdoor Nursery School, Chevy Chase, Maryland (2007 Montgomery County Champion Dove Tree)
• River Farm
• A few private yards

Devil's Walkingstick (Hercules' Club, Angelica Tree)

Aralia spinosa L. • Ginseng Family *Araliaceae*

A small, native tree or large shrub, easily identified by its stout branchlets covered with prickles.

NATIVE HABITAT AND RANGE   Moist, rich woodlands and streamsides; Delaware to southern Illinois and Missouri, south to Florida and eastern Texas. (Also introduced northward to New York, southern New England, and Michigan.)

Branchlet of Devil's Walkingstick (*Aralia spinosa*)

LEAVES   Bipinnately compound, alternate, deciduous. Large, with prickly leaflets, stalks, and petiole. Each leaflet 2 to 3 inches (5–7.5 cm) long, ovate, toothed. Dark green above; paler, glaucous, and nearly glabrous below.

FLOWERS   Small, white, in large branched clusters. Mid or late summer.

FRUIT   Small, black, berry-like drupe. Chipmunks, foxes, and many other mammals and birds enjoy the juicy fruit. Autumn.

GROWTH HABIT   Small tree or shrub.

SIMILAR SPECIES   Not likely to be confused with any other commonly planted species, due to its dense prickles. However, a closely related Asian species is planted at the National Arboretum and could be encountered elsewhere. Japanese angelica-tree [*Aralia elata* (Miq.) Seem.] is a slightly taller woody plant with leaflets that are more pubescent below. The Asian species is slightly less prickly than the native one, and a smooth form has been developed in China, according to Michael A. Dirr (*Manual of Woody Landscape Plants*).

LOCATIONS
• National Arboretum
• Some private homes
• Area woodlands

American Holly

Ilex opaca Aiton • Holly Family *Aquifoliaceae*

STATE TREE OF DELAWARE

With its evergreen leaves and bright red fruit, the American holly perfectly complements the white marble monuments of Washington. In our region, American hollies serve as host plants for Henry's elfin butterflies.

NATIVE HABITAT AND RANGE   A number of habitats, but most abundant in moist, sandy Coastal Plain woodlands; southern New England to Florida and Texas.

LEAVES   Simple, alternate, evergreen. 2 to 4 inches (5–10 cm) long. Margin with spiny outcurved teeth. Leathery. Rather dull green above, paler below.

FRUIT   Small, round, bright red, berry-like drupe, remaining on the tree through winter. The fruit is eaten by many species of birds. I once saw dozens of robins gorging on the fruit of a single snow-laden tree after a February storm.

OTHER FORMS   Many cultivars of the American holly are grown in Washington, including *I. opaca* f. *xanthocarpa*, which is among the cultivated forms with yellow to orange fruit.

SIMILAR SPECIES   The American holly is the most widely planted tree-sized holly in Washington, although many shrubby ornamental species are grown here and can reach good size. (See "Other Hollies of the Washington Area," below.) The shrubby osmanthus (*Osmanthus heterophyllus*) has similarly shaped leaves, but they are oppositely arranged.

LOCATIONS
• Jefferson Memorial and Tidal Basin
• Lincoln Memorial

- U.S. Capitol grounds
- Smithsonian Castle
- Rock Creek Park and other regional woodlands
- Common throughout the city, both in the wild and in cultivation

Other Hollies of the Washington Area

The English holly (*Ilex aquifolium* L.) and several Asian holly species, hybrids, and cultivars are planted in Washington, but they rarely become trees (although they often attain large shrub stature, and the English holly and others can be tree-like). Most non-native evergreen hollies grown here have shiny leaves, compared to the duller green leaves of the American holly (*I. opaca*). Noteworthy are 'Nellie R. Stevens' (originated from a hybrid of *I. aquifolium* and *I. cornuta*) and the following Asian species and their many cultivars: longstalk holly (*Ilex pedunculosa* Miq.); Japanese holly (*Ilex crenata* Thunb.); and lusterleaf holly (*Ilex latifolia* Thunb.). Foster's hybrid hollies (*Ilex × attenuata* Ashe. 'Fosteri') represent a cross between the American holly (*I. opaca*) and a southeastern species called Dahoon holly (*Ilex cassine* L.). Yaupon (*Ilex vomitoria* Aiton.) is another southeastern holly that could be encountered here. Shrubby hollies indigenous to Maryland, Virginia, and District woodlands include several deciduous species. Two of them are planted in Bartholdi Park of the U.S. Botanic Garden: winterberry [*Ilex verticillata* (L.) A. Gray] and possum-haw (*Ilex decidua* Walter). The National Arboretum has a noteworthy holly collection. For more information about cultivated hollies, consult Michael A. Dirr's *Manual of Woody Landscape Plants*.

Winged Euonymus (Winged Burning-Bush)

Euonymus alatus (Thunb.) Siebold •
Staff-Tree Family *Celastraceae*

A large shrub, native to Asia, easily
identified by its corky-winged branchlets; small, simple, opposite leaves;
and bright scarlet fall color. Widely
planted throughout the region and escaped from cultivation in local woodlands, where it has become invasive,
as has another member of the genus,
climbing euonymous [*Euonymus*

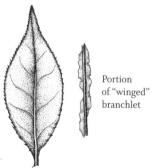

Portion
of "winged"
branchlet

fortunei (Turcz.) Hand.-Mazz.]. Two native euonymous species grow in area woodlands: wahoo or burning-bush (*Euonymous atropurpureus* Jacq.) and strawberry bush (*Euonymous americanus* L.). Both have showy fruit.

LOCATIONS
• U.S. Capitol grounds
• Rock Creek Park
• Common throughout the city and suburbs

Japanese Raisin-Tree

Hovenia dulcis Thunb. • Buckthorn Family *Rhamnaceae*

The rare Japanese raisin-tree has uniquely shaped, edible, raisin-like fruit. (See illustration.)

NATIVE RANGE   China, cultivated in Japan and India.

LEAVES   Simple, alternate, deciduous. 4 to 6 inches (10–15 cm) long. Broadly ovate to elliptic. Shallowly cordate or rounded at the base, and often unequal. Apex pointed. Margin coarsely toothed.

FRUIT   Brown and raisin-textured. Fleshy and juicy inside, with a sweet, slightly fermented flavor. Autumn.

LOCATIONS
• Tidal Basin
• Kenilworth Aquatic Gardens
• National Arboretum

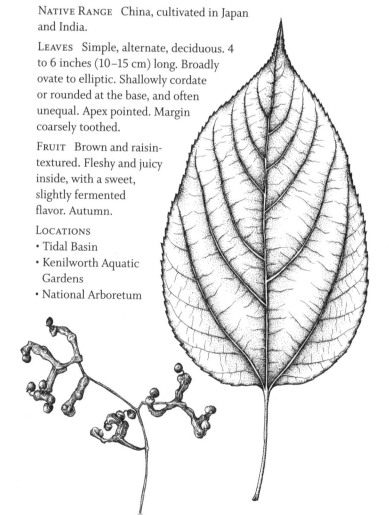

Common Jujube (Chinese Date)

Ziziphus jujuba Mill. • Buckthorn Family *Rhamnaceae*

THE NATIONAL CHAMPION JUJUBE, AS LISTED IN THE *National Register of Big Trees* (2006–7), GROWS ON THE U.S. CAPITOL GROUNDS.

Fresh, cooked, or dried, the date-like jujube is a delicious and nutritious delicacy. The fruit has also been used medicinally for centuries. The jujube is cultivated throughout the Orient and the Mediterranean. Although rare in Washington, several specimens grow on the grounds of the U.S. Capitol and the U.S. Botanic Garden.

NATIVE RANGE   Southeastern Europe, Asia.

LEAVES   Simple, alternate, deciduous. ¾ to 3 inches (2–7.5 cm) long. Ovate to ovate-lanceolate. Pointed or blunt apex; shallow rounded or pointed teeth. Three main veins radiate from the base, which is usually slightly unequal. Spine-like stipules often present.

FLOWERS   Small, greenish white or yellowish flowers in clusters. Spring.

FRUIT   Ovoid-oblong, orange-red drupe, ½ to 1 inch (1–2.5 cm) long.

LOCATIONS
• U.S. Capitol grounds
• U.S. Botanic Garden: Bartholdi Park

The Ashes

Fraxinus L. • Olive Family *Oleaceae*

The white ash (*Fraxinus americana*), a common native tree, is often planted in Washington. The green ash (*Fraxinus pennsylvanica*), a native tree of moist and wet soils, is less commonly cultivated but has grown in popularity, especially as a street tree. The other species included here are rare. Ashes have become threatened by the emerald ash borer (a pest capable of wreaking devastating damage) and ash anthracnose.

LEAVES   Odd-pinnately compound, opposite, deciduous.

FLOWERS   Small, in sometimes conspicuous clusters. Unisexual or perfect. Spring, with or before the leaves.

Fruit   Usually single-seeded samara with a terminal wing.

Distribution   About sixty-five species in the Northern Hemisphere.

White Ash

Fraxinus americana L. • Olive Family *Oleaceae*

A statuesque native tree with dark, dramatically grooved, almost braided-looking bark.

Native Habitat and Range   Rich woods; southeastern Canada and eastern U.S., south to Florida, west to eastern Texas, eastern Nebraska, and Wisconsin.

Leaves   Pinnately compound, opposite, deciduous. 7 to 13 inches (17.8–33 cm) long. Five to nine (usually seven) leaflets, 3 to 5 inches (7.5–12.5 cm) long. Oblong-lanceolate, with smooth or obscurely toothed margins. Glabrous or slightly hairy below. Petiolules ¼ to ½ inch (6–12 mm) long. Autumn color: peachy gold to maroon to almost purple.

Flowers and Fruit   Flowers in clusters. Spring, before or with the leaves. Fruit is a winged samara, 1 to 2 inches (2.5–5 cm) long. The samaras serve as food for wood ducks, quail, wild turkeys, and several species of songbirds.

BARK AND TWIGS   Bark dark gray, thick, separating into vertical, diamond-shaped ridges and furrows, and sometimes into blocks resembling the blockiness of persimmon bark. Twigs lustrous grayish green with large U-shaped leaf scars and small, round, dark brown winter buds.

GROWTH HABIT   Medium-sized to tall tree with a straight trunk and open, pyramidal, or rounded crown.

SIMILAR SPECIES   The similar green or red ash (*Fraxinus pennsylvanica*) is not as widely cultivated as the white ash, and in the wild the two can often be separated largely by habitat. (The red or green ash grows in moist or wet soils; the white ash grows in moist but not wet soils.) Although the two species are hard to tell apart, the green or red ash usually has narrower leaflets and samaras. The samaras have thinner seeds that flow into the wing (decurrent).

LOCATIONS
- U.S. Capitol grounds
- White House grounds
- The Mall, near 17th Street and Independence Avenue (Casey Trees' 2006 D.C. Champion White Ash)
- Parks, public buildings, and private homes
- National Zoo
- Rock Creek Park and woodland parks throughout the region
- Town of Chevy Chase, Maryland
- Lyon Park (2007–2008 Arlington County Co-champion White Ashes)

Green Ash (Red Ash)

Fraxinus pennsylvanica Marshall • Olive Family *Oleaceae*

Most botanists no longer recognize green and red ash as separate trees, although the more glabrous green ash used to be considered a variety of the pubescent red ash. Today the trees are lumped together under the single name *Fraxinus pennsylvanica*.

NATIVE HABITAT AND RANGE   Moist or wet woods, often along streambanks and in floodplains; Cape Breton Island, Nova Scotia, and New Brunswick south to northern Florida, west to eastern Texas, northeastern Colorado, Montana, and Alberta.

LEAVES   Pinnately compound, opposite, deciduous. 10 to 12 inches (25.3–30.5 cm) long. Five to nine leaflets, 4 to 6 inches (10–15 cm) long. Oblong-lanceolate to elliptic. Margins smooth, toothed, or toothed only above the middle. Glabrous or pubescent below. Petiolules often narrowly winged, ⅛ to ¼ inch (3–6 mm) long.

BARK   Brown, scaly and fissured; usually not quite as thick as that of the white ash (*Fraxinus americana*).

SIMILAR SPECIES   White ash usually has slightly wider leaflets and samaras. The white ash is more commonly cultivated in the city, but the green ash is planted, too, especially as a street tree.

LOCATIONS
• Kenilworth Aquatic Gardens
• National Arboretum
• National Zoo
• Barcroft Park (2007–2008 Arlington County Champion Green Ash)
• Parks and private yards
• Moist and wet woods of Rock Creek Park and other regional parks

European Ash (Common Ash)

Fraxinus excelsior L. • Olive Family *Oleaceae*

The European ash is planted in some private yards and public grounds in the city.

NATIVE RANGE   Europe, Asia Minor.

LEAVES   Pinnately compound, opposite, deciduous. 7 to 14 inches (17.8–35.5 cm) long. Nine to thirteen leaflets. Lanceolate or ovate-oblong. Margins with sharp, shallow teeth. White pubescence along the veins below.

TWIGS   Winter buds black.

DISTINGUISHING CHARACTERISTICS   The black winter buds are the best distinguishing feature of the European ash. The white pubescence along the leaflet veins is another helpful diagnostic.

LOCATIONS
• National Arboretum
• U.S. Capitol grounds
• Private yards and public grounds

Chinese Ash

Fraxinus chinensis var. *rhynchophylla* (Hance) Hemsl. • Olive Family *Oleaceae*

This tree is extremely rare in D.C.

NATIVE RANGE   Northeastern Asia.

LEAVES   Compound, opposite, deciduous. Usually five leaflets, ovate or obovate, with rounded to pointed teeth. Usually pubescent below.

LOCATIONS
• Extremely rare in Washington

Blue Ash

Fraxinus quadrangulata Michx. • Olive Family Oleaceae

Several specimens of the rare blue ash are planted on the Potomac River side of the Tidal Basin. They can be distinguished from other ashes in the area by their stout, four-sided twigs.

NATIVE HABITAT AND RANGE   Dry and moist woods of uplands and bottomlands, often in limestone soils; Midwest from southern Ontario and southern Wisconsin to Arkansas, northern Alabama, northern Georgia, and western West Virginia.

Other Ash (*Fraxinus*) Species That Could Be Encountered Here

The pumpkin ash [*Fraxinus profunda* (Bush) Bush] and the Carolina ash (*F. caroliniana* Mill.) are trees of the southeastern Coastal Plain, and the black ash (*F. nigra* Marshall) is a tree of northeastern swamps, bogs, lakesides, and streamsides. All three species are listed in Shetler and Orli's *Annotated Checklist of the Vascular Plants of the Washington-Baltimore Area* and could be encountered in or around D.C. The rare flowering ash (*Fraxinus ornus* L.), native to southeastern Europe and western Asia, has showy, fragrant spring flowers and is planted at the National Zoo.

Osmanthus (Holly Tea Olive)

Osmanthus heterophyllus (G. Don) P. S. Green • Olive Family *Oleaceae*

Large shrub with very fragrant autumn flowers.

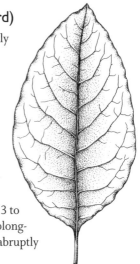

NATIVE RANGE   Japan.

LEAVES   Simple, opposite, evergreen. ¾ to 2½ inches (2–6.5 cm) long. Usually with a few sharp teeth, but sometimes smooth-margined. Lustrous dark green above, paler below. Closely resemble the hollies (*Ilex* spp.), which are arranged alternately.

FLOWERS   Small, creamy white flowers in fragrant clusters. October to November.

GROWTH HABIT   Usually a dense, full, tall, multi-branched shrub.

SIMILAR SPECIES   The hollies (*Ilex* spp.). Devilwood or wild-olive [*Osmanthus americanus* (L.) A. Gray], native to Florida's sand hills, grows in the National Arboretum's Fern Valley. Fortune's osmanthus (*Osmanthus* × *fortunei* Carr.) is cultivated in Washington. This large shrub is a hybrid of *Osmanthus heterophyllus* and *Osmanthus fragrans*.

LOCATIONS
• U.S. Capitol grounds
• Jefferson Memorial
• Fairly common throughout the city

Fringe-Tree (Old-Man's-Beard)

Chionanthus virginicus L. • Olive Family *Oleaceae*

A small tree or shrub that puts forth fragrant, cloud-like flower clusters in spring. Deer, quails, wild turkeys, and songbirds eat fringe-tree drupes.

NATIVE HABITAT AND RANGE
Woods, streamsides; New Jersey west to eastern Oklahoma and Texas, south to Florida.

LEAVES   Simple, opposite, deciduous. 3 to 8 inches (7.5–20 cm) long, ovate to oblong-elliptic. Smooth margin, gradually or abruptly pointed apex. Rounded toward base, but finally narrowly wedge-shaped. Petiole ½ to 1 inch (1.2–2.5 cm) long.

FLOWERS   White, four-petaled flowers in drooping, airy clusters. Individual flowers fringe-like, with slender, delicate petals, ½ to 1¼ inches (1.2–3 cm) long. Late April to May. (See color close-up.)

FRUIT   Dark blue-black or purple, ovoid or ellipsoid drupe, ½ to ¾ inch (1.2–2 cm) long.

BARK AND TWIGS   Bark reddish brown, broken into thin scales. Twigs rather stout, pubescent or not, with scaly winter buds and true end bud.

GROWTH HABIT   Shrub or small tree.

SIMILAR SPECIES   Asian fringe-tree (*C. retusus*).

LOCATIONS
- Smithsonian Arts and Industries Building: Mary Livingston Ripley Garden
- Mount Vernon and River Farm
- Glencarlyn Park (2007–2008 Arlington County Champion Fringe-Tree)
- Gardens and grounds throughout the city
- Rock Creek Park
- Sugarloaf Mountain, Maryland

Asian Fringe-Tree (Chinese Fringe-Tree)

Chionanthus retusus Lindl. & Paxt. • Olive Family *Oleaceae*

Native to China, Korea, and Japan. Similar to our native fringe-tree, but with shorter and relatively wider leaves that often are indented at the apex, and flowers with slightly shorter, wider petals. The cloud-like flower clusters are thicker and less airy-looking than on our native tree, but no less beautiful.

LOCATIONS
- National Arboretum
- A few public and private gardens and grounds

The Lilacs

Syringa spp. • Olive Family *Oleaceae*

The lilacs are shrubs (rarely small trees) with opposite, heart-shaped or lance-shaped leaves, and upright or drooping clusters of showy, often fragrant flowers. Many forms of lilac are grown in

Washington, with blossom color ranging from white to purple. Most bloom during early spring. The Japanese tree lilac [*Syringa reticulata* (Bl.) Hara] blooms during late spring and early summer.

LOCATIONS
• National Arboretum
• Private yards, public grounds, and parks throughout the city and suburbs

Common Lilac (*Syringa vulgaris*)

The Viburnums

Viburnum spp. • Honeysuckle Family *Caprifoliaceae*

The viburnums are a large genus of shrubs and small trees with opposite, simple leaves and usually showy flowers and fruit. The leaves may be lobed or unlobed, toothed or with smooth margins. Small, often brilliant white flowers have five-lobed corollas and are usually borne in large flat-topped or rounded clusters. Larger sterile flowers sometimes present around the outside of the cluster. The fruit (usually a berry-like drupe) is red, black, or dark blue and is eaten by many birds and mammals. The Washington area supports a large number of native and exotic viburnums. We list a few of the most commonly planted species and those that are native and naturalized in regional woodlands.

Viburnums Native to North America

Nannyberry

Viburnum lentago L. • Honeysuckle Family *Caprifoliaceae*

NATIVE RANGE   Northeastern U.S., southeastern Canada.

LEAVES   Simple, opposite, deciduous. 2 to 5 inches (5–12.5 cm) long. Ovate to elliptic-lanceolate. Rounded or wedge-shaped at the base, sharply pointed at the apex. Finely and sharply toothed margin. Glandular below. May have a slightly winged petiole.

FLOWERS Tiny white flowers in dense, rounded or flat-topped clusters.

FRUIT Dark, blue-black, sweet, and juicy, in dense clusters.

GROWTH HABIT Tall shrub or small tree.

Blackhaw

Viburnum prunifolium L. • Honeysuckle Family *Caprifoliaceae*

NATIVE RANGE Eastern and midwestern U.S.

LEAVES Similar to preceding species, but not glandular below. Some leaves may be more bluntly pointed at the apex, and petioles are usually wingless (or barely so).

FLOWERS See color close-up.

GROWTH HABIT Tall shrub or small tree.

LOCATIONS
• Indigenous to native woodlands, including Rock Creek Park
• Arlington National Cemetery (2007–2008 Arlington County Co-champion Blackhaw Viburnums)

The Maple-Leaved Viburnum or Dockmackie (*V. acerifolium* L.), Possum-Haw (*V. nudum* L.), and Arrow-Wood (*V. dentatum* L.) also are shrubby native species that grow in regional woodlands.

Viburnums Not Native to North America

The Asian species Linden Viburnum (*V. dilatatum* Thunb.), with bright red fruit, has become naturalized in regional woodlands, including Rock Creek Park, and has grown invasive.

Siebold Viburnum

Viburnum sieboldii Miq. • Honeysuckle Family *Caprifoliaceae*

A large shrub with red fruit (maturing to black). This species also escapes from cultivation and could be found growing in regional parklands.

NATIVE RANGE Japan.

Double-File Viburnum

Viburnum plicatum Thunb. var. *tomentosum* (Thunb.)
Rehd. • Honeysuckle Family *Caprifoliaceae*

Small white flowers are surrounded by a circle of larger ones.

NATIVE RANGE   Asia.

Japanese Snowball Viburnum

Viburnum plicatum Thunb. • Honeysuckle Family *Caprifoliaceae*

This viburnum bears ball-shaped clusters of small white flowers.

VIBURNUM LOCATIONS
• National Arboretum
• Lyndon Baines Johnson Memorial Grove
• Parks, private yards, and public building grounds throughout
  the city
• Maryland, Virginia, and D.C. woodlands (native and natural-
  ized species)

Seven-Son Flower (Seven Sons Tree)

Heptacodium miconioides Rehd. • Honeysuckle Family
Caprifoliaceae

This Chinese shrub or small tree has fragrant white flowers
(growing in clusters of seven) that bloom from late summer to
autumn; fruit with showy purple-pink sepals; and mottled bark
similar to the crape-myrtle. Leaves are simple and opposite.

LOCATION   National Arboretum.

Paulownia (Royal Paulownia, Empress Tree, Princess Tree)

Paulownia tomentosa (Thunb.) Siebold & Zucc. ex Steud. • Fig-
wort Family *Scrophulariaceae* [Some taxonomists place this tree
in the bignonia family (*Bignoniaceae*).]

An Asian ornamental with tall, candelabra-like clusters of tan,
fuzzy flower buds developing in autumn, and large, lavender
blossoms opening in late April and May. Named for Anna Pav-
lovna, daughter of Russian Czar Paul I and wife of Prince Willem
of the Netherlands. Anna eventually became queen consort of

the Netherlands. Her namesake tree has enjoyed a rich history in Asia, and it's currently making history in the U.S. In Japan, the wood has long been prized for making spoons, bowls, boxes, furniture, wooden clogs, and musical instruments. In recent years, American farmers have begun planting this fast-growing tree for domestic and Asian markets, and it has been planted for strip mine reclamation in Kentucky—despite the fact that Paulownia has long been considered an invasive woody plant species.

NATIVE RANGE   China, cultivated in Japan. Escaped from cultivation in the eastern states from southeastern Connecticut, Indiana, and Missouri to Georgia.

LEAVES   Simple, opposite (rarely whorled), deciduous. 4½ to 10 inches (11.5–25.3 cm) long or longer. Heart-shaped. Margin smooth (young leaves sometimes with two shallow lobes near the base). Downy all over. Petiole densely pubescent, 2½ to 8 inches (6.3–20 cm) long.

FLOWERS   Lavender flowers in erect clusters up to 12 inches (30.4 cm) tall. Twenty or more flowers per cluster, each one bell-shaped, downy, yellow and white inside, with tan, velvety sepals. Late April and May. (See color close-up.)

FRUIT   Upright clusters of woody, ovate, nut-like capsules, each 1 to 1¾ inches (2.5–4.5 cm) long, with a sharp beak at the apex, splitting in half to release many small winged seeds.

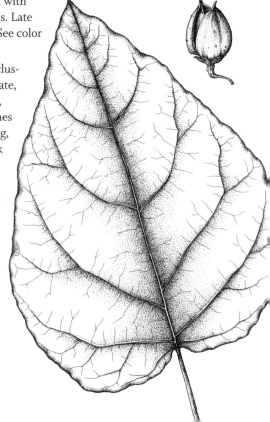

BARK AND TWIGS   Bark light brown or gray, may be slightly furrowed and/or flaky. Twigs stout, olive or reddish brown, with rounded or elliptical leaf scars. (Pith chambered or hollow.) In winter, mature trees usually have clusters of both this year's fruit and next year's flower buds.

GROWTH HABIT   Fast-growing, medium-sized tree with stout, spreading branches forming a rounded crown.

SIMILAR SPECIES   The catalpas (*Catalpa* spp.) have white or yellow flowers; long, thin, pendulous fruit; usually whorled leaves; and twigs with solid piths.

LOCATIONS
- Parks citywide, including Garfield and Montrose
- National Zoo
- National Arboretum
- C&O Canal, Georgetown and vicinity
- Private yards throughout the city
- Young trees in unused lots and along highways and railroad tracks

The Catalpas

Catalpa Scop. • Bignonia or Trumpet-Creeper Family *Bignoniaceae*

The catalpas are among Washington's most beautiful flowering trees. Two native American species are commonly grown here: the northern or western catalpa (*Catalpa speciosa*) and the common or southern catalpa (*Catalpa bignonioides*). Both trees produce many large upright clusters of white flowers. Because the catalpas are full-sized trees and bloom at a time when they have the scene pretty much to themselves, their effect in flower is dramatic. The northern and common catalpas are often con-fused with one another, but they are easily distinguished from the one Asian species commonly found in D.C.: the yellow or Chinese catalpa (*Catalpa ovata*), which produces yellow flowers.

LEAVES   Simple, opposite or whorled, deciduous. Heart-shaped, or with three to five shallow lobes.

FLOWERS   White or yellow flowers, usually marked with purple, orange, and yellow, in showy, upright clusters. Late May and June. (See color close-up.)

FRUIT   Long, thin, bean-like capsule that splits open to release flat seeds with tufts of hairs at either end.

DISTRIBUTION   About ten species in North America, West Indies, and eastern Asia.

KEY TO THE CATALPAS COMMONLY CULTIVATED IN WASHINGTON, D.C.

1a) Flowers yellow. Leaves often shallowly three-lobed, glabrous below at maturity, or with pubescence only along the veins ...
....Yellow Catalpa (*Catalpa ovata*)

1b) Flowers white. Leaves always heart-shaped, pubescent below.

2a) Leaf with a foul odor when crushed. Flowers early to mid-June, each 1¼ to 1¾ (3–4.5 cm) across. Autumn and winter capsules contain seeds with tufts of hairs coming together at tips, nearly to a point ....
.... Common Catalpa (*Catalpa bignonioides*)

2b) Leaf with no foul odor when crushed. Flowers late May to early June, each 2 to 2½ inches (5–6 cm) across. Autumn and winter capsules contain seeds with hairs not coming together at tips..
.... Northern Catalpa (*Catalpa speciosa*)

Northern Catalpa (Western Catalpa, Catawba-Tree, Cigar Tree)

Catalpa speciosa (Warder) Warder ex Engelm. • Bignonia or Trumpet-Creeper Family *Bignoniaceae*

This tree and the common catalpa (*Catalpa bignonioides*) are very difficult to tell apart. The northern catalpa comes into bloom slightly earlier than the common catalpa.

NATIVE HABITAT AND RANGE   Moist, rich soils, often along streams and lakes; southern Indiana and Illinois to northeastern Arkansas and western Tennessee. Widely cultivated and escaped from cultivation eastward and northward.

LEAVES   Simple, opposite or whorled, deciduous. 6 to 12 inches (15–30 cm) long. Heart-shaped. Apex abruptly or gradually pointed. Base heart-shaped, rounded, straight across, or barely wedge-shaped. No foul odor when crushed. Margin smooth. Pubescent below. Petiole 3 to 7 inches (7.5–17.5 cm) long.

FLOWERS   Showy white flowers with small yellow and purple spots in upright clusters. Each flower 2 to 2½ inches (5–6 cm) across. Late May to early June.

FRUIT   Bean-like capsule, 8 to 20 inches (20–50.5 cm) long, remaining on the tree into winter. Contains many flat-winged seeds with fringes of soft white hairs at either end. Hairs do not converge at tips. (See illustration.)

BARK AND TWIGS   Bark brown, reddish brown, or gray, fissured and scaly with age. Twigs glabrous, stout, brown or gray, with rounded leaf scars and small winter buds. End buds false. Pith solid.

GROWTH HABIT   Medium-sized or tall tree with a pyramidal or rounded crown.

SIMILAR SPECIES   Very similar to the common or southern catalpa (*Catalpa bignonioides*). The Asian yellow catalpa (*Catalpa ovata*) differs from the two native American species in having leaves that are often shallowly three-lobed. The paulownia (*Paulownia tomentosa*) has opposite leaves that are rarely whorled, lavender flowers, a nut-like woody fruit capsule, and twigs with chambered or hollow piths. Redbuds (*Cercis* spp.) have alternate leaves.

LOCATIONS
- Corner of E and First Streets, S.E.
- Widely planted throughout the city

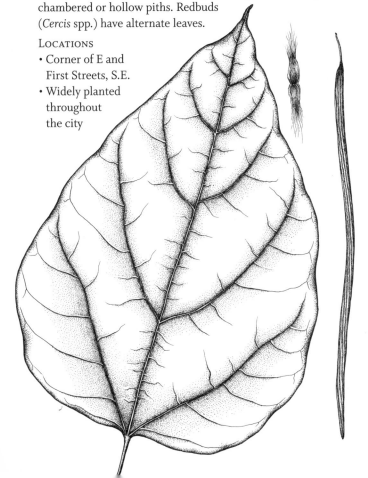

Common Catalpa (Southern Catalpa, Indian-Bean)

Catalpa bignonioides Walter • Bignonia or
Trumpet-Creeper Family *Bignoniaceae*

Common Catalpa
(*Catalpa bignonioides*)

This tree is very similar to the northern or
western catalpa (*Catalpa speciosa*). It differs from the preceding
species in the following ways.

NATIVE HABITAT AND RANGE   Rich, moist soils, streamsides, and
riverbanks; Gulf Coast states from Florida to Louisiana. (Naturalized as far north as southern New England, Ohio, and Michigan.)

LEAVES   Give off a foul odor when crushed. (Northern catalpa
leaves do not.)

FLOWERS   Individual flowers are not quite as wide as the
northern catalpa, only about 1¼ to 1¾ inches (3–4.5 cm) across,
but they are more conspicuously marked with yellow, orange,
and purple. Slightly later than the northern catalpa, early or
mid-June.

FRUIT   The bean-like fruit capsule is slightly shorter and thinner
than the northern catalpa, but the difference is nearly impercep-
tible. The best way to distinguish the two trees in fall and winter
is to split open a capsule and examine the seeds. The white fringe
of hairs on either end of the common catalpa's winged seeds
come together nearly to a point. (See illustrations.)

BARK   The common catalpa's scaly bark is not as deeply furrowed as the northern catalpa's.

SIMILAR SPECIES   See northern catalpa "Similar Species."

LOCATIONS
• Washington Monument grounds
• Common throughout the city in parks and around public build-
  ings and private homes

Yellow Catalpa (Golden Catalpa, Chinese Catalpa)

Catalpa ovata G. Don • Bignonia or Trumpet-Creeper Family
Bignoniaceae

This Asian tree, though lovely in bloom, is no match for our
native American species in stature and beauty. Frederick Law
Olmsted chose the yellow catalpa for his charming brick grotto

(or "summerhouse") on the Capitol grounds. (See Part I, page 31.)

NATIVE RANGE China. (Escaped from cultivation and sparsely naturalized from southern Ontario and Connecticut to Ohio and Maryland.)

LEAVES Simple, opposite or whorled, deciduous. 4 to 10 inches (10–25.4 cm) long, and about as wide. Similar to the leaves of the two native American species, but often shallowly three-lobed and occasionally five-lobed. Lobes sharply pointed. Base heart-shaped, rounded, or straight across. Glabrous or nearly so below, except when young. Petiole 3 to 8 inches (7.5–20.3 cm) long.

FLOWERS Yellow or yellowish white, marked with purple and orange, in upright clusters. Individual flowers up to ¾ inch (2 cm) across. Except for color and smaller size, very similar to the flowers of the two native American species. Early June.

FRUIT Capsule looks like a string bean. Very thin, 8 to 13 inches (20–33 cm) long, remaining on the tree into winter. Splits open

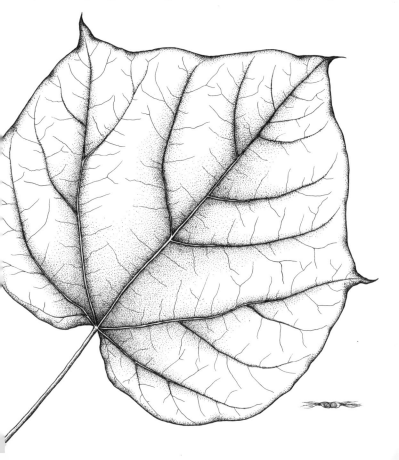

to release small, flat seeds with fringes of soft, white hairs at either end. Hairs do not converge at tips. (See illustration.)

BARK AND TWIGS   Twigs usually glabrous, similar to northern catalpa, but thinner.

GROWTH HABIT   Small tree with spreading branches.

SIMILAR SPECIES   Distinguished from the northern (*Catalpa speciosa*) and common (*C. bignonioides*) catalpas by its yellow or yellowish flowers, usually glabrous and often three-lobed leaves, and thinner fruit capsules.

LOCATIONS
• Washington Monument grounds
• National Zoo
• Tidal Basin
• Not as common in Washington as the two native American species

Chaste-Tree (Chasteberry, Monk's Pepper-Tree, Hemp-Tree, Wild Lavender)

Vitex agnus-castus L. • Vervain Family (*Verbenaceae*)

Its upright clusters of blue or purple flowers make this tall shrub or small tree conspicuous in Washington from midsummer until autumn. The common name, chaste-tree, stems from an ancient belief that properties of this woody plant could "cool the heat of lust." Chaste-tree has enjoyed a renaissance in modern herbal medicine as a remedy for premenstrual and menopausal symptoms. According to renowned herbal authority James A. Duke, writing in *The Green Pharmacy*: "The small fruits of the chaste tree have been used for menstrual disorders since Greco-Roman times."[91]

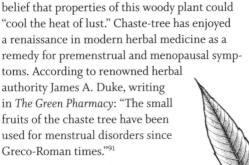

NATIVE RANGE   Southeastern Europe, western Asia; naturalized in the southeastern U.S. as far north as Maryland.

LEAVES   Palmately compound, opposite, deciduous. Five to seven lanceolate or narrowly elliptic leaflets are 2 to 5 inches (5–12.6 cm) long, with smooth or very sparsely toothed margins. Gray-green. Lower (and sometimes upper) surfaces of leaflets, petioles, and branchlets covered with close, soft, grayish pubescence. Strong, spicy aroma.

FLOWERS Attractive purple or blue (rarely white) flowers in narrowly pyramidal clusters. Midsummer to mid-autumn. (See color close-up.)

TWIGS Four-sided.

SIMILAR SPECIES Not likely to be confused with other species. The combination of late-blooming flowers and opposite, palmately compound leaves is distinctive.

LOCATIONS
• U.S. Capitol grounds
• Smithsonian Air and Space Museum
• Public and private gardens and grounds throughout the region

Banana

Musa • Banana Family *Musaceae*

While banana plants technically are not trees, we believed their presence in Washington could not go without mention. When I first moved to Washington from New England, I was impressed by the fact that there were real bananas growing in our neighborhood. Visitors to my Capitol Hill apartment were given the full tour: the Capitol, the Supreme Court, the Library of Congress— and the bananas outdoors at the Botanic Garden. These little "trees," which actually are herbaceous plants, are set out each spring in various locations. Before they are removed in autumn, they produce small bunches of bananas. The cold-hardy *Musa basjoo* has become a popular cultivated plant in the region during recent years.

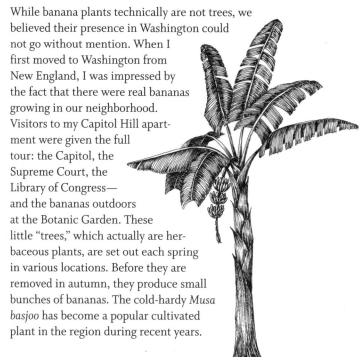

Illustrated Glossary *Text follows on page 385*

Figure G-1 ALTERNATE LEAVES

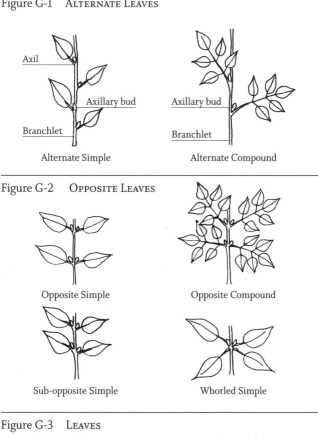

Alternate Simple

Alternate Compound

Figure G-2 OPPOSITE LEAVES

Opposite Simple

Opposite Compound

Sub-opposite Simple

Whorled Simple

Figure G-3 LEAVES

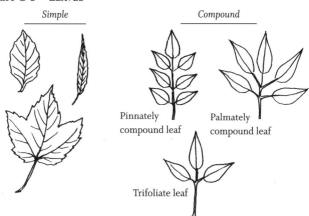

Simple

Compound

Pinnately
compound leaf

Palmately
compound leaf

Trifoliate leaf

Figure G-4   Pinnately Compound Leaves

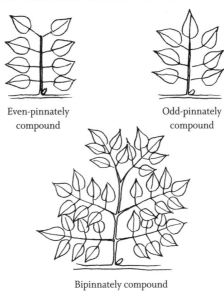

Even-pinnately
compound

Odd-pinnately
compound

Bipinnately compound

Figure G-5   Parts of a Leaf

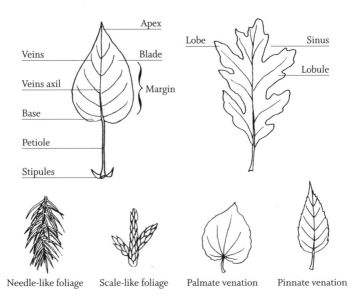

Apex

Veins

Blade

Veins axil

Margin

Base

Petiole

Stipules

Lobe

Sinus

Lobule

Needle-like foliage   Scale-like foliage   Palmate venation   Pinnate venation

Figure G-6 PARTS OF A COMPOUND LEAF

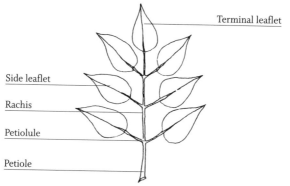

Terminal leaflet

Side leaflet

Rachis

Petiolule

Petiole

Figure G-7 PARTS OF A FLOWER

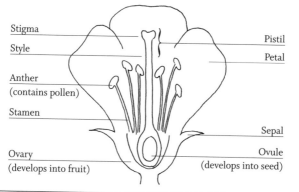

Stigma

Style

Pistil

Petal

Anther
(contains pollen)

Stamen

Sepal

Ovary
(develops into fruit)

Ovule
(develops into seed)

Figure G-8 LEAF SHAPES

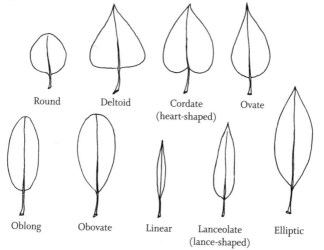

Round

Deltoid

Cordate
(heart-shaped)

Ovate

Oblong

Obovate

Linear

Lanceolate
(lance-shaped)

Elliptic

Figure G-9   LEAF BASES

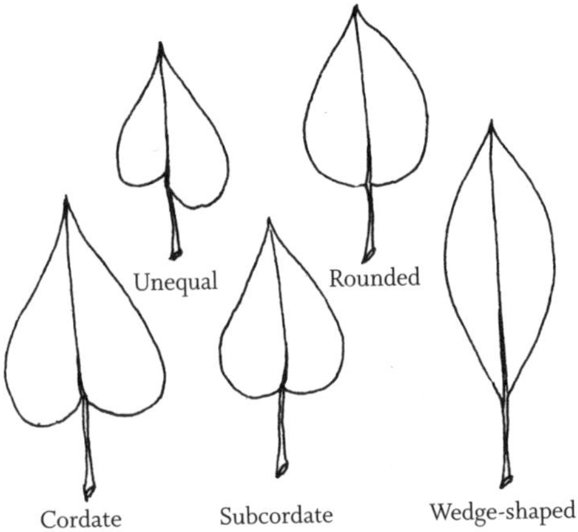

Unequal

Rounded

Cordate

Subcordate

Wedge-shaped

Figure G-10   LEAF MARGINS

Sharply toothed

Wavy-toothed

Rounded teeth

Smooth

Doubly toothed

Bristle-tipped teeth

Figure G-11   WINTER TWIGS

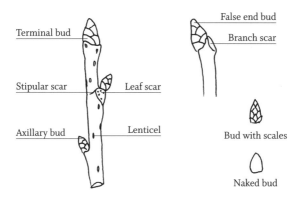

Terminal bud

False end bud

Branch scar

Stipular scar

Leaf scar

Axillary bud

Lenticel

Bud with scales

Naked bud

Figure G-12   TWIGS IN CROSS-SECTION

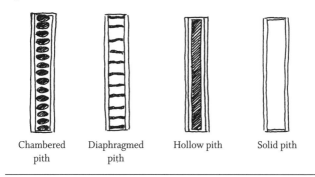

Chambered
pith

Diaphragmed
pith

Hollow pith

Solid pith

Figure G-13   GROWTH HABITS OF TREES

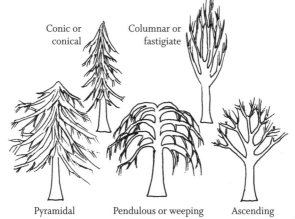

Conic or
conical

Columnar or
fastigiate

Pyramidal

Pendulous or weeping

Ascending

Figure G-14   Woody Plants

Fig. G-15   Catkins

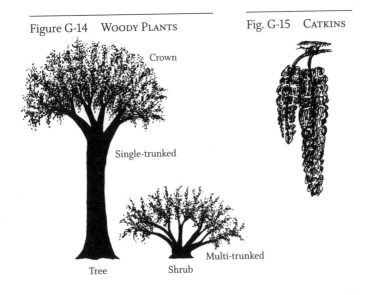

Crown

Single-trunked

Tree

Shrub

Multi-trunked

Figure G-16   Fruit and Cone Shapes

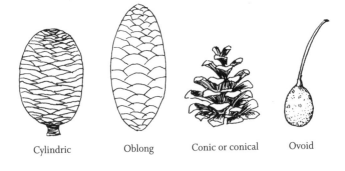

Cylindric

Oblong

Conic or conical

Ovoid

Figure G-17   Spur Shoots

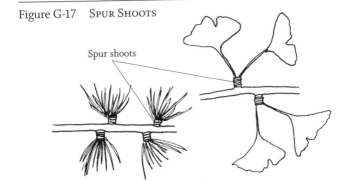

Spur shoots

Achene. A dry, one-seeded fruit that does not split open.

Aggregate Fruit. A compound fruit, developing from many parts of the same flower. *See also* Multiple Fruit

Alternate. A common leaf arrangement in which the leaves are not opposite each other on the branchlet (see figure G-1).

Angiosperm. Belonging to the class of plants that produce seeds within ovaries; most trees of the angiosperm class are broad leaved. *See also* Gymnosperm

Anther. The pollen-producing part of the stamen (see figure G-7).

Apex; plural Apices. The tip of a leaf blade, lobe, bud, fruit, etc.; the part farthest from the base (see figure G-5).

Appressed. Lying flat or close against the surface.

Arbor. Used in this volume to mean a "grove of trees."

Arboreal. Pertaining to trees.

Arboretum. A place where trees are exhibited and studied. Most frequently used in this volume in reference to the National Arboretum in northeast Washington, D.C. May also be used informally to refer to a noteworthy collection of trees.

Aril. A seed covering. Used in this volume to describe the red, berry-like covering of the yew seed.

Ascending. Pointing upward; a fairly common branching pattern (see figure G-13).

Axil. The upper angle formed where two veins or the petiole and branchlet meet (see figures G-1, G-5).

Axillary Bud. Bud located in the axil of the branchlet and petiole (see figures G-1, G-11).

Base. The part of a leaf blade, cone, or fruit that is closest to the stem or branch and farthest from the apex (see figures G-5, G-9).

Berry. Technically, a simple fruit with a fleshy or pulpy ovary. In this volume, we refer to fruit that looks like a berry but is technically some other type as "berry-like."

Bipinnately Compound. Refers to leaves that are twice pinnately compound (see figure G-4).

Blade. The large, flat part of the leaf, excluding the petiole (see figure G-5).

Bonsai. A dwarfed tree or shrub trained by pruning of the roots and limbs.

Botanical. Of or pertaining to plants, including trees.

Botanist. One who specializes in the study of plants, including trees.

Botany. The biological science of plants, including trees.

Bract. A leafy plant part sometimes located below a flower or flower cluster, or lower down the stem or branchlet. In some cases (for instance, the dogwoods), the bracts are showier than the flowers themselves.

Branchlet. In this volume, "branchlet" and "twig" are used interchangeably to refer to the leaf and flower-bearing part of the branch (see figure G-1).

Bristle-tipped. Describes a lobe, tooth, or apex of a leaf that comes to a thin, sharp, thread-like point.

Broad-leaved Tree. Flowering, fruiting tree of the angiosperm class.

Bud. A small protuberance on a branchlet that contains the shoot, leaf, and/or flower in embryonic condition; buds may be "naked" or covered with scales (see figures G-1, G-11). *See also* End Bud; False End Bud; Axillary Bud

Caducous. Falling off early; refers to sepals or other plant parts.

Calyx. The outer part of a flower, consisting of leafy or, rarely, petal-like parts known as sepals (see figure G-7).

Capsule. A dry fruit that splits open to release two or more seeds.

Catkin. A long, thin cluster of tiny flowers (see figure G-15).

Chambered. Describes the pith or center of a twig that has horizontal chambers divided by thin partitions. The center, or pith, of a twig in cross-section may be chambered, diaphragmed, hollow, or solid (see figure G-12).

Clone. A plant propagated from a single parent by means of grafting, cutting, layering, or budding; many cultivars are clones.

Columnar. Describes trees with narrow, upright growth habits (see figure G-13).

Common Name. The name or names (red oak, sugar maple, etc.) by which a tree is known to the layperson. Common names often differ from region to region and are difficult to translate into other languages; thus, Latin is the universal naming language of the botanical community. In this volume, the common name or names for a tree make up the main listing title, followed on a separate line by the tree species' scientific (Latin) name and its common and scientific family names.

Compound Fruit. A fruit with more than one ovary.

Compound Leaf. A leaf that is divided into three or more leaflets (see figures G-3, G-4).

Cone. The woody, scaly structure produced by most conifers that bears the naked seeds.

Conic, or Conical. Cone-shaped. Pointed at one end, evenly spreading outward (see figures G-13, G-16).

Conifer. Usually cone-producing trees of the gymnosperm class; seeds are naked (not enclosed in ovaries).

Cordate. Heart-shaped; may refer to the entire leaf blade or just the base (see figures G-8, G-9).

Corky Wings. Flat, woody, wing-like projections on the branches of some trees and shrubs.

Corolla. All the petals of a flower, either separate or united; the corolla is often brightly colored and showy.

Crown. The full, top part of a tree or shrub formed by the spreading branches (see figure G-14).

Cultivar. A plant variety derived by horticultural means and not occurring naturally. The cultivar name follows the species name of the plant and is presented in single quotes.

Cultivated. Describes plants, including trees, that are planted and nurtured by humans.

Cylindric. Shaped like a cylinder (see figure G-16).

Deciduous. Describes trees and shrubs that shed their leaves in autumn. *See also* Evergreen

Deltoid. Triangular (see figure G-8).

Diaphragmed. Describes the pith or center of a twig that has small horizontal spaces divided by thick partitions. The center, or pith, of a twig in cross-section may be diaphragmed, chambered, hollow, or solid (see figure G-12).

Dimorphic. Of two types. Evergreen trees with dimorphic foliage have leaves that are scale-like and leaves that are needle-like on the same tree.

Dioecious. Male and female flowers are produced on separate trees of the same species. *See also* Monoecious

Downy. Covered with fine, soft hairs.

Drupe. A fleshy fruit with a bony, single-seeded center. Peaches, for example, are drupes.

Ellipsoid. Elliptic lengthwise and round in cross-section; describes three-dimensional plant parts, such as fruit.

Elliptic. About twice as long as broad, and widest in the middle; a common leaf shape (see figure G-8).

End Bud. Bud found at the precise end of the twig; also called a terminal bud (see figure G-11). *See also* False End Bud

Erect. Standing straight up; the opposite of pendulous.

Even-Pinnately Compound. A pinnately compound leaf with an even number of leaflets (see figure G-4). *See also* Odd-Pinnately Compound

Evergreen. Describes trees and shrubs that retain their leaves throughout the year. *See also* Deciduous

Exotic. Not native to North America. Exotic trees in Washington come from Asia, Europe, and Africa.

False End Bud. Bud that forms at or near the end of the twig in the absence of a true end bud. The false end bud can be distinguished from the true end bud by the presence of an adjacent scar (see figure G-11). *See also* End Bud

Family. The gymnosperm and angiosperm classes are divided into plant families, which are subdivided into genera and individual species.

Fastigiate. A growth habit in which the branches of a tree or shrub stand erect and close together (see figure G-13).

Fissured. Vertically grooved; describes bark.

Flower. The reproductive part of a plant, which usually includes the petals (see figure G-7).

Foliage. Leaves, including those that are needle-like or scale-like.

Follicle. A dry fruit that splits along only one seam to release seeds. *See also* legume

Fruit. The ripened ovaries of a seed-bearing plant, containing the seeds; may be dry or fleshy.

Genus; plural Genera. Plant families are subdivided into genera and then individual species.

Glabrous. Hairless. Parts of trees are either glabrous or pubescent (covered with hairs); some leaves are pubescent in spring, then become glabrous at maturity.

Gland. Small structure that may secrete a sometimes sticky liquid; some leaves have small glands on their blades or petioles.

Glandular. Having small glands, sometimes visible only with a hand lens.

Glaucous. Chalky; covered with a white or bluish bloom.

Growth Habit. *See* Habit.

Gymnosperm. Belonging to the class of plants more commonly known as conifers. Gymnosperm seeds are naked (not protected by ovaries), and are usually borne beneath woody cone scales. Gymnosperm foliage is typically needle-like or scale-like. *See also* Angiosperm

Habit. The overall shape or silhouette of a tree (see figure G-13).

Hardy. Able to survive in a particular climate. A plant is not hardy in Washington if it cannot survive the cold of winter or the heat of summer.

Herbaceous. Describes plants that do not have woody stems; includes grasses, wildflowers, garden flowers, herbs, and more.

Herbarium. A plant library containing dried plants labeled and organized for scientific study.

Hollow. Having a single, unfilled cavity. The center, or pith, of a twig in cross-section may be chambered, diaphragmed, hollow, or solid (see figure G-12).

Horticulture. The science of cultivated plants, particularly those used for ornament.

Horticulturist. One trained in the science of horticulture.

Hybrid. A cross between unlike parents. Most of the hybrids described in this volume are the result of crosses between two species of the same genera.

Lanceolate. Lance-shaped; a common leaf shape (see figure G-8).

Lateral Bud. *See* Axillary Bud

Latin Name. The scientific name of a plant family, genus, or species; the Latin name is often given in italics after the common name.

Leaf. The food-producing part of the plant. On broad-leaved trees, leaves may be simple or compound; on conifers, they typically are needle-like or scale-like (see figure G-5).

Leaf Base. The portion of a leaf closest to the petiole (see figures G-5, G-9).

Leaf Blade. The broad, flat portion of a leaf, excluding the petiole (see figure G-5).

Leaflet. A leaf-like portion of a compound leaf (see figure G-6).

Leaf Margin. The edge of a leaf; may be smooth or toothed (see figures G-5, G-10).

Leaf Scar. The scar on the branchlet that remains when the leaf falls off the tree. In winter, the shape of a leaf scar can be used to help identify the tree (see figure G-11).

Legume. A dry fruit that splits along two sides to release seeds. Members of the pea family are said to be "leguminous."

Lenticel. Variously shaped markings on the bark or branchlets of trees or shrubs; lenticels serve as pores, allowing gases to pass in and out of the tree's interior.

Lobe. A portion of a leaf blade that may be rounded or pointed and is separated from other lobes by deep or shallow sinuses (see figure G-5).

Lobule. A small lobe, which is often part of a larger lobe (see figure G-5).

Margin. The edge of a leaf; may be smooth or toothed (see figures G-5, G-10).

Monoecious. Male and female flowers are produced on the same tree. *See also* Dioecious

Monotypic. The sole member of its group, such as the only species of a genus and family.

Mucronate. Tipped with a short, sharp, slender point.

Multiple Fruit. A compound fruit, developing from many different flowers. *See also* Aggregate Fruit

Naked bud. A bud with no scales (see figure G-11).

Native. Growing in the wild; indigenous.

Native Habitat. The region where a plant occurs naturally.

Naturalized. Escaped from cultivation and established as an independent population in the wild. Some Asian species, for instance, have become naturalized in the eastern United States.

Needle-like. Describes the needle-shaped foliage of many conifers, such as pines and spruces.

Nut. A hard, one-seeded fruit, like an acorn, that does not split open.

Nut-like. Resembling a nut but not fitting the technical description.

Oblanceolate. Inversely lanceolate (or lance-shaped); broader at the top.

Oblong. About three times as long as wide, with nearly parallel sides (see figures G-8, G-16).

Obovate. Inversely ovate (see figure G-8).

Odd-Pinnately Compound. A pinnately compound leaf with an odd number of leaflets (see figure G-4). *See also* Even-Pinnately Compound

Opposite. Describes leaves arranged opposite each other on the branchlet; also includes whorled and sub-opposite leaf arrangements (see figure G-2).

Ovary. The part of the pistil that develops into the fruit and contains the seeds (see figure G-7).

Ovate. Egg-shaped; a common leaf shape (see figure G-8).

Ovoid. Egg-shaped; usually refers to fruit or cone (see figure G-16).

Ovule. A plant's "egg," contained in the ovary, which after fertilization develops into the seed (see figure G-7).

Palmately Compound. Leaflets arranged in a pattern shaped like an open hand (see figure G-3). *See also* Pinnately Compound

Palmate Venation. Leaf veins arranged in a pattern shaped like an open hand (see figure G-5).

Peltate. In this volume, describes cone scales that are attached at the center rather than the base of the cone.

Pendulous. Describes hanging branches, fruit, etc. (see figure G-13).

Perfect Flower. A flower that possesses both male and female parts.

Petals. Flower parts that surround the center of the blossom (see figure G-7). Petals are usually colored, and often are fragrant. Their primary function is to attract insects in order to facilitate fertilization.

Petiole. The leafstalk (see figures G-5, G-6). *See also* Petiolule; Rachis

Petiolule. The stalk of a leaflet that attaches to the petiole or rachis (see figure G-6).

Pinnate. *See* Pinnately Compound; Pinnate Venation

Pinnately Compound. Leaflets arranged in a feather-like pattern (see figures G-3, G-4). *See also* Palmately Compound

Pinnate Venation. Leaf veins arranged in a feather-like pattern (see figure G-5).

Pistil. The female part of the flower, including the ovary, the stigma, and the style (see figure G-7).

Pith. The inner core of a twig. In order to examine the pith, cut the twig in half lengthwise with a sharp knife. The pith may be chambered, diaphragmed, hollow, or solid (see figure G-12).

Pod. A dry fruit that splits open to release seeds. *See* Legume

Pollen. Male seed (usually a fine powder) produced within the anther of a flower (see figure G-7).

Pome. A fleshy fruit, like the apple or pear, that contains several seeds. *See also* Drupe

Pubescent. Covered with hairs. Parts of trees are either glabrous (without hair) or pubescent; some leaves are pubescent in spring, then become glabrous at maturity. Pubescence may be obvious—as when the entire lower surface of a leaf blade is covered with hairs—or it may be visible only with a hand lens. Frequently, hairs are borne only in the axils of leaf veins.

Pyramidal. Shaped like a pyramid; a common growth habit of trees (see figure G-13).

Rachis. A term used in this volume to describe the portion of the petiole on a compound leaf that bears the leaflets (see figure G-6). *See also* Petiole; Petiolule

Radiate. To spread outward from a common point.

Resinous. Containing or covered with resin, a usually sticky liquid exuded by some trees.

Samara. A dry, winged fruit that doesn't split open; maples and elms bear samaras.

Scales. Most often used in this volume to describe the woody "leaves" of cones; also describes broken sections of outer bark.

Scaly. Most often used to describe bark that is broken into many small, flaky sections.

Seed. The fertilized, mature ovule (see figure G-7).

Seedling. A tree, shrub, or herbaceous plant grown from seed, as opposed to grafting or other horticultural means.

Sepal. A portion of the calyx, or outer part, of the flower. Most flowers have a circle of petals (which are usually brightly colored) surrounded by a smaller, inconspicuous circle of sepals (see figure G-7). Sepals are usually leafy and green, but in some cases they are petal-like.

Sessile. Having no petiole or stalk.

Shoot. Used in this volume to describe the newest growth at the end of a branchlet.

Shrub. A multi-trunked, woody plant that usually stands no higher than 20 feet (about 5½ meters) (see figure G-14).

Silky. Covered with fine, soft hairs.

Simple Fruit. Fruit that contains a single ovary.

Simple Leaf. A leaf that is not divided into leaflets (see figures G-1, G-2).

Sinus. The recess between the lobes of a leaf (see figure G-5).

Smooth Margin. A leaf margin with no teeth (see figure G-10).

Solid. Having no internal cavity. The center, or pith, of a twig in cross-section may be chambered, diaphragmed, hollow, or solid (see figure G-12).

Species. An individual member of a genus; may be divided into varieties or cultivars.

Spine. A sharply pointed woody projection that is a modified leaf or stipule.

Spur Shoot. A short branchlet bearing clusters of leaves (see figure G-17).

Stamen. The male part of the flower, which includes the pollen-bearing anther (see figure G-7).

Stigma. The part of the style that receives pollen from the anther (see figure G-7).

Stipular Scar. The scar left on a twig where a stipule has fallen off (see figure G-11).

Stipule. A leaf-like appendage at the base of the petiole; not present on all species (see figure G-5).

Style. The long portion of the pistil, between the stigma and the ovary.

Subcordate. Shallowly heart-shaped; describes the leaf base (see figure G-9).

Sub-opposite. Describes a leaf arrangement in which the leaves are nearly opposite on the branchlet (see figure G-2).

Sucker. A sprout arising from the roots of the tree; some species are more apt to produce suckers than others.

Terminal Bud. Bud found at the precise end of the twig; also called an end bud (see figure G-11). *See also* False End Bud

Terminal Leaflet. The leaflet located at the apex of a pinnately compound leaf; when the terminal leaflet is present, the leaf is odd-pinnately compound (see figure G-6).

Thorn. A stiff, sharply pointed woody projection that is a modified stem.

Toothed. Describes a leaf margin with teeth (see figure G-10).

Tree. A usually single-trunked woody plant that stands more than 20 feet (about 5½ meters) high (see figure G-14).

Trifoliate. Describes a compound leaf with three leaflets (see figure G-3).

Trunk. The main stem of a tree that connects the roots with the crown.

Twig. Used synonymously with branchlet to refer to the leaf-bearing part of the branch; often used to describe the branchlet in winter (see figure G-11).

Unequal Base. Describes a leaf base in which the two sides of the base do not attach to the petiole at opposite places (see figure G-9).

Unisexual. Of one sex only. Some trees bear separate male and female flowers, rather than perfect flowers.

Variety. A naturally occurring variance that is not considered a separate species and yet has characteristics that differ from those typical of the species.

Veins. The slender vascular bundles that transport sap through the leaf (see figure G-5).

Venation. The arrangement of the veins in a leaf (see figure G-5).

Wavy-toothed Margin. A leaf margin with undulating teeth (see figure G-10).

Wedge-shaped. Shaped like the narrow end of a piece of pie; describes the leaf base (see figure G-9).

Weeping. Describes the crown of a tree in which the branches are pendulous (see figure G-13).

Whorled. A leaf arrangement in which three or more leaves are attached to the branchlet opposite one another (see figure G-2).

Wing. A thin, woody appendage on the branches of some woody plants.

Winter buds. Buds that develop during summer or fall and stay on the tree throughout winter, until they unfurl the following spring.

Woody plant. A tree or shrub.

Woolly. Covered with short, soft hairs.

Blooming Calendar

March

April

FLOWERING TREES IN BLOOM

Black Locust *Robinia pseudoacacia*
Bladdernut *Staphylea trifolia*
Bradford Pear *Pyrus calleryana* 'Bradford'
Buckeye, Hybrid *Aesculus* × *hybrida*
Buckeye, Ohio *Aesculus glabra*
Buckeye, Red *Aesculus pavia*
Buckeye, Sweet or Yellow *Aesculus flava*
Carolina Silverbell *Halesia carolina*
Cornelian Cherry *Cornus mas*
Crabapples *Malus* spp.
Dogwood, Flowering *Cornus florida*
Dogwood, Stellar *Cornus* × *rutgersensis*
Dove Tree (Handkerchief Tree) *Davidia involucrata*
Fringe-Tree *Chionanthus virginicus*
Fringe-Tree, Asian *Chionanthus retusus*
Golden Chain Tree *Laburnum anagyroides*
Hawthorns *Crataegus* spp.
Horse-Chestnut, Common *Aesculus hippocastanum*
Horse-Chestnut, Red *Aesculus* × *carnea*
Japanese Flowering Cherry Trees
   Akebono *Prunus* × *yedoensis* 'Akebono'
   Fall-Blooming Cherry *Prunus subhirtella* 'Autumnalis' (also
      blooms in November and December)
   Gyoiko (Rare) *Prunus serrulata* 'Gyoiko'
   Kwanzan *Prunus serrulata* 'Kwanzan'
   Weeping Cherry *Prunus subhirtella pendula*
   Yoshino or Somei-Yoshino *Prunus* × *yedoensis*
Laburnum, Common (*see* Golden Chain Tree)
Laburnum, Voss's *Laburnum* × *watereri*
Magnolia, 'Elizabeth'
Magnolia, Kobus *Magnolia kobus*
Magnolia, Lily *Magnolia liliflora* (*Magnolia quinquepeta*)
Magnolia, "Little Girl Hybrids"
Magnolia, Saucer *Magnolia* × *soulangeana*
Magnolia, Star *Magnolia stellata*
Magnolia, Umbrella *Magnolia tripetala*
Magnolia, Yulan *Magnolia denudata* (*Magnolia heptapeta*)
Maple, Red *Acer rubrum* (and other early-blooming maples)
Paulownia or Princess Tree *Paulownia tomentosa*
Pawpaw *Asimina triloba*

Peach *Prunus persica*
Pear *Pyrus* spp.
Plum, Purple-leaved or Pissard *Prunus cerasifera*
   'Atropurpurea'
Redbud *Cercis canadensis*
Redbud, Chinese *Cercis chinensis*
Rowan Tree (European Mountain-Ash) *Sorbus aucuparia*
Serviceberry, Shadbush, or Shadblow *Amelanchier* spp.
Snowbells *Styrax spp.*
Spice-Bush *Lindera benzoin*
Tamarisks *Tamarix* spp.
Trifoliate Orange *Poncirus trifoliate*
Tulip-Tree (Tulip Poplar, Yellow Poplar) *Liriodendron*
   tulipifera
Viburnums *Viburnum* spp.
Witch-Hazels *Hamamelis* spp.

May

FLOWERING TREES IN BLOOM
  Black Locust *Robinia pseudoacacia*
  Bladdernut *Staphylea trifolia*
  Buckeye, Hybrid *Aesculus* × *hybrida*
  Buckeye, Ohio *Aesculus glabra*
  Buckeye, Red *Aesculus pavia*
  Buckeye, Sweet (Yellow) *Aesculus flava*
  Carolina Silverbell *Halesia carolina*
  Catalpa, Northern (Western) *Catalpa speciosa*
  Catalpa, Yellow (Golden) *Catalpa ovata*
  Cherry, Black *Prunus serotina*
  Chestnut, American *Castanea dentata*
  Chestnut, Chinese *Castanea mollissima*
  Chokecherry *Prunus virginiana*
  Crabapples, Flowering (*Malus* spp.)
    Some commonly planted flowering crabapples:
    Carmine *M.* × *atrosanguinea*
    Dorothea *M.* × 'Dorothea'
    Hopa *M.* × 'Hopa'
    Japanese Flowering *M. floribunda*
    Katherine *M.* × 'Katherine'
    Purple *M.* × *purpurea*
    Siberian *M. baccata*
    Southern *M. angustifolia* (*Pyrus angustifolia*)

Dogwood, Flowering *Cornus florida*
Dogwood, Kousa (Japanese) *Cornus kousa*
Dogwood, Stellar *Cornus × rutgersensis*
Dove Tree (Handkerchief Tree) *Davidia involucrata*
European Smoke-Tree *Cotinus coggygria*
Fragrant Snowbell (Big-Leaf Storax) *Styrax obassia*
Fringe-Tree *Chionanthus virginicus*
Fringe-Tree, Asian *Chionanthus retusus*
Golden Chain Tree (Common Laburnum) *Laburnum anagyroides*
Hawthorns (*Crataegus* spp.)
    Some commonly planted hawthorns:
    Cockspur Thorn *C. crus-galli*
    English May *C. laevigata*
    Paul's Scarlet *C. laevigata* 'Paul's Scarlet'
    Washington Thorn *C. phaenopyrum*
Honey-Locust *Gleditsia triacanthos*
Horse-Chestnut, Common *Aesculus hippocastanum*
Horse-Chestnut, Red *Aesculus × carnea*
Japanese Snowbell *Styrax japonica*
Kentucky Coffee-Tree *Gymnocladus dioicus*
Lime (*see* Linden)
Linden, European *Tilia × europaea*
Linden, Large-leafed *Tilia platyphyllos*
Linden, Silver *Tilia tomentosa*
Linden, Small-leafed *Tilia cordata*
Magnolia, Bigleaf *Magnolia macrophylla*
Magnolia, Cucumber (Cucumber Tree) *Magnolia acuminata*
Magnolia, Southern (Bullbay or Evergreen) *Magnolia grandiflora*
Magnolia, Sweetbay *Magnolia virginiana*
Magnolia, Umbrella *Magnolia tripetala*
Paulownia (Royal Paulownia, Princess Tree) *Paulownia tomentosa*
Redbud *Cercis canadensis*
Redbud, Chinese *Cercis chinensis*
Rowan Tree (European Mountain-Ash) *Sorbus aucuparia*
Snowbells *Styrax* spp.
Spice-Bush *Lindera benzoin*
Trifoliate Orange *Poncirus trifoliata*
Tulip-Tree (Tulip Poplar, Yellow Poplar) *Liriodendron tulipifera*

Viburnums *Viburnum* spp.
Voss's Laburnum *Laburnum* × *watereri*
Yellowwood *Cladrastis kentukea* (*Cladrastis lutea*)

June
FLOWERING TREES IN BLOOM
Catalpa, Common *Catalpa bignonioides*
Catalpa, Northern (Western) *Catalpa speciosa*
Catalpa, Yellow (Golden) *Catalpa ovata*
Chaste-Tree *Vitex agnus-castus*
Chestnut, American *Castanea dentata*
Chestnut, Chinese *Castanea mollissima*
European Smoke-Tree *Cotinus coggygria*
Golden-Rain-Tree *Koelreuteria paniculata*
Japanese Raisin-Tree *Hovenia dulcis*
Kousa Dogwood (Japanese) *Cornus kousa*
Lime (*see* Linden)
Linden, American *Tilia americana*
Linden, European *Tilia* × *europaea*
Linden, Large-leafed *Tilia platyphyllos*
Linden, Silver *Tilia tomentosa*
Linden, Small-leafed *Tilia cordata*
Magnolia, Bigleaf *Magnolia macrophylla*
Magnolia, Southern (Bullbay or Evergreen) *Magnolia grandiflora*
Magnolia, Sweetbay *Magnolia virginiana*
Mimosa (Silk-Tree) *Albizia julibrissin*
Rowan Tree (European Mountain-Ash) *Sorbus aucuparia*

July
FLOWERING TREES IN BLOOM
Catalpa, Common *Catalpa bignonioides*
Chaste-Tree *Vitex agnus-castus*
Chinese Chestnut *Castanea mollissima*
Crape-Myrtle *Lagerstroemia indica*
European Smoke-Tree *Cotinus coggygria*
Golden-Rain-Tree *Koelreuteria paniculata*
Japanese Pagoda Tree (Chinese Scholar Tree) *Sophora japonica*
Japanese Raisin-Tree *Hovenia dulcis*
Linden, American *Tilia americana*

Magnolia, Southern (Bullbay or Evergreen) *Magnolia grandiflora*
Magnolia, Sweetbay *Magnolia virginiana*
Mimosa (Silk-Tree) *Albizia julibrissin*
Rose-of-Sharon *Hibiscus syriacus*
Sourwood (Sorrel-Tree) *Oxydendrum arboreum*

August

FLOWERING TREES IN BLOOM
Chaste-Tree *Vitex agnus-castus*
Crape-Myrtle *Lagerstroemia indica*
Franklin Tree *Franklinia alatamaha*
Japanese Pagoda Tree (Chinese Scholar Tree) *Sophora japonica*
Magnolia, Southern (Bullbay or Evergreen) *Magnolia grandiflora*
Mimosa (Silk-Tree) *Albizia julibrissin*
Rose-of-Sharon *Hibiscus syriacus*
Sourwood (Sorrel-Tree) *Oxydendrum arboreum*

September

FLOWERING TREES IN BLOOM
Crape-Myrtle *Lagerstroemia indica*
Franklin Tree *Franklinia alatamaha*
Japanese Pagoda Tree (Chinese Scholar Tree) *Sophora japonica*
Magnolia, Southern (Bullbay or Evergreen) *Magnolia grandiflora*
Rose-of-Sharon *Hibiscus syriacus*
Sourwood (Sorrel-Tree) *Oxydendrum arboreum*

TREES BEARING CONSPICUOUS FALL FRUITS IN WASHINGTON, D.C.
Black Locust *Robinia pseudoacacia*
Buckeyes and Horse-Chestnuts *Aesculus* spp.
Catalpas *Catalpa* spp.
Chinese Chestnut *Castanea mollissima*
Crabapples *Malus* spp.
Dogwoods *Cornus* spp.
European Filbert *Corylus avellana*
Fig-Tree *Ficus carica*
Golden-Rain-Tree *Koelreuteria paniculata*
Hackberries *Celtis* spp.

Hawthorns *Crataegus* spp.
Hickories *Carya* spp.
Hollies *Ilex* spp.
Honey-Locust *Gleditsia triacanthos*
Japanese Pagoda Tree *Sophora japonica*
Kentucky Coffee-Tree *Gymnocladus dioicus*
Magnolias *Magnolia* spp.
Oaks *Quercus* spp.
Osage-Orange *Maclura pomifera*
Paulownia *Paulownia tomentosa*
Persimmons *Diospyros* spp.
Planes (Sycamore) *Platanus* spp.
Sourwood (Sorrel-Tree) *Oxydendrum arboreum*
Sweetgum *Liquidambar styraciflua*

October

Flowering Trees in Bloom

Franklin Tree *Franklinia alatamaha*
Osmanthus *Osmanthus heterophyllus*
Rose-of-Sharon *Hibiscus syriacus*
Witch-Hazel, Common *Hamamelis virginiana*

October Fall Color in Washington, D.C.

American Beech *Fagus grandifolia*
Ashes *Fraxinus* spp.
Buckeyes, Horse-Chestnuts *Aesculus* spp.
Dogwoods *Cornus* spp.
Elms *Ulmus* spp.
Hickories *Carya* spp.
Maples (particularly Sugar Maple) *Acer* spp.
Oaks *Quercus* spp.
Sourwood (Sorrel-Tree) *Oxydendrum arboreum*
Sweetgum *Liquidambar styraciflua*
Tulip-Tree *Liriodendron tulipifera*
Tupelo *Nyssa sylvatica*
Witch-Hazels *Hamamelis* spp.
Zelkovas *Zelkova* spp.

November

FLOWERING TREES IN BLOOM
>   Fall-Blooming Cherry Tree   *Prunus subhirtella* 'Autumnalis'
>   Osmanthus   *Osmanthus heterophyllus*
>   Witch-Hazel, Common   *Hamamelis virginiana*

NOVEMBER FALL COLOR IN WASHINGTON, D.C.
>   American Beech   *Fagus grandifolia*
>   Bradford Pear   *Pyrus calleryana* 'Bradford'
>   Elms   *Ulmus* spp.
>   European Beech   *Fagus sylvatica*
>   Ginkgo   *Ginkgo biloba*
>   Hickories   *Carya* spp.
>   Maples (particularly Red, Sugar, Japanese, and Norway
>   Maples)   *Acer* spp.
>   Oaks   *Quercus* spp.
>   Sourwood (Sorrel-Tree)   *Oxydendrum arboreum*
>   Sweetgum   *Liquidambar styraciflua*
>   Witch-Hazels   *Hamamelis* spp.

December

FLOWERING TREES IN BLOOM
>   Fall-Blooming Cherry Tree   *Prunus subhirtella* 'Autumnalis'
>   Witch-Hazel, Common   *Hamamelis virginiana*

CONSPICUOUS WINTER FRUIT IN WASHINGTON, D.C.
>   Bladdernut   *Staphylea trifolia*
>   Catalpas   *Catalpa* spp.
>   Hawthorns   *Crataegus* spp.
>   Hollies   *Ilex* spp.
>   Kentucky Coffee-Tree   *Gymnocladus dioicus*
>   Paulownia   *Paulownia tomentosa*
>   Planes (Sycamore)   *Platanus* spp.
>   Tulip-Tree   *Liriodendron tulipifera*

A Special Message from Casey Trees about Planting and Caring for Trees in Washington, D.C.

Planting

Planting trees is a wonderful way to contribute to your community as well as our urban landscape. When planting, learn as much as you can before digging the hole. It is important to select the right tree for your space. Trees need ample room for their roots and canopy, as well as proper amounts of nutrients and water to develop fully. In addition, considerations such as the depth of the tree hole, the addition of nutrients, and care for the tree's roots while planting are important.

If you want to learn how to plant trees with an organization, consider volunteering with Casey Trees or another group that does community-based tree planting. Also, consider spending time at the National Arboretum and our many nature centers and public gardens.

Maintenance and Stewardship

New trees, like young children, need special care. Ample watering and mulching over the course of the tree's first three years in a new location are the most important things to ensure that your new tree will survive and mature. Watering is especially important during warm months when soils can readily dry out.

Proper mulching also is vital to your new tree's success. Mulch helps conserve water and protect the soil from compaction, and it provides a safety zone around the tree, reducing the risk of damage to the trunk from lawn mowers or other equipment. Maintain the depth of mulch at about three inches and keep it from touching the trunk to avoid rot damage.

CITIZEN PARTICIPATION

There are many ways of getting involved. The trees and forests of Washington need citizen stewards to care for individual trees. Citizens are also important to provide well-thought-out planning and advocacy for open spaces. For those who like to get their hands dirty and wet, opportunities abound for planting and watering trees and removing invasive species. If you like organizing, you may decide to gather neighbors or a community group to plant on private or public grounds. Perhaps you are a community advocate who can lend a voice for trees and landscape design at public meetings where development projects and infrastructure upgrades are discussed. All these activities rely on stewards and directly enhance the forests of our city.

Notes

1. Frederick Gutheim, *The Potomac,* Maryland Paperback Bookshelf Series (Baltimore: Johns Hopkins University Press, 1986), 28.
2. Ibid., 27.
3. William M. Maury, *Washington, D.C., Past and Present: The Guide to the Nation's Capital* (New York: CBS Publications, in cooperation with the U.S. Capitol Historical Society, 1975), 41.
4. Elizabeth S. Kite, *L'Enfant and Washington, 1791–1792: Published and Unpublished Documents Now Brought Together for the First Time* (1929; repr., New York: Arno Press, 1970), 23.
5. Erle Kauffman, *Trees of Washington, The Man—The City* (Washington, D.C.: Outdoor Press, 1932), 56.
6. Constance McLaughlin Green, *Washington: Village and Capital, 1800–1878* (Princeton, N.J.: Princeton University Press, 1962), 105–6.
7. Mary Cable, *The Avenue of the Presidents,* foreword by Nathaniel Alexander Owings (Boston: Houghton Mifflin, 1969), 113.
8. Peter Henderson, "Street Trees of Washington," *Harper's Magazine,* 1889.
9. Kauffman, *Trees of Washington, The Man—The City,* 57.
10. George J. Olszewski, *History of the Mall, Washington, D.C.* (Washington, D.C.: U.S. Office of History and Historic Architecture, Eastern Service Center, 1970), 51.
11. Lady Bird Johnson, speech given at Yale University, 1967.
12. www.caseytrees.org.
13. "Washington, the Nation's Capital," *National Geographic,* March 1915.
14. "In the White House Looking Out," *U.S. News & World Report,* April 8, 1935.
15. Wolf Von Eckardt, "Verdant Vista Is Memorial to J.F.K.," *Washington Post,* May 31, 1964.
16. *Washington, Design of the Federal City* (published for the National Archives Trust Fund Board by Acropolis Books, 1981), 14.
17. Ibid., 6.
18. Olmsted Brothers—Landscape Architects, "Report to the President of the United States on Improvements and Policy of Maintenance for the Executive Mansion Grounds" (1935), 62.

19. "Historic Trees on the White House Lawn," *Washington Post Magazine,* December 3, 1933.

20. Lonnelle Aikman, *The Living White House,* foreword by Rosalynn Carter, 6th ed. (Washington, D.C.: White House Historical Association with the cooperation of the National Geographic Society and its Special Publications Division, 1978), 124.

21. Ibid.

22. *Washington Star,* March 25, 1928.

23. Wolf Von Eckardt, "Verdant Vista Is Memorial to J.F.K.," *Washington Post,* May 31, 1964.

24. Ibid.

25. Maxine Cheshire, "Only Her Name Could Grace Glowing Greensward," *Washington Post,* April 23, 1965.

26. Rosalynn Carter, "The White House Gardens and Grounds" (brochure distributed during the Carter administration to visitors to President's Park, 1977–81).

27. Margaret Bayard Smith, *The First Forty Years of Washington Society* [portrayed by the family letters of Mrs. Samuel Harrison Smith (Margaret Bayard), from the collection of her grandson, J. Henley Smith; edited by Gaillard Hunt] (New York: C. Scribner's Sons, 1906), 11–12.

28. "Historic Trees on the White House Lawn," *Washington Post Magazine,* December 3, 1933.

29. "In the White House Looking Out," *U.S. News & World Report,* April 8, 1935.

30. "Historic Trees on the White House Lawn," *Washington Post Magazine,* December 3, 1933.

31. Washington newspaper story (source unknown), Washingtoniana Division, Martin Luther King Jr. Public Library, Washington, D.C.

32. "Historic Trees on the White House Lawn," *Washington Post Magazine,* December 3, 1933.

33. *Washington Post,* August 25, 1933.

34. Virginia Burgess Warren, "White House Trees," *American Forests,* March 1958.

35. Ibid.

36. Wauhillau La Hay, "L.B.J. Plants for the Future," *Washington Daily News,* October 17, 1964.

37. Frederick Law Olmsted, report contained in the Annual Report of the Architect of the United States Capitol (Washington D.C.: Government Printing Office, 1882), 13, Files of the Architect of the Capitol.

38. Ibid.

39. Ibid., 14.

40. Ibid.

41. Ibid., 15.

42. Ibid., 17.

43. Ibid., 16.

44. Ibid., 17.

45. Ibid., 15.

46. Ibid., 6.

47. Speech by Senator Edward Kennedy, 95th Cong., 2nd sess., *Congressional Record* 124 (June 27, 1978).

48. Author interview with Sylvia Ripley, 2006.

49. Paul Russell, *The Oriental Flowering Cherries,* Circular/U.S. Department of Agriculture, no. 313 (Washington, D.C.: U.S. Department of Agriculture, 1934), 2.

50. Author interview with Robert DeFeo, 2006.

51. Ann McClellan, *The Cherry Blossom Festival "Sakura Celebration"* (Boston: Bunker Hill Publishing in association with the National Cherry Blossom Festival, 2005), 2.

52. Russell, *The Oriental Flowering Cherries,* 1.

53. Ken Ringle, "Where the City Gets Together," *Washington Post,* August 7, 1975.

54. *Washington Star,* January 19, 1913.

55. Ibid.

56. Letter dated June 27, 1927, Washingtoniana Division, Martin Luther King, Jr., Memorial Library, Washington, D.C.

57. Eastern National Park and Monument Association, *The Lyndon Baines Johnson Memorial Grove on the Potomac* (Washington, D.C.: National Geographic Society, 1977), 3.

58. Ibid., 25.

59. Ibid., 3.

60. *The Diaries of George Washington,* ed. Donald Jackson and Dorothy Twohig (Charlottesville: University Press of Virginia, 1976–79), 4:299 (entry for March 26, 1786). The diaries are also available online at http://memory.loc.gov/ammem/gwhtml/gwseries1.html#D.

61. Taylor Biggs Lewis Jr. and Joanne Young, *Washington's Mount Vernon* (New York: Holt, Rinehart, and Winston, 1973).

62. Kauffman, *Trees of Washington, The Man—The City,* 5.

63. Mount Vernon Ladies' Association of the Union, "The Mount Vernon Gardens" (pamphlet, 1973), 9.

64. Lewis and Young, *Washington's Mount Vernon.*

65. Ibid.

66. Charles Sprague Sargent, *The Trees at Mount Vernon* (report to the Council of the Mount Vernon Ladies' Association of the Union, 1926,) 3.

67. *The Diaries of George Washington,* 4:75, 78 (entries for January 12, 1785 and January 19, 1785, respectively).

68. E-mail interview with Dean Norton, 2007.

69. Ibid.

70. *The Diaries of George Washington,* 4:160, 164 (entries for July 6, 1785 and July 13, 1785, respectively).

71. E-mail interview with Dean Norton, 2007.

72. Author interview with Dean Norton, 2006.

73. Mount Vernon Ladies' Association of the Union, *Mount Vernon, Virginia: An Illustrated Handbook* (Mount Vernon, VA: The Association, 1974), 28.

74. Sargent, *The Trees at Mount Vernon,* 6.

75. *The Diaries of George Washington,* 4:184 (entry for August 18, 1785).

76. Randle Bond Truett, ed., *Washington, D.C.: A Guide to the Nation's Capital*, new rev. ed. (New York: Hastings House, 1968).

77. Janine Guglielmino, "Natural Capital—Trees of Washington, D.C.," *American Forests*, Spring 2001.

78. Georgina Masson, *Dumbarton Oaks, A Guide to the Gardens* (Washington, D.C.: Trustees for Harvard University, 1968), 6.

79. E-mail interview with Stan Shetler, 2006.

80. E-mail interview with Carole Bergmann, 2006.

81. Theodore Roosevelt letter, June 21, 1904, files of the Maryland–National Capital Park and Planning Commission (courtesy of Carole Bergmann).

82. E-mail interview with Cris Fleming, 2006.

83. Michael A. Dirr, *Manual of Woody Landscape Plants: Their Identification, Ornamental Characteristics, Culture, Propagation, and Uses*, 5th ed. (Champaign, Ill.: Stipes, 1998), 753.

84. Melanie Choukas-Bradley, "Under the Spreading Chestnut Tree, a Band of Volunteers Stands," *Washington Post*, December 18, 2003.

85. "Lindens Stretch Seven Miles on Famous Avenue in Capital," *Washington Star*, August 12, 1923.

86. Dirr, *Manual of Woody Landscape Plants*, 903.

87. Ibid., 540.

88. Oliver E. Allen, "A Tree Grows in America," *American Heritage*, April/May 1984.

89. Dirr, *Manual of Woody Landscape Plants*, 761.

90. Ibid., 20.

91. James A. Duke, *The Green Pharmacy: New Discoveries in Herbal Remedies for Common Diseases and Conditions from the World's Foremost Authority on Healing Herbs* (Emmaus, Pa.: Rodale Press, 1997), 441.

Selected Bibliography

Aikman, Lonnelle. *The Living White House.* Foreword by Rosalynn Carter. 6th ed. Washington, D.C.: White House Historical Association with the cooperation of the National Geographic Society and its Special Publications Division, 1978.

———.*We the People: The Story of the United States Capitol, Its Past and Its Promise.* 11th ed. Washington, D.C.: United States Capitol Historical Society in cooperation with the National Geographic Society, 1978.

Andresen, John W. "The Greening of Urban America." *American Forests,* November 1978.

Ayensu, Edward S., and Robert A. DeFilipps. *Endangered and Threatened Plants of the United States.* Washington, D.C.: Smithsonian Institution, 1978.

Bean, W. J. *Trees and Shrubs Hardy in the British Isles.* 8th ed., fully rev. 4 vols. London: J. Murray, 1970–80.

Beauty for America. Proceedings of the White House Conference on Natural Beauty, Washington, D.C., 1965. Washington, D.C.: Government Printing Office, 1965.

Brown, Russell G., and Melvin L. Brown. *Woody Plants of Maryland.* Baltimore: Port City Press, 1992.

Cable, Mary. *The Avenue of the Presidents.* Foreword by Nathaniel Alexander Owings. Boston: Houghton Mifflin, 1969.

Chadbund, Geoffrey. *Flowering Cherries.* London: Collins, 1972.

Choukas-Bradley, Melanie. *An Illustrated Guide to Eastern Woodland Wildflowers and Trees.* Illustrations by Tina Thieme Brown. Charlottesville: University of Virginia Press, 2004.

———. "Every Tree Counts: A D.C. Census of What Grows Where." *Washington Post,* May 30, 2002.

———. "Jackson's Magnolias Lose Their Currency." *Washington Post,* January 14, 1999.

———. "Lessons Along Rock Creek." *Washington Post,* July 2, 2006.

———. "On This Historic Day, Hail to the Leaf." *Washington Post,* January 20, 2005.

———. "Under the Spreading Chestnut Tree, a Band of Volunteers Stands." *Washington Post,* December 18, 2003.

Clepper, Henry. "George Washington's Trees." *American Forests*, August 1976.

Committee for a More Beautiful Capital. "Beautification Summary." Washington, D.C.: 1965–68.

Crockett, James Underwood, and the editors of Time-Life Books. *Flowering Shrubs*. Watercolor illustrations by Allianora Rosse. 1972; reprinted, New York: Time-Life Books, 1977.

Dirr, Michael A. *Manual of Woody Landscape Plants: Their Identification, Ornamental Characteristics, Culture, Propagation, and Uses*. 5th ed. Champaign, Ill.: Stipes, 1998.

Duke, James A. *The Green Pharmacy: New Discoveries in Herbal Remedies for Common Diseases and Conditions from the World's Foremost Authority on Healing Herbs*. Emmaus, Pa.: Rodale Press; distributed in the book trade by St. Martin's Press, 1997.

Eastern National Park and Monument Association. "The Lyndon Baines Johnson Memorial Grove on the Potomac." Washington, D.C.: National Geographic Society, 1977.

Eberlein, Harold Donaldson, and Cortlandt Van Dyke Hubbard. *Historic Houses of George-Town & Washington City*. Preface by Richard Hubbard Howland. Richmond, Va.: Dietz Press, 1958.

Elias, Thomas S. *The Complete Trees of North America: Field Guide and Natural History*. New York: Outdoor Life/Nature Books; distributed by Van Nostrand Reinhold, 1980.

Evans, James Matthew. *The Landscape Architecture of Washington, D.C.: A Comprehensive Guide*. Washington, D.C.: Landscape Architecture Foundation, 1981.

Fairchild, David. *Exploring for Plants*. From notes of the Allison Vincent Armour expeditions for the United States Department of Agriculture, 1925, 1926, and 1927. New York: Macmillan, 1931.

"5000 Brave Rain to See Crab Apple Blossom Parade." *Washington Post*, April 19, 1953.

Fleming, Cristol, Marion Blois Lobstein, and Barbara Tufty. *Finding Wildflowers in the Washington-Baltimore Area*. Foreword by Stanwyn G. Shetler. Baltimore: Johns Hopkins University Press, 1995.

Garland, Mark S. *Watching Nature: A Mid-Atlantic Natural History*. Art by John Anderton. Washington, D.C.: Smithsonian Institution Press, 1997.

"General Hains." *Washington Star*, April 13, 1946.

Gleason, Henry A. *The New Britton and Brown Illustrated Flora of the Northeastern United States and Adjacent Canada*. 3 vols. New York: New York Botanical Garden, 1952.

Gleason, Henry A., and Arthur Cronquist. *Manual of Vascular Plants of Northeastern United States and Adjacent Canada*. 2nd ed. Bronx, N.Y.: New York Botanical Garden, 1991.

Gray, Asa. *Gray's Manual of Botany: A Handbook of the Flowering Plants and Ferns of the Central and Northeastern United States and Adjacent Canada*. 8th (centennial) ed., largely rewritten and expanded by Merritt Lyndon Fernald, with assistance of specialists in some groups; corrections supplied by R. C. Rollins. Portland, Ore.: Dioscorides Press, 1950.

Green, Constance McLaughlin. *Washington: Village and Capital, 1800–1878.* Princeton, N.J.: Princeton University Press, 1962.

Griswold, Mac K. *Washington's Gardens at Mount Vernon: Landscape of the Inner Man.* Photography by Roger Foley. Boston: Houghton Mifflin, 1999.

Guglielmino, Janine. "Natural Capital—Trees of Washington, D.C." *American Forests,* Spring 2001.

Gurney, Gene, and Harold Wise. *The Official Washington, D.C. Directory: A Pictorial Guide.* New York: Crown Publishers, 1977.

Gutheim, Frederick. *The Potomac.* Maryland Paperback Bookshelf edition. Baltimore: Johns Hopkins University Press, 1986.

Harlow, William M. *Fruit and Twig Key to Trees and Shrubs: Fruit Key to Northeastern Trees and Twig Key to the Deciduous Woody Plants of Eastern North America.* New York: Dover Publications, 1946.

———. *Trees of the Eastern and Central United States and Canada.* New York: Dover Publications, 1957.

Hermann, Frederick J. *A Checklist of Plants in the Washington-Baltimore Area.* Washington, D.C.: Conference on District Flora, Smithsonian Institution, 1946.

Heywood, V. H., et al. *Flowering Plant Families of the World.* Updated and rev. Buffalo, N.Y: Firefly Books, 2007.

Higgins, Adrian. "Magnolias Flowering in Their Own Time." *Washington Post,* March 21, 2002.

———. "Rallying Around the Flowering Dogwood." *Washington Post,* April 21, 2005.

———. "Spring in the Gardens of Georgetown, Starting with Tudor Place." *Washington Post,* May 9, 2002.

———. *The Washington Post Garden Book: The Ultimate Guide to Gardening in Greater Washington and the Mid-Atlantic Region.* Washington, D.C.: Washington Post Books, 1998.

Hillier and Sons. *Hilliers' Manual of Trees & Shrubs.* 4th ed. Newport, England: Yelf Brothers, 1974.

Hitchcock, A. S., and Paul C. Standley. *Flora of the District of Columbia and Vicinity.* Washington, D.C.: Government Printing Office, 1919.

Huyck, Dorothy Boyle. "Washington—City of Trees." *American Forests,* March 1974.

Jefferson, Roland M. *History, Progeny, and Locations of Crabapples of Documented Authentic Origin.* Washington, D.C. National Arboretum Contribution, no. 2. Washingtin, D.C.: Agricultural Research Service, U.S. Department of Agriculture, 1970.

Jefferson, Roland M., and Alan E. Fusonie. *The Japanese Flowering Cherry Trees of Washington, D.C.* Washington, D.C. National Arboretum Contribution, no. 4. Washington, D.C.: Agricultural Research Service, U.S. Department of Agriculture, 1977.

Jefferson, Roland M., and Kay Kazue Wain. *The Nomenclature of Cultivated Japanese Flowering Cherries (Prunus): The Sato-zakura Group.* Washington, D.C. National Arboretum Contribution, no. 5. Washington, D.C.: Agricultural Research Service, U.S. Department of Agriculture, 1984.

Johnson, Hugh. *The International Book of Trees: A Guide and Tribute to the Trees of Our Forests and Gardens*. New York: Simon and Schuster, 1973.

Judge, Joseph. "New Grandeur for Flowering Washington." *National Geographic*, April 1967.

Kartesz, John T., and Rosemarie Kartesz. *A Synonymized Checklist of the Vascular Flora of the United States, Canada, and Greenland*. The Biota of North America Series, vol. 2. Chapel Hill: University of North Carolina Press, 1980.

Kauffman, Erle. *Trees of Washington, The Man—The City*. Washington, D.C.: Outdoor Press, 1932.

Keene, Donald, comp. and ed. *Anthology of Japanese Literature*. New York: Grove Press, 1960.

Kite, Elizabeth S. *L'Enfant and Washington, 1791–1792: Published and Unpublished Documents Now Brought Together for the First Time*. 1929; reprinted, New York: Arno Press, 1970.

Klots, Alexander B. *Eastern Butterflies*. Peterson Field Guide Series. Boston: Houghton Mifflin, 1951, 1979.

Lanham, Clifford. *The Tree System of Washington*. Washington, D.C.: Judd and Detweiler, 1926.

Lewis, Pauline. "In Spring in the Capital, Fancies Turn to the Arboretum." *New York Times*, May 14, 1978.

Lewis, Taylor Biggs, Jr., and Joanne Young. *Washington's Mount Vernon*. New York: Holt, Rinehart, and Winston, 1973.

Li, Hui-Lin. "The Discovery and Cultivation of Metasequoia." Morris Arboretum *Bulletin*, December 1957.

———. *The Origin and Cultivation of Shade and Ornamental Trees*. Philadelphia: University of Pennsylvania Press, 1963.

Little, Elbert L., Jr. *Sixty Trees from Foreign Lands*. Washington, D.C.: Forest Service, U.S. Department of Agriculture, 1961.

Martin, Alexander C., Herbert S. Zim, and Arnold L. Nelson. *American Wildlife & Plants: A Guide to Wildlife Food Habits: The Use of Trees, Shrubs, Weeds, and Herbs by Birds and Mammals of the United States*. 1951; reprinted, New York: Dover Publications, 1961.

Masson, Georgina. *Dumbarton Oaks, A Guide to the Gardens*. Washington, D.C.: Trustees for Harvard University, 1968.

Mattoon, Wilbur R., and Susan S. Alburtis. *Forest Trees of the District of Columbia: Including Some Foreign Trees, How to Know Them, Where to See Them*. Washington, D.C.: American Forestry Association, 1926.

Maury, William M. *Washington, D.C., Past and Present: The Guide to the Nation's Capital*. New York: CBS Publications, in cooperation with the U.S. Capitol Historical Society, 1975.

Mazzeo, Peter M. *Trees of Shenandoah National Park in the Blue Ridge Mountains of Virginia*. 1967; reprinted, Luray, Va.: Shenandoah Natural History Association, 1979.

McAtee, Waldo Lee. *A Sketch of the Natural History of the District of Columbia Together with an Indexed Edition of the U.S. Geological Survey's 1917 Map of Washington and Vicinity*. Washington, D.C.: Press of H. L. and J. B. McQueen, 1918.

McClellan, Ann. *The Cherry Blossom Festival "Sakura Celebration."* Boston: Bunker Hill Publishing in association with the National Cherry Blossom Festival, 2005.

Mitchell, Alan. *A Field Guide to the Trees of Britain and Northern Europe.* 1st American ed. Boston: Houghton Mifflin, 1974.

Mitchell, Henry. "Georgetown Gardens." *Washington Post,* April 17, 1977.

MCFB (Montgomery County Forestry Board), *Register of Champion Trees.* Published biannually in odd years (most recent count at time of writing, 2007).

Mount Vernon Ladies' Association of the Union. *Mount Vernon, Virginia: An Illustrated Handbook.* Washington, D.C.: Judd and Detweiler, 1974.

National Register of Big Trees. Published annually by American Forests, Washington, D.C., and available online at www.americanforests.org/resources/bigtrees/.

National Register of Historic Places Inventory—Nomination Form for Federal Properties (East and West Potomac Parks). Washington, D.C.: U.S. Department of the Interior, November 30, 1973.

O'Hara, Mike. "Trees of Capitol Hill." *American Forests,* August 1976.

Ohwi, Jisaburo. *Flora of Japan.* Edited by Frederick G. Meyer and Egbert H. Walker. Washington, D.C.: Smithsonian Institution, 1965.

Olszewski, George J. *History of the Mall, Washington, D.C.* Washington, D.C.: U.S. Office of History and Historic Architecture, Eastern Service Center, 1970.

———. *The President's Park South.* Washington, D.C.: U.S. Office of History and Historic Architecture, Eastern Service Center, 1970.

Pardo, Richard. "Our National Bonsai Collection." *American Forests,* December 1977.

Pariser, Ursula R., and Noëlle Blackmer Beatty. *The Dumbarton Oaks Gardens: Their History, Design, and Ornaments.* Washington, D.C.: Dumbarton Oaks; distributed by Acropolis Book, 1978.

Petrides, George A. *A Field Guide to Trees and Shrubs: Field Marks of All Trees, Shrubs, and Woody Vines that Grow Wild in the Northeastern and North-Central United States and in Southeastern and South-Central Canada.* Illustrations by George A. Petrides and Roger Tory Peterson. 2nd ed. Boston: Houghton Mifflin, 1972.

Phillips, Roger. *The Random House Book of Trees of North America and Europe: A Photographic Guide to More than 500 Trees.* New York: Random House, 1978.

Preston, Dickson J. "The Rediscovery of Betula Uber." *American Forests,* August 1976.

Preston, Richard J., Jr. *North American Trees (exclusive of Mexico and tropical United States): A Handbook Designed for Field Use, with plates and distribution maps.* 3rd ed. Ames: Iowa State University Press, 1976.

"The Rambler" (newspaper column written by J. H. Shannon). *Washington Star,* 1915–24.

Randall, Charles Edgar, and Henry Clepper. *Famous and Historic Trees.* Washington, D.C.: American Forestry Association, 1976.

Rehder, Alfred. *Manual of Cultivated Trees and Shrubs Hardy in North America: Exclusive of the Subtropical and Warmer Temperate Regions.* 2nd ed., rev. and enl. New York: Macmillan, 1940.

Ruben, Barbara. "Kenwood: Home of the Other Cherry Blossoms." *Washington Post,* April 12, 2003.

Russell, Paul. *The Oriental Flowering Cherries.* Circular/U.S. Department of Agriculture, no. 313. Washington, D.C.: U.S. Department of Agriculture, 1934.

Sargent, Charles Sprague. *The Trees at Mount Vernon.* Report to the Council of the Mount Vernon Ladies' Association of the Union, 1926.

Seale, William. *The White House Garden.* Photographs by Erik Kvalsvik. Washington, D.C.: White House Historical Association, 1996.

Seeber, Barbara H. *A City of Gardens: Glorious Public Gardens In and Around the Nation's Capital.* Sterling, Va.: Capital Books, 2004.

Shetler, Stanwyn G., and Sylvia Stone Orli. *Annotated Checklist of the Vascular Plants of the Washington-Baltimore Area.* Part I. *Ferns, Fern Allies, Gymnosperms, and Dicotyledons.* Washington, D.C.: Department of Botany, National Museum of Natural History, Smithsonian Institution, 2000.

Sites, Maud Kay. *The Japanese Cherry Trees in Washington, D.C.* Baltimore: Norman T. A. Munder, 1935.

Smith, James Payne, Jr. *Vascular Plant Families: An Introduction to the Families of Vascular Plants Native to North America and Selected Families of Ornamental or Economic Importance.* Illustrations by Kathryn E. Simpson. Eureka, Calif.: Mad River Press, 1977.

Smith, Margaret Bayard. *The First Forty Years of Washington Society.* [Portrayed by the family letters of Mrs. Samuel Harrison Smith (Margaret Bayard), from the collection of her grandson, J. Henley Smith; edited by Gaillard Hunt.] New York: C. Scribner's Sons, 1906.

"Southeast Cheers Crab Apple Blossom Festival and Parade." *Washington Star,* April 25, 1954.

Spilsbury, Gail. *Rock Creek Park.* Baltimore: Johns Hopkins University Press, 2003.

Spirit of a Native Place: Building the National Museum of the American Indian. Edited by Duane Blue Spruce. Washington, D.C.: National Museum of the American Indian, Smithsonian Institution, in association with National Geographic, 2004.

Supplement to the Dictionary of Gardening: A Practical and Scientific Encyclopaedia of Horticulture. Edited by Patrick M. Synge. 2nd ed., rev. Oxford: Clarendon Press, 1969.

Tamulevich, Susan, with photographs by Ping Amranand. *Dumbarton Oaks: Garden Into Art.* New York: Monacelli Press, 2001.

Thomas, Lindsey Kay, Jr. *Geomorphology and Vegetation of Theodore Roosevelt Island.* Washington, D.C.: Conservation, Interpretation, and Use, National Capital Region, National Park Service, U.S. Dept. of the Interior, 1963.

Trees of Washington, D.C., compliments of Forestry Division. [List of native and cultivated varieties, by botanical name, with parks where found; and detail for grounds of Agriculture Department, White House, and Lafayette Park.] Washington, D.C.: , 1891.

Truett, Randle Bond, ed. *Washington, D.C.: A Guide to the Nation's Capital.* New rev. ed. New York: Hastings House, 1968.

Viertel, Arthur T. *Trees, Shrubs and Vines: A Pictorial Guide to the Ornamental Woody Plants of the Northern United States Exclusive of Conifers.* Syracuse, N.Y.: Syracuse University Press, 1970.

Ward, Lester F. *Guide to the Flora of Washington and Vicinity.* Bulletin of the U.S. National Museum, no. 22. Washington, D.C.: Government Printing Office, 1881.

Washington, Design of the Federal City. Published for the National Archives Trust Fund Board by Acropolis Books, 1981.

The White House Gardens and Grounds. [Booklets developed and distributed by the White House during spring and fall garden tours, 1981–2006]

Williams, George Livingston. *The Gardens of Hillwood, A Guide Book with Map.* Washington, D.C.: Corporate Press, 1965.

Wilson, Ernest Henry. *Plant Hunting.* Boston: The Stratford Company, 1927.

Index

Boldfaced page numbers refer to detailed, usually illustrated, descriptions of trees. (Boldfaced page numbers are used only with the common names of trees; however, most page numbers following the scientific names also send you to detailed tree descriptions and illustrations.)